THE AARONSOHN SAGA

SHMUEL KATZ

THE AARONSOHN SAGA

Shmuel Katz

gefen

publishing house בית הוצאה לאור

JERUSALEM • NEW YORK

Layout: Marzel A.S. — Jerusalem
Cover Design: S. Kim Glassman

ISBN: 978-965-229-416-6

Edition   1 3 5 7 9 8 6 4 2

Gefen Publishing House Ltd.
6 Hatzvi St.
Jerusalem 94386, Israel
972-2-538-0247
orders@gefenpublishing.com

Gefen Books
600 Broadway
Lynbrook, NY 11563, USA
1-516-593-1234
orders@gefenpublishing.com

www.israelbooks.com

Printed in Israel

Send for our free catalogue

Contents

Introduction 1

Chapter 1.   Kirkwall, Scotland 5

Chapter 2.   "The Mother of Wheat" 11

Chapter 3.   The Clash with Rothschild 27

Chapter 4.   And Now — Geologist! 51

Chapter 5.   Cold Winds 63

Chapter 6.   The World War — Volunteers for Britain 69

Chapter 7.   The Odyssey 95

Chapter 8.   British Doors Open 111

Chapter 9.   Aaron and Alexander 125

Chapter 10. "Nili" 131

Chapter 11. "Aaronsohn Is Running GHQ" 155

Chapter 12. Who Was Who — and How — in Nili 173

Chapter 13. General Allenby Takes Advice 187

Chapter 14. A Myriad of Problems 203

Chapter 15. Weizmann's London Political Committee 219

Chapter 16. Sarah — The Leader of Nili 227

Chapter 17. The Pigeon Errant and the Blunder Human 241

Chapter 18. The Death of Sarah 263

Chapter 19. Hangings in Damascus 277

Chapter 20. Avshalom and Yosef — Postmortem 297

Chapter 21.   Grandiose Plans 303

Chapter 22.   Great Hopes 321

Appendix 1:   Sarah's Last Letter (October 9, 1917) 333

Appendix 2:   Turkish Defenses on Palestine Mediterranean Coast
                 as Reported by Aaron Aaronsohn in July 1916 335

Appendix 3:   Churchill's Concurrence on the Strategy Urged
                 by Aaronsohn 337

Appendix 4:   Colonel Richard Meinhertzhagen on T. E. Lawrence . . . 339

Appendix 5:   The Mysteries Surrounding Aaronsohn's Death 340

Appreciations 343

Bibliography 345

Index 349

Introduction

More than a quarter of a century ago I decided to write a biography of Aaron Aaronsohn. I had written of him in my book *Battleground* as one of the three great Jews (with Weizmann and Jabotinsky) who had stood out in the First World War. But Aaronsohn's role in 1917 in the British campaign in Palestine has been ignored both by the British historians, for reasons that can be guessed at, and by the Jewish establishment — for their own astonishing reasons. The absence of a comprehensive biography of Aaronsohn left a broad gap in Jewish and indeed in British military annals.

In fact Aaronsohn's early career, with its amazing achievements in the world of science, was surely important enough for a biography. (In May 1999, a gathering of scientists was held at Zichron Ya'akov to commemorate him on the eightieth anniversary of his death.)

As my research progressed and deepened, I found I must reconsider the simplistic title (*A Biography*) I had chosen for the book. The reason was the story of his sister Sarah. It is impossible to see and write of Sarah only as a lesser player — as Aaron's deputy — in the drama of Nili (the secret pro-British spy organization founded by Aaron), or even as merely Nili's commander-in-the-field. That task itself demanded qualities of a very high order. They soon revealed themselves — and revealed that Sarah was a great historic personality in her own right.

How to reflect in a title the interaction of two such personalities? Hence we have *The Aaronsohn Saga*.

Two major works in Hebrew had appeared: *Nili: Toldoteha shel he-aza medinit* (Nili: A story of political daring) by Yosef Nedava and Eliezer Livneh, with Yoram Efrati as editor (Tel Aviv, 1961); and a biography by Livneh, *Aaron Aaronsohn: Ha-ish u-zmano* (Aaron Aaronsohn: The man and his times, Tel Aviv, 1969).

1

Both had been preceded in 1959 by Anita Engle's groundbreaking *The Nili Spies* — in English.

All the authors had come too soon to be able to examine relevant British official documents relating to crucial intelligence operations in the Palestine campaign. These were released only early in the seventies. The relevant volumes of Chaim Weizmann's letters and papers were published only in the late seventies, and not least important, the diary of Shmuel Tolkowsky was published (in Hebrew) only in 1981.[1] Tolkowsky was a member of the committee that helped Weizmann during the negotiations with Britain before and after the issuance of the Balfour Declaration. His diary contains an amazingly detailed account of its deliberations — and throws much light on the relations between Aaronsohn and the Zionist Establishment in London.

The main research resource has naturally been the Aaronsohn House Museum in Zichron Ya'akov, where, over the years, Rivka (the youngest survivor of the family) succeeded, despite the depredations of the Turks, in accumulating an astonishingly large collection of documents: letters, Aaron's scientific writings, memoirs of members of Nili, and reports from the field.

The concentration of this material in the Aaronsohn House has obviated the need for a multitude of reference sources. A simple subject catalogue covers the available material, and a verbal request will ordinarily ensure the delivery of the required document within minutes.

I am deeply grateful to the manager of the Aaronsohn House, Esther Deckel, who, by her ready assistance throughout the many months of my work, eased my lot considerably.

An auxiliary source was at the Central Zionist Archives in Jerusalem. In addition to relevant required documents, the full volumes of Weizmann's letters are to be found there.

Essential research had to be done at the Public Record Office in London (at Kew), specifically in the War Office Intelligence reports. There I had the welcome boon of guidance by Mr. John Fisher to a series of invaluable British intelligence reports from 1917. In Israel there was my friend the late

---

1. Shmuel Tolkowsky, *Yoman Tziyoni medini: London, 1915–1919; Li-kerat Hatzharat Balfur uve-'ikvoteha* [Zionist political diary: London, 1915–1919; On the making of the Balfour Declaration], ed. Devorah Barzilay-Yegar (Jerusalem: Hassifriya Hatziyonit, 1981).

Yehoshua Bension who, with characteristic care, read the early manuscript and made some important observations.

Others to whom my thanks are due are Harry Sessler, Michael Shapiro (London), David Shoham (Tsilla Feinberg's son since dosist), Ann Swersky, Professor William Van Cleave (Springfield, Missouri) and Dr. Laurence Weinbaum. I deeply regret that Harold Blumberg, the former manager of the Aaronsohn House, who guided me to some useful sources, did not live to see the finished work.

CHAPTER 1

Kirkwall, Scotland

On October 16, 1916, two years after Ottoman Turkey entered the World War on the side of Germany, Aaron Aaronsohn, a Turkish citizen from Palestine, boarded the neutral Scandinavian-American passenger boat *Oskar II*, sailing from Copenhagen to New York.

The ship was fully booked, but Aaronsohn had succeeded in procuring passage. For this he had to thank two Americans, one of whom was an old friend. He was a Reform rabbi named Judah L. Magnes, returning to New York with a younger colleague, educationalist Dr. Alexander Dushkin. They had been carrying out a war-relief mission to Eastern Europe on behalf of an American charitable organization.

The two-bunk cabin allotted to them also contained a day-sofa, and on this Dushkin volunteered to sleep, giving up his more comfortable bunk to Aaronsohn. That night he and Magnes may well have regretted their hospitality for, as Aaronsohn remarks in his diary, they were surely kept awake by his snoring.

Dushkin's nocturnal discomfiture was sharpened during the next two days, for his good friend Magnes spent many hours on deck with Aaronsohn, absorbed in conversation from which Dushkin was pointedly excluded. It was only some days later that Magnes told him what he and Aaronsohn had been talking about.

Aaronsohn, a forty-year-old bachelor, sought out other company on the boat as well — and discovered a "lovely" young German woman, "the prettiest woman on the ship, described in her passport as Mademoiselle Olga Bernhardt." They fell into friendly conversation. Evidently impressed with him, and learning that as a Turkish citizen he qualified as an ally, she had told him "some of her secrets."

He concluded from her talk that she was no friend of Britain.[1]

On October 22 the boat put in at the Scottish port of Kirkwall, where it was boarded for routine wartime examination by a British military unit. The interrogation of the passengers was not severe, but when Aaronsohn's turn came, the officer commanding the unit gave him a "queer" look and invited him to go below. After a while he came back on deck, under close escort. The British officer formally informed the ship's captain that a search of Aaronsohn's cabin had found it "full of German stuff" — and Aaronsohn was under arrest.

The passengers crowding the deck gazed in astonishment as Aaronsohn was taken off the ship under guard. Most moved at this spectacle, as Aaronsohn noted in his diary, was a dismayed Olga Bernhardt. She called out to him from the rail: "When I get to New York I shall tell what they are doing to you." She was as good as her word. The day the *Oskar II* docked in New York, a report describing Aaron Aaronsohn's arrest as a dangerous Turkish spy was prominently displayed in that city's *Evening Post*.

On shore at Kirkwall, Aaronsohn was handed over to a sergeant-major who told him that he was not in fact a prisoner but, as his case was "irregular," he must remain under guard. Under guard, then, he was given permission to go to a hotel in town for a cup of tea. That night he slept in the guardroom of a sergeant-major; and the next morning, escorted by a colonel and a captain, he traveled to London.

There he was driven from the railway station directly to Scotland Yard; but evening had fallen and there was nobody at the Yard authorized to deal with him. He was consequently told to return at noon the next day. His escort left him to his own devices.

He was not entirely a stranger to London, for in the year before the war he had spent a month there. Hotels all seemed to be full until, with the help of a taxi driver, he found lodging at the First Avenue Hotel in High Holborn. He registered — giving his name as William Mack — and went for a long walk in the darkened city, blacked out against possible German Zeppelin air raids. Unwittingly that evening he broke the law under which enemy aliens were

---

1. Aaronsohn, *Diary*, Oct. 20, 1916. Quotes from Aaronsohn's diary taken from *Yoman Aaron Aaronsohn, 1916–1919* [Diary of Aaron Aaronsohn, 1916–1919], ed. Yoram Efrati (Tel Aviv: Karni, 1970).

prohibited from being abroad after 10PM. Nobody stopped him, and he reached the hotel after midnight.

At noon the next day Aaronsohn was subjected to interrogation by Sir Basil Thomson, the deputy superintendent of Scotland Yard. Thomson was also deputy to the head of the Naval Intelligence Division, Admiral Sir Reginald Hall, in charge of British counterespionage. The interrogation lasted four hours that day, and was concluded in a second session only five days later.

In his memoirs, Thomson described Aaronsohn's arrival in London as "one of the most romantic incidents in the war experience of Scotland Yard."[2] First, Aaronsohn revealed to him the genesis of the comedy at Kirkwall. He was a scientist with contacts at the very highest level of the Ottoman regime, and had been given permission in that capacity to leave Turkish territory for allied Germany. There he proposed to continue research on a project to produce a heavier type of sesame oil, which he claimed could enhance the Turkish national food supply.

He spent several weeks in Germany, where he sought out colleagues in his fields of agronomy and botany, and impressed them with a detailed description of his nonexistent sesame plan. He then turned to the German authorities, and to the Turkish embassy in Berlin, to enable him to travel to neutral Sweden and Denmark where, he claimed, relevant experts would help him in his research.

To bolster his appeal, he mobilized an old Berlin friend, mentor and professional colleague — highly respected botany professor Otto Warburg, who innocently testified to Aaronsohn's bona fides, and the importance of such research. His wish was granted. He duly visited Sweden and Denmark, again met several old scientific colleagues, and then, in Copenhagen, exercising great caution, he made his way to the British legation.

For his talk with the British minister, Sir Roger Paget, he needed some kind of introduction. It arrived in the form of a telegram from the Secretary of Agriculture in Washington. Mr. Aaronsohn was in fact a "collaborator" of the US government "Bureau of Plant Industry" and thus officially on the staff of the Department of Agriculture. His presence, Sir Roger was informed, was urgently requested in Washington. Would Sir Roger be good enough to help

2. Basil Thomson, *Queer People* (London: Hodder and Stoughton, 1922), p. 201.

Aaronsohn procure passage on a boat bound for New York? He would have to obtain an assurance from London that Aaronsohn would not be challenged as an enemy alien when the boat passed through Kirkwall. This assurance was required by the shipping company — the Scandinavian-American Line — before they allowed any alien to travel on one of their vessels.

What Paget was persuaded to arrange with London, however, was rather more complex. In addition to the assurance to the shipping company that Aaronsohn would not be troubled at Kirkwall and would be enabled to continue the voyage to America, London was asked to be good enough to arrange a public violation of that assurance. By having Aaronsohn arrested with great fanfare, removed from the boat and prevented from traveling to America, news of which certainly reached Constantinople, the British would provide a pleasant surprise for the Turkish authorities: this highly respected scientist had evidently decided to become a spy for his government. Were it not for the arrest at Kirkwall, Aaronsohn's failure to return to Turkish territory would have dire consequences for his family at the village of Zichron Ya'akov in Turkish Palestine. And here he was in Sir Basil Thomson's office at Scotland Yard.

Aaronsohn's account of his odyssey, however, was only a foretaste of the war experience which he was to provide for Scotland Yard. It is likely that Thomson had seldom, perhaps never, heard a tale that seemed at first glance so wildly improbable. Here was a man who claimed that a small village in northern Palestine called Zichron Ya'akov was the center of a group of young men and women who on their own initiative had decided to help Britain win the war by gathering information from behind Turkish lines. Aaronsohn's purpose now was to reach Egypt, there to establish contact with the British military authorities — the Egyptian Expeditionary Force — and to arrange with them a means of regular communication with the group of which he was the leader.

Contact had in fact been made the previous year by Aaronsohn's right-hand man, Avshalom Feinberg, with a British intelligence officer in Cairo, Lieutenant Leonard Woolley, who had promised to make the arrangements for the execution of the project. Inexplicably, however, the contact had been broken off. After a long wait Aaronsohn had decided to make another try; hence his long, hazardous roundabout journey. Now he wanted London's cooperation to bring him to Egypt.

Thomson evidently satisfied himself that Aaronsohn was not a Turkish spy. When Aaronsohn came to Scotland Yard for a second meeting five days later Thomson told him that his inquiries had revealed the reason for Woolley's silence. He had been captured during an operation off the Syrian coast and was now a prisoner of war. He had unfortunately not passed on to his superiors any report of his conversations with Feinberg.[3]

Thomson also told Aaronsohn that the restrictions on the movements of aliens in London would no longer apply to him.

Even before that second meeting at Scotland Yard, however, Thomson had cleared him for a meeting at the War Office with the head of the Turkish desk — Major Walter Harold Gribbon — and so Aaronsohn was escorted to the War Office.

There took place an immediate meeting of minds. Gribbon was a genial man with a broad knowledge and understanding of Turkey and the Turks, his special expertise. In Aaronsohn he was startled to discover a mind of encyclopedic range on every conceivable subject relating to Turkey as a whole, as well as keenly analytical on the issues of the day. He boldly voiced criticism of the British conduct of the war. Shining through Gribbon's own later writing is a powerful empathy towards Aaronsohn and to the cause he was serving — an empathy which he extended to Aaronsohn's family after Aaronsohn's death, and indeed to the end of his life nearly three decades later.

---

3. After the war, archaeologist Woolley gained fame as the discoverer of Ur of the Chaldees.

CHAPTER 2

"The Mother of Wheat"

It may be said that the first link in the tortuous chain of circumstances which ultimately brought Aaronsohn to burst upon the British war scene in the autumn of 1916 was forged ten years earlier, in the late spring of 1906, on a windy height in the Galilee. On June 18 thirty-year-old botanist Aaronsohn made a discovery that brought him resounding fame throughout the world of science.

Generations of botanists had agonized over the theory that physical samples of the wild wheat growing in some arid zone of the world might, by means of hybridization with cultured wheat, make possible the production of a new strain of wheat in soils previously found inhospitable. The economic and social effects in less developed areas of the world could be considerable. The scientists had known for many years that such a sample of that "mother of wheat" — triticum dicoccoides — did exist. An Austrian scientist, Professor Kotschy, had actually found an ear of the "mother of wheat" in the year 1855, had failed to identify it, but cautiously deposited it in the Vienna Science Museum. There it lay, unconsidered, until it was seen and recognized fourteen years later by the German botanist Friedrich Koernicke.

Kotschy had made his find at Raschaya on the northwestern slope of Mount Hermon, which thus became the focus of search by many botanists. One of them, the noted American George Post, actually lived for some years at Raschaya. None of them had any success.

In 1902 Aaronsohn, by then already a scholar of repute, was visiting Berlin. There he was pressed by a group of distinguished botanists, among them Otto Warburg, Paul Ascherson, Friedrich Koernicke himself and George Schweinfurth — the noted botanist-geologist-African explorer — to try to find the elusive plant. During the next three years, Aaronsohn

11

accordingly — though not very energetically — added the search for wild wheat to his other activities.

In the summer of 1905 Aaronsohn, visiting Berlin, was again urged by Schweinfurth and Ascherson to resume the search in his zone. Sometime later, however, it was reported that Professor Post and another noted botanist, Bornmuller, had given up the search "in despair"; Aaronsohn was about to follow their example. Just then however he met with Professor Post, who explained that he had not "despaired"; he simply did not have "the time, the energy or the money" needed for the search.[1] Aaronsohn, however, did not resume the search immediately. He was busy with geological research. It was thus on June 18, 1906, in an orchard in the village of Rosh Pinna in the Galilee, when he was explaining to a companion the eocene origin of the region, that his eye caught, in the interstices of a rock, an ear of what turned out to be the wheat he was looking for. Search as he might, however, he found no more in the vicinity. Aaronsohn consequently decided to make a further attempt on Mount Hermon. He rode out on horseback, surveyed again the western slopes of the mountain — and found nothing. Then, almost as an afterthought, he rode around to the further eastern slope — and into a full field of wild wheat.

He was able later to ponder over the degree of chance that had helped him. Had he postponed for a few weeks the latter phase of his search he would have found nothing, for it soon became apparent that the wheat's season ended with the onset of the summer.

Aaronsohn's news from Palestine was greeted by an outburst of joy from the scientists who had urged him to make the search. What lent a special aura of drama and of unusual popular interest to the find was an ongoing dispute that was then being waged among scientists in both the botanic and humanistic fields as to the location of the cradle of our civilization. The argument was that our civilization had begun with the beginning of agriculture; and agriculture was born with the finding of the original wild "mother of wheat." For Professor Schweinfurth, Aaronsohn's discovery pointed to a confirmation of a long-held belief that civilization had begun in the Fertile Crescent centered on Syria-Palestine.

---

1. Aaronsohn to Koernicke (Bonn), March 28, 1907. Aaronsohn's letters, as mentioned in the introduction, are immediately accessible at the Aaronsohn House Museum in Zichron Ya'akov, and all letters referenced in this work were seen there.

Aaronsohn shared this broad assessment as well as the hope of immediate practical results from a cross-culturation of the wild wheat with modern wheat. As it turned out these hopes were not fulfilled. Experiments in cross-culturation, carried out in the United States, by Aaronsohn in Palestine, as well as by Koernicke in Germany, proved barren. As time went by the theory in its botanical context remained a subject of inconclusive debate.

"It is difficult to determine," wrote a later Israeli scientist, "to what degree there is an intellectual 'quantum leap' from the concept of improvement, by means of hybridization between cultivated plants, to the concept of transmission of characteristics from the wild to the cultivated. If there is such a leap, Aaronsohn was one of the first to make it independently."[2]

Aaronsohn's find, and its timing, however, signalled a sharp turn in his own life. Schweinfurth became most active in spreading the news. His account of the find and its significance appeared not only in scientific journals and in the Zionist periodical *Altneuland* (November 1906), but even in the influential German daily newspaper *Vossische Zeitung* (September 1906). Then aged seventy, Schweinfurth asserted that Aaronsohn's discovery was the most important he had heard of in his lifetime. In his enthusiasm he also sent the news to colleagues in the field. Among them was David Fairchild, of the United States Department of Agriculture, the agricultural explorer in charge of the Bureau of Plant Industry, nicknamed the "plant hunters." Their duties included precisely the seeking out of plants that might be accommodated in the soil of the United States.

The reaction from Washington came swiftly. Fairchild opened a correspondence with Aaronsohn, who was able to supply quantities of wild wheat from the Hermon for experimental use. Fairchild soon learned however of the vast scope of Aaronsohn's scientific resource; during the years of intensive research he had amassed a tremendous herbarium, and his knowledge of plant life throughout most of the Near East was unique.

A lively exchange ensued with requests for the supply of various plants required by Fairchild in his department. Fairchild invited him at an early

---

2. Dr. Shaul Katz, "Aaron Aaronsohn: Reshit ha-mada ve-reshit ha-mehkar ha-hakla'i be-Eretz Yisra'el [Aaron Aaronsohn: The beginnings of science and the beginnings of agricultural research in Eretz Israel]," *Cathedra*, no. 3 (1977): 3-29. See also Aaronsohn's own article "Le blé, l'orge et le siègle à l'état sauvage," *Bulletin of the Botanical Society of France* 61 (1909).

stage to visit the United States, but his research preoccupations (described in chapter 4) were such that he was able to do so only in 1909 when, for good reason, his journey was funded by the Zionist Organization.

Fairchild, in his memoirs (written more than thirty years later), describes the astonishing impact of that first encounter:

> I soon discovered that I was in the presence of an extraordinary man. Although Aaronsohn had never been there, his knowledge of California almost equalled his knowledge of Palestine. No foreigner had even been in my office who had so keen an understanding of the soils, climates, and adaptability of plants to their environment as had this friend of Schweinfurth. He had studied at the School of Agriculture at Montpellier, France,[3] but was largely self-educated, having collected a comprehensive library at his home in Haifa. His grasp of dry-land agriculture problems was astonishing.

Equally astonishing to Fairchild was Aaronsohn's capacity for communication:

> The speed with which Aaronsohn picked up English was amazing. In a week's time I heard him carrying on technical conversations, comparing the flora of Palestine and California.

His store of information proved so unusual that he was requested to write a bulletin on the cultivated plants of Palestine. He was one of those rare pioneer minds that quickly leaped at the essentials, and he sat down and in short order drafted an article covering a wide range of useful plants which, in his opinion, should find a congenial home in America.[4]

> Inasmuch as he had not seen the Pacific coast, we arranged a trip for him that summer, and put him in touch with the agricultural investigators of our western states. This trip proved a great success...[5]

---

3. Fairchild's error — it was Grignon.
4. Aaron Aaronsohn, "Agricultural and Botanical Explorations in Palestine," US Dept. of Agriculture, Bureau of Plant Industry Bulletin, no. 180 (Washington: Government Printing Office, 1910).
5. David Fairchild, *The World Was My Garden: Travels of a Plant Explorer* (New York and London: Charles Scribner's Sons, 1938).

This was an understatement. His tour can only be described as a triumph. His addresses, both to academics and to practical farmers, drew large audiences, and the regular reports he sent to his young sisters — Sarah, then nineteen, and seventeen-year-old Rivka who kept order in his herbarium and records — reflect a sense of great achievement. Two events on the tour, which lasted from the end of June to the end of October and covered all the western states, proved to be of special significance.

He came to the University of California at Berkeley, which was then the premier seat of learning in the field of agronomy and botany. Its reputation had been built up largely by the renowned Professor Hilgard. Hilgard was now over eighty years old, and had been relieved of his teaching duties. Aaronsohn came to pay his respects, and Hilgard expressed interest in his work, much of which had — as he demonstrated — been influenced by Hilgard.

The old professor did not hide his surprise at Aaronsohn's account. He started to question him more closely, and soon they were engaged in broad-ranging scientific discussion. Manifestly intrigued, Hilgard showed him around his extensive laboratory and urged him to lengthen his stay at Berkeley for a few days. He offered to have him shown around the vicinity of the university, which had much to offer to an observant scientist. "Thus," wrote Aaronsohn to his sisters:

> I went walking with a Professor Osterhout. We spent two days in the
> hills and we touched on thousands of scientific subjects.

After all that, he adds, "they admitted that they had played a trick on me." They had simply been putting him through a test, and discovered that they had finally found the right man to succeed the great Hilgard. The search for a worthy successor had been going on for two years. The next day the president of the university formally offered Aaronsohn the position.

Sarah and Rivka were most excited by the news. This was the most prestigious position that could be offered a scholar in his field, and financially attractive to boot. Aaronsohn turned down the offer. He pointed out to his sisters the many jealousies and enmities such an appointment to a much-courted post would create. In any case not only did he want to live in Palestine, but he had a dream: he meant to establish an agricultural experiment station of international standard within a stone's throw of their home village of Zichron Ya'akov.

He even mentioned his plan for an experiment station when two months later he lectured at Billings, Montana. Indeed the public highlight of his tour was the reaction to that address — given at a "dry-farming" conference. It turned out to be the central feature of the conference,[6] attended not only by the nine hundred dry-farming delegates, but six hundred more people including (as Aaron gleefully wrote) senators, diplomats and professors.[7] Overstepping the twenty minutes allotted to him, he was cheered on by the audience not to break off — and he spoke for a further twenty-five minutes. He was unanimously elected to serve as a vice president at the next conference. The conference, moreover, passed a number of special resolutions calling on the US Department of Agriculture to ensure that the lessons of Aaronsohn's lectures should receive practical application. To top it all off, the conference expressed its understanding of the importance to US agriculture of the experiment station that Aaronsohn projected in Palestine.

He had come to America with the raw idea of finding funds for its realization. Indeed, soon after his arrival in Washington, he had broached, to the friends he had made in the Department of Agriculture, the proposal that, because of its certain value to American agriculture, the US government should underwrite the project. The government however turned down the proposal. It was then that Aaronsohn decided to approach some of the famously rich Jews of America.

He of course did not know any American Jewish millionaires. It seems clear however that he enlisted Fairchild in the cause, and that his first contact through Fairchild was not indeed with a millionaire, but with a famous

---

6. "Wild Dryland Wheat of Palestine and Some Other Promising Plants," published in the *Dry Farming Congress Bulletin* 3, no. 190, pp. 161–71.
7. Letters to Sarah and Rivka, August 28 and October 14, 1909.

scholar, Dr. Cyrus Adler, then president of Dropsie College in Philadelphia. Adler then introduced Aaron to Oscar Strauss, a member of the famous family of philanthropists.

That was the beginning; one after another some of the wealthiest Jews in America fell under the spell of his personality. They were astounded by a broad general knowledge such as none of them had ever encountered, and an ease of manner which they, as very rich men, did not expect from a youngster of thirty-three. The very fact however that he had come from the "back-woods" of Turkey, added to the romance of his discovery of the wild wheat, captured their hearts. Still, this did not guarantee their putting up substantial sums for a project whose potential practical significance they perhaps did not entirely grasp. Aaronsohn showed considerable practical common sense when he enlisted Fairchild not only to effect introductions, but to plead his case.

"I was curious to know," recalled Fairchild, "why Aaronsohn wanted these introductions, and he explained to me that if he went himself with his story of the wild wheat, they would not believe him...." Aaronsohn was rather more precise in explaining to his sisters that these assimilated Jews would be impressed most of all by the recommendations of an important Gentile, and one moreover who had an American government department behind him.

Fairchild did not share Aaronsohn's oft-expressed optimism about the revolutionary consequence of the discovery for the world economy. He and a colleague, Walter Swingle, with whom too Aaronsohn soon established a warm rapport, were more enthused by Aaronsohn's vision of the experiment station's potential for American agriculture. "It was highly desirable," wrote Swingle, "to have an up-to-date Experimental Station and plant breeding garden somewhere at the eastern end of the Mediterranean...." From it "we could learn more about the agricultural crops of that region and their suit-ability for cultivation in California."

While still on tour, Aaronsohn met the business magnate Julius Rosenwald[8] and thereafter it was plain sailing for his project. A trustees' committee was formed. Among its members, in addition to Rosenwald and Nathan Strauss, were Supreme Court Judge Louis D. Brandeis, Judges Felix Frankfurter and Julian Mack as well as Rabbi Judah L. Magnes. Henrietta Szold, later the famous founder of Hadassah, took on the task of secretary.

---

8. Founder of the firm of Sears, Roebuck.

Two of the members served in Europe: Otto Warburg and Selig Soskin. There were only three declared Zionists among them: Warburg, later indeed president of the World Zionist Organization, Miss Szold and Soskin. The initial capital was organized among them. The station was registered as an official American institution.

These assimilated rich Jews were usually prepared to contribute for some philanthropic or even educational project, but objected to any hint of Zionism — that is to the idea that the Jews were a nation with a national homeland. As it turned out it was on this issue that Aaronsohn struck a snag. One of Rosenwald's friends, the famous philanthropist Jacob Schiff, did not immediately promise to participate, and it was evidently only after the intervention of the great and good Professor Hilgard that Schiff joined the committee. Then, one day, his representative on the committee, Professor Loeb, reported to him that the land for the station had already been made available by the Jewish National Fund, the Zionist fund for acquisition of land and, among other things, for afforestation of the denuded country.

Indeed the idea for a station had, at Aarohsohn's urging, been adopted several years earlier at a Zionist world congress, and the JNF had there and then announced its gift of the land — at Athlit on the coast near Haifa. It was because the Zionists were unable to allocate funds for the setting-up of the station that Aaronsohn had taken on himself the task of finding funds in America.

On hearing the report, Schiff exploded in anger. He was being involved in a Zionist project! This was out of the question. He would have none of it. On second thought, however, not wishing to withdraw from what was after all an important, healthy, educational project, he offered a compromise: he would purchase the land from the Jewish National Fund and gift it to the station. The JNF however was by its constitution strictly forbidden to sell land.

When Aaronsohn heard of Schiff's attitude, he did not mince words. "The source of the station," he wrote on October 3, 1909, to Warburg, "is Zionism.... Thanks only to Zionism have these philanthropists been given the opportunity to join in the venture." He described Schiff's rejection of the Jewish National Fund's offer as an insult. He concluded on a defiant note, "as somebody is going to have to give way, and as it is not I who is going to do so, Mr. Schiff had better accept the situation."

Schiff did give in. What pressure was exerted on him we do not know.

Fortunately for this outcome the debate was not conducted in any face-to-face encounter with Aaronsohn.

The Jewish Agricultural Experiment Station was established the very next year, 1910, at Athlit some ten miles south of Haifa. Maybe the proximity of the Aaronsohn home at Zichron Ya'akov influenced Aaronsohn's choice of site, but undoubtedly the main reason was that, for the experiments he had in mind, the variety of soils on that coastal stretch were particularly suitable. Parts were poor — just the kind to encourage plants whose demands on the soil were minimal. Good results from a poor soil, he wrote to the trustees in New York, were more impressive than heavier yields from fertile ground. On the other hand, parts of the station's acreage were swampy, with promise of great fertility.

Aaronsohn, through years of meticulous observation and research, had by this time acquired a tremendous grasp of the botanical and agricultural potential of the small but multifaceted country. Now he had at his command an essential tool for putting that potential to work.

He needed only a small staff of professional scientists, and he was able to call on the services of members of his family, primarily his young sisters. Both were not only of high intelligence but had long been inducted into the lore of plant discovery. Indeed Rivka was the official custodian of his large and evergrowing herbarium; and it seems that she and Sarah even participated in some of Aaron's searches, as did another assistant, his close friend and disciple Avshalom Feinberg.[9]

The station was an immediate functional success, best evidenced by the service it was able to render to the US Department of Agriculture. The volume of surviving correspondence between Athlit and Washington reflects an enormous weight of data and of physical plant samples that reached Fairchild and Swingle and their colleagues — as well as the quantity that they, for their part, were able to send to Athlit. The efforts they had invested in

---

9. See the favorable comment on Aaronsohn's researches by a noted botanist of the next generation, Professor H. R. Oppenheimer, in the foreword to *Tsemah ma'arav hayarden* [Flora west of the Jordan] (Tel Aviv, 1940), p. 136.

promoting Aaronsohn's plan for the station among the American Jewish millionaires was vindicated many times over.

Aaronsohn was the first nature scientist to grasp the fact that California was the "main source for the import of agricultural knowledge to the agriculture of Eretz Israel." Writing seven decades later, Israeli botanist Shaul Katz added that the Californian role "has been to this day a prime element in the development of agriculture and of agricultural research in this country."[10]

What is more, the fame of the experiment station spread far and wide throughout the world; and a steady flow of correspondence developed from all the continents — requests for information on plants and on dry farming — from scientists, farmers, universities, government departments and agricultural institutes. These indeed were proclaimed objectives of the station. The results of its research and experiments, initiated by its director, were destined to be made available for all the arid and semi-arid areas in the world. Similarly oriented for universal application were Aaronsohn's ideas and recommendations in the agricultural field. Their direct and immediate impact however was naturally in Palestine itself. Here the mandate of the station was to disseminate instruction and advice (in Hebrew, Turkish and Arabic) for the guidance of agriculturalists, and to reach the community as a whole through the children. Aaronsohn thus devoted special attention to the school teachers.

An eloquent evaluation of Aaronsohn's impact on them is contained in the description of the groundbreaking summer study conference of teachers that he organized at Zichron Ya'akov in 1912. Among those who participated was Israel Reichert, later professor of agriculture at the Hebrew University of Jerusalem and noted as an expert on plant conservation:

> Before Aaronsohn's advent there was no established teaching of nature studies, nor any [lessons in] observation of the periphery of the school. The teacher himself was ignorant of his surroundings.... Teachers had no knowledge of the natural phenomena of the land. Those "summer lessons" for the first time opened to the teacher the

---

10. See Shaul Katz, "Aaron Aaronsohn: Reshit ha-mada." See also N. Y. Nuttson, "Agriculture Climatology, Physical Belts, and Crop Ecology of Palestine and Transjordan and their Analogues in the United States," American Institute of Crop Ecology (Washington, 1947).

enchanted palace of nature study.... The glory of the flora and the
mountains was brought home to us...the way they breathed, their
structure, their very names.[11]

Soon, however, Aaronsohn ran into a wave of very serious criticism. In disre-
gard of the unequivocal policy — indeed the ideology — of the Zionist movement, Aaronsohn employed Arab workers on the land. A more grievous sin
against the Zionist idea could not be imagined. Beyond the revival of Jewish
national independence, a no less crucial purpose of Zionism was to correct
and normalize the lopsided economic structure of the Jewish people. Born of
discrimination in many parts of the Diaspora, one of its two most important
components (the other was the prohibition of bearing arms) was the exclusion of Jews from owning land. Thus the physical return of Jews to the
national homeland was signalled by the purchase of land — and by working
it.

That movement had begun long before the advent of Herzl and the birth
of the Zionist Organization at the First Zionist Congress in Basel in 1897 (it
became the World Zionist Organization [WZO] in 1960). The new rural
township (*moshava*) of Petah Tikva, and an agricultural school, Mikve
Yisrael, near Jaffa, were established in the 1870s. In the 1880s the "back to the
land" movement received a great boost. An organization for that specific
purpose was established in Eastern Europe; perhaps even more significant
was the historic entry onto the stage of a Rothschild, Baron Edmond of Paris,
who established a small "empire" of villages, from the far north of the country
almost to the borders of the Negev, where groups of Jewish pioneers
(*halutzim*) began to till the land.

Rothschild laid down rules for his workers, and one of the most stringent
was the imperative that only Jews must work the land. Significantly, Arabs
could be, and were, employed in Rothschild's administration — but not on
the land itself. There every square inch was sacred to the ideal of righting the
historic distortion of centuries.

It was consequently in a mood of great expectancy — tempered at first by
some scepticism — that the promise of an agricultural experiment station
was greeted by the community. Great was the shock when it was learned that

11. Y. Reichert, "L'zecher Aaron Aaronsohn [In memory of Aaron Aaronsohn]," *Hed
Hahinukh* (1943-44): 11-12.

not all the work places would be reserved for Jews. True, there were also individual Jewish farmers who employed Arabs on the land. They were
constantly being admonished — indeed their behavior was a regular subject
of angry debate. They, however, were all private people; the station, though
also in fact private, was seen as a semi-public institution. And had not even its
land been gifted by the Jewish National Fund?

Aaronsohn remained unmoved by the criticism.[12] He did not question
the force of the Zionist purpose. Indeed he was angered by the imputation
that he was violating it. He claimed, however, that it did not have to be applied
rigidly and universally. He saw his own pragmatic considerations as serving
the Zionist aim. Employing a number of Arab workers, he calculated, would
enhance the quality of Jewish farming. There was much, he asserted, that the
Jews, with their more modern methods and machinery, could teach the
Arabs; but there was also much that the Jews could learn from the Arabs,
some of whose primitive methods were still effective. It would be foolish to
forego this contribution to the upbuilding of Jewish agriculture.

Aaronsohn himself published some examples; by all independent
accounts there was considerable merit in his views. There is the story of the
"Palestinian plough." "The founders of Petah Tikva," later wrote a science
historian, "agonized over the question of what kind of plough they should use
to break up the soil. They saw the 'poor' plough of the Arab fellah (peasant)
— consisting of a wooden body with a sharp edge of iron — and they mocked
it. That was why their first efforts were made with European ploughs unsuit-
able for working the soil of the land. In time, the old plough, with some
improvements by a young blacksmith, was restored to its former glory."[13]

Aaronsohn expressed his view in precise and forceful terms:

> Not only is the European method not useful but it is harmful to the
> crops. I wished to emphasize the value of the Arabs' agricultural
> traditions. Even now (1912) I continue to learn from them. I don't
> pay attention to their reasons and their explanations because they are

---

12. Some of it was plainly malicious. When Julius Rosenwald was visiting Palestine in
    1914, the journal of the Labor movement, *Hapoel Hatza'ir*, complained that
    Aaronsohn was employing only Arabs and was disseminating information only to
    the Arabs.
13. Shmuel Avitzur in *Etmol* 1, no. 2 (June 1975): 8–10.

usually wrong, but I respect their agricultural experience and I reckon with it. If I was offered a faculty in California it was not because of knowledge I acquired in Europe, and if I was invited by the American Department of Agriculture to lecture on dry farming it was only because I live in an ancient land where this system was created.[14]

He was even more explicit with the writer Yosef Klausner (later famous as a historian and professor at the Hebrew University of Jerusalem). Klausner, on a visit from Russia in 1912, was enthralled by Aaronsohn. He took him to task however for employing Arabs. Aaronsohn retorted: "Wherever I can employ Jews I do so. There are swamps around us and the Jewish workers come down with malaria. The Arabs are accustomed to the bad climate. You can't do everything you'd like to do. Without Arabs I'm not sure I'd be able to maintain the station." And he added, "We are surrounded by Arab villages, and we must live at peace with them."[15]

However, even his friends remained unconvinced — and an incident provided him with dramatic evidence. At the end of the teachers' summer school it was decided to make a tour of the station (some eight miles away). One of the participants described how, on their way to Athlit, Aaronsohn "aroused our wonderment with his knowledge and his love for every plant and every bush, every stone and every hill. He knew everything — everything above the ground and everything in the bowels of the earth; and great was our love for him."

But when the teachers saw the many Arabs working at the station, love turned quickly to hostility — at least in the hearts of those who were members of the Hapoel Hatza'ir labor movement. At their initiative a very stern resolution was passed at the closing ceremony of the school. Aaronsohn's policy, it asserted, "weakened the Jewish position in the country, conflicted with the strivings of the nation" and with "the work of national education at which we are toiling."

Aaronsohn replied with evident reason that his experience in the field

---

14. K. Y. Silman (Mimeila), "Summer Lessons for Teachers at Zichron," *Hapoel Hatza'ir*, no. 24 (September 1912).
15. Eliezer Livneh, *Aaron Aaronsohn, Ha'ish u-zmano* [Aaron Aaronsohn: The man and his time] (Jerusalem: Bialik Institute, 1969), p. 164.

was greater than that of those who had created the term "Jewish labor." The issue could not be forced. "If we wish to introduce Jewish labor, we must move forward gradually. We [at the station] are trying to do this…. We all have the same aim, but our methods are different. The day will come when we shall achieve that common purpose."[16]

The conflict — with logic on each side — remained unsolved. His critics in the labor movement, evidently unwilling to admit that there was an honest second side to the dispute, decided to demonize their antagonist. They pretended that his advocacy and employment of a proportion of Arab labor was not dictated by practical and positive reasons which he believed would benefit Zionism and the Jewish community — but by "hatred for the Jewish workers."

This circumstance lends significance to the case of one important labor maverick. In early 1915, Rahel Lishansky (Yanait), a young but already prominent member of Hapoel Hatza'ir who had been studying agronomy for two years at Nancy, France, came to learn and work at the station. She had been made fully aware of the extreme hostility of her fellow Socialists to Aaronsohn, but when she met him and had taken his measure she decided that he was "a proud Jew," and she dismissed totally as nonsense that he was "an enemy of the Jewish workers." She was shocked, and said so, by the large (though then reduced) number of Arabs employed there. However she did not allow this to deter her. Upbraided by some of her fellow Socialists, who repeated the ready-to-hand charge that Aaronsohn was "an enemy of the Jewish workers," she retorted: "If the station were situated in a monastery in some obscure corner of the country I would go there to study the nature of our land and its cultural products."[17]

It would be futile to try to measure the positive elements of Aaronsohn's policy against the fierce but understandable opposition which it aroused.

---

16. *Hapoel Hatza'ir* (20 Elul 5672 [September 3, 1912]).
17. Rahel Yanait Ben-Zvi, *Anu olim* [We go up] (Tel Aviv: Am Oved, 1959), p. 221. She later married Yitzhak Ben-Zvi, who became the second president of the State of Israel.

Moreover the conflict was heated by an ongoing state of friction and mutual denigration between the labor element of the "Second Aliyah" (1905-14) and the families of the "First Aliyah" among whom the Aaronsohns were seen as the "leaders." The hatred toward Aaron pursued him to the end of his days — and beyond.

The life of the station turned out to be brief. Its significant scientific activities slowed down with the onset of war in 1914, and came to an end by 1916; most of its contents were destroyed by the Turks in 1917. As a scientific institution its impact was consequently fleeting, and a sympathetic and scientifically knowledgeable commentator writing in the 1970s mourned: "Thus came the end to the pioneer of institutes of research in the nature sciences and agriculture in Eretz Israel. The outstanding remnant of the Jewish Agricultural Experiment Station is the long avenue of Washingtonia palms east of Athlit."[18]

Another truth, however, another history, emerged from that station. Through it a group of young Jewish men and women acquired a broad universal training in what may be called Palestinology. Something, maybe much, of the unique catholicity of Aaronsohn's own autodidactically acquired knowledge was certainly transmitted to his young assistants and pupils. In the four years before the World War, these young people, nearly all native born, soaked up an intricate knowledge of the country, its hills and valleys, its highways and numerous byways, its flora and its fauna. All this was topped by their perfect knowledge of Turkish and Arabic, of the folk habits of the Arab peasants, of the abilities, pretensions and weaknesses of the Turkish officials.

Looking back on those years from a distance of eight decades, one's imagination must conjure up a far-seeing mind which, several years before the World War, foreordained a succession of unrelated events that would bring about a seemingly inconceivable result. Foreseeing that this group of young people in Ottoman Palestine would in the not distant future serve as the members of an intelligence organization behind the Turkish lines to help the British invader fight the war, that mind would have carved out precisely the preconditions in Palestine that would prepare them for their mission — including the experiment station as their headquarters.

18. Shaul Katz, "Aaron Aaronsohn: Reshit ha-mada," p. 23.

CHAPTER 3

The Clash with Rothschild

Efraim Fishel Aaronsohn and his wife Malka came to Palestine from Romania in the autumn of 1882, bringing with them six-year-old Aaron. The family was part of a group of four hundred and fifty souls, who were simply Jews "going up" to their ancient homeland. Their idea was to "return to the land," which meant to become farmers, build for themselves, and collectively help build the land for their people. The idea — alive for nineteen centuries — had not yet been given its modern name: Zionism.

The reception the land gave them was most inhospitable. Whatever descriptions they may have heard or read of its wild and near-barren landscape were only too fully realized in their own experience. A member of the group, Batya Liebman, described their arrival in a book on the early history of Zichron Ya'akov written by one of the group's descendants:[1]

> The journey [from the port] lasted all day. Some of us rode mules, others in wagons drawn by oxen. In the evening we reached the foothills of the Samarian mountains. In those days there were no roads. A narrow path led to the summit of the wild mountain. As we stood at its foot the land was shrouded in darkness. The oxen refused to go further. Two men began to hack with axes at the thick bushes, but in vain. In the end they had to take the wagons apart and loaded their parts and their contents on their shoulders. The oxen, having been persuaded to move, were driven ahead while behind them trailed the women with their infants in arms. We climbed for several hours,

---

1. Aryeh Samsonov, *The Book of Zichron Ya'acov* (Zichron Ya'acov, 1940).

surrounded by darkness and deathly silence — a silence broken only
from time to time by the howling of jackals.[2]

The ground on which the pioneers proposed building their houses and which
they intended to work was covered by rocks. Much of it was unbreakable even
to the indigenous Arab plough. Actually settling in had to be postponed.
They soon were forced to evacuate the women and the children, who were
lodged temporarily in Haifa while the men painfully cleared the ground and
built dwellings.[3]

Their money began to run out: they had had to pay for their plots of land.
They tried pooling what remained in a "commune," but this promised no
rational solution. Hungry and nearly desperate, they were salvaged by the
helping hand of Baron Edmond Rothschild, who took them under the wing
of his remarkable, probably unprecedented, personal major colonizing
project. A fascinating description of the prelude to Rothschild's intervention
is described by Aryeh Samsonov in his *Book of Zichron Ya'akov*. In the days of
their greatest need a Mr. Venitziani Hirsch, visiting from Paris, informed the
pioneers that he was empowered to make them an offer from Baron Hirsch,
the German-Jewish tycoon. Hirsch was promoting the salvation of the Jews
of Eastern Europe by establishing them in the Argentine.

He now proposed through Mr. Hirsch that the Zichron Jews join the
Argentine venture. Apart from other benefits, the offer included traveling
expenses. The offer was met at first by stony silence, but in a free discussion
the Zichronites explained their idealistic motives. Thereupon Hirsch urged a
close confidant of Baron Rothschild, Rabbi Tsadok Cohen, to bring their
plight to his attention. There were no doubt other influences, but the Baron
himself, on his later visit to Zichron, declared that it was Tsadok Cohen who
had influenced him. It was not an act of charity that he was performing, he
declared, but a contribution to the rehabilitation of Jewish national culture,
endangered as it was by the conditions of the Jews in Eastern Europe.

---

2. The eerie sense of silence in the whole country comes through in the reports of trav-
    elers from Europe of the late eighteenth and early nineteenth centuries. See for
    example Mark Twain, *Innocents Abroad* (New York, 1869), and Alphonse de
    Lamartine, *The Holy Land; Or, Recollections of the East* (London: George Virtue,
    1845), pp. 268, 308.
3. It was only a decade later that the village was cleared of its rocks by eighteen hundred
    workers (Livneh, *Aaron Aaronsohn*).

(Zamarin,[4] the Arab name for the village, was later named after Baron Edmond's father Yaacov.) As part of the Rothschild structure, the Zichron pioneers, like many hundreds of other pioneers in Palestine of the late nineteenth century, were enabled in time to stand on their own feet. The aid the Baron gave them was carefully channelled by his officials, whose relations with the settlers, however, were often as stony as the ground they worked on. Many years of hard struggle lay ahead.

It was as a child then that Aaronsohn imbibed many of the hard and demanding lessons of pioneering life in Palestine. He also imbibed, however, the spirit of resistance, in reaction to the incredible hardships and tribulations suffered by his father and mother. A study of the photograph of his father rather suggests an unusually sweet personality. It does not reflect the hardy endurance of difficulties, and the accommodation to hardship, nor his fierce, even obesssive attachment to the land. Efraim Fishel Aaronsohn was up every morning at dawn to rush off to morning prayers in the synagogue, and from there to his orchard and his fields. Aaron would bring his breakfast to him out in the field. Maybe it was his extreme diligence and the love of his labors that made it possible for him to be the first settler to come to the Baron's agent, Eliyahu Scheid, after five years to tell him that he no longer needed the Baron's aid.

The impact of the harsh beginnings is more obviously imprinted in the photograph of Aaron's mother, Malka. The features are strong and not without a touch of bitterness. By the testimony of her son Alexander[5] she was shrewd and kind. Like the girls of her time in Eastern Europe she had not had much formal schooling. She was however an inveterate reader and had no inhibitions about expressing her opinion on any subject that arose. Then she revealed a sharp humor. "What's the use of learning?" she would say, "give me character!" or, "Don't judge a cobbler by his present occupation; first find out whether he intends to remain a cobbler."

Malka Aaronsohn is accorded a special mention in Samsonov's account. "Her wise and industrious hands turned her poor house into a modest peaceful habitation; whitewashing the walls inside and out, she hangs over the

---

4. *Zamarin*, a corruption of the Hebrew *Shomron*, Samaria.
5. Alexander was the youngest son, born after Zvi and Shmuel (Sam). The girls, Sarah (1891) and Rivka (1893) came later.

'windows' — they are actually holes in the wall — a masterpiece of curtains made from remnants of bedsheets. When her husband comes back from the fields, tired out by the day's toil, every corner of the house shines with light and joy...."[6]

Yet in the wrenchingly crucial decisions of those awful days, it was surely her toughness that provided an inspiration to Aaron — and not to him alone. There came a time (in 1899) when the Baron transferred his holdings and his authority to the colonizing organization that had meanwhile grown up, the Jewish Colonization Association (ICA, renamed in 1924 the Palestine Jewish Colonization Association, or PICA). Its officials decided to cut expenses, and to convert some of the pioneers from aspiring independent farmers to wage laborers. Some of them left. At a meeting held at the Aaronsohn home to decide what to do, it was suggested that the purpose of the ICA officials was precisely to reduce the number of settlers. At this point in the proceedings, Malka, who was busy serving tea, made what became a famous pronouncement: "Even if we have to gnaw stones we're not moving anywhere."

The curriculum at the village school was limited to three subjects: Hebrew, Arabic and French. There Aaron, like all his fellow pupils, completed his formal education at the age of eleven, and went to work for the Baron. However, neither during his four years at school as laid down by the Baron, nor afterwards, did his parents accommodate themselves to those limitations. They provided him with private lessons. The teachers, mostly pioneers themselves, had never attended a university or a teachers' training college, but they were all excellent. The Baron did not want any professional teachers. Aaron thus learned Talmud from Leib Eizenstein; Jewish history from Ze'ev Yavetz; Bible and "advanced" Hebrew from Moshe Hurwitz, previously a good farm laborer; French from Haim Tsifrin, a former master carpenter who was the school's headmaster; and Arabic from a young man named Mograbi from Haifa. Aaron's command of a juicy Yiddish he "received" from his mother.

From morning to evening he would ride about on his horse, Abir.

Gaining at an early age his first experience of practical farming, he at once felt drawn to it. He evidently excelled, for after a year's labor, he was appointed assistant to the works supervisor. It was hard and responsible

---

6. Samsonov, *The Book of Zichron Ya'acov.*

work, visiting all the points of activity in the colony and its environs, watching with a growingly observant eye the planting of vines and olives, a variety of fruit trees, eucalyptus and pine. Guided by gardeners who were brought as experts from France, he learned the lore of agriculture in all its aspects.

Yet it cannot be far from the truth to say that it was from his father that he absorbed that special intimacy with the land that later often stunned his listeners — a belief in the mutuality of a loving nurture of the land, to which it responded by the gift of its fruits, its flowers, its trees, its insects, its rocks. "It was," his brother wrote, "as though he heard its voice, which he alone could hear."[7]

The work however did not enslave him. With his friends in the village, "in the free hours, on festivals, at night, they would race their horses to nearby and distant surroundings. To the tents of Beduin, to Arab villages, to Caesaria and Sidna-Ali (on the coast). They would meet Arab friends and go out riding with them, competing, quarrelling, making-up..."[8]

From among the sons of his villages, the Baron would choose promising youngsters to be sent abroad to France for further training. Thus at the end of 1893 Aaron was sent to study for two years at the Agricultural College at Grignon. Two years and no more. The Baron did not want his protégés to earn a diploma which might induce them to seek their fortunes in France. Moreover, he kept regular track of their studies, and he had them adhere strictly to the living rules he had laid down. He made them an adequate monthly allowance, which also covered some entertainment. It had to be spent that month; no savings were allowed. (They might otherwise be applied to some unapproved Parisian self-indulgence.) On one occasion he discovered that Aaron and a fellow student had remained with a balance of twenty francs. He simply deducted twenty francs from their next month's budget. However, he encouraged and made possible their exposure to the glories of French culture, of music, of painting, of architecture, of theater. Aaron had long been in love with French literature. French was the "language of European culture" in Zichron. Now its immediacy was a manifest joy. The French experience fortified his broad knowledge of French history — and sharpened his sense of the struggle that still lay ahead for the renewal of his own people.

---

7. Livneh, *Aaron Aaronsohn.*
8. Ibid.

Further stimulus in that direction was provided by the monstrous Dreyfus case, which exploded on the French scene precisely during the two years, 1893–95, that Aaron spent at Grignon. Horrified he was but, in his innocence, he wrote in a letter to his parents: "How is it possible that a nation that has produced a Zola, a Clemenceau and a Picard could also nurture a fanatic like Drumont?" His studies at Grignon evidently proved fruitful. Before leaving for home he was informed by Eliyahu Scheid, the head of the Baron's administration in Palestine, that he had been appointed agricultural instructor at the new colony of Metulla in the Galilee.

Aaron revered the father figure of the Baron. Like all the children of the Baron's villages, he had been brought up to the knowledge that Rothschild was a bountiful fabled prince to whom their families owed a tremendous debt of love and respect, and whose only precondition for his bounty was that they work hard and live as good Jews. Now, twenty years old, Aaron was filled with profound gratitude for having been given a scientific education which had expanded considerably his store of knowledge, broadened his intellectual horizons, and would surely give direction to his innate talents.

In several conversations he was briefed in Paris personally by the Baron on the special duties that awaited him in Palestine.

Metulla, established a year earlier on lands bought from Druze villagers, was to become a new model for the management of the Baron's ventures. The envisaged new policy was simple in its essence. It can be easily summarized: instead of spoonfeeding the farmers with loans over an indefinite number of years they would be provided with the means for making a livelihood; but they must stand on their own feet at the end of one year.

Personal initiative and resourcefulness would become dominant elements in their lives; and Aaronsohn, the agricultural director of the project, was being given the most responsible task in its implementation. Brimming with enthusiasm he arrived at Metulla on August 23, 1896, shortly after his twentieth birthday. Ten months later, on June 15, 1897, after a bitter exchange, he sent in a letter of resignation to the Baron. Though they did meet many years later, no close relationship was ever restored between them.

It had not taken long for Aaron to discover that the Baron's senior staff in charge of his Galilee operation was riddled with corruption. Yet four months went by before he drew any conclusions. One can surmise why he waited. In the first place, his revelations only served to confirm what was common knowledge throughout the community. Indeed he writes in his diary, (November 19, 1896):

> My impressions on arriving in Metulla were the same as always in the Baron's colonies. Here as always he has been cheated…. He has been imposed upon….

Then, it certainly was not his personal duty to report to the Baron on the wrongdoings of his agents. But when the fulfillment of his duties and the implementation of the Baron's new policy for Metulla were undermined, he had no alternative but to report to his employer on the difficulties he was encountering.

The Baron was being robbed. The thousand dunams of grassland which he had told Aaron would be at his disposal did not exist. What he found was a rocky hill. Furthermore, each settler farmer (so the Baron had told him) was to be given two hundred dunams for producing field crops. Careful measurement revealed to Aaron that what each farmer would receive was little more than half the intended allotment — one hundred seventeen and a half dunams. Two flour mills which, the Baron had assured him, would yield an income of four thousand francs, did indeed exist, but both were in a state of extreme disrepair. When repaired they might conceivably yield an income of four hundred francs.

Equipment required for ploughing with horses and new ploughs — all of which Aaron had been promised that he would find on arrival at Metulla — were not there. Later, when wood and leather accessories arrived, Aaron found that they were made of low quality materials. The merchant through whom all the accessories had been purchased was the brother-in-law of the head of the Baron's administration in the Galilee. To top it all, the Druze from whom the land had been bought had been underpaid, and they threatened trouble.

The income from the land and the mills, according to the details of Rothschild's plan, would have provided a living for each farmer. Failing these essential prerequisites, Aaron was soon compelled to ask for funds for a specific task (planting of olives). This was refused; and he was even rebuked by the Baron (through his administrator, Scheid). The Baron, he was told, regarded a request for funds as a return to the old system.

It was only then that Aaron wrote to the Baron in tones of controlled anger:

> We are too well aware of the failings of the old established settlements
> to want to introduce them in Metulla…. We know that the Baron
> wished Metulla to be a model colony, but to achieve this purpose it is
> essential that Metulla should in fact receive what it was promised in
> principle.

This and later reports by Aaronsohn were sent to Rothschild through the hierarchy of the guilty administrators. Thus attacked, they took the opportunity of accusing Aaron of several misdemeanors. Aaron defended himself vigorously, always by letters that went through Scheid and Ovsievitz (the head of the operation in the Galilee).

The Baron's reply came nearly three months after Aaron's first letter (March 16, 1897). It consisted of a blistering attack. He described Aaron's letters as "most ridiculous." He charged him with being a "youngster just out of school who poses as a reformer and big chief…. At your age one should be more modest." He should learn, the Baron continued, to obey and follow the advice of experienced people. Worst of all, he charged him with lying and exaggeration. He hoped that the letter would serve as a cold shower.

Aaronsohn could not be certain why the Baron accepted automatically the word of tried, trusted and "experienced" servants against that of a mere "whippersnapper." Was it because he was actually ignorant of the wrongdoing of those servants, or was it because he knew, but was too proud to admit, that he was being duped and robbed?

Rothschild was, after all, a complex character. He was not at that time merely the greatest living benefactor of the Jewish people, but used his great wealth according to a grand design. He was a great man by any criterion; and great men have their faults. He was an autocrat, open to ideas, but very self-opinionated. Aaronsohn was caught somewhere in that complex.

Aaronsohn did not refrain from viewing the overall problems of the Baron's organization, but he kept his conclusions to himself — in his diary. There he wrote (on November 19):

> Since my arrival in Metulla I have already come to the conclusion
> that the Baron has not yet been successful in his colonies

substantially through his own fault, but enormously more because of the falseness of his empowered appointees.

It is possible that Aaronsohn's letter did have an effect, though seemingly unrelated. Ovsievitz was soon transferred to a position outside the Galilee, and Scheid left the Baron's organization altogether. Aaronsohn, meantime, having been told that the Baron refused to receive further letters from him, wrote one long, sad letter (March 15, 1897), again in due deference, but reaffirming the veracity of all he had written. "I would be dishonest, a liar and despicable," he wrote, "if I did not warn my noble protector…. At Metulla and in Upper Galilee there exists a gang of officials, wonderfully organized to deceive you…and abuse your trust."

He pleaded for ten minutes of the Baron's time in Paris. When this was not granted, he resigned from the Baron's service (June 15). He was 21 years old, and out of work.

If he did not change his ways and did not do as he was told, the Baron had written him, "You will have to go back to your father and work in his vineyard." Aaron did indeed go home, but did not return to the vineyard. While pondering over his future, he unburdened himself of his bitterness in letters to his friends. Dramatically enough, within weeks of his resignation, he was made aware of the fate of his successor, his friend Belinki who, falling foul of the officials, had confronted the Baron's agent in Paris and had been refused an audience with the Baron. He too resigned in disgust. In Metulla he had nourished the mollifying belief that the Baron was unaware of the misdemeanors of his employees. Now in Paris he discovered how mistaken he had been, and was even planning to write a book on his experiences. Aaronsohn received the idea approvingly but abjured him: "Say what you like about the others, but don't hurt the Baron's name."

His own reputation did not suffer as a result of his break with the Baron. On the contrary, he was received with enthusiasm by the community in the Baron's domains; they had all partaken of his officials' bitter herbs. Nor, despite Scheid's refusal to give him a reference, did he remain for long without offers of employment. Indeed, within weeks of his departure from Metulla, he faced a difficult choice between two proposals.

One of the great landowners of the region, the Sursouk family of Lebanon, invited him to come and manage their large estate at Chtaura in the

Bek'a. It was professionally a very attractive offer, and there was no apparent reason why he should not jump at its challenge, its status and the generous emoluments it promised. He was sorely troubled however by its implications. It was clear to him that the ambitious Sursouks, impressed as they undoubtedly were by his capacities, must certainly be interested in learning through him the innards of the Baron's modern farming methods, then already mechanized, particularly in the developing field of winery. Aaron would thus become an instrument of the Sursouks for competing with the Baron.

That was not all. He could not obliterate the recollection of his original debt to the Baron, nor could he suppress the fear that he would be helping to undermine the infant Jewish economy as a whole. He asked the advice of his close friends. Most of them favored acceptance of the offer, but in his heart of hearts he doubtless knew he would not take the post if the Baron disapproved. He consequently wrote the Baron, setting out the reasons for declining the offer, and asking for the Baron's opinion. The Baron replied that there was no reason to decline. However, he did not send his reply direct to Aaronsohn, but to one of his agents at Zichron — Ben-Shmuel (a friend of Aaron's) — who delayed its delivery. By this time, however, Aaronsohn had decided on his own to reject the offer.

The alternative proposal came from an old friend of the Grignon days, Ben-Dano. He had just resigned as manager of the estate of the French family Couzeniera in Anatolia in order to take up the management of Baron Hirsch's farming colony. Hirsch was moved, like Rothschild, by the idea of returning Jews to the land, except that he believed the right place for this was in the Argentine. Ben-Dano was now prepared to recommend Aaronsohn to the Couzeniera family for the vacant post.

The family had extensive interests in both agriculture and industry, they were well known for progressive business methods — and Aaronsohn could discover no moral objection to working for them.

Thus at the end of September 1897, little more than two months after his leaving Metulla, he set out — with fare money borrowed from friends — for Jehan Pacha, the Couzeniera estate near the town of Magnesia in Anatolia. On his way he stopped over at Beirut for a friendly visit to the Sursouk family.

For two years his career at Magnesia evidently proceeded to mutual satisfaction. Two circumstances brought it to a sudden end. One was foreseeable. In spite of interesting and variegated responsibilities on the estate, from which he found much to learn, he was homesick. There was nothing in the life of the Jewish community at Magnesia to attract or challenge him. To the contrary: its shallowness and a pervasive atmosphere of nepotism and corruption disgusted him. He did however maintain a lively correspondence with his friends in Palestine and was kept up-to-date on all the gossip, especially that surrounding the Baron's officials. Aaron's enemies had been ousted, and the Baron was preparing to dismantle the bureaucratic structure over which he presided and to place his whole venture in the hands of the ICA organization. There the Baron would play a much diminished role. A sense of satisfaction at these developments did not lessen Aaron's loneliness. Moreover, while on a visit to Zichron to buy cattle for the Couzeniera estate, an effort he made to find some satisfactory employment proved fruitless.

It was the other circumstances — more complex and most unpleasant — to which he succumbed. Ben-Dano had not been successful in Argentine. Aaronsohn, through various connections he had established, tried in vain to find work for him, both in Turkey and in Palestine. Precisely at this juncture his expanding responsibilities called for the appointment of an assistant. Not very wisely he proposed Ben-Dano. The Couzenieras agreed — and an impossible situation, which he might have foreseen, was created. Soon Ben-Dano was criticizing his working methods, and it was not long before he was passing on his criticisms directly to their employers (who were Ben-Dano's personal friends). Then he confronted Aaronsohn with the retrospective charge that he had "always" been a "false friend."

Aaronsohn wrote to the employers: "It seems that Mr. Ben-Dano wants to regain his position. I think it is my duty to resign." Thus was he rewarded for his efforts to help Ben-Dano — and he wrote a bitter letter to his close friend Dr. Hillel Joffe, on man's inhumanity to man.

It is possibly hindsight that suggests that the turn of the century was followed by a period of restlessness or lack of orientation in Aaronsohn's life. He needed to make a living, and his logical tendency was to find an occupation in which he could exercise his agricultural expertise. He offered his services to the administrative head of the Jewish Colonization Association (ICA), to whom Baron Rothschild had turned over his projects in the country; but despite an acknowledgement of his talents, he was turned down. It was suggested to him that he had been abrasive in some encounter during his service in Metulla.

He was annoyed by the attitude of the ICA officials. To Dr. Hillel Joffe he complained: "They believe they have a monopoly of the living resources in Eretz Yisrael." Consequently "they ought to be shown that one can live here without depending on their support."

At the same time he was not unhappy over his rejection by the ICA. As he explained to Dr. Joffe he found the idea of "individual pioneering" more attractive, "especially in view of my character, which does not take kindly to discipline."

He then decided to go into business, and joined the firm of A. Dick, a German importer of agricultural accessories — machines, implements, seeds, fertilizers and other farmers' requirements. Aaronsohn would acquire the most suitable products and give technical advice to the purchasers. The partnership was short-lived. The partners were not compatible, they did not develop mutual trust; there were moreover disagreements on policy. Aaronsohn held that the best machines for their purpose were French made. Dick's patriotic feelings demanded German products. The partnership ended in litigation.

He went into a similar import business with a Jewish partner, David Haim, which ran smoothly in the five or six years before his scientific activities claimed him for their own. He was however never really at ease with the commercial side of agriculture; he missed the managerial role with which he could conceive ideas for experiments in mixed farming. Thus he undertook commissions to investigate conditions and prospects on farms established by the Hibat Zion movement,[9] or private farms with absentee owners (usually Zionists in Russia).

In some of these ventures he was taken in as an associate by a friend, Dr. Selig (Evgeny) Soskin. He continued to serve as a consultant for a variety of ventures; he worked towards calculated improvement and modernization of the slowly growing Jewish agricultural economy. Scientific passions were however gradually dominating his life and, though originating naturally from the same Zionist purpose, they set him off in a new direction. A crucial role in this development was played by a young woman who in fact opened the door to his botanical research. Her name was Rahel Joffe — the sister of the physician — and she has been described as probably the first Palestinian botanist.

---

9. *Hibat Zion*, "Love of Zion," a forerunner of political Zionism.

She had been a brilliant student under the tuition of Professor Flahaut at the University of Montpellier in France.

Aaron later acknowledged wholeheartedly his debt to her. "Only thanks to Rahel Joffe, under her guidance and following her instruction, did I arrive at botanical research and begin to collect plants and herborize." He, after all, had had no university education in botany, nor any experience in the field. Rahel — a few years his senior — took him for long walks in the Galilee and Samaria, taught him to identify plants, and how to collect and preserve them.

She succeeded not only in drawing him into the fascinating world of plant life but lit up in him the passion of research. He has gone down in history as the greatest botanist in the annals of Palestine science, while Rahel Joffe (later Rogoff) is hardly remembered. Yet there was a moment in their relationship when Aaronsohn's thoughts and passions strayed — to the field of geology; and in Rahel's letters to him one finds appeals, themselves in passionate terms, for him to come back to botany. She writes of herself as having neglected botany while he was abroad traveling. "Aren't you sorry for this poor creature (that is, botany), have you no affection for the poor lonely one?... Help me to raise her spirits."

The fact is of course, as emerges from her letters to Aaron, that beyond the botany she was head over heels in love with him. In one letter she writes: "I shortened my journey and waited for you in vain on Tuesday and Wednesday. The two days spent here...alone and without you made me sad." She is unhappy at his involvement with geology. "I am jealous, of course, I don't hide my weakness from you.... Come and herborize."

There is no indication whatsoever that Aaronsohn saw in their cooperation (and indeed in the recognition of his indebtedness to her) anything more than a platonic relationship. Regrettably, her brother Hillel — an important figure in the community — and his wife were offended by his indifference to Rahel; and this, it so happened, proved to be the beginning of the breakup of Aaronsohn's longtime friendship with the physician. Rahel herself, in her outspoken fashion, made no secret in her letters of her unhappiness; but, evidently well balanced as she was, a couple of years later (in 1906) she married and became Mrs. Rogoff. Not surprisingly it was then that her correspondence with Aaronsohn was renewed on the subject of botany — and she followed with interest his travels and his meteoric career in the field into which she had introduced him. Reading her letters of that time, one senses something of the pleasure of a teacher whose pupil has won renown; but also at least a hint of recollected passion.

Aaronsohn lost none of his affection and respect for her. On a visit to Montpellier he sent her a photograph of her teacher, Professor Flahaut. She was overjoyed. In her reply she recalled her youthful student days. She added: "Do you know, Mr. A., you have written me many letters, some of them very interesting and full of spirit, but there was never among them a letter so pleasing as your latest one. Do you think it is because you wrote from Montpellier? Maybe, but not only for this reason."

Later, in 1909, he invited her to participate in the reorganization of his herbarium — "a wonderful opportunity of getting absorbed once more in the flora of our land." She replied, "I am tempted but I don't think I can accept."

It was perhaps a failure of her woman's intuition that made her try to wean Aaronsohn from his "straying" from botany to geology. He was not straying at all. What was working in him was a rare quality of personality. It was a quality graphically described by his closest friend and colleague at the time, Selig Soskin. In a memoir written six years after Aaron's death he wrote:

> We worked together in the fields of botany, of geology and agriculture. His talents in botany were phenomenal…and he had a deep understanding of geology as well. He sensed the relationship between the flora and the earth — the earth which is the final result of geological creation. To him they were links in the same chain. It was as though his whole being went into the plants and the earth and became part of them. From his trips he always came back loaded with stones and plants, which he tried to understand.

Strangely similar was the impression made on Aaron's young sisters by his attitude or, perhaps more precisely, by his relationship to nature and the earth. "Our big brother," wrote Sarah (then sixteen) and Rivka (fourteen),

> never goes out without returning loaded with various plants, stones, metals, etc. He looks after them as though they were pearls, writes down on a slip of paper the place where he found each object. One could almost say that he hugs and fondles them. He really loves their

company, it's his great joy to sit among them. Little by little we are being infected with this sickness.[10]

Selig Soskin and Aaron first met in 1896 at Metulla when Aaron was in charge of the village for the Baron. They took to each other at once; but Aaron left soon afterwards for Turkey. It was only when he returned to Zichron in 1900 that they became fast friends and collaborators. In the years that followed, Soskin — the older by four years — discovered that Aaron was a very restless person. "He needed little sleep, four or five hours," he recalled. "His stormy spirit could not tolerate rest. At four in the morning — or, latest, at five — he was up reading books on geology or botany, or he would go out on scientific excursions…. Aaronsohn knew how to survey the land."

"It was through our friendship that I acquired, inter alia, my own knowledge of the land." Unlike their contemporaries, he wrote, "we explored the Arab areas. Horse riding served as our means of travel and thus in our excursions, we were able to reach the most remote corners of the land — and to learn."

The result of those excursions was a number of articles on their observations and impressions which they published under their joint authorship in *Die Welt* (the Zionist journal established by Theodor Herzl) in Vienna.

Then, in 1902 they published their article on "Road Communications in Eretz Israel," for "we knew of roads other than the beaten tracks connecting the various villages. We envisaged a chapter in a work on the general geography of the country — which we never completed." Also in 1902 they published in *Palastina* (one of whose founders was Otto Warburg) their comprehensive research on the "future of growing silk in Eretz Israel."

In the German journal *Truppenflanzer* they contributed an exhaustive work, "The Orchards of Jaffa." In addition, so wrote Soskin, "as a result of our joint surveys, an article appeared in *Altneuland* (under my editorship in Berlin, after I had gone to live there) on 'Es Salt, City of Raisins.'"

The eminently respectable volume of serious studies and indeed the specific excursions on which they were based came to birth as part of a most ambitious venture. Aaron and Soskin teamed up with a dedicated young immigrant from Germany, Yosef Treidel, a surveyor and water engineer, to

---

10. *Hahashkafa* (27 Kislev 5667 [December 3, 1906]).

establish an institution whose inspiration was the Zionist dream in the
crucial field of agriculture. They named it the "Agronomisch-Kultur-
Technische Bureau fur Palastina."

Its functions would be variegated, its prospectus breathtakingly far-
reaching: planning and managing agricultural undertakings, plantations,
farms and settlements, organizing scientific missions to the land; drying out
swamps by drainage and plantation. The list of potential projects was
published in journals throughout Europe in five languages — Hebrew,
German, French, Russian and English. Its purpose was to encourage investors in Eretz Israel agriculture.

Measured by their intensive efforts and by their hopes, the venture was an
almost complete failure. Most of the few successes they enjoyed fell to Treidel.
Land development requires surveyor's measurements and these commissions
were offered to Treidel not by prospective immigrants or private investors
from abroad, but from existing colonizing bodies: the Hovevei Zion of
Russia, or the ICA. The income from this work, however, did not provide
Treidel with a living. After a year and a half of struggle, at the end of 1902, he
went back to Europe. As for Soskin and Aaron, they were indeed called in as
counselors or acting managers to help existing shaky farms or villages to
survive; but these cases were, strictly speaking, not connected with the
bureau. The only tangible success of their publicity campaign derived from
the final paragraph of their advertisement: their offer of advice free of charge.
The response to this from all over Europe, in all five languages, was considerable...

The diminished partnership did not last. Shortly after Treidel's departure,
Soskin fell seriously ill and was compelled to move to Germany for treatment.[11]

Had the group had serious capital behind them, they might conceivably

11. He remained in Germany for many years, and meetings with Aaronsohn were neces-
    sarily infrequent, but the friendship remained warm till the end of Aaronsohn's life.
    In 1903 Theodor Herzl included Soskin in the study mission sent to examine coloni-
    zation possibilities in the El Arish zone of Sinai. After a spell of editing the Zionist
    journal *Altneuland* (which replaced *Palastina*), Soskin spent a number of years as an
    agricultural expert in German colonies in various parts of the world. He returned to
    Eretz Israel in 1924 and subsequently was associated with Jabotinsky in the Revi-
    sionist movement. He was the inventor of the hydroponics system of agriculture.

have sweated it out. They had however no financial support. The whole venture was set up on a shoestring in the yard of Efraim Fishel's house; and Soskin recorded that they had lost "some thousands of francs."

Yet that bureau in retrospect takes on a significant role in Aaronsohn's development. It helped establish an element of organization in his activities — arguably thanks to Soskin. It is conceivably not a coincidence, moreover, that it was just then that Aaronsohn began putting down in writing — indeed, reporting seriously, for the first time his observations on his excursions, his surveys and his studies.

From Soskin's descriptions of these joint excursions, and how he himself had learned from them, it is pretty certain that the essence of those resulting articles was Aaronsohn's work, but that the prodding to write them came from Soskin. That Aaronsohn had earlier had no urge to write and report for publication is evidenced by the fact that his only previous venture into public writing had been ten years earlier as a youth of sixteen in a letter to a Hebrew journal in Europe — *Hamelitz* — on the study of Hebrew as a central feature of life in Zichron.[12]

It was that phase of his activities that later earned him the title "Father of Palestine Science and of Agricultural Research." It reflected the stark fact that Aaronsohn was the first son of the Palestine soil (he missed being actually born there by six years) to explore and research the land and record his findings.

There is but one parallel case, in another field: the work of musicologist A. Z. Idelson, who sought to understand the relationship between ancient and modern Jewish musical traditions in Palestine, and how ancient Palestine Jewish liturgy influenced the later music of various Jewish and Christian communities.[13]

Foreigners had visited and researched the land for hundreds of years. Records have been found going back to the fourth century. Professor Rodenheimer identified 150 researchers between the years 1553 and 1931. None of them ever communicated or cooperated with local scholars; and the local scholars simply learned from them what there was to be learned from

---

12. February 1891.
13. Shaul Katz, "Aaron Aaronsohn: Reshit ha-mada," p. 12. See also *Encyclopedia Judaica*.

their writings. Now for the first time "one of our own" appeared on the scene with the voice of knowledge that was absolute and an authority that was perhaps unique.

It was undoubtedly those articles, authored jointly with Soskin, some of them published in scientific journals, that first brought Aaronsohn onto the international map as a serious and original scholar.

For two or three years, however, there was an important observer who had been following Aaronsohn's career and, it may almost be said, waiting for an opportunity to help him fulfill the promise he had detected in him. It was Professor Otto Warburg, the famous botanist and an active and imaginative member of the entourage of Zionist leader Theodor Herzl.

He had met Aaron together with Soskin when visiting Palestine in 1900, and had heard from them details of their program with Treidel for the projected technical institute. He was most impressed. Thereafter they were in frequent touch. When Soskin was forced, by the need for specialized medical attention, to leave the country, the contact was maintained with Aaronsohn.

Warburg's personal interest in Aaronsohn was colored and deepened when he discerned his intense Zionist patriotism and his strongly held belief in the vital importance of scientific research for the future of the land — a belief that dictated much of his own Zionist activity. His interest was inevitably enhanced by the thought of the sheer loneliness of Aaron's work. He was now the only botanist of any note in the country. Rahel Joffe had moved out of his orbit; there was simply nobody with whom to discuss or to compare notes, and there was no botany library nearer than Europe. When he needed a book, he had to order it from abroad. When he had a question to ask, he had to write to Professor Flahaut at Montpellier, to whom Rahel had introduced him, and then it might take months to get a reply from the good professor.[14] It may be said then that, alert to the unusual qualities revealed in Aaronsohn, Otto Warburg plucked him out of the wastes of this Ottoman backwater whenever it was feasible, in order to bring him into touch with some of the great scientific minds in his field in the world.

It was thus that Aaronsohn was received when he visited Berlin in 1902, warmly welcomed by Warburg and, through Warburg, enabled to meet a

---

14. Letter to Koernicke, March 28, 1907.

number of famous botanists — Koernicke, Ascherson and Schweinfurth, who all asked him to help in the search for the "mother of wheat."

In the few years before he made that discovery he was drawn into an experience fascinating and fulfilling, not only enriching his life as a scientist, but making a tremendous contribution to the scientific panamora of the land. Once again it was the discerning Warburg who opened a door. At their meeting in Berlin in 1902, where Aaronsohn met the botanists, Warburg also introduced him to Professor Max Blanckenhorn. It is highly likely that he already then envisaged a possible relationship between the two.

Blanckenhorn was not a botanist, but a famous geologist. He had for some years been researching the geology of the Land of Israel; and his travels in the Judean desert, the northern Negev and eastern (Transjordanian) Palestine had yielded the discovery of phosphatic and bituminous rocks and the phosphates of the Dead Sea.[15] It was Blanckenhorn's researches, about which Warburg told Theodor Herzl, that inspired Herzl's vision of an industrialized "Altneuland."

A year after Aaronsohn's meeting with Blanckenhorn, Warburg revealed what must have been his purpose in bringing it about. He had founded, under Zionist auspices, "the Committee for the Exploration of Eretz Israel," and in the summer of 1903 he initiated a decision to send a mission to explore the metallurgical possibilities of the country. Blanckenhorn was to head it, and as an assistant they would appoint a scientist with experience of Palestinian conditions who was a committed Zionist — in short, a position tailored for Aaronsohn.

In the letter of appointment he was told that he would be responsible for the economic side, for communications, and for the political aspects of the research to be done — that is, to have his eye on the Zionist aspect of the expedition's findings. He, the letter said, would "represent our interests."

It had been intended that the mission would begin towards the end of the year (1903) but because of an outbreak of typhoid fever, it was delayed till

---

15. See L. Picard, "History of Mineral Research in Israel," *Israel Economic Forum* 6, no. 3 (1954): 10-38.

February 1904. Aaronsohn in this interval had no doubt more leisure to contemplate the triple blow that had befallen him with the departure of Soskin and the realization that he would not be coming back in the foreseeable future. He had lost the intimacy of a rare close friend; his departure had sealed the fate of the bureau; and with Soskin had gone his wife Sonia, with whom Aaronsohn was hopelessly in love.

They had met in 1900, when Aaronsohn returned to Zichron from Turkey and renewed his friendship with Soskin. Sonia, like Selig, had come to Palestine as a dedicated Zionist. Indeed they even lived a frugal pioneering life. Livneh remarks (in his biography of Aaron) that white bread was seldom to be seen on their table; but they had permitted themselves the one luxury of bringing a piano from Russia. She was an accomplished pianist; later, in Berlin, she made her debut on the concert platform.

For Aaronsohn this was a heavy fall into love at first sight. For Sonia, a highly intelligent young woman (like Aaron she was twenty-four), it was inevitably an exciting intellectual, spiritual and perhaps flattering encounter. The rock on which their relationship was built was their acceptance of the fact that in return for his love she could offer him no more than deep admiration — and a passion which can be most closely described as sisterly.

She did not fail to remind him from time to time that she was very much in love with her husband, and that she knew how dearly Selig loved her. In truth the Soskins were a very happily married couple.

Soskin knew of Aaron's feelings towards his wife (Aaron's brother Alex wrote later that Aaron had "confessed" his love to Selig), but this did not lessen the singularly warm relationship between the two men. Years later, Soskin wrote that one-third of his being was taken from him when Aaron died, and another third by the death of Sonia.

A striking expression of the romantic nature of his feelings was recalled years later in a reminiscence of his sister Rivka.[16] Sonia had revealed to her that one day, on opening the door of her room, she had found the floor carpeted by a thick layer of roses — which it must have taken Aaron hours to pick. Touched by the sight, she had reverently taken off her shoes and stockings before stepping into the room.

---

16. In conversation with Eliezer Livneh, Aaron's first biographer (see Livneh, *Aaron Aaronsohn*).

Unable to return Aaron's love, she yet did not want to let him go out of her life. On the contrary, she enjoyed his visits to Berlin (over the years, he paid a number of visits in connection with plans or projects put forward by Warburg, usually in association with Soskin). She rebuked him, however, when she felt that a proposed visit was something he could not afford. He was planning a scientific "grand tour" of Europe and was considering working on some job in Berlin; she wrote to him:

> Why do you want to come to Berlin at any price? It's foolish to come here and to earn at most 250 marks a month.... When are you going to be more serious, and when will you forget the nonsense that you've taken into your head.... It upsets me. Think first of all where to earn money, and only afterwards about your feelings.... Be healthy and logical.... Otherwise I won't love you. You character, you!

He evidently took her criticism in his stride and sent her a reassuring reply. Four weeks later she withdrew her objections: "Do you know, my friend, you can be very convincing. Don't misunderstand me. If I oppose your coming it's only for fear of your not succeeding. I can't doubt your ability, but I don't know whether your knowledge would earn you money here. So let us hope [your plans] will be successful." And she goes on to make plans for his stay in Berlin.

"You'll teach me French and German," she writes, "won't you? For nobody will succeed in teaching me, only you, with your great and infinite patience towards me."

She treasured the special friendship with him with such determination that she was even jealous of his male friends. Writing of his relations with his very good friend Dr. Naftali Weitz, she complains that Weitz "takes away something of you.... True, you are a great man and one can share you. But you know how jealous I am. If at least it was a woman! But male friendships are more solid and more logical...."[17]

From the beginning, he appears to have had no secrets from her. She was kept informed of Aaronsohn's rejection of Rahel Joffe and of the consequent resentment of Rahel's brother and sister-in-law. Sonia was angered by their attitude and the pain this apparently caused Aaron. "Whoever hurts you," she

17. March 10, 1906.

writes protectively, "will have me to deal with." No less. He soon became her mentor in many ways. His wide erudition in his own scientific field and well beyond, his capacity in recounting experiences and explaining ideas must surely have captivated her. Something of her feelings for Aaronsohn — she was never in love with him — can be gleaned only from the handful of her letters that survived. They maintained a lively correspondence which — begun after the Soskins went off to Berlin — continued through the next decade. All but one of her letters come from the middle period, 1905-07.

None of his letters to her from that period have survived, but something of their essence is revealed through her replies. None of her letters written after 1907 have survived — until 1913 when the strange idyll came to an end. Almost precisely covering the intervening period (1909-12), a handful of his letters surfaced recently (in the Central Zionist Archives in Jerusalem), and they reflect sharply the enduring nature of his feelings for her. Coincidentally, among his papers is a short poem by a French writer, which Aaron copied out on September 2, 1909 at El Portal during his visit to California.

The Old Bridge

On the old bridge, greened with moss
And all worn away by russet lichen,
Two lovers were talking in low voices
And it was we.

He leaning towards her tenderly,
Spoke of the love and the trust
That he bore in his faithful heart,
And it was I.

She seemed pale, uncertain,
Trembling, yet unafraid,
Listening to this distant voice,
And it was I.

On the old bridge, always the same,
Two lovers were meeting.
He spoke, she believed he loved her
And it was no longer we.

There is no indication as to whether he sent a copy to her. But in light of the contents of his letters at that time she would not have found such a gift unbecoming.

She does not ever deny that she is fully conscious of the depth of his passion and the source of his anguish. "I don't forget for a moment that you have a miserable life," she writes in May 1905. A year later: "I have been the cause of all your suffering.... When I think of you, your eyes, my heart is sore.... I beg you again to be my brave friend." Another year later he had written that his love for her would never be quenched, and she replies: "Let us not talk about it."

Of his feelings for her she was once fortuitously afforded physical testimony. She was crossing a busy street in Berlin when straight at her came a couple of runaway horses drawing a carriage. He rushed into their path, grabbed their harness and turned them away. He was, it should be said, a strong man and, for all his bulk, unexpectedly nimble.

In a lighter vein, she did everything, perhaps unwittingly, perhaps not, to remind him of her charm: how young she felt, in her new hat, or a new frock with its frills, how well received was her performance on the concert platform, and she even went on about admirers and their (justified) compliments on her looks, which she accepted with unaffected pleasure.

Withal her letters reflect the day-to-day concerns of two good friends. He sent her, from Zichron, from Tunis, from California, full accounts of his activities. In the years to come she was able to follow, at first hand, the great leaps forward of his scientific reputation. But throughout their relationship there ran the constant counterpoint in his mind — the love he bore for her. On April 12, 1912, he relates that a planned visit to the US had been postponed to 1913 by the trustees of the Jewish Agricultural Experiment Station.

"I accepted," he writes, "because I shall be able to speak more with you."

The breach was sharp when it came — and it was never explained. It remained forever their secret. It is reflected in a letter she wrote on November 20, 1913, when the Soskins were living in Hamburg. It is a bitter letter, but she recognized that whatever ills derived from their relationship, the blame was as much hers as his.

> Your letter of November 4 affects me differently from the effect on the doctor [the way she always referred to her husband]. I deserve a

cruel attitude, but the doctor?... He hasn't done anything to you and he loves you. Such a letter might cause him much suffering. I deserve a cruel letter from you, but you have permitted yourself to insult me in astonishing fashion.... I pity you, my old and unhappy friend. How you must be suffering if you can say such things. We live in order to cause each other anguish, as though those we love were created in order to hurt us.

One may conclude that she did not show this letter to Selig. That the rift was healed at some point we shall learn from Aaron's wartime activities. From Soskin's memoir it can be deduced that relations between the men remained unaffected.

The unusual relationship had engaged Aaron's emotions for thirteen years. He was now thirty-seven; nine months after the break came the war in Europe, and two months later Turkey had joined in. Throughout the tremendous tensions of the years that followed there is no slightest hint of his forming any new attachment. Livneh, researching in the 1960s, was able to interview two people who had been close to him in the last eighteen months of his life: Lucy Philipsberg (the daughter of Sonia's brother Mr. Berman), who had known him at close quarters as a child in Zichron, and Israel Sieff, colleague of Chaim Weizmann, who worked with him in the Zionist field. Both attested that he was particularly reserved and uncommunicative in his attitude to women.

Be that as it may, we know from his diary[18] of one incident in which he took notice of an attractive woman, and that he appears to have affected her strongly. However, whatever momentary or fleeting relationships he may later have had, there is no evidence that he ever fell in love again.

---

18. See chapter 1.

CHAPTER 4

And Now — Geologist!

There were wrinkles in the role assigned to Aaronsohn in the Blanckenhorn expedition. Warburg's Zionist committee saw him as their representative and he was expected to ensure the maximum secrecy of the expedition's objectives, its work and its findings. Snares, however, proliferated. There were rivals in the field, German and British, aiming at acquiring mining rights, who would welcome any "inside" information from a prestigious Blanckenhorn expedition; there were Ottoman bureaucrats with their keen nose for secrets that could be sold, or suppressed, for a cash consideration; there were leaders of the Jewish community who were not known for their discretion.

Indeed Aaronsohn was careful, throughout those weeks, to keep away from the Jewish quarters of Jerusalem. Then there was Blanckenhorn himself: in a convivial mood he was prone to gossip, innocent and potentially devastating. Last but not least, the Ottoman government itself could frustrate the whole enterprise if it should learn that it was sponsored by the Zionists. Aaronsohn evidently passed this test with flying colors: there were no leakages.

It was Aaronsohn who compiled the thirty-one-page report for the Berlin committee on "the expedition undertaken in Spring 1904 with a view to studying the exploitable minerals of Palestine." It covered the detailed survey they had made of the Judean desert, of areas east of the Dead Sea into the heart of Transjordan, and of Samaria.

Their findings were positive on the prospects of economic exploitation of the phosphate deposits they had discovered, and Aaronsohn consequently urged on Warburg the desirability of applying to Constantinople for mining rights. Warburg, however, had to reject the idea. His vision, Zionist and scientifically vindicated, foundered on the existing financial realities. When a decision had to be made it was found that the Zionist Organization lacked the funds for the further necessary research and for investment in the prospective exploitation. Warburg may have miscalculated from the start, but the fact is that the Zionist Organization was plunged that summer (July 1904) into a state of overwhelming crisis and near-paralysis by the sudden death of its leader, the legendary forty-four-year-old Theodor Herzl.

In historic irony Warburg's failed plan for further research opened a new phase in Aaronsohn's scientific development, which had a major impact on the future of science in the country. There was always an obsessive element in Aaronsohn's researches. Over the years, after all, they had covered large areas of the country. Yet it seems that that month with Blanckenhorn, with its intensive studies on the ground — as much for understanding its geological treasures as for expanding the tremendous volume of his herbarium — gave a new impetus to his work. Not the least element in his deepened motivation was the revelation that through Blanckenhorn's cooperation and his guidance in the field, botanist Aaronsohn manifestly achieved (overnight as it were) the stature and status of a mature and even authoritative geologist!

When Blanckenhorn, having fulfilled his commitment, went back to Germany, Aaronsohn set out in June for a second tour — on his beloved horse — again into the Galilee as far as the Litani River. During this trip he records being joined by Daniel Saporta (the Zichron Ya'akov manager of the ICA) to whom he "explained the geology" of the area. This did not complete his stint for the year. He was back again in the north for brief surveys in August and September.

From the heights and joys of creative scientific research and discovery, Aaronsohn (who never enclosed himself in an ivory tower) was constantly forced, by circumstances and perhaps no less by his own supercilious attitudes, into involvement in quarrels, disputes and misunderstandings. True, the fences between him and ICA had been gradually mended in the course of his independent activities as an expert and advisor in agriculture and the use of land; indeed he was often called upon and offered commissions by the ICA. Beyond ICA, however, wide areas of friction and animosity developed.

The generation of pioneers that had come to the country in the 1880s were motivated by Zionist inspiration. They were collectively known as *Hovevei Zion* (Lovers of Zion) and their organization was called Hibat Zion

(Love of Zion). But love was seldom accompanied by knowledge of Zion in the specific field in which most of them were to become active: agriculture. Nor did they have foreknowledge of the character of the Turkish rulers of the country. Then, most of them came from Eastern Europe, Romania or the Russia of the tsars, while the headquarters of the Zionist Organization, at first established by Herzl in Vienna, was moved after his death in 1904 to Berlin. There Otto Warburg became a dominant figure — with a very active agenda for developing the land. Disagreements were inevitable between him and the Russians who shared his Zionist zeal but were not equally qualified by knowledge or experience in the field.

Warburg had intended that Aaronsohn and Dr. Soskin should work in tandem as his representatives; but with the departure, through ill health, of Soskin, Aaronsohn in effect remained the predominant professional executive of the ideas and projects propounded by Warburg and his Eretz Israel committee. It was to Aaronsohn that they turned for advice on the feasibility of ideas and projects under consideration — including proposals emanating from the local Zionist establishment.

In the frictions that arose, whatever decisions by Warburg were disliked by the Russians, it was Aaronsohn — the resident on-the-spot expert — who became the central target for criticism, and worse. Probably the most significant episodes related to the Anglo-Palestine Bank, the first Zionist financial institution, which naturally was responsible for the fostering of economic enterprise. It served as the financial arm of the Berlin committee and so its managing director in Palestine, Zalman David Levontin, had a guiding role to play.

It was a legitimate function for him to pass forward to Berlin any projects of his own; it was also essential that every proposal should be examined for feasibility by Aaronsohn. Levontin's ideas were varied. One of them, eminently logical in principle, was for the building of a railway between Jaffa and Haifa; another was for a railway from Gaza to the heart of Samaria. They both said much for Levontin's Zionist vision, but they were economically premature and beyond the resources of the Zionist Organization, and so they were turned down.[1]

---

1. The second — in a form similar to Levontin's proposition — was built years later by the Turkish government; the first was laid down two decades later by the British Mandatory government.

Levontin, however, did not restrict himself even to the broad role of a banker in an era of economic hustle. In January 1905 he informed Aaronsohn that he had acquired important concessions from the Turkish authorities. Aaronsohn was taken aback. It was one thing to put forward ideas, feasible or otherwise; it was another to discuss them, let alone negotiate them, with the Turks — and that moreover, manifestly without relevant study or preparation. Most pertinently, Aaronsohn realized at once that Levontin, through inexperience and out of his depth, had been misled.

One of the concessions that Levontin claimed had been granted was for the exploitation of all the Jordan waters and the springs, as well as for working and planting on the land at Jericho, enough for settling five hundred Jewish families. The land was "Jiftlik" — state-owned, meaning it belonged to the Sultan himself — but the one question Levontin thought to put to Aaronsohn was whether the climate at Jericho was tolerable.

Aaronsohn's report to Berlin was scathing. The objective conditions in the area, such as climate, were indeed intimidating, but the political achievement in such a concession would surely make the offer attractive. The drawback however was, as he realized at once, that no such offer had come from Istanbul. Unlike Levontin, he knew his "customers," and it was clear to him that here was a ploy by the local *mutasarif* (governor) at Jerusalem. So it turned out to be: there had in fact been no such offer. What was most unfortunate was Levontin's straying into the very sensitive area of diplomacy.

That was not all. The second concession reported by Levontin almost horrified Aaronsohn. When he and Blanckenhorn had surveyed the area for metallic deposits, they had taken every possible precaution against word of their work or its economic aspects reaching the Turkish bureaucracy. Evidently some hint had reached Levontin, for a member of his staff had talked to the *mutasarif* precisely about metals and told him that Aaronsohn was an expert in the field. The *mutasarif* consequently asked Aaronsohn to come and see him.

Aaronsohn reported to Berlin on that meeting. Clearly, he wrote, the *mutasarif* was looking for personal profit out of any information he might obtain. Aaronsohn had to impress upon him that he had no connection with the bankers and evidently satisfied him that he did not know what they were talking about. The effect on his relations with Levontin may well be imagined.

Nor were relations improved when, a year later, Levontin proposed to Warburg the planting of a forest on Mount Nevo across the Jordan as a memorial to Theodor Herzl. Aaronsohn's comment was derisory. Nobody had done any research, he wrote, and the proposers had never in their lives as much as seen Mount Nevo. Even Warburg who, unlike Aaronsohn, was a placatory soul, gave vent to his frustration. He believed the banker should stick to banking. He would have established a separate institution for development, but, as he wrote to Aaronsohn, the scope of the Zionist Organization's operations did not yet warrant it.

In the tiny community in Palestine however, where there were no secrets, a climate distinctly hostile to Aaronsohn was created. Somehow he and Warburg were seen as working against the communal interest. Of gossip there was surely no lack; and even a grotesque notion had been bruited that they were really serving German interests!

But Aaronsohn was altogether more closely involved than faraway Warburg in the affairs of the community, and so was much more exposed to the slings and arrows of criticism and denigration. His association with such a personality as Warburg — which was an undoubted blessing to the community — in any case heated the hostility towards him. Nonetheless, a substantial contribution to that hostility was made by Aaronsohn's own abrasiveness.

The next year Blanckenhorn (with whom a correspondence had developed), on his own initiative, invited Aaronsohn to join him, and they set out on a lengthy and far-ranging tour in November and December 1905. Again they went north to the Galilee, across to the Jordan Valley. The climax of the venture was a nine-day exploratory mission along the length of the Hedjaz railway from Dera'a (Edrei) to Ma'an — traveling most of the way in stages by train, but on horseback where necessary. Thus, off the beaten track they also visited Petra, combing the area for plants and rocks and fossils.

Blanckenhorn was overjoyed by Aaronsohn's performance as a geologist; at one point of the journey he urged Aaronsohn to do a doctoral thesis on nomolites and offered his help (as a professor). Aaronsohn records the suggestion in his diary (December 7, 1905) but does not refer to his reply which must have been negative. After all, he might well have said to himself, he was often referred to as Doctor A. anyway, and his knowledge was probably sufficient to earn him two or more doctorates; why then should he have to work on a thesis as well?

Blanckenhorn was, of course, only the first to recognize Aaronsohn's genius as a geologist. He was blessed by later generations of students, and tribute was paid to his unique achievements by the later doyen of geological studies at the Hebrew University, Professor L. Pickard. "Aaronsohn," he wrote, "was the first to make the important discovery of nomolites in the mountains of Efraim"; and "he was the first to see the signs of the Eocene Age in Gilboa."[2]

Pickard wrote exhaustively on Aaronsohn's great contribution to the development of the country's metals:

> Aaronsohn formulated with clarity the economic importance of the various natural resources.... He expressed justified doubts about a number of Blanckenhorn's proposals, such as the question of sulphur and asphalt in the Dead Sea region; and he regretted that the appearance of copper and iron deposits between Eglon and Petra had not been researched.

Pickard named a number of other discoveries by Aaronsohn, and he concluded: "Were it not for Aaronsohn's tours, large parts of the country — especially in the north — would have remained unknown until the geological map by Blake."[3]

Pickard's tribute was supplemented by H. R. Oppenheimer, who wrote in similarly glowing terms of Aaronsohn's contributions to the study of the geographical features of the area.[4] Three months after returning to Zichron, Aaronsohn was "on the road northward" once more — indeed three times more. It was on the third tour, on his way back during a walk in a vineyard at the village of Rosh Pinna, that he made the discovery that made him famous throughout the world community of scientists.

The discovery of wild wheat and the worldwide recognition Aaronsohn gained from it added force to a long-cherished dream. The more his knowledge of Palestine and his insights into subjects well beyond the confines of

---

2. Ibid., pp. 38, 56.
3. L. Picard, "Geological Studies of Aaron Aaronsohn," *Mad'a* (August 1959).
4. Heinz Richard Oppenheimer, "The Scientific Enterprise of Aaron Aaronsohn" (1944).

Palestine deepened and broadened, the more painful became his sense of frustration at the almost complete absence of scientific intercourse in the Ottoman Palestine backwater. It was essential for him to go out, broaden his horizons and perhaps, from the tremendous storehouse of his own ideas and accomplishments, help others to broaden their horizons.

For Aaronsohn 1907 was thus to be the year of decision. He would visit North Africa and Europe and finally, he hoped, the arid areas of America, which he had studied from afar. He would make the "grand tour." Though America beckoned — David Fairchild at the US Department of Agriculture had invited him — and he was itching to see its arid areas, he could not yet definitively include that visit in his plan. He did not have the funds.

However, preparing for a long absence from home, he began freeing himself of his professional and business obligations. He resigned from his business partnership with David Haim, from his position as manager of farms in Hadera (remnants of his association with Soskin) and from his management of an oil-producing venture, Yitshar, which he had established in 1903 with seven of his friends.

Precisely at this juncture, in the summer of 1907, he received an offer from Blanckenhorn to join him in a new expedition. The Ottoman government had proposed that Blanckenhorn carry out a survey of metallurgical prospects in the Dead Sea area, and promised that he would be permitted to visit Hedjaz. Blanckenhorn's offer to Aaronsohn was accompanied by letters from both Schweinfurth and Ascherson urging him not to refuse. Aaronsohn had no need of urging. He was fascinated by the idea — not only because he was presented with a new and virgin field of research. Hedjaz, home of the cities holy to Islam — Mecca and Medina — was forbidden territory to non-believers, and he was thrilled at the notion of a Jew and a Christian together breaking the taboo.

Ascherson was particularly keen. Himself a convert from Judaism to Christianity, he now proved himself an erudite student of Muslim as well as Jewish scriptures. He advised Aaronsohn to study not only the Bible for references to plants in the Dead Sea (which he emphasized was not "dead" at all), but also the Koran where "there are many references," including some plants recommended by Muhammed himself for medical purposes.[5]

---

5. January 25, 1908.

Ascherson's advice reached Aaronsohn almost simultaneously with the news that the Ottoman authorities had cancelled the visit to the Hedjaz. The excuse they gave was an outbreak of cholera. The expedition, however, though denied the plum in the pudding, went ahead, and it seems to have been the most comprehensive of the series. Blanckenhorn and Aaronsohn were assisted by zoologist Y. Aharoni, his ornithological assistant Mr. Barzilai and a cartographer — Aaron's old friend and colleague Yosef Treidel. This time, in all logic, they were accompanied by a representative of the Ottoman government, Dr. Muhram Effendi.

As a kind of prelude to the "official" survey, Blanckenhorn spent the preceding month (February 1908) in a survey on his own of the Dead Sea area.

The area they covered was again a considerable part of both western and eastern Palestine. They consequently prepared a comprehensive report and brought it to Constantinople. What followed was an astonishing charade. They were taken in hand by one of the highest officials in the land, Izzet Pasha, secretary of the sultan's inner cabinet, who treated them like a couple of foreign potentates on a junket.

He presented them to the sultan (Abdul Hamid II), showed them around all the wonders of Constantinople (now Istanbul) and its palaces, and took them to view Smyrna (now Izmir). Then he made a practical proposal: that they come to work for the government, specifically in the sultan's personal cabinet. This was in effect the ministry responsible for the Dead Sea and the Hedjaz railway — the area they had researched.

Neither of them was inclined to consider this proposal, and towards the end of June Blanckenhorn returned to Germany. Aaronsohn stayed on till August and took the opportunity of herborizing around Constantinople and the Sea of Marmora, but the real reason for his remaining was quite different: throughout the weeks of their stay together in Constantinople they never succeeded in getting a penny out of the government for the work they had done. Aaronsohn, now on his own, had no more success. The only change that took place was that Izzet suggested to Aaronsohn that he cooperate with him in falsifying the accounts. The question that then arose was whether Izzet had embezzled the money owed to the expedition. The question was never answered. Precisely then the government was overthrown, the "Young Turks" (the Committee of Union and Progress) took over the government, and Izzet Pasha fled the country.

The new government refused to recognize the sultan's debts, and it took Blanckenhorn (who bore this burden alone) four years of litigation (with the help of the German embassy) before he was awarded a part of the money. Aaronsohn however now embarked on the project he had long nurtured and whose details he had brought with him to Turkey. From Constantinople, then, he set out — for a comprehensive tour in the West whose climax would be in the United States.[6] There he would at last see for himself the arid areas about which he knew so much.

He opened his tour in Berlin. His best friends were there, Warburg and Soskin, George Schweinfurth and Paul Ascherson. He spent some six months there, even serving as a lecturer at the agricultural college and at various museums. There is no evidence of any other scientific commitment. If an explanation is needed for such a lengthy stay in Berlin, delaying his visit to America, it must be sought in the presence there of Sonia Soskin.

Indeed, he writes of her to his sisters and, with a touch of pretended irritation, describes her efforts, in collaboration with Mrs. Warburg, to interest him in matrimony. "The young ladies they talk about," he says, "are afflicted with a surfeit of money, but they are not interesting."

Sonia could hardly have expected any serious results from this initiative, for who knew as well as she how deeply Aaronsohn was in her thrall. He proved predictably unhelpful. He even took an opportunity (at a dinner party at Warburg's home) to come down hard on one of their presumably prospective candidates for his hand. The young lady (so he wrote) had

> permitted herself to say that Yiddish is a disgusting language — I told her warmly but politely, that she was a silly goose and Yiddish is a great treasure of the Jewish people. I praised the beauty of the language and its poetic elements.... Soon the professors and

6. Where he ultimately obtained funding for his expedition we cannot know. Perhaps he managed to receive payment from the sultan after all, or perhaps he borrowed. In any event he was able to make the trip.

scientists at the party began paying attention to what I was saying —
and they all expressed agreement with me.

The young lady was of course not alone in showing contempt for Yiddish.
Many of the German Jewish intelligentsia, while doubtless not using offensive epithets, looked down on Yiddish as a jargon, a patois, earthy, unscien-
tific. Being ignorant of the language, they never experienced its multifaceted
human expressiveness. To Aaronsohn Yiddish was his real mother tongue,
and the day-to-day tool of discourse of the great mass of his people in the
Western world. Moreover, he had a number of social allergies, among them
one to "fools," and he sometimes gave them colorful expression. He was the
last person in the world in whose presence the Yiddish language could be
insulted with impunity.

A fortnight was spent in Vienna, where he delivered lectures, on botany to
academics, on Zionism to Jewish groups. Vienna was perhaps the most
important center of German antisemitism. It was appropriately a German
journalist, Wilhelm Marr, who coined the term *antisemitism* to describe the
various manifestations and gradations of hatred for Jews. Aaronsohn's visit
coincided with a particularly vicious period of anti-Jewish propaganda, and
he evinced an understandable self-satisfaction when he wrote to his sisters on
February 19, 1909: "Here the antisemites will be compelled to listen to a
nationalist Jew speaking of sensational discoveries in our country. How painful for their ears." By the same token his lectures to Zionists were received
with exceptional enthusiasm, notably by the students' organization "Theodor
Herzl."

Then — on to France, where nostalgia for his youth now mingled with the
respectful acclaim with which he was received in the scientific world. "You
can't imagine how pleasant it is to be in France," he wrote. In his letters he
never mentions the Baron, but he did have a long and friendly talk with the
old man's secretary, Wormser. Yet it seems that his most rewarding experience in France was the few days that he spent at the University of Montpellier.
There he met the famous botanist Charles Flahaut, with whom he had had
correspondence (and whose photograph he sent to Rahel Joffe Rogoff). Here
he encountered a truly kindred spirit. Flahaut, too, came from a family of
farmers, and he spoke of the land in terms of intimacy that Aaron identified
instantly: the land was part of Flahaut's being, just as it was to Aaron and his

father. As he was also a warm, caring personality, he would certainly have an inspirational effect on his students: it was no wonder that Rahel had spoken of him so lovingly.

At Montpellier (where he lectured) he made another discovery. Old and famous as the university was, it practiced a severe economy in its structure and facilities. There was no surplus space. Here was an approach diametrically opposed to what he expected to find — and later did indeed find — in America.

His next port of call was Tunisia — then French colonial territory. Indeed it was to participate in the Congress of the French Botanical Society that he hed come. Here he was most enthusiastically welcomed by the press and fellow delegates, and he participated in the delegation that called on the local regional governor — who was delighted to find a delegate who spoke a perfect Arabic.

One of the functions offered by the authorities was a tour of the country, and Aaronsohn enjoyed his days of study in the Sahara desert. He took advantage of the opportunity to cross into Algerian territory and was able to excite his Tunisian host by reporting that their farming was already more modern and efficient than that of Algeria.

Back to Europe, through Italy to Germany, on June 1 he boarded a boat at Bremen for New York. He took with him a lesson he claimed he had only now learned. He described it later in a letter to his sisters: A Jew's excellence is not recognized by a second Jew unless it has been affirmed by a Gentile![7]

It was a truth he would discover once more in the United States. Having achieved his tremendous success, admired and celebrated on all sides, he nevertheless needed the recommendations of Fairchild and Hilgard in order to persuade the Jewish millionaires to put up the funds to set up the experiment station at Athlit.

---

7. Letter to Sarah and Rivka, June 30, 1909.

CHAPTER 5

Cold Winds

While Aaronsohn was occupied with consolidating the work of the experiment station in its first stages,[1] with a clear program and an efficient staff — spreading information and illumination far and wide to enquirers in four continents, though naturally most extensively from America — he did not neglect his own studies. He continued his lively tours throughout the whole zone. Now he was busy in the Judean landscape south of Jerusalem — he had long before made for the Zionist Organization a study-in-depth of agricultural prospects in the Negev — now he went north through Lebanon and Syria. In October 1911, in response to a request by Fairchild, he spent two whole months in Egypt, examining varieties of dates, in order to recommend kinds that might be suitable for acclimatizing in the dry southwestern region of the United States.

During his absence he left a stand-in who proved eminently suitable — Avshalom Feinberg. This poet and romantic who, several years earlier as a student in France, had attracted the attention and won the friendship of such intellectual giants as Jacques Maritain and Charles Péguy, was yet a farmer, devoted to the land, its love and its secrets. He proved perfectly capable moreover of managing the station, its workers and its students.

The US Department of Agriculture had long before enlisted Aaronsohn as a "dollar-a-year" man, and by 1911 had appointed him a "collaborator" of the department at a fee of three hundred dollars a year. He was to find that appointment a godsend at a most critical moment in his life.

There were other such commissions from Washington, which he conscientiously fulfilled. When, however, he was asked by Washington in summer

---

1. As described in chapter 2.

1912 to study citron-growing in Albania and on the island of Corfu, he declined. He had good reason.

It would interfere with his planned lengthy visit to Western Europe — to Paris, Berlin and, for the first time, to England — where he arrived in September 1912. He spent much of his time there luxuriating in the botanic wonders of Kew Gardens. However, his observations were not only botanical. In his diary he pays a backhanded compliment to the equestrians in Hyde Park. "The gentlemen and the few Amazons," he writes, "look ridiculous on their horses. Maybe they know all about etiquette, but they don't know how to ride a horse."

He did not go home from Europe. While there he received an invitation from the Department of Agriculture to revisit North America. He was asked to address that year's International Dry-Farming Congress in Alberta, Canada, and then to do a study tour along the Pacific coast. He thus spent several weeks in San Francisco and its environs — providing a heavy crop of notes on the flora and fauna and even labor relations in the region. Again he lectured at the University of Berkeley and once more was able to enjoy the warm welcome of the old Professor Hilgard. In California he was joined by Walter Swingle who, like Fairchild, had become a firm friend. He went on to Chicago, where he lectured both at the university and to a general audience. His acknowledged successes moved him to write to his sisters: "My name is capturing hearts."

Not least important, seen retrospectively, was the deepening of his personal relationships, especially with Rosenwald and Judge Frankfurter, with Judge Julian Mack and with the secretary of the Jewish Agricultural Experiment Station trustees' committee — Henrietta Szold. Through Frankfurter, he met and became a friend of the man who was to be the central figure, at a historic moment, in the Zionist Organization of America, Judge Louis Dembitz Brandeis. Brandeis, who rose to membership of the Supreme Court, was a confidant of then newly installed President Woodrow Wilson. This relationship was to attain singular significance when, five years later, the future of Palestine became an issue of international importance. Meantime, however, he and Aaronsohn found themselves discussing the economics of Zionism.

They both — each from his own viewpoint — saw dangers inherent in trying to build the country by public funding. They agreed that a healthy economy could and should be built by private enterprise.

So impressed was Brandeis by his meeting with Aaronsohn that several weeks later he told a public meeting about the work of Aaronsohn, whom he described as one of the most interesting and brilliant people he had ever met.[2]

Perhaps Aaronsohn's most piquant experience was his meeting with recently defeated President Theodore Roosevelt. Aaronsohn described the encounter in his diary. When Roosevelt asked to be enlightened on the colonizing activities of the Zionists, Aaronsohn replied in a lecture that "lasted an hour and forty-five minutes.... Everybody who knows the colonel (Roosevelt) was surprised. I shall henceforth be known as the man who succeeded in shutting the colonel's mouth for a hundred minutes."

It was during this tour, in a talk to a group of Jews and Christians — among them Julian Mack, Fairchild, Swingle and Cook — that Aaronsohn gave expression to his political feelings and his vision of Palestine's future. He warned against the spread of inimical German influence, and expressed the hope that Palestine should be taken over by Britain. The year was 1912.

Aaronsohn's second tour of America was thus once again a triumph. He was listened to with enhanced respect in the highest academic and intellectual circles, he had strengthened his relations with his friendly colleagues at the Department of Agriculture, he had disseminated his belief, as a scientist, in the innate vitality of Palestine and the certainty of its revival despite the neglect of centuries, and he had won some of the best minds in America for the Zionist cause. Shortly before his departure however he was accorded a sudden whiff of the cold winds that blew about him persistently in his homeland.

In his diary on March 14, 1913, he writes: "I learn from Miss Szold that [Louis] Lipsky and other members of the Zionist leadership have declared a boycott against me because of my attitude in the question of Jewish labor."

The boycott (whatever that might mean) by a handful of critics was of little importance and could be ignored. His policy at the station had been approved after all, by the trustees (including their two European colleagues — Otto Warburg and Selig Soskin, both famous Zionists and scientists), and

---

2. Speech at Chelsea, May 18, 1918, quoted in the Zionist monthly *Maccabean* (June 1919).

they were kept informed of the professional success his ideas had achieved: the successful application of some elements of primitive Arab farming methods (as against the failure in Palestine of some more modern European methods) and, as the lessons were absorbed, the gradual reduction of the Arab work force on the land.

What was significant in the news of such a "boycott" was the success abroad, albeit limited, of the propaganda of Aaronsohn's enemies in the workers' movement in Palestine.

The background to the workers' hostility was broadening at that very time. It was developing from what could be described as an "episode" into a full-scale parochial class war — in Zichron Ya'akov — between workers of the Second Aliyah (the wave of immigration from Eastern Europe between 1904 and 1914) and the children of the First Aliyah (1880-1904). Most of the members of the Second Aliyah breathed not only heroic pioneering Zionism but also Socialist ideas, which they had imbibed in the heady debates in Russia heralding the Russian Revolution of 1905. They — as European sophisticates — looked down on the "rustics" of the First Aliyah and their offspring, most of whom were now farming their own land.

These offspring were by no means a soft and pampered generation. Most of them had endured the horrendous difficulties and raw conditions against which their parents had struggled in those early days of the 1880s and 1890s. They were seen as inferior because they had no "ideology." Undoubtedly some of the labor sophisticates were dreaming — understandably — of becoming farmers themselves. On the other side, the Zichron Zionists were not blameless. They described these Zionist Socialist newcomers disparagingly as "foreigners" or "Moscoby" (Moscovites).

They had moreover another cause for resentment. The girls of Zichron, who had much more free time than the young men, also had more sophisticated interests. They read more books, discussed ideas and literature — subjects not included in the routine of the hardworking boys. They consequently tended to take a feminine interest in the men on the "other side of the tracks." In short, seen in retrospect, there was material here for a comic opera.[3]

Alexander Aaronsohn, Aaron's youngest brother, made an effort for

---

3. See Livneh, *Aaron Aaronsohn*, p. 174.

cooperation — in the cause of improvements in the village and in the development of lands outside. Most of his offers were rebuffed, and he set about establishing a group which would do on its own what had to be done. It was named the Gideonites. The best notion of the relations between them and the Socialists is to be found in an article by Ya'akov Zerubavel, one of the Socialist leaders, in the journal *Ha'ahdut* ("The Unity") on May 5, 1914:

> In truth, the Gideonites have performed many useful functions; they have brought order to the courtyard of the cemetery, they have cleaned out the runnels (imagine, the grandchildren of the Baron cleaning out runnels!)…. The young men of Zichron are accustomed to working, and they love work — but that is all…. The same social boorishness…the same empty life, lacking aspiration or ideals and, especially, the same deadly hatred of the "foreigners."

These were strange ideas coming from the pen of a Zionist worker, but Socialism was then all the rage — in Tsarist Russia.

No more serious clash seems to have occurred between the parties; and the First World War six months later put an end to the episode. Its only importance lies in the fact that although Aaron was away in the United States when the Gideonites were formed, and never joined the group, the propaganda of the workers against the group, couched in extreme language, was directed against "the Aaronsohn brothers."

Much more serious and of lasting impact was Aaron's new quarrel, at precisely that time, with the Zichron community at large. Its origins were in the field of public health. On his first visit to America Aaronsohn had persuaded the millionaire philanthropist and public health activist Nathan Strauss to set up in Jerusalem a public health institute which would place the malaria scourge at the head of its agenda. Aaronsohn's own practical interest in public health, and his study of the gruesome impact of the disease, had led him to institute a regulation at the station that every worker must take a quarter of a gram of quinine every day. Some of the workers chafed at this order but the result was that there were no cases of malaria at the station.

Strauss, who was a member of the station's trusteeship committee, put up all the funds for the establishment of the health center, which was to be administered in the name of the committee and managed by Aaron. It was opened in 1912. Aaron, intending to appoint a medical director, had already in 1910 discussed the matter with his old friend Dr. Hillel Joffe (Rahel's brother). He was startled however to learn from Joffe that he knew nothing about the anopheles mosquito. He admitted that in all his twenty years in the country he had never seen an anopheles mosquito!

Here was a dilemma. Aaronsohn saw however that he could not possibly appoint as head of the campaign against malaria a man ignorant of one of its crucial carriers. Moreover he had at hand a young doctor, Ze'ev Brinn, two years in the country after qualifying in Germany as a specialist in tropical diseases. When Aaronsohn announced the appointment of Brinn the roof fell in. Joffe himself was devastated. He had no doubt that his seniority and general experience made him an automatic choice. He felt personally insulted. As Joffe was a popular family physician in the community — where Aaronsohn had enough enemies as it was — Aaronsohn was attacked on all sides. Explanations did not help. Even another close friend, Naftali Weitz, himself a physician, believed Aaronsohn had made a grievous error. Aaronsohn, conscious of his obligation to the founder of the center to provide the best professional service, was not to be moved from his decision.

The lines of battle were carried abroad. Joffe was well known and liked throughout the Zionist movement, and even the current leader of the movement in Russia, Dr. Yehiel Tchlenov, wrote Aaronsohn in his behalf. Aaronsohn was adamant. He offered a full explanation of his decision, but it did not help. Not only Joffe, but Tchlenov too became a lifelong enemy. Nor were they alone — the denigration of Aaron Aaronsohn spread throughout the upper echelons of the world Zionist movement. Otto Warburg was, it seems, the only one who did express support for Aaronsohn. But Aaron's "mistreatment" of Dr. Hillel Joffe was added to the burden of "sins" that Aaron carried with him into the era of the World War.

CHAPTER 6

The World War —
Volunteers for Britain

From the moment Turkey entered the European war in October 1914, its government treated the Syrian-Palestinian provinces as though they were enemy-occupied territory. As Aaronsohn wrote later to Judge Julian Mack (October 9, 1916): "No enemy ever more ruined an invaded, conquered country and ill-treated its inhabitants than the Turks ruined the country and ill-treated the inhabitants of Syria and Palestine."

The Turks indeed lost no time in launching a policy of comprehensive requisitioning. More correctly described, most of this was sheer confiscation. They denuded farms of their produce, their implements, their machinery, their animals, their medicaments. Even water pipes were torn out of the ground. Stocks of foodstuffs were confiscated. Stocks of flour which had but recently been bought from the government itself were taken away by the government. Food production decreased, as did imports; the main markets for the country's exports — in the West — notably of vegetable oil and citrus fruits, were closed to them. Other regular sources of aid and investment from the West dried up. The signs of deprivation soon began to show in the population.

The Ottoman Empire's plight could not be kept secret from the world outside. Emboldened by the long period of permitted intervention — by way of the capitulations treaties — in the affairs of Turkey, the United States offered to send in supplies to relieve the developing famine. The Turks repelled the gesture; their sense of sovereignty was offended. No less potent however was their pragmatic calculation that accepting foreign bounty would create the unfortunate impression that the all-knowing "Young Turks" did not know how to feed their people.

A substantial quantity of "unofficial" aid did reach Palestine. The Jewish community at least could turn for help to the Jews of America, and the response was generous.

Philanthropists Jacob Schiff and Nathan Strauss and the Zionist Organization of America bore the main burden of donation. Delivery of the aid (including cash which amounted finally to a total of one and a quarter million dollars) was effected by the United States government. Until it entered the war, the United States sent loads of these supplies — thirteen times in all — by warship.

At both ends, the handling of the aid was regulated. In the United States, a Zionist emergency committee was set up and several groups cooperated in organizing and dispatch. At the receiving end, a relief committee was set up to oversee the distribution. Headed by Dr. Arthur Ruppin, representing the World Zionist Organization, its two other members were Efraim Cohen, representing the German-oriented anti-Zionist Ezra organization — and Aaronsohn, whose appointment was requested by the Americans. The committee divided the country into three regions; Aaronsohn was allotted the responsibility for distribution in the northern region. Some of the aid was passed on to the Arabs.

The trio worked in reasonable harmony for more than a year. Aaronsohn, however, was troubled constantly by the pressures of vested interests to make changes, to their pecuniary advantage, in the distribution of the aid. But in the spring of 1916, Ruppin was forced to leave — he was driven by the Turkish authorities into internal exile in Constantinople — and his place was taken by Dr. Joshua Thon. Aaronsohn, already sickened by the corrupt pressures, did not succeed, moreover, in establishing the same rapport with Thon as he had had with Ruppin. He decided to resign.

At first it might have been said that in bringing about mass privation, the Ottomans were evenhanded in their behavior towards their citizens. If, in execution of their policy of plunder, they were more active and brutal towards the Jews, this could be attributed to their belief that the Jews were the wealthier section of the population. It soon became apparent however that they were pursuing a purposeful campaign against the Jewish community, even if ostensibly only against manifestations by that community of a Jewish national identity — that is, Zionism.

In an incredibly short time the Turks abandoned the historic attitude of benevolence and hospitality which, since their welcome of the refugees from the Spanish Inquisition in the sixteenth century, had traditionally characterized their policy towards the Jews. No sooner had they denounced the capitulation treaties — which assured various foreign nationals of "protection" by their governments — than the Turks launched their campaign, ostensibly against Zionism.

Within weeks of Turkey's entry into the war, every public manifestation of Zionism had been uprooted: Hebrew shop signs had been removed, Hebrew schools were closed, even the Anglo-Palestine Bank was forced to shut its doors.

Most comprehensive were the measures against the direct beneficiaries of the capitulations, predominantly Russian Jews. They were told they must naturalize, become Ottomans or face expulsion, never to return. Large numbers did so, but already in December 1914, many hundreds were deported at a moment's notice and sent off to Egypt. (There they were taken care of by the British military authorities and the Jewish community).[1] Some applied for "Ottomanization" but were rejected; others who had already been naturalized had their naturalization revoked. All these were deported. The Jewish community, in addition to widespread confiscation of their possessions, were subjected to a stream of harassments. Leaders of the community found themselves summarily under arrest, their homes and offices searched; they were interrogated and just as summarily released. Some were deported from their homes in Jaffa-Tel Aviv to the north of the country or to Syria.

Not the least significant act of hostility — indeed contempt — towards the community was the exclusion of the Jewish recruits to the army from the combat units. Though initially issued with arms, these were suddenly taken from them; they were transferred to non-combatant units and put to work in

---

1. Egypt, then under British protectorate rule, housed the headquarters of the army's Egyptian Expeditionary Force. Refugees from Palestine, urged by Vladimir Jabotinsky, Joseph Trumpeldor and the British colonel John Henry Patterson, volunteered for service with the British army in the hoped-for liberation of Palestine. The volunteers were formed into the historic Zion Mule Corps, which served with great distinction in the ill-fated Gallipoli campaign (under the command of Patterson and Trumpeldor) and later constituted the core of the Jewish Legion in Palestine. See J. H. Patterson's *With the Zionists in Gallipoli* (London: Hutchinson & Co., 1916) and Vladimir Jabotinsky's *Story of the Jewish Legion* (New York: Bernard Ackerman, 1945).

the hard labor groups, building roads in harsh conditions usually forced on convicted felons.

The only saving grace for these men was the possibility of bribing their way out. One of these fortunate ones was Alexander Aaronsohn, Aaron's youngest brother.[2]

It was the brutalities of the Turks that finally impelled Aaronsohn in the spring of 1915 towards active revolt — though not without much heart-searching. The idea had been occupying his mind for some time. Long before the war, he had nurtured two separate beliefs on the future of the Jewish people. One was that its best hope was that Britain should take Palestine under her wing as a protectorate. In the letter he sent from Copenhagen to Judge Julian Mack in October 1916, he recalled to the judge how, during his visit to the United States in 1912, he had expressed this belief to him (in the presence also of his friends Fairchild, Swingle and Cook of the US Department of Agriculture):

> I remember very clearly, you, Judge, asking me: But why do you not submit your project to the British authorities? and I answered only, that on account of my being an Ottoman subject, it was not as much a delicate matter for me as a dangerous one for others. Should the Turks get knowledge of such a step by a Palestinian Jew, our whole work could be ruined.

The other relevant belief that he had long harbored was that there was an essential brutality in the makeup of the German nation. Again, he recalled to Mack:

> Did I not see long ago how deep the German poison lay? And did I not, *à propos et mal à propos*, always warn my American friends and colleagues even against the poisoned German science, a thing so many people have recognized now to have been right and timely?

---

2. Alexander Aaronsohn, *With the Turks in Palestine* (Boston: Houghton Mifflin, 1916).

Did I not, in private talks and public lectures warn against the German danger?

Until the war came, the notion of a British takeover remained a dream. There was even no merit in talking about it. But, Aaronsohn confessed:

> When the European war broke out, I bitterly regretted having to stay in Palestine and maintain the work of the station, but I remained stoically where I was. Then came the horrible days of November 1914, and I was horrified in getting an entirely unsuspected aspect of the Turkish methods.

His instinctive reactions ranged further afield. In November 1914 he had "got the conviction," he wrote, "that Jewish massacres were in sight, were planned by the government, and I acted on that conviction." His conviction was fortified nearly two years later, shortly before he wrote to Mack from Copenhagen: "I got written evidence from official circles in Berlin that I was right in my conviction."

However that may be, what is certain is that the reports from Turkey of a massacre of Armenians that was actually in progress played an important part in his coming to the conclusion that it was crucial for the Jews, for whom a similar fate might be in preparation, that Turkey should be defeated.

Precisely at the time these ideas were maturing Aaronsohn had a meeting with Djemal Pasha. It was arranged by the American and Italian consuls, but it was certainly at Aaronsohn's initiative. His agenda for the meeting was simple and conservative. He explained to Djemal how the so-called requisitions from the farmers were harmful to the economy of the country and not just to the Jewish agriculturalists. It affected seriously all the farmers, and indeed the whole population, whose standard of living had already plummeted dangerously.

Aaronsohn was doubtless the only personality in the country who could speak to Djemal in these terms. Djemal had to see him as a scientist famous in his field, and (more important) one who enjoyed excellent relations with the American government. The Jewish Agricultural Experiment Station which he headed was a registered American institution. These considerations evidently laid the groundwork for some alleviation in Djemal's overall policy, and for further meetings between them. It did Djemal no harm in the eyes of Washington that he treated Aaronsohn with respect.

Another outcome of their meeting was less positive. Aaron's relations with the Jewish communal leaders in Jaffa and Jerusalem were quite unnecessarily worsened. They were passing through a most difficult time. They and the community as a whole were under constant harassment by the local Turkish authorities. They were being humiliated as Jews and chastised as Zionists. Their houses and businesses were searched, several of them had been deported, others were being detained and interrogated without explanation, then released — again without any explanation. The threat of further deportations hung over all of them. That one prominent member of the Jewish community should have been courteously received by the fearsome governor seemed to suggest the promise of some relief for their battered nerves, and maybe from their fears for the future of the community.

Thus when the idea was broached to send a delegation to Constantinople, they invited Aaronsohn to meet with them. They asked him to tell them of his meeting with Djemal and, being admittedly inexperienced, asked for advice. As recorded that day in the diary of the senior member of the community, Aaronsohn responded with an outburst that was both arrogant and downright insulting.

> You only know how to listen to what Djemal Pasha is saying, but I forced him to listen to what I wanted to say to him.... Whom will you send to Constantinople, and who among you is capable of going?[3]

Though the communal leaders knew that Aaronsohn had a low opinion of their capabilities, this unprovoked outburst stunned them. "This is not the man to lead us... [;] the man is completely lacking in modesty and refinement. What a pity!"[4]

Aaronsohn's further meetings with Djemal developed into a relationship friendly in tone but not lacking in intimidating undertones. They found expression in real or pretended jocularity. "I ask myself," said Djemal, "what would you say if I ordered you to be hanged?" The heavily built Aaronsohn

---

3. Mordechai Ben-Hillel Hacohen, *Milhemet ha-amim* [War of the nations] (Tel Aviv: Tarpat, 1929), vol. 1, p. 95.
4. Ibid., p. 93.

retorted: "What should I say, Your Excellency? The weight of my body would break the tree, and the noise would be heard in America."

Overnight, Aaron's relationship with Djemal was catapulted to a higher level. Literally from the heavens came a strange visitation: a swarm of locusts invaded the country. The Bible-oriented Jews at once recalled the prophet Joel's horrendous description of the locust invasion in his time. Visually, it is as though a heavy cloud, dense enough to blot out the sunshine, comes to earth, covering everything in sight with a deep carpet of the insects, and within a very short space of time, everything green in the area has disappeared — grass and flowers, leaves and crops.

There was nobody in the country who knew from experience how one dealt with locusts. Djemal automatically called in Aaronsohn as the only scientist of standing in the country and appointed him to organize a war against locusts. Aaronsohn thereupon mobilized some fifty young men from the agricultural settlements and placed them under the command of his deputy at the station, Avshalom Feinberg, who himself took charge of the forward area of the anti-locust front in southern Transjordan. Aaronsohn records that the Zionist office and Jewish communal bodies provided the funds for the operation.[5]

The locusts' offensive was characteristically fierce, though some areas were not touched. The prospective danger, however, lay in the eggs they laid — possibly millions — and left behind under the top layer of earth. Aaronsohn's fighters, whose numbers were increased by a contingent of schoolchildren, had to dig and burrow in order to collect the eggs. Aaronsohn went out on an extensive survey instructing, advising, lecturing, demonstrating in the field, and negotiating with the local Turkish officials in each district.

It was not long however before he resigned his commission (April 28, 1915). He had not succeeded in gaining the cooperation of the local Turkish officials. Not one of them, he noted in his diary, "understands the gravity of the case." Feinberg records that many of them simply shirked their duty. Yet Djemal, who had placed at Aaronsohn's disposal the resources of the army and police, and the postal, telegraph and railway services, angrily sided with his officials. It was probably out of sheer solidarity, but it may also be that the

5. Aaron Aaronsohn, *Diary*, March 30, 1915.

officials whispered to him that the whole operation was not worth the effort, seeing that as against the obvious damage they caused, the locusts had positive economic value: they could be eaten — they were said by the rural Arabs to be very tasty when fried.

Meanwhile, however, among Aaronsohn's locust fighters there were some young men who, clothed with the authority of the government, had in the course of their official duties been roaming over the countryside, visiting army installations, alert to the movement of men and stores, and to any other items of information that could be useful to an invading army.

It was after Aaronsohn's resignation from the anti-locust operation that he finally set about preparing to offer the British the service of an intelligence group working behind the Turkish lines. In fact, the group had actually been taking shape during the anti-locust campaign, when Aaron had been in frequent conclave with his brother Alex and with Avshalom Feinberg.

Feinberg, then only twenty-five, was one of the most colorful personalities in the country. His parents, Yisrael and Fanny, were among the pioneers of 1882; the family was of a mold both heroic and scholarly. His father was one of the founders both of Rishon Lezion — south of Jaffa — and of Hadera (between Zichron and Haifa) in an area of malaria-ridden swamps. To fight this plague the early settlers feverishly planted groves of eucalyptus trees, but the curing process was horrendously slow, and family after family was dying out. There the Feinbergs settled. At one stage Yisrael sent his wife and children back to Rishon, himself continuing with his fellow founders the struggle against malaria in Hadera. Subsequently the family returned, but after many doctors' warnings, made their way back to Rishon. The battle finally was won, however, and the Feinbergs settled down to a "regular" farming life in Hadera.[6]

Notwithstanding these wanderings and tribulations, young Avshalom

---

6. Hadera today, a century later, a medium-sized undistinguished town in the midst of flourishing farm lands, indeed represents one of the most dramatic and tragic examples of the heroism of the early Zionist pioneers a century earlier. Both families paid the price of their early hardships. Aaron's mother Malka, barely sixty years old, died in 1912 and Avshalom's father in 1913 at forty-eight.

was acquiring as rich an education as was conceivable. In addition to elementary studies at the French-oriented school of the Alliance Israélite Universelle he had four excellent teachers. Grandfather Meir, erudite and dedicated, gave him a thorough grounding in the Bible; uncle Yisrael Belkind, a famous Hebraist, taught him the language at a time when modern Hebrew was still in a state of gestation; an Arab sheikh taught him formal Arabic (his spoken Arabic, like that of his contemporaries, was perfect); and an aunt, Olga Belkind, advanced his knowledge of French.

In all his studies Avshalom had demonstrated a high level of excellence. The Arab sheikh described him as the best pupil he had ever had. His parents decided to advance him further in his command of French, then universally recognized as the European language of truly educated people. At fifteen, then, Avshalom came to France. He fell in love with his curriculum, and indeed immersed himself thoroughly in French culture.

Yet in contemplating the future of Palestine and the hope of restoring the Jewish patrimony it was not to France, but to England that his youthful thoughts turned. To him it was clear that one day England would have to take Palestine from the backward Turks — and turn it into a modern country. When war came, therefore, Britain's role in bringing about the downfall of the corrupt and decrepit Ottoman Empire became a realistic prospect. But the consummation of that prospect needed help — which he and others like him should be ready to offer. He was delighted to discover at some stage of his relationship with Aaronsohn, that to Aaron, too, liberal Britain was the preferred candidate for furthering the Jewish future in Palestine.

He had first met Aaron, thirteen years his senior, in 1911 when he was appointed his assistant at the experiment station. Powerfully influenced by Aaron's encyclopedic intimate knowledge of Palestine and the whole zone, as well as by his strong character, he became his ardent admirer. The attraction was mutual, and a meeting of minds developed into a friendship of fraternal warmth.

With Avshalom's help Aaronsohn established a branch of the experiment station at Hadera and placed Avshalom in charge. Living in Hadera, Avshalom soon found a home away from home in the Aaronsohn house at nearby Zichron. It was not long moreover before he fell in love with the younger Aaronsohn girl, Rivka, who became the focus of much of his poetry. They became an engaged couple.

According to Aaron, the first practical proposal for action to help the British came from Avshalom, who was seconded by Aaron's younger brother Alexander.[7] Many years later Alex, in a letter to Harold Gribbon, recalled how Aaron, wrestling with his doubts about the morality of working against his country, "walked to and fro like a caged lion, in the yard of our house at Zichron and the courtyard of the station at Athlit."

Their first thoughts had been of a regular military unit, but they soon realized that the idea was simply chimerical and it became clear that the most useful — indeed the only — way they could help the British was by intelligence. When the decision was finally made, they had in their hands a substantial amount of preliminary intelligence material gathered during their campaign against the locusts which, after all, had laid their eggs indiscriminately, not excluding military camps and zones; any intelligent tour in and around these sites and areas, including inevitable casual conversation with Turkish soldiers, could be fruitful. No less helpful was their freedom to travel on roads along which moved Turkish guns and men and materiel — not to mention their obviously unequalled knowledge of every nook and cranny in the country.

How was contact to be established with the British in Egypt? Somebody would have to go there. Alex was picked for the task, and Rivka was to accompany him. Aaron had laid down that she must be removed from whatever troubles might come down on the family.

Leaving the country proved comparatively simple. American warships were regularly calling at Beirut in neighboring Lebanon and taking many non-Ottoman subjects out of the war zone. The only snag was that all the Aaronsohns were Ottoman subjects, and the American officers on the ships were understandably scrupulous in preventing Ottoman citizens from coming aboard. Alex however knew his way around, and acquired forged Spanish passports. On July 8, 1915, he and Rivka sailed from Beirut aboard the American warship *Des Moines*. The vessel however paid leisurely visits to several Mediterranean ports, and reached Alexandria in Egypt only after twenty-five days — on August 2.

The problem of making contact with British military intelligence was

---

7. Between Aaron and Alexander were two other brothers: Tzvi (Hirsch) and Shmuel (Sam).

solved in almost miraculous fashion. Alex was a gifted writer and, with reams of important information at his command, he offered a series of articles on the situation in Palestine to the English-language newspaper in Cairo, the *Egyptian Gazette*. The first of these appeared on August 11, 1915, the last on August 31. They contained information that should have shaken up the British military establishment.

Essentially they reflected the weaknesses of the Turks. No less important, they pointed to the feasibility of a landing on the Syrian-Palestinian coast. The Turkish coastal defense positions were lightly manned. Between Gaza and Beirut there were thirty observation posts, with ten to fifteen soldiers in each. In the interior of the country there were eight thousand men. It was likely, Alex wrote, that a major cause of the paucity of manpower was the locust invasion — which had resulted in severely depleted food supplies even for the army. Of necessity therefore the army had been thinned out.

Through Charles Boutagy, a Christian Arab from Palestine living in Egypt who was employed by British intelligence, these articles were brought to the attention of the intelligence headquarters, and an appointment was arranged for Alex to meet a major named Newcombe.

The result was disastrous. Newcombe treated Alex's story with open distrust. He manifestly could not believe that there were people who were prepared to serve the British cause without payment. Names like Aaronsohn and Feinberg no doubt sounded too German or, perhaps, too Jewish. Moreover, just then, Newcombe was one of a group of British intelligence officers who were busy setting up what would be named the Arab Bureau. Its master plan was to promote the concept of a comprehensive Arab federation under British tutelage throughout the whole area of what was then called the Near East. The idea of a Jewish Palestine could be given no part in this grandiose scheme.

Newcombe not only gave Alex short shrift, he recommended to his superiors (the British were the actual rulers of Egypt) that Alex and Rivka be ordered to leave the country. They sailed for the United States on September 3.

Aaron and Avshalom waited impatiently for news from Alex. They did not have even a notion of the length of the voyage to Alexandria. They had evidently taken it for granted that whether the mission failed or succeeded, they would soon learn the result. Without knowing what had become of Alex and Rivka, and feeling unable to wait any longer for news, they decided to make another try. This time Avshalom would have to go.

His preparations for traveling were similar to those of Alex. He too armed himself with a forged foreign passport — in the name of a nonexistent Hersh Narunsky — and a twenty-day-old beard. These survived the careful scrutiny of the United States consular official on the ship. This time the voyage took eight days in all, traveling through Crete to Alexandria. Avshalom stepped ashore on September 6, 1915 — three days after Alex and Rivka had sailed for the United States.

He met with early success in his mission. Through Charles Boutagy, he was brought to the headquarters of British naval intelligence — where Boutagy was employed — and there introduced to Lieutenant Leonard Woolley.

Immediate rapport was established. Woolley entertained no suspicions. He evidently knew the essentials about Zionism; he grasped immediately what the Zichron group might be able to do and its importance. He set out a list of subjects on which it would be important for Cairo to be informed.

It hardly differed from the schedule they had already been following — military (heavy armament and personnel) and economic (crops, food prices). Woolley specified, too, the importance of information on projected Turkish military plans, and on prisoners of war.

On arrival in Egypt Avshalom had soon found himself without money. Because of the financial straits of the station he had taken from its treasury a minimal sum, expecting to be able to receive help from Aaron's friends in America. When, however, he sent a telegram to Henrietta Szold asking for two thousand francs, he got no reply. A second telegram was equally unproductive. He nearly starved when he was seeking contact with the British. A kind of miracle intervened: Alex wrote to him from the United States,[8] and learning of Avshalom's problem, sent him a sum adequate for his personal expenses, as well as for the purchase of some much-needed supplies for the households in Zichron.

---

8. As Avshalom had sent a long letter from Egypt to Henrietta Szold, it is no doubt through her that he obtained Alex's address.

The arrangement with Woolley for the agreed-on transmissions of information was to be accomplished through a British naval vessel which would
sail periodically along the coast, and by agreed signals to and from the boat
when it came abreast of the experiment station. On such a boat, the *St. Anne*,
Woolley arranged for Avshalom to be brought discreetly home. It sailed on
November 8, 1915, and arrived opposite the station at Athlit late that night. A
rowboat from the *St. Anne* manned by Syrian Arabs brought him and his
parcels to land. The parcels were secreted in nearby bulrushes, and Avshalom
walked the short three-kilometer distance to the station.

The station's watchdogs recognized him and refrained from barking. He
awakened the sleeping Aaron. Together, after collecting the parcels, they rode
in a station cart to Zichron and were home at five o'clock in the morning.
Avshalom described all this in detail in a letter to Leonard Woolley, but he
could not send such a letter except by the promised naval vessel, which did
not come; he never heard from Woolley again.

On Feinberg's return, Aaronsohn put together the substantial quantity of
intelligence material they had for months been amassing. Much was recorded
in Aaronsohn's intimate diary, page after page of detailed information —
some of it outdated by that time but all of it reflecting the tremendous variety
and scope of his interests, his inquiring mind, his sharp eye, and behind it all,
the background of his unequalled knowledge of the land.

There was information on Turkish army units, bases, communications,
camouflage, economic data, profiles of Turkish personalities — in the case of
Djemal Pasha views and assessments as they had emerged in his meetings
with Aaronsohn. Essentially, Aaronsohn knew what to look for and where to
look, and understood at once the meaning of what he found. It all lay waiting
to be redeemed.

Soon after Avshalom's return to Zichron, Aaron spent time in the north.
He notes in his diary (November 23, 1915), "in the descent at Haritia what
looks like a forest of thistles [he details the botanic variety] but which is in
fact a disguised trench, on the face of it a haven of rural peace, without a sign
of arms or ammunition."

Elsewhere, he engages in casual admiring conversation with a bridge builder, who tells him the specific weight of the artillery that the bridge is intended to carry.

The intelligence material mounted up. The British naval vessel did indeed patrol in view of the coast at Athlit, and did several times send the agreed signal — to which the prearranged reply, "all clear," was signaled — but did not approach the shore to land the expected emissary. It was only a year later that Aaronsohn, in Egypt, was given an explanation for the mystery. Evidently there had been some mix-up in the signals. For more than a month, together with one of Aaronsohn's assistants at the station, Menashe Bronstein, they took turns in frustrating nightly watch for the British ship, then gave up in despair.

Aaronsohn turned the failure to one advantage. The several signals from the British vessel aroused suspicion in a Turkish coastal patrol. A resident of Athlit, Binyamin Davidescu, was detained by the Turkish soldiers and beaten. Aaronsohn, in a show of anger, used his easy access to the Kaimakam at Haifa to protest at this harassment of unoffending citizens. The reporting sergeant and his men were duly punished and warned against "interfering with civilian transport."

By this time Feinberg had lost patience. He decided to make a new attempt to reach Egypt, this time overland by way of Sinai. It was clearly a most hazardous undertaking, yet he all but succeeded. Pretending that he was still part of the team — which had long been dissolved — searching for locusts' eggs, he managed to deceive the Turkish officers he encountered, until he came into No Man's Land in the desert. There, even the least knowledgeable of Turkish soldiers could be expected to see through his thin pretense — it was not likely that any intelligent locust would come down to eat sand in the desert.

Such a Turkish patrol questioned him. He was arrested, sent to Beersheba and, understandably, accused of spying. For three weeks the threat of trial and summary execution hung over his head. To his good fortune the news of his arrest almost immediately reached a friend of his, Yosef Lishansky, who headed a security organization, Hamagen, operating among the communities in the south, and enjoyed good relations with Turkish officials. Through such an intermediary he arranged a means of communication — by an exchange of written messages on slips of paper — between Avshalom and his cousin Na'aman Belkind at Rishon Lezion. Avshalom was thus able to inform

Na'aman and, through him, Aaronsohn as to which official could be effectively bribed. The gravity of the charge called for a heavy sum. It was duly furnished by Avshalom's family and Aaronsohn, and in return Avshalom was moved to a "lighter" jail, in Jerusalem. The account however had even then not been settled. A new bribe, as required perhaps further up the administrative scale, achieved his release and the quashing of the charge. On January 10, 1916, he was free — and home in Hadera.

But he would not give in. He went off to Zichron with a new plan in his mind. Aaronsohn however was not in Zichron; he had gone to Damascus for a meeting with Djemal Pasha. Instead, Avshalom was overjoyed to find Sarah — who had returned home on December 16 after nearly two years' absence in Constantinople.

Sarah had had no foreknowledge of the scheme for pro-British intelligence that her brothers and Avshalom had decided upon some time in the spring of 1915. Moreover, it may be assumed that had she then been in Zichron she would have been sent out of the country together with Rivka. Now, Avshalom found that she had already been briefed, brought up to date by Aaron, and that she had "enrolled" at once. With Avshalom she set out for Damascus to meet Aaron and discuss Avshalom's new project.

Aaron was fretting no less than Avshalom at the continued absence of contact with the British. He agonized over what he saw as the grievous blunder of the Allies in not launching the campaign to liberate Palestine by an attack on the coast. He believed that the information his group could supply, especially on the weakness of Turkish defenses, would induce them to place such a move on their strategic agenda. He accepted Avshalom's proposal.

Avshalom proposed taking a long way around. He would travel by train from Constantinople to Berlin in order, as he would tell the Turkish officials, to visit his younger sister Tsilla who was studying there. From Berlin, he would ask for permission to travel to Romania, and thence, Romania being neutral, he should be able to get to Britain and to Egypt. He set out for Constantinople to make his application to the Ottoman administration, while Aaron and Sarah returned to Zichron.

Sarah had brought with her to Zichron a tale of unparalleled horror. Her journey by train from Constantinople had taken three whole weeks, and on the way she had witnessed how the Turks were murdering masses of

Armenians. In a memorandum prepared later that year for the British Foreign Office, Aaronsohn recounted Sarah's experience.[9]

Already committed to work for the defeat of Turkey, Aaronsohn was now confronted by the gruesome new evidence of the validity of his fears for the future of the Jewish community. If the Turks could wreak such cold, brutal barbarity on their Armenian citizens, there was no reason to trust them not to mete out a similar fate to the Jews. Nor did he ignore the significance of the silence of the Turks' German allies.

Despite his intuitive sense of a barbaric strain in the German character, he rationalized in his memorandum their failure to stay the hand the Turks were laying on the Armenians, or even to reprimand them. He was certain the Germans would explain their passivity by "reasons of state." Had his life been prolonged, he would have witnessed, less than two decades later, the development of an active state policy of antisemitism in Germany coming to full flower and reaching an apocalyptic climax in the Holocaust — a terrifying vindication of his early insight.

In any case, however, in 1915 and later where Turkish policy towards the Jews was concerned, the German government actively intervened to prevent excesses. One might speculate what German reactions might have been had the Jews, like the Armenians, been a completely helpless minority, unable to call on active sympathy and succor from the United States. But Berlin had another important incentive for keeping a door open to the Jewish people at large. There was considerable sympathy in America for the German cause, some of it derived from well-grounded hatred for oppressive, antisemitic Tsarist Russia. Most of the Jews in the United States at that time had come in the great wave of emigration from Russia between 1880 and 1914. Indeed within Russia itself there could not but be an accumulation of similar sentiments hostile to the regime. Berlin therefore had begun to think along lines similar to those in Britain: Why not win the support of the Jews by offering some form of recognition of Jewish national aspirations in Palestine?[10]

Sarah's report grimly enhanced the urgency of Aaronsohn's

---

9. "Pro-Armenia," London, November 1916. Aaronsohn House Museum archives.
10. For a comprehensive discussion of German policy with its unavoidable inner contradictions see Isaiah Friedman, *Germany, Turkey and Zionism, 1897-1918* (London: Oxford University Press, 1977).

determination to work for an end to Turkish rule. It is likely that that is what triggered a new and surprising approach to Djemal Pasha. Precisely towards the end of 1915, reports had been coming in that a renewed locust invasion was imminent. Soon after Sarah's return to Palestine, Aaronsohn conveyed to Djemal a plan of action. In consequence not only did a cordial meeting take place between the two in Haifa on January 9, 1916, but Aaronsohn was invited to spend three weeks at the headquarters of Djemal's Fourth Army in Damascus! There Aaronsohn's plan was discussed with officials in the Ottoman Department of Agriculture.

Aaronsohn achieved his objective. He did not propose himself for the task of heading the execution of the plan. It was Djemal who made the overture. Aaronsohn pleaded that he should not be chosen — because he had failed in his earlier campaign. Djemal however rejected his argument and, supported by his professional officials, pressed Aaronsohn to accept. Aaronsohn then put up a significant condition which, astonishingly, was accepted by Djemal. He would not be appointed, but an agreement would be signed between "His Excellency Minister Djemal Pasha, Commander of the Fourth Army, and Mr. Aaron Aaronsohn, Director of the Jewish Agricultural Station." It laid down that "in case of a renewed locust invasion, Aaronsohn will serve as the technical director of the committee for the war on the locusts."

Aaronsohn's prerogatives were defined specifically: "The director and his staff will be provided with authority to visit military positions throughout the whole area of the operations." Moreover, local telegraph offices would be instructed to "convey telegrams relating to the operations like war telegrams."

Sending news of the agreement to the trustees' committee in New York, Aaronsohn pointed out the boost it would give to the prestige of the station.

Meanwhile, Avshalom continued with his efforts in Constantinople to obtain the permits that would enable him to reestablish contact with British military intelligence in Egypt.

What had Sarah been doing in Constantinople? She had gone to live there in 1914, some months before the war broke out, after her marriage to a well-to-do Constantinople businessman, Haim Avraham. Facts about this development in her life are sparse. What is known and what has been guessed at make a complex and somewhat sad tale. Its beginning is in the love story between Avshalom and Rivka. It was common knowledge inside the family — and outside — that they, not so secretly, were betrothed.

A reading of Avshalom's letters, almost from his first encounter with the Aaronsohn family in 1911, and sometimes at the rate of one a day when he was not working in Zichron, reveals the intricacy of the relationship, its passion and its poetry.

A close friendship however had also grown up between Avshalom and Sarah. Indeed some of his early letters — all written in romantic language — were addressed to both sisters. An easy, warm relationship developed among the three of them, but the close-knit ties between the two sisters remained as strong as they had ever been since childhood.

How long could this situation continue? It seems likely that Sarah was herself in love with Avshalom, and the familial relationship among the three could hardly have been free of pain. More pressing was the circumstance that she was an obstacle in the way of her sister's marrying. It was not acceptable in a Jewish orthodox home that a younger girl should marry before her older sister. Until Sarah married, Rivka would have to wait.

There is an element of mystery about the marriage to Haim Avraham. She was not in love with him, and moving to Constantinople meant a complete break in her life, a break with her beloved family, a break with the pioneering home where she was born, indeed with the whole idea of home. If she felt she had to make Rivka socially free to marry by getting married first, there were certainly, by all accounts, many other more suitable candidates for her hand closer to home.

If it be said that marrying any one of them would have meant a loveless marriage, that after all was what she had accepted as part of the sacrifice she was making. But the questions persist: why Avraham, and in faraway Constantinople? There is not much information available on Avraham, and questions that arise are not easily answered. Avraham, it is true, was a devoted Zionist, but he was also reputed to be a skinflint. He was furthermore substantially older than twenty-three-year-old Sarah — a contemporary photograph shows a well-to-do man close to forty. Moreover, his business affairs were far-ranging, into Western Europe, involving long absences from home. Where, then, in Constantinople, a milieu notably backward in its notions of women's emancipation, would Sarah find congenial society? She could not have had many illusions about the sea-change that living in Constantinople would bring into her life.

She was a famously vibrant personality in her community. True, like all the girls of that time and place it was at age twelve that she had completed all the formal schooling that was available. She continued however as an avid reader to give herself an eclectic education. Her favorite subjects were the Bible, Jewish history and French literature — with brother Aaron as her mentor.

Her Constantinople experience turned out to be worse than might be expected. Her own letters of the first year of her stay have not survived, but it is from a letter written to her by Avshalom as early as June 17, 1914, in reply to one of hers, that some light is shed on the domestic scene. Clearly Avraham was neglecting her, was moreover claiming that he was making a "sacrifice" for her, and this (wrote Avshalom) was "sufficient to make up for the lack of homeland, family and friends… [;] he thinks very little of us."

Viewed in retrospect, from a distance of nearly a century, the only rational explanation for the mystery is that Sarah's marriage was, from the outset, planned as a fiction. It is reasonable to speculate that it was initiated by Aaron — who was on particularly friendly terms with Haim Avraham. It can be assumed that in family conclave late in 1913 or early in 1914 a timetable was surely laid down providing for "reasonable" intervals between the acts. The plan would open in spring 1914 with Sarah's marriage. With little delay, and allowing for a reasonable interval, Rivka and Avshalom could marry in the fall. With Rivka married, Sarah and Avraham could then decide on the procedure for dissolving their marriage (unless by that time they decided to remain married after all).

In August 1914, however, came war in the West, with the havoc it brought to many plans and projects. As it happened, some of the most authoritative personalities in the West were forecasting a short war ("home by Christmas," they were saying).[11] Come the fall, Turkey entered the war, and tribulations came down hard and fast on the Jewish community. Sarah must have satisfied herself that it was still only a question of a little time before Rivka and Avshalom would take their step. But Avshalom's life, like Aaron's, was disrupted by the campaign against the locusts. By April 1915, Aaron resigned

---

11. See Barbara W. Tuchman, *The Guns of August* (New York: Macmillan Co., 1962).

from the task and Avshalom too was "demobilized." She could meantime be calculating — another month, another month!

Knowing nothing of the revolutionary plan that was hatched that spring of 1915 for Zichron to enter the war on Britain's behalf, she was startled when she suddenly received a letter from Rivka — sent from Beirut — of her impending departure not with Avshalom, but with her brother Alex, on a voyage which would take her out of the danger zone and bring her to America! They left on July 9, 1915.

It was then that the dam burst. However strong Sarah's resolve had been to make a success of her self-inflicted exile, she realized now that circumstances had entrapped her, and she gave vent to her despair. On August 8, she writes to Avshalom's sister Tsilla:

> I would like to tell you something interesting, but I have nothing that is likely to interest you. My life is monotonous and I am cut off from everything. I don't visit anybody, I find no pleasure in anything and am indifferent to everything. I look forward to the happy day when I shall return home and we settle down among those that are dear to us. If you think, my dear, that I am involved in the affairs of Eretz Israel and what is happening in our families, you are mistaken. They don't write to me, and my nerves are racked…. This life, far from my family, has become intolerable. Meantime the family home has become empty, and my poor father remains all alone. My heart aches for him. I can't continue writing, my tears are streaming, and my heart is breaking…

She was on the verge of decision. Some days after this outburst when, fortuitously or otherwise, Haim left on a business trip for Vienna and Berlin, she began making preparations for return to Zichron. Tiresome as were the bureaucratic delays in the issue of the permit required for travel from the imperial center to the Palestine province, the real problem lay elsewhere. It was unthinkable for a woman to make the journey alone. Fortunately a young man from Eretz Israel whom she knew — Yitzhak Hoz, a member of Hashomer — was in Constantinople. He had been sent by his organization to try to have fellow members Yisrael and Manya Shochat freed from Turkish internal exile. He was returning home; and so they took the train together, he disconsolate at the failure of his mission, she beginning to see herself again amidst the rolling hills of Zichron Ya'akov.

In letters to Haim after reaching Zichron, she declares her intention to return to Constantinople after three months, before the Passover festival. In her writing there are, too, expressions of longing and affection — but they seem to be contrived. This impression is reinforced by a letter from Aaron to Haim a month after her return (January 23). Evidently Haim had asked for (or demanded) Sarah's return to Constantinople: "You are permitted to come to see her...but as for sending Sarah to you, forget it!"

The high-handed interdiction did not result in a visit by Avraham to Zichron; but, no less significant — to judge from Aaron's letters to Avraham later that year — it did not affect in the least the friendly relations between the two men.

In those early months of 1916, Sarah was inducted into the practical tasks of the intelligence project. Rahel Yanait, in her fascinating book of memoirs,[12] recalls her frequent meetings with Sarah after her return to Zichron and how high were her spirits. "Sarah looked happy to have returned to the bosom of her family. Her blue eyes shone with good humor."

Meanwhile, she waited with Aaron at Zichron for news from Avshalom, struggling in Constantinople. Overcoming Turkish bureaucratic resistance was no easy task but, wonderful to relate, the exit permit and the German visa were granted towards the middle of March. He began making preparations to travel to Romania en route to Britain. Precisely at that moment the whole plan turned topsy-turvy. On the morning of March 14 two members of the staff at Athlit found a letter attached to the shafts of a wagon in the grounds of the station. It had come from Woolley. An overjoyed Aaron sent a telegram to Avshalom recalling him to Zichron. "It was my first happy moment in four

_____

12. Ben-Zvi, *Anu olim*, p. 428.

anxious months," he wrote in his diary. "Woolley's letter was wonderful…a sign that he maintained his faith in us and wished to resume contact."

There was consequently no need for Avshalom to undertake the problematic journey to Europe. He returned to Zichron early in April to find that the nightly vigil at Athlit had been renewed.

Again, shockingly, to no avail. No passing British vessel anchored at Athlit. Many months later Rafael Aboulafia, whom Avshalom had "recruited" in Egypt, reported to Aaron that Woolley had told him that he was washing his hands of the whole project. His letter had remained without a reply, and he had concluded that the people at Athlit were not seriously interested!

In fact, the young emissary, who had been paid twenty Egyptian pounds for delivering the letter, had not tried to find Avshalom or Aaron. Arriving at the yard he had been attacked, as he reported, by one of the station's dogs — who did not know him — and he had simply fled back to the boat which had brought him, leaving the letter to be picked up.

For all his understanding and goodwill, Woolley — probably a very harassed intelligence officer — was by all accounts short-tempered and impetuous. His letter created a misunderstanding: at Athlit they were certain that at last, after all their vain vigils, the boat would arrive. Woolley, despite the fact that this is what had been agreed with Feinberg, assumed that Athlit would reply to his letter promptly by return post. It is probable that he never learned the truth of what had happened. Later that year, on a hazardous mission off the Syrian coast, he was captured by the Turks and spent the rest of the war in a prison camp.

Throughout the first months of the war, all the talk and the thinking by the group in the little village of Zichron Ya'akov were purely theoretical: the British had no intention of confronting the Turks in Palestine. In Britain indeed the debate was raging between "Westerners," who believed that the war would be decided in Europe, and "Easterners," who believed, especially in light of the heavy losses in the European stalemate, that an eastern front would draw off German forces from Europe, ease the pressure on the Western allies and could be crucial for victory. But the dominating personality of

Lord Kitchener, war minister and a historic national hero, blocked the Easterners' strivings.

There were however many minds in the British establishment that saw the desirability of a specific great stroke that could bring the Turkish capital itself, Constantinople — a tremendous prize — within the Allies' grasp. They dreamt of forcing the Dardanelles, the narrow stretch of water connecting the Aegean Sea with the Sea of Marmara. To its west lies the protruding finger of the Gallipoli Peninsula; to the east, the coast of Asia.

The idea of a naval conquest of the Dardanelles — the ancient Hellespont — had wandered around in military minds for centuries. Earlier in the twentieth century British naval and military experts had examined the problem and come to the conclusion that, though not impossible, it would be a most hazardous enterprise. Nevertheless, three months after Turkey entered the war on Germany's side, the problem passed from the theoretical to the immediate. An urgent appeal came from the Russian ally. The Turks had launched a massive surprise offensive against them in the Caucasus, and their whole eastern front seemed to be in danger of collapse. They wanted their allies in the west to launch a diversionary attack on the Turks; and so the Dardanelles idea came to life. The British response to the Russian appeal was to plan an attack on that narrow stretch of water.

By the time the British (with their French allies) could reasonably open such a campaign, the Russians' appeal had become irrelevant. Contrary to their panicky fears, they had achieved a tremendous victory in the Caucasus. It was, it so happened, a vicarious victory — reminiscent perhaps of an earlier Russian victory, when in 1812 Napoleon's invading armies were defeated by the winter snows — for the hundred-thousand-strong frostbitten Turkish army had been almost literally wiped out by the cold. The idea of forcing the Dardanelles however had fired British imaginations, and the planning of a campaign began.

Its tortuous progression through a complex of British Cabinet debates, though a fascinating subject, is not relevant to this volume. What is relevant is that the Gallipoli expedition, as it was launched finally, might well have succeeded but for the ambivalence of British statesmen and the incredible blunders of the men in the British military establishment.

They discovered early on that they were unable to achieve their objective by naval action alone. The Turks' basic defense of the narrow entrance to the

Dardanelles consisted of mobile gun batteries on both shores, and the straits themselves were heavily mined. The mines were thus protected by the guns; the ships could not make progress until the mines were swept away — and the mine-sweepers could not make progress until the guns were silenced. "This," wrote an authoritative modern historian, "was the problem confronting any purely naval attempt to force the Dardanelles. It was a situation never fully grasped by the British... [who] persisted in treating the forcing of the Dardanelles in terms of knocking out the established batteries at the narrows."[13] Moreover the whole operation was bedevilled from beginning to end by conflicting instructions from London and little knowledge of the targets to be attacked.

It thus became necessary to launch a campaign on the Gallipoli Peninsula itself. The extreme difficulty of this operation was compounded by a most lamentable ignorance of the terrain. It is enough to mention that when General Sir Ian Hamilton, appointed at short notice to the overall command, was about to open the campaign, he was given an out-of-date textbook on the Turkish army, two small guidebooks on western Turkey, a pre-war Admiralty report on the Dardanelles defenses, an out-of-date map and some very brief instructions from Secretary for War Lord Kitchener. This in spite of the fact that in the dark recesses of the War Office there lay a considerable amount of information, collected over the years, relating to Turkish armaments, details of the Turkish defenses and "important data concerning the topography of the Gallipoli Peninsula and the Turkish shore." All this remained untouched, and the author of the then most recent reports, though available, was not consulted.

The muddle that characterized the opening of the campaign was matched by many of the events that followed. Muddle, as so often happens, was accompanied by bad luck. A sober commentator, Foreign Secretary Sir Edward Grey, later described the upshot: "Nothing so distorted perspective, disturbed impartial judgement and impaired the sense of the strategic values, as the operations on Gallipoli."[14] The many deeds of great valor performed by the troops — including the French participants and not forgetting the six-hundred-strong Zion Mule Corps, which earned a special mention by

---

13. Robert Rhodes James, *Gallipoli* (London: B. T. Batsford, 1965), pp. 15–16.
14. Ibid., pp. 53–54.

General Sir Ian Hamilton — do nothing to mitigate the sense of a major disaster. The Gallipoli campaign lasted nine months and its cost in casualties, dead or wounded, has been estimated at a quarter of a million.

The trauma caused in the minds of military planners affected directly the campaign for Palestine and Syria. Once such a campaign was contemplated it seemed to be logical and militarily feasible to land on the Syrian or Palestinian coastal plain, rather than to move an army up from Egypt — where the British expeditionary force was stationed — through the Sinai desert.

The thought however of another combined operation, landing troops on a hostile shore, though largely free of the topographical difficulties of Gallipoli, had an overwhelmingly deterrent effect. When Eliezer Livneh, visiting London in the late 1960s for material for his biography of Aaronsohn, was given access to the papers of Sir Wyndham Deedes, who had served as a senior intelligence officer in the eastern zone, he found confirmation of this assessment.

It emerges, wrote Livneh, that at the end of 1914 serious consideration was given to a proposal for a landing from the sea into the heart of Turkey through the Gulf of Alexandretta. Deedes supported this plan. It was rejected however in favor of the idea that it would be possible to demolish Turkey by a single blow — a landing at the Dardanelles. When the Dardanelles campaign failed, all eagerness for other landings went sour.

Aaron Aaronsohn's insistent emphasis on the desirability of a British landing on the Syria-Palestine coast thus finds unexpected intellectual support.

On the very eve of operations on the Palestine front, no less an authority than the chief of the Imperial General Staff himself, General Sir William Robertson, recalled in a memorandum on December 29, 1916, the views of the Admiralty, as expressed in a General Staff paper dated October 19, 1915, while the Gallipoli campaign was still in progress. It was there explained that "under favorable conditions military landings might no doubt succeed at various points — about Acre and Haifa, for instance — at Jaffa and even possibly at Gaza." But the memorandum added, "the winter is coming on, and any one of these disembarkation operations might be interrupted at any moment."

However in an appendix (no. 3) to this paper, the Admiralty War Staff turned down the whole idea, for the reason that "it would be unwise to repeat the experience we have undergone and are now suffering from [i.e., at Gallipoli]."

Hence Robertson concluded, in his 1916 memorandum:

> In view of these opinions, the landings of any considerable force on the coast of Syria is out of the question. An invasion, if undertaken at all, must therefore be carried out by an advance from the Sinai Peninsula.[15]

---

15. PRO/WO 106/715.

CHAPTER 7

The Odyssey

While Avshalom was still busy struggling to obtain his travel permits, Aaron, on his return from Constantinople, had been occupied with the preparations for "war" on the expected new locust invasion. It turned out however that this invasion was much less heavy than the previous year's. By the month of April it seemed to have petered out. It is not clear however whether the agreement between Djemal and Aaron was formally cancelled.

What with Avshalom's two failed attempts to make contact through Sinai with the British in Egypt, he was manifestly disqualified for a new effort. Now Aaron, the only one of the trio who had yet to implicate himself and the originator of the whole venture, would have to make the trip himself. The decision to leave the country at war was fraught with far-reaching implications apart from its inherent dangers. He was after all committed to his own creation, the experiment station, and he had specific obligations to the philanthropic American committee sponsors of the venture. He could foresee unpleasantness with them, maybe even crisis, but he believed that he needed no more than a matter of weeks to put the arrangement with Woolley on track. Thus he did what he could from Zichron to put that problem on the back burner: he wrote in half truth to Henrietta Szold, the secretary of the committee, that he was about to travel to Europe. That indeed was to be the first target of his odyssey. Once in Europe he would decide how best to communicate more explicitly with his American friends.

How to achieve his object in Constantinople was not entirely clear to him before he left Zichron, but the details of his cover story evolved as he went along. He had after all to produce for the Ottoman authorities particularly weighty reasons for leaving the country.

One serious setback struck immediately, even before setting out from home: he fell off his horse and broke several ribs. Doubly impatient, he found himself able only on July 7 to leave Zichron for Beirut, his first port of call. Still in pain, he took Avshalom with him. Fortunately he was friendly with the wali of the district, Azmi Bey, who had once visited the station at Athlit and now greeted Aaronsohn with a warm tribute to the work being done there. Aaronsohn expansively explained to him the reasons for his urgent need to leave for Europe: in his researches, he told him, he had discovered a new type of sesame containing a concentration of oil double the percentage hitherto known. He must consequently confer with professional colleagues in Europe in order to check his findings and evolve a formula for exploitation of his discovery. The wali, he urged, would easily recognize the importance of the matter to Turkey's war economy.

Azmi certainly did, and immediately set to arranging with the police commander of the district for travel passes to Constantinople for him and Avshalom. It was not within his competence however to arrange for the issue of a passport for leaving the country. That would have to be done in Constantinople.

Aaron thus needed no more than three days in Beirut — and off he was on his way to Damascus. To Azmi he had made no mention of Djemal Pasha; the last thing he needed was an encounter with him, which would certainly cause delay and possibly abort the whole expedition — if for example Djemal took it into his head that his favorite scientist must not leave the country.

Arriving in Damascus in the very early morning of July 14, Aaron learned that Djemal had arrived late the previous night, to take part in a national celebration. With Avshalom's help, and in all haste performing several essential chores, he managed to leave Damascus at noon the very next day; he arrived at the railway station in a rush five minutes before the train left.

Here he parted company from Avshalom who was to return to take over management of the station. He was replaced by a young friend, a tried member of the group, Levi Yitzhak Schneierson.[1]

Avshalom hastened back to Athlit. No sooner had he arrived there than he carried out a quiet "coup." It involved Rahel Yanait. In the nearly eighteen months that she had worked at the station, she had become completely integrated. She had even been enabled to board at the station. The joy of working

---

1. A scion of the famous family that founded the modern Habad movement.

on the land under the unique guidance of Aaronsohn had soon overcome —
though it did not dissipate — her distaste for Arab labor. Beyond her own
access to knowledge and practical experience, she became aware of the extensive service the station had been and was still rendering to the development
of the country's agriculture, and which, up to the outbreak of war, had been
serving as a model for dry farmers in the United States, and indeed throughout the world.

As for Aaron, he found in her not only a most intelligent pupil but a
kindred spirit. She shared his vision of the future, from a scientifically based
agriculture to the wonders to be accomplished by afforestation of the long
neglected land — "covering the nakedness of the mountains."

In that spring Aaronsohn had been sunk in the extreme gloom of almost
paralyzing shortages — of tools and seeds and plants and fodder, indeed food
— which restricted the work of the station to a minimum (and necessitated
the closure of the branch at Hadera). The woes of wartime were much aggra-
vated by the incomprehensible niggardliness of the trustees in America. Yet
in his report to them he mentioned two slightly compensatory factors — his
good relations with the Turkish army (which to them must have seemed a
puzzling irrelevance) and the excellent work of Rahel (Lishansky) Yanait in
her research on the pathology of plants. Under the pressures of denigration in
the community, he found in Rahel a sympathetic listener, and a personal
friendship developed between them, in which Sarah joined when she
returned from Constantinople in January 1916.

It is hard to believe that a swift and propinquitous intelligence like Rahel's
did not begin to put two and two together. It is possible even that Aaron gave
her some hint of the brewing of the spy group. There is no indication of any
attitude whatsoever towards Rahel by Avshalom, deputy to Aaron and, in
Aaron's absence, acting director of the station. However, whatever may have
been his reason, as soon as he came back from Damascus he asked Rahel to
leave the station.[2]

Aaronsohn's journey of 1,650 kilometers to Constantinople took seven
full days. It was not all done by rail: there were gaps in the line and changes
from train to train. At one of them he and Schneierson had to run, dragging
their luggage for a mile to a second train. They barely scrambled aboard as

2. Livneh, *Aaron Aaronsohn*, p. 183.

the train began to move. At another gap they transferred to a wagon drawn by three horses, lacking brakes and driven by an "insane driver," downhill racing madly and uphill falling back to the edge of the abyss. There were other delays and stoppages, and Aaronsohn traveled throughout in severe pain. They reached Constantinople by train on July 22.

It was in Constantinople that Aaron learned facts about Sarah's marriage that startled him. They are reflected in the diary notes at the beginning of his stay. He arrived in the afternoon and even before taking a bath, which he needed badly after his gruelling journey, he telephoned Haim Avraham. The next morning he and Haim went shopping; but in the afternoon he visited the Blumberg family — friends of Sarah in the Cazareto Quarter. He was manifestly shocked at the neighborhood. "That my poor Sarah agreed to live here for more than a year boggles my mind!" And he, Aaron, had not known!

That evening (evidently together with Levi Yitzhak "Liova" Schneierson) he had dinner with the Avrahams — Haim and his brother Morris — and after dinner they all went for a stroll in the Petit Champs. The next morning, he writes in his diary: "After nine o'clock we go along with Ronya [Morris Avraham's wife] to inspect Sarah's home." Haim is manifestly not present. "We have the keys of the front door, but all the other doors are locked, and we have to call in a locksmith to break them open. We find the house in disorder, but Mrs. Blumberg takes it upon herself to set things straight."

Sarah's house? Locked doors and no keys left with Haim? Yet it seems that it was only the poverty of the neighborhood that shocked Aaron. He shows no surprise at the manifest disconnection between Sarah and Avraham, apparently maintained during the whole period of her sojourn in the city. He evidently did expect, and certainly understood that, with or without Haim's approval, Sarah had seen to it that the marriage should not be consummated.

What remain to be explained are the expressions of affection and "pining" in Sarah's letter to Avraham after her return to Zichron. It had to be assumed that the letters were read by the Turkish censor. An omission of normal terms of endearment in a letter between wife and husband would draw attention, perhaps suspicion.

For four full weeks Aaron labored in the Turkish capital. At first it was the Turkish bureaucracy that delayed him, not because of opposition to his departure, but because of the hallowed principle that nothing could ever be done the same day. There was always a "come back tomorrow" — tomorrow, the Turkish equivalent of the Spanish *mañana*, the Arabic *bukra*, which meant a string of tomorrows — waiting for the passport. The problem however arose with the German and Austrian consular service. From them he needed entry visas. He learned from his experience of those weeks that citizens of the Ottoman Empire wishing to visit the territory of their German ally were to be subjected to humiliation and delay.

Aaronsohn was told that he should have cleared his application for a visa through the German consul at Damascus; why the senior consular official in the capital needed authority from the consul in the provinces was never explained. And then the provincial official was in no hurry. A telegram was sent to Damascus, but Aaronsohn was kept waiting two weeks, day after frustrating day, before a reply came. However, it was positive when it came.

As for Schneieron's visa, his application was refused outright. He remained in Constantinople, and Aaron decided that he could serve as a way station for indirect communication from Aaron to Zichron.

At last Aaron took the train to Berlin — but not without a new scare at almost the last minute. Staring out at him from the July issue of the popular American journal *Atlantic Monthly* was a chilling article. It was entitled — no less — "Our Swords Are Red, O Sultan," its content was a fierce attack on the Ottoman government, and it was written by his brother Alex. Shocked beyond measure, he could hardly blame the Turks if in their anger they would take investigative steps which would at the very least delay indefinitely his departure for Europe. No less frightening, they might quite logically come to the family home at Zichron and turn everybody and everything inside out. Miraculously, nothing of the sort happened, and on August 21 Aaronsohn arrived in Berlin.

A pleasant surprise awaited him: there on the platform as the train pulled in was an old and dear friend, American Reform Rabbi Judah Leib Magnes. A warm friendship had sprung up between them during Aaronsohn's long stay in America in 1909. Magnes had joined the trusteeship committee for the experiment station, and helped organize Aaronsohn's later lecture tour in 1913. Their political views were often in conflict, and from time to time Aaronsohn's ill-wishers, like Dr. Joffe, or members of the Labor movement (because of his views on Arab labor) had complained to Magnes about Aaronsohn's behavior or his opinions. The friendship however was not affected. Indeed, Norman Bentwich, who knew both of them well, expressed surprise at the relationship between "two men so different."[3]

Magnes, who was about to leave for Poland with a colleague, Dr. Alexander Dushkin, on an aid mission to the Jewish community, had learned of Aaronsohn's impending arrival in Berlin from Dr. Theodor Zlocisti, a German Zionist personality with whom Aaronsohn had but recently been in touch in Constantinople. Now Magnes was to be the first "non-member" to learn of the true nature of Aaronsohn's venture into espionage. Aaronsohn was overjoyed at the meeting which, he saw at once, could also be helpful in solving an immediate problem: Magnes would soon be returning to America and could serve as courier. Indeed, that very night Aaron wrote to Sarah that the meeting with Magnes "makes a great change in my plan, and it's a change for the good…"

Aaron spent four weeks in Germany. His diary is blank for that period, but it emerges from surviving letters that, as he had represented to the officials in Turkey, he did visit and confer with scientific colleagues and did discuss with them his researches in the realm of sesame. Practicing deception on his good friends in Germany was not a happy experience. Least of all could he have enjoyed his meetings with Otto Warburg, his friend and mentor for so many years, who in 1903 had opened the door for him to the European scientific community — and thence to his rise to international fame.

Precisely from Warburg he needed a very specific favor. He needed German permission in order to leave Germany for neutral Denmark and Sweden. He had impressed upon the Turkish and German authorities in Constantinople that there were famous botanists in Scandinavia as well, whose cooperation he wanted for his work on sesame. He turned to Warburg for a recommendation to the German government. Warburg acquiesced immediately. Indeed he was enthused by Aaronsohn's report on his research, and Aaron relates in a letter to Feinberg that innocent Warburg, who caught him studying "the rust on cereals at the laboratory of one Dr. Ericssen,"

---

3. In conversation with Eliezer Livneh (Aaronsohn's earlier biographer) in London, 1960. Bentwich (a Zionist from Britain) served the British Mandatory administration as attorney general in the 1930s. The Bentwich family set deep roots in Zichron Ya'akov early in the century.

reproached him for neglecting his research on sesame. Warburg, pointing out to the German authorities the economic potential if Aaronsohn's researches bore fruit, duly seconded Aaron's application; the exit permit was granted, and it was probably on the strength of German acquiescence that the Turkish embassy also made no difficulties.

Aaronsohn took great care that it should be clearly understood that his request was made to Warburg as a scientist and in no sense as a Zionist leader. (He had succeeded David Wolffsohn as president of the World Zionist Organization.) On no account did Aaron want the Zionist movement to be suspected of even the remotest involvement in what he was doing. Moreover, Warburg probably was, personally, pro-German like many other Zionists; the Zionist Organization as such had proclaimed itself neutral in the war and maintained that position with maximum punctiliousness.[4] When, later, Warburg was taxed with his assistance to Aaronsohn, he answered in absolute honesty that he had done so as a scientist, and had not the faintest notion of what Aaronsohn was up to outside the field of science.

The American embassy in Berlin helped as well. Aaron had over the years maintained friendly contact with the embassy in Constantinople. He was, after all, an official "collaborator" with the Department of Agriculture. Indeed when Avshalom's funds were running low during his earlier efforts in Constantinople to obtain an exit permit, Aaron had had no hesitation in asking American Ambassador Morgenthau to make him a loan. During his own sojourn in Constantinople, he had found new friends in the embassy and one of them, Philip Montgomery, traveling ahead of him to Berlin, had informed Ambassador Gerard of his impending arrival.

Gerard welcomed him with open arms both at the embassy and at his home. He placed the embassy's diplomatic bag at his disposal, and Aaron used it judiciously to inform Fairchild in Washington of his planned visit to Scandinavia.

In Berlin, through the providential presence there of Avshalom's sister Tsilla, he was enabled at once to organize a channel of communication with Zichron. Tsilla was a highly intelligent young woman and wholeheartedly devoted to the common cause. She regarded him as her leader; her nickname

---

4. With such punctiliousness that it had expelled Jabotinsky from its ranks for pursuing his campaign for a Jewish Legion to help the British liberate Palestine.

for him was "rabbi," and sometimes he signed his letters to her that way. They worked out a simple name code. He could thus, through her, transmit information that she, the carefree student, would encapsulate in letters to her big-sisterly dear friend Sarah, and to big brother Avshalom. Ironically, she had been given a job — which helped pay for her education — in the German postal censorship![5]

It seems certain that already there in Berlin Aaron revealed to Magnes the essentials of his plan. Whether or not Magnes was comfortable with the far-reaching purpose of the Zichron group, he behaved like a true and faithful friend then and later — and beyond Aaron's death.[6]

There in Berlin Magnes assured Aaron that if he was able to leave Copenhagen by October 19 he would have a bed available to sleep in the over-crowded *Oskar II*, on which Magnes and Dushkin had already secured passage.

He paid two more visits in Germany, each for two days, at the home in Hamburg of Selig and Sonia Soskin. He was there (as he wrote to Avshalom) towards the end of August, when they celebrated their twentieth wedding anniversary, and again on his way to Copenhagen. Was his love for Sonia, the one great passion of his life, completely dead? Had their quarrel in 1913 — the secret of whose cause died with them — then merely been patched up? All we know of the meeting in Hamburg comes from the nostalgic memoir written in 1925 by Selig.[7] There he reveals that Aaron told them of the existence of the Zichron group, and of his need to reach Egypt to meet the British and set the wheels of the plan turning again.

Arriving in Copenhagen on September 16, Aaron dutifully called on Professor Johannsen, then traveled to Svalof in Sweden to meet Professor Nielson. (He did not speak only science to them: he discovered Johannsen was pro-British, Nielsen pro-German.) Back in Copenhagen he set about solving the crucial and most difficult of his problems.

The cover story that had brought him to Scandinavia was exhausted. He

---

5. She was evidently resourceful in her own right. She managed to convey some of her messages on the backs of postage stamps.
6. Magnes was the first rector of the Hebrew University of Jerusalem, established in 1925. Very unpopular in the community for his minimalistic views on Zionism, he behaved with immaculate fairness and loyalty towards students and colleagues alike.
7. *Hayishuv* (May 14, 1925).

had however worked out a new cover story and a plan to bring him to England. In his contacts with the American diplomats in Constantinople and Berlin he had mentioned the possibility of visiting America. His entry there was of course guaranteed by his status in the Department of Agriculture. Now he made arrangements as though he did intend to travel to America. A vessel sailing from Denmark in those wartime conditions would on its way have to submit to examination at the British port of Kirkwall in Scotland. Passengers needed, in addition to an American visa, a British guarantee of safe passage at Kirkwall.

It could not be expected that an "enemy alien" — Aaronsohn's status — would be given a berth on board a ship without a British guarantee to the shipping company that he would be allowed to complete the voyage to New York. It was only through his special status in the eyes of the American administration that he was able to achieve this. It seems that he first communicated with Henrietta Szold, who consulted David Fairchild. Fairchild brought to his chief, the secretary for agriculture, Aaronsohn's cabled request that the British government be asked to provide safe passage which would enable Aaron to travel to America — on the grounds that he was needed there by the administration!

At first the secretary tended to refuse to cooperate. He recalled resentfully Aaronsohn's rejection of an American offer, passed on through Ambassador Morgenthau early in 1915, to take him out of Ottoman territory on an American ship. However, reminded no doubt of Aaronsohn's notable services to American agriculture, he finally succumbed to Fairchild's persistence; the telegram was sent.

Aaronsohn, taking all possible precautions to avoid being followed in the streets of Copenhagen, succeeded in reaching the British Legation. There he told the minister, Sir Ralph Paget, the full story of how the intelligence venture was born, of the contact that had been established with Lieutenant Woolley, and the capacity of this small group in the backwoods of Palestine to help the mighty British Empire.

Paget was also not immediately helpful. Aaronsohn, in one of his letters to Zichron, suggests that Paget did not approve of "Woolley's profession" (that is, he did not like "spies"). He proposed that Aaronsohn should rather proceed to America and from there more conveniently recross the Atlantic to England! Aaronsohn, angry at the idea of losing more time, and horrified at the notion of turning up in America where he would have to explain himself to all his old friends, firmly rejected the suggestion. Fortunately Paget did not have to accept responsibility which, after all, could be left to London; and so sent to London Aaronsohn's request (with Washington's official backing), together with Aaronsohn's own memorandum recounting the genesis and history of the Zichron project. There, in London, the claim of the contact with Woolley could be checked, together with Woolley's reactions and his arrangement with Avshalom.

The project on the face of it seemed to be a fantasy. A group of unknown young Jews from a remote village in the heart of enemy territory, albeit with an older, intelligent and articulate scientist at their head, might well be seen as actors in a piece of theater; or it might, as like as not, consist of Turkish-trained intelligence agents. When the proposal reached London even the first question that arose could not be answered: Woolley was not in Egypt. Now languishing in a prisoner-of-war camp, he had left neither message nor instructions relating to any intelligence group in Palestine.

There was consequently considerable scratching of heads in London. The absence of verification of the claim of an arrangement with Woolley might have resulted in a dismissal of the project out of hand. It was undoubtedly saved by the proof of Aaronsohn's standing with the American government. He was obviously a serious personality if his presence was required by Washington. Yet what the Americans were not being told was that the sole purpose of the "safe conduct" was to get the shipping company to give him a berth on the boat. They were not told that, once achieved, the "safe conduct" would not be used at Kirkwall at all.

No doubt at this point the problem was simplified for the British authorities. Aaronsohn, taken into British custody at Kirkwall, would be sent to London for exhaustive questioning and subsequently watched carefully. If he proved to be genuinely pro-British, with a group under his command, the British would have gained an ally. If his relations with the American administration were so good, it could be left to him, when the time came, to explain to his friends in Washington why he had had to deceive them.[8]

Weighing both possibilities — as to which side he was on — the directors of the British War Office decided to take what they would no doubt describe

---

8. Research hitherto has not revealed any complaint by Washington.

as a "sporting chance," and to accept the proposal of this very persuasive Ottoman Jew.

The British deliberations however necessarily took up time, and as day after day went by without a reply from London, Aaronsohn was in a fever of frustration. Not the least of his fears was simply the likelihood of bureaucratic procrastination, of lazy, indifferent officials, of his memorandum lying around on some undusted shelf. He did not realize — and it was only later when he reached London and recounted the experience of those anxious days in Copenhagen, that he was reminded — that Britain was a nation at war. Every official in the War Office was, to start with, overloaded with a plethora of problems perhaps even more pressing than his. Moreover, his case — the potential value of his offer, so clear to him — was quite problematic to almost everybody else. Meantime, he bit his nails, and waited.

Not that his time was wasted. He expanded the fulfillment of his original undertakings to the Turkish and German officials by paying visits to several more scientists to talk about sesame. One of them, Professor Warming, had joined him in 1909 on a herborizing expedition in the Sahara.

He treated himself to tours of a variety of museums — archeological, geological and botanical — where he was welcomed as a colleague. He was taken to see "the largest quarry in Denmark" and hoped to enrich himself with "a large collection of fossils." All this was very useful if (as he believed) he was being followed by German agents, and excellent material for his diary.

At the US embassy he bumped into Ambassador Gerard from Berlin who, he gathered, was engaged in an effort to prevent America's entry into the war — the policy to which President Wilson still clung, proclaiming "we are too proud to fight."[9]

He went for drives in the beautiful environs of Copenhagen, finding congenial companions for these outings, including one Mr. Heck, a US embassy official from Constantinople on a surprise visit to Denmark, and an "intelligent twenty-eight year-old widow, Mrs. Von Mendelsohn."

Copenhagen had become a Zionist center. The world headquarters were established there in the interests and emphasis of strict neutrality. There the interim leadership made its policy decisions and did its utmost to keep the local territorial branches toeing the neutralist line. It could not, and did not,

---

9. The US declared war on Germany over five months later, on April 2, 1917.

succeed everywhere. In Berlin, Jewish community leaders undoubtedly kept in touch with high officials, discussing the possibility of a German proclamation in favor of a Zionist policy towards Palestine.[10] In London Weizmann was developing his effort for such a British declaration, while Jabotinsky's public campaign for specific Jewish participation in the war had made significant headway. Aaronsohn in Copenhagen — a Zionist and an Ottoman citizen — took care not to lend political color to his claim of scientific research, by the few unavoidable meetings he had with Zionist friends; but he willingly made use of the Zionist office for writing his letters and keeping his diary up-to-date.

It was in that office that he toiled to write the crucial letter to his American friends in which he revealed the great secret that was dominating his life. He addressed the letter to Judge Julian W. Mack, whom he saw as the American closest to him, and asked him to show it to some of his other friends. Delivery of the letter to Mack he entrusted to Magnes. He boldly entitled it "The Confession."

Its tone throughout was passionate, but its content was incisive. It began with a description of the Turks' behavior, the way they had denuded the country — both the Syrian and Palestinian provinces — and ravaged the people. At the time he was writing, fifty thousand people had died of starvation — none of them Turks. Traveling to Damascus in July of that year he had seen hundreds of "aimlessly wandering, starving people and dozens of dead bodies bordering the main arteries." When, in Damascus the next day, he had sounded out the feelings of Djemal Pasha's chief of staff who, with Djemal himself had traveled along the same road a day earlier, he was — incredibly — upbraided for being influenced by the "crocodile tears of half a dozen mendicating women."

The Jewish community, though subjected to the same treatment (without actual bloodshed) had not fared as badly as the Muslims and Christians. Jews were possessed of a greater natural resilience and resourcefulness and were moreover receiving help from abroad, particularly from the American Jewish community. The main onslaught by the Turks had been directed at the Jewish nationalist movement, trying "brutally and methodically" to destroy everything that had been built up by Zionist endeavor — even though it was

---

10. See Friedman, *Germany, Turkey, and Zionism*.

beneficial also to the Turkish Empire. The Turks aimed at destroying Jewish national identity. "They wanted to enslave us," he wrote. "We were to become 'Turks of the Mosaic confession.'"

At the same time, he concluded from the massacre of the Armenians that the threat of a similar fate hovered over the Jewish community. Consequently it became imperative to fight the Turkish regime:

> As long as our lives, at least, were safe under the Turkish misrule, I did not feel the right to take a hand in the destruction of the Turks. But when it became clear to me, above the shadow of a possible doubt, that our lives depended on the caprices of a Djemal, or any other Turk suffering from sadism, then I felt the strong duty to draw the conclusions, and that I did.
>
> I went over, mentally at least, to the "enemy" from that moment. If I did not cooperate with the English before then, it was simply because of mere material impossibility. But at that time already, before my conscience, I undertook to work with them. To do all in my power to rid our country of the Turkish scourge. What I undertook to do, I still was going to do in a private capacity, but I knew for a certainty, that all our Jewish people in Palestine would approve of me. I did not like to have them share the responsibility, but I was sure of the moral support.[11]

He went on to describe the efforts made to establish relations with the British in Egypt, beginning with Alex's failed mission. At this point, while full of praise for Alex's qualities, Aaron manifests disappointment at Alex's failure to return home and join in the struggle. He describes Avshalom's two attempts to reach Egypt, the first successful, the second having brought down on him the dire threat of being hanged by the Turks. The issues were quite clear. But would the group of Jews living in distant free America — who, after all, had invested only money in the experiment station — feel that what was happening in Palestine justified the abandonment of his obligations to them and, horror of horrors, his becoming a spy?

Concluding the confession he declares that the purity of the cause

---

11. It turned out that he was wrong about the massive "moral support" — as becomes clear later in this narrative.

helps me to feel no loss of self-respect in the work I undertook. In order to avoid any misrepresentation, neither I myself nor anyone of my collaborators touched a penny for his services. I have put in the enterprise every cent I possessed and so did my collaborators. Nobody can say we were doing it for the sake of vile money; leave that for Arab spies. We are not doing it for honors either, for nobody is more conservative, in this respect, than the Britisher, and we do not see the showering of honors on spies, no matter how great the services. We are not even sure of their confidence; they may think us capable of betraying them just as we were of betraying the Turks. We do not do it for vengeance; we do it because we hope we are serving our Jewish cause. We did not even ask for promises. We considered it our duty to do our share and we are still foolish enough to believe in right and justice, and recognition of the cause we are serving.

I am glad of the opportunity I had to tell you all that. It was preying on my mind. I felt from the beginning the necessity that you of all men, should know as early as possible; I could not keep you in ignorance. It is up to you to form your own opinion and to give your verdict; is it adieu or au revoir? Please express your opinion in all frankness. If you approve of me I shall surely feel uplifted; if you disapprove, I am cynical enough to admit that, no matter how deeply sorry I shall feel, I will not change my attitude nevertheless.

He added a personal letter to Mack — telling him to whom he wanted the letter shown. He exhibited considerable percipience in the reactions he expected. He writes first of Felix Frankfurter:

He is open-minded, free and prudent and has such a wonderfully subtle mind. I owe him the truth. I would like you to show him the letter.

I understand that both you and he had adhered (more or less) lately to the Zionist Movement. As I have, no doubt, a part in your conversion, I want you to know where my nationalism landed me. It may do me personal harm in your opinion, but cannot possibly harm the cause, can it?

Speaking of converts, I should feel the necessity of having Justice Brandeis informed. From Mrs. Rosenwald's report I gather that

Brandeis publicly declared me somewhat responsible for his conversion. But I do not believe it is going very deeply with him. He has not, in my opinion, to draw much, in this matter, on his own remarkable mental resources. Therefore I see no necessity of informing him, unless you judge otherwise.

There is Miss Szold. You know I think of her not only as a very sweet soul but as the greatest Jewess it was my lot to know. But I am afraid it will be such a shock to her. Even you and Felix will get a shock, but will recover. But what of her? Maybe give her the news in homeopathic doses and as she is so nicely womanly and *raisonne avec le coeur* [reasons with her heart] she may some time recover her balance.

The hardest case for me is with Mr. and Mrs. Rosenwald. They ought to know, but here I hesitate. With you and Felix, I am glad of the first opportunity to tell you and have a clear situation. With the R's, to whom I owe so much, it is much harder; they are so bourgeois in their thinking that maybe it is better to keep them in the dark till it ends. Here again it is up to you and Felix to judge.

I may be wrong but it seems to me that Albert and Anna Loeb would more easily understand my case. Albert, though a multimillionaire, has still somewhat of the spirit of an anarchist....

I think that J.H.S.[12] would drop dead. I understand he is more "Jew and German and American" than ever.... He will certainly despise a spy! And will find a post factum justification in the dislike he always felt for me.

I care much for the opinion of Louis Marshall and am afraid of him too. He is a good lawyer but too much of a lawyer. He will see the legal side only. I cannot expect him to be mild. I am sorry, but here again I shall bear it.

That is about all. Curious, is it not, when it comes to such a serious situation, when it may be turning your back on all you loved and respected during a lifetime, there are, of the hundreds of people you like and approached, about half a dozen you really but deeply care about.

---

12. Jacob Schiff.

Whatever your verdict is I hope to hear from you at least once
again.

With the burden of the confession off his mind, he remained face-to-face
with the uncertainties of the complex stratagem he had to employ in order to
come within reach of his immediate goal — and what the consequences
might be if the British authorities failed to cooperate. Eight days of anguish
followed — but on October 17 he was informed that his requests were being
met. He could leave by *Oskar II* on the 19th. Cautious as ever, he adds in his
diary "without molestation at Kirkwall." Yet a difference with the British
Legation at the last moment nearly upset his whole plan. He applied to the
legation for the "safe conduct" document. The proud British diplomat told
him loftily that his verbal assurance was enough. With this Aaron went back
to the shipping company. They would not hear of it. They insisted on a document from the legation. Telephoning the legation, Aaronsohn did not mince
words. He even accused them of lying.

Finally satisfaction was achieved by a telephone call from the legation to
the company. It was October 18. At eight o'clock that evening Magnes and
Dushkin reaffirmed their promise to let him join them in their cabin; and
Oskar II sailed the next afternoon.

CHAPTER 8

British Doors Open

It is to Major Walter Gribbon (later brigadier general) that we owe the clearest reflection of the impact Aaronsohn made on his British hosts. Gribbon's own reaction to Aaronsohn recalls the effect on David Fairchild seven years earlier when he met Aaronsohn at the Department of Agriculture in Washington. He was overwhelmed. Whatever briefing Gribbon received from Basil Thomson, he was hardly prepared for a towering personality of such dimensions.

Gribbon was the War Office expert on Turkey, and was deputy to the director of military intelligence, General George MacDonogh. There is no indication that Aaronsohn was informed at this stage of Gribbon's double role. Later, after the war, he was attached to the personal staff of Prime Minister Lloyd George in the discussions and negotiations on the disposition of a dismantled Ottoman Empire. He did expect to receive from this visitor from Turkey useful information on the Turkish side of the still inactive Palestine front; as it turned out, he was enriched by an encyclopedic range of knowledge — scientific, scholarly, well organized — which had been amassed over years of study, research and observation.

Aaronsohn presented Gribbon with a multifaceted picture of the Ottoman regime — political and military — of its structure for defense against a prospective British invasion, and of Ottoman society in the context of a war economy.

Aaronsohn records in his diary that he found Gribbon well informed about Turkey. He was manifestly sufficiently well informed to recognize immediately the authenticity of what Aaronsohn told him. Moreover he was not troubled by doubts about Aaronsohn's motivation — and he took immediate advantage of Aaronsohn's gift of communication. The hour they spent that first day (October 26) was followed by five hours of conference the next day. By the third day Gribbon had already prepared a report for his superiors in the War Office, and its content would be forwarded without delay to the headquarters of the Egyptian Expeditionary Force (EEF). There, he said, were a number of officers who were well informed on the subject of Turkey, but they lacked "certain information." "This," wrote Aaronsohn in his diary, "will be helpful to our concerns and cause them to decide to take action." "Action," of course, meant that they would enable him to come to Egypt.

To Gribbon indeed he explained the need for haste. So much time had been lost, because of the failure of the authorities in Egypt to follow through on the arrangement between Woolley and Avshalom Feinberg. His colleagues at home were continuing to collect intelligence — with all its accompanying dangers — and if their sense of working in a vacuum persisted, they might well throw in the towel.

After all, he had made the long and hazardous journey with the idea of spending no more than a few days in London and then the few days in Cairo that would be needed to activate the arrangement. As far as he was concerned he could leave for Egypt the next day.

He did not know that the situation was not what he had envisaged. First of all, at his next talk with Basil Thomson he was informed that a thorough inquiry in Egypt had revealed that there was no record whatever of the arrangement with Feinberg. Woolley had left neither report nor instructions nor information. He had gone off on an intelligence mission to the Syrian coast. There, near Alexandretta, his ship *Zaida* had been hit by a mine and sunk. Woolley had been rescued by Turks, and was now inaccessible at a prison camp at Kistamuni. The War Office, then, having conveyed to Cairo all the information it had about Aaronsohn, was now waiting for GHQ in Egypt to make up its mind, purely on the basis of Gribbon's report, as to what it suggested doing with him.

Aaronsohn's next surprise was one he brought on himself — by his impact on Gribbon. Their long meeting on the second day was interrupted by visitors — who obviously had been invited by Gribbon to "drop in." One was Sir Mark Sykes, a political personality well within the corridors of power, working on high-level intelligence and diplomacy in and about the East. He had been a close aide to Lord Kitchener, and had traveled far and wide in the East, amassing a great deal of information (on various levels of authenticity) on which he built a structure of views and policy.

The previous year he had negotiated with the French the secret treaty that was to become famous — or infamous, as many both inside and outside the British government would have it — as the "Sykes-Picot Agreement" for the division of Palestine.

Sykes had long regarded himself as an antisemite. His reasons were specific. He saw the Jew as the embodiment of international capitalism, and he despised what he saw as the rootlessness of the wealthy assimilated Jews whom he encountered in Britain. On Zionism his knowledge was superficial. He had read the memorandum submitted by Herbert Samuel — then home secretary — to Prime Minister Asquith early in the war on the desirability of establishing a Jewish state in Palestine; Samuel himself had introduced him to a well-known Zionist, Rabbi Moses Gaster. His interest in Zionism was casual, however, and indeed irrelevant to his concerns. The Zionist idea was incompatible with the content of the Sykes-Picot Agreement, which envisaged breaking up Palestine into British and French zones. The notion of any substantive connection between the Jewish people (the people of the Bible) and the Holy Land had manifestly not occurred either to him or to the French. Nor, evidently, was he aware of the fascinating nineteenth-century phenomenon of British Christian support for the restoration of the Jews to the Land of Israel.

At Gribbon's office, Sykes questioned Aaronsohn about his ideology: to what branch of Zionism did he adhere? As his visit to the office was necessarily brief, he invited Aaronsohn to visit him at his home two days later (on October 30). There, Aaronsohn elaborated on his view that a British offensive should be launched by a landing on the Palestine or Syrian coast — and not from Sinai. He could not know that the commander-in-chief of all the British forces, General Robertson, was about to submit a memorandum to the War Office ruling out an attack from the sea. He would have been startled by one of the two reasons raised by Robertson. One, understandably, was the trauma that still persisted both in the army and amongst the public of the disaster in Gallipoli. But the second reason adduced by Robertson was the "strength of the Turkish coastal defenses."

This was simply a figment of the imagination — presumably of whoever had briefed him. Before leaving Palestine in July, Aaronsohn had exploited the freedom of movement which he had been granted by Djemal in 1915 and, precisely because he favored an attack on the Mediterranean coast, he had made a tour of the Turkish positions along the whole coast from Jaffa northwards.

He had listed them and brought the list with him to England. There was no sign of strong defenses. The total number of Turks along the whole Palestine coast, including coastguards, was about four hundred.

From Aaron's laconic references in his diary it is not clear whether Sykes agreed with his proposed strategy. Having been identified with Kitchener's "Western" school and its emphatic rejection of an eastern offensive, Sykes may well have found it inconvenient to discuss the crucial question of strategy with a mere civilian, and an Ottoman subject to boot. That is probably why, when he invited Aaronsohn to his home a second time, he found he had an urgent appointment elsewhere, and Aaronsohn remained alone with a man who had accompanied Sykes at both earlier meetings. This man had expressed support for Aaronsohn's view.

His name was Gerald Fitzmaurice and behind that name hangs a strange and significant tale. He had been the chief dragoman at the British embassy in Constantinople. The designation understates his real position and influence. He was in fact the recognized expert and the chief adviser to the ambassador on Turkey and Turkish affairs. Thus on May 29, 1910, the ambassador, Gerald Lowther, claimed in a long memorandum to his chief at the Foreign Office that he had uncovered a conspiracy organized by an international coalition of Jews, Freemasons and Zionists with the "Young Turks" — that is, the Committee of Union and Progress, which was governing Turkey.[1] He claimed that in fact the committee itself was dominated by Jews, and that the objectives of the conspiracy were hostile to Britain. He did not name his sources for this farrago of nonsense. The real author of this report was undoubtedly Fitzmaurice.[2]

---

1. Historical record has revealed that of all the Young Turk leaders only one had a connection, extremely remote, with Judaism — with the seventeenth-century followers of the false messiah Shabtai Zvi.
2. Elie Kedourie, "Young Turks, Freemasons and Jews," *Middle Eastern Studies* 7 (January 1971). See also Mim Kemal Oke, "Jews and the Question of Zionism in the Ottoman Empire," *Zionism* (Fall 1986): 199–218; PRO/FO 383/599/222.

The report, despite such suspicious credentials, was spread far and wide throughout the British foreign services, and from time to time it surfaced unexpectedly. It was perhaps pure coincidence that on the very day of Aaronsohn's arrival in London (even before he was received by Basil Thomson) a senior official in the Foreign Office, George Kidston, wrote in a memo to his chief:

> It is notorious that the Committee of Union and Progress and indeed the whole Young Turkish Movement originated with the Jews of Salonica and that Jewish influence has always predominated in it; it was the Jewish element which transformed an admirable movement for freedom into the unscrupulous reign of terror which the Committee now exercises with German assistance.

Kidston's own chief, Lord Hardinge, the permanent undersecretary for foreign affairs (the real head of the Foreign Office for many years) seems not to have reacted at all to Kidston's outburst, but three decades later he reveals in his memoirs that he too had uncritically swallowed the antisemitic slander. He wrote unabashedly that the situation of Turkey under the Young Turks was dominated by "a corrupt committee of Jews and aliens."[3]

It may well be that it was the very idea of this mythical Jewish power that led Fitzmaurice, once the war broke out, to the conclusion that it might be profitable for Britain to come to terms with the "powerful" Jews by a deal on the future of Palestine. It is apparent also that the catalyst for his embrace of Zionism was the impact of Aaronsohn — as was happening with Fitzmaurice's associate Sykes.

Sykes's active progress towards identification with the Zionist idea began with Aaronsohn. His meeting with Aaronsohn shook him. It changed his generalized view of Jews, and forced him to consider the role that Zionism could play on Britain's side in the war. Aaronsohn, indeed, in his personality and his outlook, projected the answer to Sykes's prejudices. He was their complete antithesis. He was no money-grubbing capitalist, but a hardy, hard-working son of the soil, a brilliant scientist to boot, who was manifestly abandoning his career and endangering his life for the sake of his people; and he

---

3. Charles Hardinge, *Old Diplomacy: The Reminiscences of Lord Hardinge of Penshurst* (London: John Murray, 1947), p. 175.

was not alone. The story he told of the Zichron Ya'akov group (all, as it happened, members of pioneering farming families) presented a Jewish picture completely new to Sykes.

Some weeks after his meetings with Aaronsohn, he sought out the effective leaders in Britain of the Zionist movement, Chaim Weizmann and Nahum Sokolow; he met them on January 28, 1917. He asked them for a statement of Zionist aims, and to this end a second meeting was fixed for February 7. Fortuitously it was just a week earlier that Vladimir Jabotinsky, with Joseph Trumpeldor, had sent a memorandum to Prime Minister Lloyd George[4] with the proposal for a Jewish Legion to fight for the liberation of Palestine.

At the second meeting with Sykes, Weizmann and Sokolow were accompanied by Herbert Samuel (who had left the government on Lloyd George's accession) as well as by Lord Rothschild; Joseph Cowan, the president of the British Zionist Federation; and James Rothschild, son of Baron Edmond in Paris. They gave him a memorandum containing a comprehensive statement of the Zionist proposals: recognition of the Jews as a nation, Britain to take over Palestine, and a Jewish chartered company empowered to develop the country and to organize immigration.

Sykes, respecting Aaronsohn's need for secrecy — which had kept him away from any Zionist contacts — did not reveal to them that he had had talks with Aaronsohn.[5] Nor did he tell them of the Sykes-Picot Agreement; he commented only that their ideas would probably cause difficulties with the French. Herbert Samuel who, as a cabinet minister at the time of the agreement with Picot, knew its contents, now loyally kept the secret from his Zionist colleagues.

Sykes did however spring a surprise on his Zionist hearers. He had been shown the Jabotinsky-Trumpeldor memorandum sent to Lloyd George the previous week and, he told them, he would support the plan for a Jewish

---

4. Lloyd George had taken office in December 1916 with the fall of the government of H. H. Asquith.
5. Aaronsohn was so circumspect in his behavior in London that he even cut short a visit to Whitechapel's Jewish quarter, lest he should bump into somebody who, as he put it in his diary, would not be "a blessing."

Legion. No clearer indication could have been given of the way Sykes's mind had suddenly begun making progress in the Zionist direction.

The series of Aaron's conversations with Gribbon was reinforced by two meetings — in fact, hearings — arranged for him at the War Trade Intelligence Department (WTID). All Aaronsohn's verbal information, together with his written notes, were encapsulated in a memorandum of thirty-one pages, edited by Gribbon and sent by his chief, General George MacDonogh, the director of military intelligence, to the permanent undersecretary of the Foreign Office. There it was circulated to the whole senior staff. It was headed "secret," entitled "Report of an Inhabitant of Athlit, Mount Carmel," and was marked "this is of considerable interest." It was organized in subchapters and covered a wide range of information on Turkey in a variety of fields, economic and military.

This memorandum was followed by a detailed commentary by an officer of the WTID, who was able from personal experience in the East to confirm enough of the facts gleaned from Aaronsohn to authenticate the accuracy of the whole. There was however a cautionary sting in the tail of the commentary:

> The person in question talks most freely and well and is very correct in his statements wherever they could be controlled. Of course we do not know the object of his visit to this country, but he might be just as observant of things here as he has been in Turkey and a purveyor of information of the conditions in England, if he could get back to Turkey.[6]

Though the commentary dealt briefly with Aaronsohn's remarks on the general disposition of the Turkish forces, it ignored the crucial section — on the coastal defenses — which sheds light on the strange misinformation on this subject in the memorandum submitted a few weeks later (December

---

6. PRO/FO 371/2783/236593.

1916) by Commander-in-Chief General Robertson.[7] This is what Aaronsohn wrote:

> XI. Coast Defenses Between Jaffa and Beirut.
>
> There are no real permanent defenses. In July (1916) there was not a single coast defense gun between Gaza and Beirut.
>
> The German General Reclam is in charge of the whole coastal defense of Turkey, including Constantinople. He inspected the Syrian coast in the winter of 1915.
>
> Captain Brusse (2nd in command of the [warship] *Goeben*) also visited Alexandretta and Haifa early in January 1916. He also inspected the coast further south.
>
> Nowhere are there more than light earthworks.
>
> The coast is lightly patrolled between Haifa, Tyre, Sidon and Beirut. Patrolling is slack.
>
> Signal fires are arranged along the coast, and revolvers are used, firing flash cartridges of different colors.
>
> The general arrangement appears to be a system of weak posts and patrols with very small local reserves at intervals of about 20 miles, while a main reserve is maintained in the Jeideh-Nazareth area, connected by telephone with Haifa and with not very complete defenses prepared on the slope of Mount Carmel.
>
> The defenses appear to flank the road leading inland from Haifa.
>
> The strength of the reserve would appear to be about half a division, there is no telephone service along the coast.

Aaronsohn's labors did not end there. The doors had been opened to what were clearly some of the most influential minds in British wartime officialdom and he realized that he was carrying with him a large volume of knowledge altogether unknown to them. To his good fortune, his official "host" — Walter Harold Gribbon — turned out to be possessed of a mind highly intelligent, open and generous, and only too willing to enable Aaronsohn to broaden the horizons and affect the thinking of the officials of the War and

---

7. Turkish defenses, monitored by the Zichron group, were not reinforced in the five months between Aaronsohn's survey and Robertson's memorandum — nor even later on.

Foreign Offices; and Aaronsohn continued to produce information on Turkey and on a variety of its wartime problems.

He had conveyed to Gribbon some of the information he had amassed on the Turks' massacre of their Armenian fellow citizens, and he now submitted a comprehensive memorandum on the subject to the director of military intelligence. He labelled it "Pro-Armenia." In it he included the experience of his own sister Sarah who, early in 1916, traveling from Constantinople to Palestine, had witnessed from the train the mowing down of masses of Armenians. He added a number of facts which he had noted during his own travels through Turkey: the looting and robbery, the driving of large numbers into exile and the inevitable spread of disease.

A significant revelation in his narrative related to the behavior of Djemal Pasha who intervened, with much publicity, to save the lives of a hundred thousand Armenians — thus earning plaudits for his humanity. The act was followed by his dispatch of the hundred thousand to remote concentration camps where they were put to work in intolerable conditions — with the inevitable consequence that many of them did not survive.

Aaronsohn's memorandum was also distributed among the Foreign Office officials, but two passages had been taken out: his criticism of the Germans for not having pressed the Turks to put a stop to the horrors, and his prognostication that the Turks might deal in similar fashion with other Christian minorities in their midst — and with the Jews.

Meantime, the days passing without word from Egypt were increasing Aaronsohn's agony of mind. He supplemented his daily exhortations to Gribbon on the need for haste by writing a memorandum for the director of military intelligence on the urgency of setting in train the organization of communication between Egypt and Athlit. "Even if there were no other reasons than saving the colleagues who have cooperated with me," he wrote, "I would press for the early restoration of the previous connection."

Puzzlement was added to frustration. Out of the blue Gribbon proposed that he, Gribbon, would organize from London the line of communication between Cairo and Athlit. Thus Aaronsohn need not go to Egypt at all. On the face of it the idea had come from the intelligence officers in Egypt. Aaronsohn did not ask for an explanation. He simply rejected the idea out of hand.

He now suffered another blow. He was banking on being able to communicate with Tsilla Feinberg in Berlin, with whom he had worked out a code for communicating with Zichron Ya'akov, but he records in his diary that the person he had chosen in neutral territory (presumably Denmark) had refused to help.

His mood was not improved by the fact that he had no money left. He had made it a rule, for himself and for all his followers, not to accept any remuneration from the British authorities. They could be reimbursed for expenditures, but there was to be no question of being "employed" by Britain. He had consequently rejected an offer of payment by Gribbon. He did ask Gribbon however to cable on his behalf to Henrietta Szold in New York to send him five hundred dollars. Finally, the money not having arrived by the eve of his departure from London, he asked Gribbon for a loan of a hundred pounds sterling.

He relieved his tensions by long walks, a regular exercise covering on most days twenty kilometers or more — and duly recorded in his diary. He was ever acutely conscious of his too bulky body, and now he found that walking also diverted his thoughts from his troubles. "Otherwise," he wrote on November 11, "I would go out of my mind."

Then, three days later, a change came over Gribbon's behavior. Inviting Aaronsohn for 4PM, he was held up in a meeting and arrived after five. He excused himself, and declared that an expected letter had not arrived. Clearly, however, a reply must have arrived from Egypt, for he added that Aaronsohn should be leaving on a P&O liner due to sail two days later.

Aaronsohn foresaw with relief the end of his long wait. But how could he travel without knowing what the British authorities in Egypt were offering him, what degree and what nature of cooperation? He asked Gribbon to give him an hour in order to discuss the details. "Gribbon," he writes, "does not like this, but as I insist, he puts me off till tomorrow."

The next day, on arrival at Gribbon's office, he found no Gribbon. Another officer, Major Maugham, directed him to a subordinate, Captain Traill, who repeated to him what Gribbon had said: Aaron could sail the next day. However, Traill had evidently been given details on the projected arrangement in Egypt, and these he conveyed to Aaron. In sum, contact at Athlit would be made as arranged between Woolley and Avshalom — by a boat traveling along the coast. But he, Aaronsohn, would not be allowed to land at Athlit. He could signal from the boat to his friends on shore to come aboard.

He was flabbergasted. "After losing three weeks of waiting, to leave now in haste without being promised anything, to go out on a wild goose chase?" No, he was not prepared to arrive in Egypt empty-handed, with permission "to stick my tongue out from the boat to my friends. This would simply be a crime." On no account would he leave without talking to Gribbon; and he told Traill he had decided not to sail on the P&O liner.

"Gribbon," he added in his diary, "has certainly not done this deliberately, but he has wounded me in an ugly way."

Gribbon's dilemma is understandable. Himself under orders, he had obviously been told to give nothing to Aaronsohn and simply to get him off to Egypt, where the army authorities would be completely free to exploit in whatever way they found necessary his and his group's readiness to serve the British cause. Aaronsohn's refusal to travel as though by order, forced the War Office to put their cards on the table. Gribbon must certainly now have pressed his superiors — and probably gained the support of Sykes — to straighten out relations with Aaronsohn. The next day they met for what one may describe as a showdown.

Aaronsohn did not mince words. The only acceptable relationship, he declared, had to be one of cooperation — "maybe modest, but cooperation." It was not acceptable that "on the one side were people who were risking everything, working wholeheartedly, while the people on the other side who were receiving everything, were promising nothing and what was more, treating you with suspicion." In short, he insisted on the status of an ally — tiny but independent.

Gribbon's reply was well thought out. He did not explain his own behavior, but he made plain where Aaronsohn stood. The people in Egypt were impressed with his report, and were prepared to put him to the test. In Egypt he would have to face further questioning. Now, however, because of the standing he had achieved for himself in London, where his work and his capacities had become known to so many important people, he would be able to operate at that level in Egypt. He urged Aaronsohn indeed to ask immediately on arrival to see General Gilbert Clayton, the senior political officer at General Headquarters in Cairo. Beyond that, circumstances would dictate.

Evidently he was to be given a letter of recommendation as well, for he adds in his diary, "they will also write that if necessary I shall go on shore."[8]

This was, Aaronsohn now told himself, a great advance. After all, of prime importance was the fact that the British government was agreeing to give him and his comrades the opportunity to carry out the plan he had put forward. In the memorandum explaining that plan (and recounting the efforts they had made to put it into operation, from Feinberg's brave efforts to his own odyssey around half the world) he had written that his group were unable to offer military assistance but they could help in the field of intelligence and supply, and could offer important political assistance. If British cooperation were successfully achieved, they would also be able to mobilize two thousand men capable of bearing arms.[9]

Adding to Aaronsohn's peace of mind, Gribbon unburdened himself further. He declared himself a friend and that he "gave his advice as a friend." Captain Traill now set about making arrangements for his departure on the next available boat, and he placed a lieutenant at Aaron's disposal.

On reflection the next day Aaronsohn was again assailed by bitter thoughts. He bewailed again and again the "waste of time" against which he had been able to do nothing. The month in Constantinople, a month in Berlin, the month he had been held up in Copenhagen, and now a month in London — and "for what I achieved in London three days or less would have been enough."

He was of course aware that his bona fides had not been universally accepted, but he did not know the size of the obstacles he had overcome, like the antisemitic proclivities of some of the men he had met, nor apparently the pervasive undercurrent of antisemitism throughout the British officer-class and the upper echelons of British civil officialdom. He naturally did not know of the perfectly legitimate query in the commentary from the WTID on his memorandum which in simple language meant: "Maybe this man with his very useful information is in fact a Turkish spy." He would have been shocked

---

8. Aaronsohn, *Diary*, November 16, 1916, pp. 130-31.
9. From the report on Aaronsohn's memorandum "Why it is urgent to re-establish the connection between Athlit and Egypt," conveyed by the DMI to the Foreign Office, PRO/FO 371/2783/221220. Original in Aaronsohn archives, Zichron Ya'akov AAR.ART.2C/15.

if he had known that a Zionist fellow Jew had whispered in Mark Sykes's ear that Aaronsohn might be working for the Turks.[10]

Sykes had broken Aaronsohn's confidentiality and told Rabbi Gaster — of all people — of Aaronsohn's presence in England. Sykes, in his turn, was no doubt unaware that Gaster was a spiteful, secretive and jealous man. When he had first met this important British personality he had kept him to himself. He did not inform his fellow Zionist activists Weizmann and Sokolow; and Vladimir Jabotinsky relates that when Herbert Samuel, then still home secretary, had asked Gaster (who had never met Jabotinsky) to give him some information about Jabotinsky, he had dismissed him simply with "he's only a talker."[11]

Aaronsohn, however, turned his mind to the challenge of the future, and confided to his diary: "First we shall get to Egypt, renew the contact... and start work.... Then... whether our friends are happy or saddened, we shall speak in different tones..."

Boarding the *S.S. Karmala* on November 24, Aaronsohn reached Port Said in Egypt on December 12, 1916.

---

10. Gaster's diary, November 14, 1916, quoted by Leonard Stein, *The Balfour Declaration* (London: Vallentine, Mitchell, 1961), pp. 292–93.
11. Jabotinsky, *The Story of the Jewish Legion*, p. 175.

CHAPTER 9

Aaron and Alexander

In his diary entries during the voyage to Egypt on the *Karmala*, Aaronsohn refrained from any mention of his activities, his concerns or his plans. It was manifestly a necessary caution against the boat being sunk. German submarines were active both in the Atlantic and in the Mediterranean. Passengers saved and objects salvaged by the enemy from torpedoed ships' lifeboats could yield documents or other objects useful to the screening eyes of enemy's intelligence.[1]

Aaronsohn had enough concerns to trouble him. He had thus far had no reaction from the United States to the letter of "confession," addressed from Copenhagen to Judge Julian Mack, which he had entrusted to Magnes. In fact Judge Mack was at this time dutifully making the rounds of the American friends and sponsors of the experiment station. He was, it appears, making a valiant effort to defend Aaronsohn's behavior against some of the virulent comments of members of the American group.

Writing to Magnes (January 6, 1917), Mack reports that Louis Marshall, a prominent lawyer who had joined the group of trustees, was most distressed by the news. He saw the creation of the anti-Turkish intelligence organization as an act of treachery (towards Turkey), a criminal act endangering the Jewish community in Palestine, as well as a breach of faith with the experiment station (and its sponsors). He read and reread Aaronsohn's letter with its

---

1. At this very time (early 1917), the British were preparing to reveal to the US government the contents of a German telegram deciphered by means of a code book salvaged from a torpedoed German ship. The contents of that telegram played a large (some believe, crucial) part in tilting US President Wilson into declaring war on Germany in April. See Barbara W. Tuchman, *The Zimmermann Telegram* (New York: Ballantine, 1966), p. 12.

description of the horrendous behavior of the Turkish authorities, and of the ongoing travails of the Jewish community, but remained adamant. Mack, it appears, did succeed in softening Marshall on the "treachery" and "criminal" charges, but Marshall insisted that the trustees must send no money to Aaronsohn.

Rosenwald was even more excited than Marshall. He not only refused to countenance any money being sent to Aaronsohn, he washed his hands of the station entirely. He added the argument that as the station was an American institution, sending money to Aaronsohn (which would help him fight the Turks) would be an infraction of America's policy of neutrality in the war in which Turkey was engaged.

The one case of appreciation and understanding mentioned by Mack came from the Loeb family; it was they who had taken Rivka into their home. Loeb represented Jacob Schiff on the trustees' committee, but evidently did not share Schiff's animosity towards Aaron and was presumably pro-British in his sympathies.

Had Aaronsohn known of this report, he would not have been surprised.

A more immediate concern was the behavior of his brother Alex. Aaron, for his part, had remained silent on this subject throughout the months before he reached London. There, at last, he unburdened himself. As soon as he had settled down, he wrote a letter (October 28, 1916) addressed to Alex and Rivka. It was a cautious combination of elder-brother-to-beloved-siblings with, towards Alex, a dose of restrained yet severe criticism. From its content it is clear that throughout his odyssey there had been no exchange of correspondence between them. Now he wrote to them of the relief that had come over him in England — his sense of freedom from German and Turkish censors "breathing down my neck." He related also the friendly attention he was being accorded by the British personalities he had met. But this, he points out, did not lessen his anxieties about what might be happening in Palestine.

Realizing that they would be wondering as to how he had succeeded in leaving Ottoman Turkey and being allowed into England, he referred them to Magnes. If Alex was upset by not having been updated earlier, he could have sought for a reason in Aaron's sharp recall of the shock Alex had inflicted on him in Constantinople. There he had read Alex's bitter attack on the Ottomans in the *Atlantic Monthly* — an article that could have resulted in shutting the door to Aaron's leaving Turkey and thus extinguishing the whole Zichron plan. "What realistic purpose," he now asks Alex, "do you want to achieve with your writing? I have had no news from home, but it's possible that the articles in the *Atlantic Monthly* have terribly angered Djemal Pasha at me, and I pray his anger will not go further."[2]

He reminded Alex that while they had always been in agreement on the principle that they should never allow fear of tyrants to dictate their behavior, the benefits of any act of defiance on their part would have to be very weighty indeed to justify the risk it involved. "Are you sure," he asks, "that you did not sacrifice too much for the sake of a sensational headline?"

He went much further. "What," he asks, "have you, Alex, been doing with your brilliant capacities throughout the year-long? I cannot pass judgement as I lack the information. From here I can see only your inactivity, your failure in Egypt (whose cause I do not know).... But you can imagine with what impatience I await your detailed report — frank, bold and worthy of you — and of all of us."

That he regarded a straightening out of their relations as urgent is emphasized by an appeal to Rivka. He asks her to keep pressing Alex — "who is sometimes unconcerned and indifferent — until he sends me the detailed information I am asking for."

It was not only for clearing the air that he was so insistent. He felt that he needed Alex's help for the execution of his operational plan as soon as the essential line of communication with the British authorities in Egypt was established. That contact, he explained, would be handled by Avshalom Feinberg. At the Egyptian end he would set up an office at Port Said (the port of departure of the intelligence vessel) and there he would install their brother Sam (who had also gone off to the United States). For Alex he reserved the task he had himself initiated in London — relations with the British government authorities, the friends he had made there in the War Office and outside.

With that said, however, he felt the need to put a crucial question to Alex and Sam. He writes bluntly: "Shall I be able in case of need to depend on you? Will you still be ready to give up the good and comfortable life in the United States for the [life of] abnegation, the risks and perhaps the dangers of our

---

2. Djemal evidently never reacted to the article.

undertaking? I ask," he concluded, "for a clear and categorical reply." There is no record of what reply, if any, he ever received from Alex to his specific questions.

It was only six weeks later, after he arrived in Egypt, that he had word from Alex. It was in a cable Alex had sent to London, now forwarded to Cairo. There Alex expressed his agreement to go to London — evidently to take on the diplomatic task Aaron had assigned to him.

When Major Gribbon told Aaronsohn that the officers in Egypt were impressed by his memorandum, Aaronsohn may have seen this as a positive preface to the reception he would expect in Cairo. Actually Gribbon was understating. The memorandum had so impressed the political officers at General Headquarters, that they actually lifted a substantial portion of it and had it reproduced in the next number of the *Arab Bulletin*,[3] a secret publication of the Arab Bureau — for limited circulation among senior officials and officers.

The Arab Bureau was born in mid-1916 out of a concept shared by a number of the senior members of the British colonial establishment, and its military arm centered on Egypt. Sir Mark Sykes, at that time still engaged on his far-flung eastern travels, was apparently its main progenitor. Other influential enthusiasts from the outset were the governor-general of the Sudan, Sir Reginald Wingate — who, before the end of 1916, was appointed high commissioner in Egypt — and two of his subordinates, Gilbert Clayton and Ronald Storrs. They envisaged a "federation of semi-independent Arab states under European guidance and supervision…owing spiritual allegiance to a single Arab primate and looking to Great Britain as its patron and protector."[4]

In its wartime context it was based on two premises. The first was that Sharif Hussein, the factual ruler of the Hedjaz (now Saudi Arabia) — or more accurately its governor subject to the Ottoman administration — was capable of heading a revolt throughout the Arab communities against his Turkish

---

3. No. 33, December 4, 1916. Its contents were faithfully attributed to "a resident of Athlit." Four later memoranda of Aaronsohn's that can be traced as appearing in the *Arab Bulletin* are no. 38 (January 12, 1917), no. 48 (April 21, 1917), no. 50 (May 13, 1917) and no. 64 (September 27, 1917).
4. Wingate to Lord Hardinge, August 26, 1915, Wingate Papers, School of Oriental Studies, Durham University; quoted by Kedourie, *The Chatham House Version and Other Middle Eastern Studies*. (London: Weidenfeld and Nicolson, 1970), p. 17.

masters; that, at his call, thousands, indeed tens of thousands of Arabs serving in the Ottoman armies, perhaps as many as one-third of all the Arab
soldiers, would desert and flock to his call. The second premise was that
Hussein would need finance in order to launch and maintain his revolt —
which would moreover be sustained by the operations of the British armed
forces.[5]

The second premise was indeed fulfilled. Hussein received from the British government over the next two years some eleven million pounds sterling
worth of gold (equivalent in 2006, to nearly five hundred million dollars),[6]
while the Arab revolt went into history. More accurately it went into the
history books and as a dominant factor in the many territorial gifts made to
the Arabs. As for the revolt itself, Hussein did issue his call to the Arabs
throughout the Ottoman Empire. But nobody, apart from a handful including some prisoners of war, responded.

Whatever fighting took place was done by Hussein's own meager Hedjazi
forces — some six hundred regular soldiers in all, led by his son Feisal — and
a collection of tribesmen numbering perhaps as many as twenty thousand,
suited marginally for spasmodic guerilla warfare but with neither the training, the discipline, the motivation nor the psychological conditioning of
regular soldiers. Already in May 1917 — in no. 52 of the *Arab Bulletin* — the
head of the Arab Bureau, David George Hogarth, dismissed their military
weight in a few words. "It was never in doubt," he wrote, "that they would not
attack nor withstand Turkish regulars."

The Arab revolt, however honest the intentions harbored by both Hussein
and the British planners, turned out to be perhaps the greatest hoax of the
First World War. The British officer, in later propaganda feted as a great
national hero who — often suitably dressed in Arab desert clothing (*a'agal*

---

5. On the basis of Hussein's undertaking, the British — through their chief representative in Egypt, High Commissioner Sir Henry McMahon, Wingate's predecessor —
   made promises of concessions of territory to be captured by the Allied forces. The
   debate as to what was promised and what was not promised continued for many
   years; but throughout all these years, what was conveniently "forgotten," both on the
   British and the Arab side, was that these undertakings and money were given as a
   prize for Hussein's revolt, and that, as the revolt never actually took place, the British
   owed him nothing.
6. Assessed by Col. Ronald Storrs in his memoirs, *Orientations* (London: Ivor Nicholson & Watson, 1937), pp. 167–68.

and *khefiyeh*) — was celebrated as, in effect, the mastermind of the "revolt," was Thomas Edward Lawrence ("Lawrence of Arabia"). He was a consummate weaver of relevant fairy tales. He later confessed that the whole revolt had been a "side-show of a side-show."

The success of the hoax was made possible by the deliberate British policy of attributing British military successes to Hussein's Sharifian Arabs. An Arab historian described the technique. The British laid down the principle that in any area "emancipated from Turkish control by the action of the Arabs themselves, the British would recognise complete and sovereign independence."[7]

Lawrence and the Sharifians then set out to apply the technique. It has been described by another Arab historian: "Wherever the British army captured a town or reduced a fortress which was to be given to the Arabs it would halt *until the Arabs could enter and the capture be credited to them.*"[8] (Emphasis added.)

Thus the British, who had projected an Arab revolt as the opening to their grand plan of a British-controlled Arab federation, found that they could achieve the same result from the pretense of a revolt. They could thereby achieve their immediate pressing objective — to put a stop to French competitive claims to territory which could be described as having been captured "by the action of the Arabs themselves."

7. Muhammed Kurd Ali, *Khitab el Sham* (Damascus, 1925), vol. 3, p. 154; quoted by Kedourie, *England and the Middle East* (London: Bowes & Bowes, 1956), p. 21.
8. Quoted by George Antonius, *The Arab Awakening: The Story of the Arab National Movement* (London: H. Hamilton, 1938), p. 271. See also Richard Aldington, *Lawrence of Arabia: A Biographical Inquiry* (London: Collins, 1955), and Kedourie, *The Chatham House Version.*

CHAPTER 10

"Nili"

Aaronsohn arrived in Egypt on December 12, 1916, five months after setting out from Zichron Ya'akov. The plan of action which he had carried in his mind throughout his odyssey, and which he had intended to implement on his arrival in Egypt, had been altered radically during his stay in London. What he had wanted was to see the resumption of the contact between Egypt and Athlit and then — within days — to be back himself in Athlit. But by the time he left London it was clear that the War Office, after consultation with Cairo, had accepted the project itself but would not enable him to land at Athlit.

In retrospect it would be most surprising if the British had not accepted Aaronsohn's help. All that has come to light on the state of British intelligence at that time in the zone and in Palestine in particular, presents a sad picture of ignorance, of muddle and misdirection. The credibility of the military intelligence on Palestine, supplied by the agents they had at their disposal — mainly Syrians in the north, Bedouin in the south — was pitiably low. It was matched by a broad lack of background knowledge of the officers handling it. These officers were often even incapable of assessing it; they nevertheless, in the guise of experts, generated far-reaching decisions. Also, until the spring of 1917, they were bedeviled by the existence of a plurality of authorities.

London was then still suffering from the terrible trauma of the disaster at Gallipoli, to which faulty intelligence had made no mean contribution. Then it was reflected in the ruins of a major illusion, fostered and sustained by the naiveté and the misplaced self-assurance of Cairo experts — the "Arab revolt," which was conceived as a major weapon for the overthrow of the Ottoman Empire but which never really took off, except as a series of minor operations, which made no impact on the course of the war. Now, the London planners were on the eve of launching the long-debated strategy: to achieve victory through a military campaign in Syria-Palestine. Precisely at that moment Aaronsohn, arriving out of the blue, offered them a strongly motivated, well-educated, potentially effective intelligence unit of young Jewish Ottoman citizens on their home ground behind the Turkish lines. Aaronsohn's offer must have seemed a heaven-sent strategic windfall.

It is clear however that, beyond the military intelligence Aaronsohn's followers might possibly provide, his interlocutors found that they had struck it lucky in the overwhelming personality of Aaronsohn himself. In those first conversations with Gribbon, with Sykes and Fitzmaurice and in his memoranda, he had demonstrated that he had at his fingertips an incredible range of knowledge on broad swaths of war-related subjects. They had discovered a perhaps unique source of reliable intelligence and, no less, of strategic insights. Hence they saw him as a tremendous asset, a kind of super-adviser; and they decided to keep him in Egypt, or even in London as, at one point, Gribbon suggested.

His first meetings with British intelligence officers in Egypt reawakened the angry suspicions he had voiced to Gribbon. Here he was met, not by shapers of major policy, but with planners and organizers in the marine transport unit, responsible on this front only for the dispatch and control of the boat that would receive and bring back the reports assembled at Athlit.

On his third day in Egypt he was introduced to the head of the unit, Colonel Simpson — and Simpson's first message was that he, Aaronsohn, would not be permitted to travel on the ship to Athlit. Again he burst out in protest as he had done in London. This again, he said, meant that he was not trusted and, if so, "it would be better to drop the whole thing."

Simpson denied the charge. "After all," he declared, "if we didn't trust you we wouldn't have brought you to Egypt." The crux of the matter, he explained, was that they could not take risks with his safety or his life. "You are," he said, "too valuable for us."

Simpson having to leave on a mission to Salonika, the subject was pursued by his deputy, Captain William Edmonds, who would be Aaronsohn's regular contact at the headquarters of the unit — Eastern Mediterranean Special Intelligence Bureau (EMSIB). They talked the next day for nearly three hours. Aaronsohn had to tell his story all over again, to explain the behavior, no doubt puzzling to these pragmatic British ears, of a group of

Jews volunteering their services and prepared to face extreme dangers in the cause of Britain. He told him of Zionist motivation, of Turkish oppression — and of the vital need for speed in reestablishing contact with the group.

Edmonds evidently digested only part of the message. He did, three days later, report progress. It had been decided, he said, to send the boat with an emissary, but Aaronsohn was "meantime" to remain in Egypt. Aaron had by now resigned himself to not landing at Athlit, but insisted that he should be on the boat. Edmonds was adamant. To avoid more delay, Aaron gave up his resistance; but he warned Edmonds that, while he would provide the emissary with all the necessary directions, if any accident should befall he would "never forgive them." "They don't want to understand us," he noted in the diary, "or they are still being cautious…. It makes cooperation between us annoying and even impossible." Bitterly he adds, "If it were not a matter of saving our people whose lives are in danger in Eretz-Israel, I would take leave of the English gentlemen."

That was not all. Aaronsohn had to raise the question of reimbursement of expenses he had naturally incurred in making his way from Palestine. The principle had been accepted in London. Now Edmonds behaved with unseemly discourtesy and parsimony. When Aaronsohn, who kept accounts, claimed that he had spent one thousand five hundred pounds (Egyptian), Edmonds at once declared that it seemed too much. As for current expenses, Edmonds — who spoke in Simpson's name — offered one pound a day — which Aaronsohn rejected.

He felt this was the last straw. "To this day," he wrote in the diary, "I have heard nothing from them but hidden thoughts and suspicions — and on top of it all, this niggardliness. I shall try to control my nerves in order to renew the contact with Avshalom. Then, if he so wishes, he can carry on; I've had enough. I won't continue working in these conditions."

There was, however, more to follow. The British had their rationale for preventing Aaron from landing at Athlit; they had less understandable reasons for his not being allowed even to travel on the boat. Both arguments however took on a specious look when it became clear that they were also planning to take out of his hands the choice of the emissary who was to make the personal contact at Athlit.

Aaron, unsuspecting, had called on Rafael Aboulafia, a close friend of Avshalom, to find a suitable emissary from among the Palestinian expatriates. Aboulafia had found his way to Egypt in 1915 and joined the Zion Mule Corps. Wounded in Gallipoli, he had been evacuated to Egypt, and there Avshalom had found him, confided in him, and had even introduced him to Woolley. Now he informed Aaronsohn that he had found a young man whom he could recommend. Aaron at once informed Edmonds.

Later that day Aaron, at Edmonds's request, came to the office.

There Edmonds blandly told him that he had been informed on the telephone that "they" (presumably Captain Smith, in charge at Port Said) had found a suitable emissary. They "wanted to know if I have anything special to convey."

He was flabbergasted. He was to be sidelined, no less. "This," he writes, "is too hard a blow. It's what I was afraid of. These people suspect us and want to use my knowledge in order to send some blundering fellow who may bring disaster down on our people and destroy our whole undertaking."

He did not mince words. He told Edmonds "all I thought about this suspicious attitude," and that he refused to continue any cooperation whatsoever. Edmonds had a reply which only helped to confirm Aaron's charge. "If we don't trust you," he said, "you after all also don't trust us."

Aaron explained the difference. "Our doubts," he said, "arise from your lack of diligence and your tardiness, but we don't doubt your good faith." There he evidently left the matter but that night (as he records in the diary) he had feelings of remorse as to whether he may not have been too harsh, and thereby forfeited the British cooperation which, though accompanied by contempt and suspicion, was essential for the sake of his colleagues. "But," he writes, "I cannot change my character at my age."

The next day he delivered a note to Edmonds, pointing out that they had no right to use, against his will, information he had provided. That day he also wrote a letter addressed to Gribbon in London and enclosed it in the envelope with the letter to Edmonds.

It can safely be said that the kindly Major Gribbon, a senior officer in the War Office, had never seen such a drubbing administered to his fellow officials.

Aaronsohn recalled the near-break in relations in London because of the lack of mutual understanding, and the conclusion he and Gribbon had reached — that reliance and trust had to be mutual:

You are aware that since I first came in touch with your Minister in

Copenhagen up to the day I left London I had to stand a good deal more than my self-respect could bear, and it is even worse since I left London. Were I alone, I confess I would have long ago given you up in despair. But I have behind me lots of men whom I induced to give their energies, their last pennies, their lives, for a work which we supposed could be of help for you and for us. And in order to rescue them from the clutches of the Turks... It is as well to be hard of hearing as it is to possess a blind eye on occasion. You made me swallow a good deal, but I can swallow no more. Neither myself nor, I am sure, any one of my men will agree to be rescued when looked upon as contemptible...

You will remember, dear Major, that we spoke at some length of the way I thought proper to reestablish the connection between my place and your office. I considered that it is an unavoidable necessity to direct the plan myself. You kindly promised me to write personally to Egypt about that. You will surely remember also that I always wondered at the failure of the several attempts, of which I happened to know, your office here had made to get in touch either with us or with other people; they have always failed, bringing not infrequently calamity on innocent people on shore....

And now the office here has reached a decision to send again some Syrian messenger whom it is considered better to hide from me; the Carmel map you promised to send, the Admiralty charts, which are here, are denied me when I want them to give fuller explanations....

It is therefore my duty to prevent this dangerous scheme to be put into operation. And that is why I severed my connection with your office and why I insist to make it understood there that they have no moral right whatever to do a thing which would not merely be a breach of confidence but an enormous crime towards the people in Palestine.

We were candid enough to suppose that when people volunteered as sincerely as we did, their services would be gratefully accepted and they themselves would have no reason to feel hurt in their dignity, in their self-respect. I am sorry to see now, when it is too late, that we were mistaken. I am sorry to see that you cannot understand us, we went into this enterprise whole-hearted and we expected to collaborate cheerfully. I quit broken-hearted.

But there is at least one thing I am glad of. Instinctively I always resisted the offers of money made from your side, I have not soiled my hands with a penny of yours. Whatever construction you put on our motives, we have given you no possibility of suspecting us of being mercenary as the Jew is supposed to be. Here at least you will have to look for another explanation if psychological puzzles do interest you.

As though perhaps to emphasize this point he asked Gribbon to cable Henrietta Szold to send him five hundred dollars.

It is doubtful whether the letter, which was of course read at EMSIB, was ever sent to Gribbon. Its effect was electric. Five hours after he had handed in the two letters in the one envelope, a telephone call came from Edmonds asking him to come to the office. He was received there by Colonel Simpson, who appeared relaxed; there was no strain in the air, nor any reference to the letters. Simpson simply had "good news" for Aaron.

"Since we last met," he said, "I've had the devil of a time to assuage the fears of the Chief of Public Security. After much debate when I reminded him of all that we knew about you people, and that the impression you had made in London was of the best…I convinced him of the identity of our interests, and it was decided that we are placing ourselves entirely in your hands." Recording this speech in the diary, Aaronsohn concludes blandly: "All I could do was thank him."

There was more "good news" to follow. Simpson went off to an urgent engagement and Aaronsohn was left to Edmonds, who at once raised the question of Aaron's expenses. "The Colonel," he said, "agreed to pay you more than a pound a day for your expenses."

As for the problem of the emissary to be sent to Athlit, he asked Aaronsohn to give him the name and the photograph of the young man recommended by Aboulafia — and to report together with him to Captain Smith at Port Said two days later, on December 22.

With Simpson's promise in mind, all should now have been plain sailing — but Aaronsohn discovered that he still had Captain Smith to deal with. In Port Said he bought a quantity of provisions to bring to Athlit: powdered milk, cocoa, chocolate, cereals, tea, coffee and kerosene, weighing altogether about one hundred kilos. Smith refused to allow them on board. By some strange calculation he made out that not Aaronsohn, not Aboulafia, nor the emissary Baruch Skaletsky, but only the packages would attract attention; they alone would be a breach of the strict security they were aiming at.

It was in any case a lame excuse. From the second day of his arrival in Egypt Aaronsohn had begun fortuitously to encounter old friends and acquaintances among the exiles from Palestine. Attempts at concealment would be futile. His diary records almost daily meetings, luncheons, dinners, lectures and outings with friends.

He revealed to Smith that when Avshalom Feinberg, whose voyage in 1915 had been organized by Lieutenant Woolley, arrived at Athlit, he was loaded with four hundred kilos of goods. Smith stood firm. Aaron, in desperation, suggested a "deal." If the provisions were taken on board and it was discovered at Athlit that nobody was starving, they would not be landed. Smith's retort was, "Let them starve, what do we care?" Smith got "the reply he deserved," writes Aaronsohn; but the provisions remained in Port Said.

They set out on a French fishing vessel, the *Goeland*, on the afternoon of December 24. Soon Aaronsohn was given reason to question Smith's efficiency. He had urged him that morning to bring a pair of binoculars adequate for viewing details on the shore from the ship. Smith however insisted that the binoculars on board were adequate. They were not. When the *Goeland* came abreast of the experiment station at Athlit the sea was too rough for an approach; and then they saw a figure come out onto the balcony of the station holding a black sheet. The negative signal was clear, but with those weak binoculars the person could not be identified. Smith admitted he had been wrong.

In hopes of an improvement in the weather, the *Goeland* sailed northwards as far as Haifa, put to sea and then came back two or three times. Now a heavy storm was brewing, with winds and thunder and lightning. Each time the black sheet was shown, now held up by two persons; but who were they? Aaronsohn could make only a wild guess. He was moved beyond words by this proof of the steadfast loyalty and determination of his friends and followers, keeping watch day after day, throughout the long months of isolation and frustration. Even Smith said words of praise.

Then on the second night the sky cleared. The sea was still rough, but

Abdullah, the Syrian veteran sailor, decided a boat could be lowered. Aaron begged Smith to allow him to go along.

Neither Aboulafia nor Baruch Skaletzky knew the geography at Athlit. He, Aaronsohn, knew every inch, could give directions, expedite the whole operation, and be back on the *Goeland* in two hours. Smith angrily refused; the boat set out; after an hour it returned. The sea had been too rough and Abdullah was afraid the boat would capsize. A swimmer could make it to the shore, Skaletzky was willing, but Abdullah refused to hang around in the open stormy sea for two hours, waiting for Skaletzky's return. He suggested that Skaletzky should remain on shore. As this would not solve any problem, Skaletzky came back to the ship. Aaronsohn bowed to the inevitable.

Early next morning, after much putting about, the French captain of the *Goeland* announced there was still no hope of a successful operation, and set sail for Port Said. Not however without a new altercation between Aaron and an unbelievably insensitive Smith. Aaron asked him to signal to the shore a warning of the dangers they must be aware of if caught by the Turks. Smith refused out of hand. "We are not interested in the dangers," he said, "because the subject does not influence the military situation. Only military information is important."

What was surely much more important at that moment was that a signal could be sent to announce that Aaron had reached Egypt and was in touch with the British authorities. Did Smith refuse to send such a message, or did it not occur to Aaronsohn to ask? In his diary there is no mention of such a request.

"Without anger," he wrote in his diary, "I pointed out to him the difference between volunteers who offer cooperation and people who have been bought for money and have no obligations beyond the agreed price."

Smith was unimpressed. That afternoon they were back at Port Said. When he reported to Edmonds a week later, he lied. Skaletzky, he claimed, could have gone on shore if he had wanted to…

For five days Aaronsohn kicked his heels in Alexandria in renewed frustration. Was it not enough that a month had been wasted in Copenhagen with Paget waiting for a reply from London, and then the month in London waiting for a decision from Egypt? "Only somebody who has no nerves, nor warm blood, can work with these people." Again he threatens in his diary to give it all up and hand over to Avshalom as soon as contact is established.

And so he concludes his diary entries for the month. On December 28 tea with Dr. Weitz, his old friend from Zichron; evening with Mrs. Berman, sister-in-law to Sonia Soskin, and young Miss Berligne, daughter of a communal leader in Jaffa. On December 29 a visit to the Greco-Roman museum. On the 30th — a morning at the municipal library; in the evening with Weitz and the Bermans. On the 31st — a walk through the Nuzha gardens. They are well kept, he writes, but they are manifestly run empirically, with a special eye to making a good impression.

Nineteen-seventeen opened with a message from Edmonds, delivered by a Captain Jones; he was to move to Cairo, to set up residence and work there. In the course of conversation however Jones suddenly came out with "You're the very man I'm looking for." He was seeking information on the roads of Palestine (and had with him "a bad map"). Here was an exciting hint for Aaronsohn: was finally a British offensive in the offing? Jones moreover went on to ask him for a list of personalities in southern Palestine. The list he prepared in the coming days duly appeared later on (May 1917) in a "most secret" bulletin of the Arab Bureau.

He was discovering daily the degrees of inefficiency and lack of coordination in the British military establishment. In London they had arranged his voyage to Egypt. They had told him to make contact with Colonel Simpson and with General Gilbert Clayton who, as head of all the British intelligence services in Egypt, was the natural authority for providing the necessary political contacts if Aaronsohn's unique stores of knowledge, information and insights were to be exploited.

Weeks had gone by. No word had come from Clayton, nor from any of his subordinates in the political units — the very people who, as Gribbon had told him, had been impressed with his memorandum. It was by chance that, one whole month after he landed at Port Said, he at last met one of them. A friend active in Jewish communal affairs in Cairo, banker Jacques Mosseri, who had contacts in the British military establishment, mentioned to Captain Ormsby-Gore, a Member of Parliament who was the head of the political unit in the intelligence structure at General Headquarters, that Aaron Aaronsohn was in Egypt. He met Ormsby-Gore, then, on January 15, 1917.

Ormsby-Gore apologized: He had not been informed that Aaronsohn was in Egypt, and he and his colleagues had been impatiently waiting to meet him. He was full of praise for the memorandum Aaronsohn had compiled in London.

Even more emphatic was Captain Philip Graves, the head of the overland transport unit to whom Ormsby-Gore introduced him. Graves volubly lost his temper at those (and specifically Simpson) responsible for Aaronsohn's presence not being revealed to the people who needed him most.

Complaints completed, both Ormsby-Gore and Graves got down to business immediately. Ormsby-Gore wanted details of the important personalities in all the communities in Palestine. Graves wanted information on Gaza. From hints dropped in the course of conversation, Aaronsohn was able to record in his diary a broad but fairly accurate guess at the content of the secret agreement between Britain and France for the postwar disposition of Palestine. The British would control the territory south of Acre, Jerusalem would be British and Protestant, Nazareth and the Galilee would be French. This was to become famous — or infamous — as the Sykes-Picot agreement. "For us," Aaronsohn commented, "this will be a disaster, but we are too weak to be able to express our opinion."

Ormsby-Gore thought that Aaronsohn should be attached to his unit. Three days later, however, after he had consulted with Major Malcolm (deputizing for Colonel Simpson), he found that Aaronsohn would have to be available to both their units, as well as to Captain Graves' overland transport unit.[1]

From the warmth of Ormsby-Gore's office Aaronsohn went to the frosty atmosphere of Edmonds' — who at once took the opportunity of repeating the ban on Aaronsohn's landing at Athlit. This time he explained how much more dangerous it would be for Aaronsohn, dressed in civilian clothes, than for a soldier. Then he turned to the subject of money — the reimbursement of expenses. Three hundred Turkish pounds that Aaronsohn was due to receive would be paid to him in three installments.

His suspicions that Edmonds was still suspicious of him were strengthened that very week. Captain Norman Bentwich, a Jewish officer in the Camel Corps, disclosed that Edmonds had been questioning him about Aaronsohn's precise standing in the Palestine community. Bentwich, it so

---

1. Graves, as a correspondent of *The Times*, was the first to expose, in 1920, the fabricated antisemitic "classic" *Protocols of the Elders of Zion*.

happened, was no stranger to Zichron Ya'akov, where he had close family connections.[2]

Thus began a new era in Aaronsohn's relations with the British. In the marine transport unit, Edmonds and Smith continued to be unfriendly and manifestly insensitive to the problems of the group operating under the nose of the Turks; but the men with whom Aaronsohn now began meeting were of a very different stamp — not only highly intelligent, but politically sophisticated. They were at the level of the personalities he had met in London: Sykes, Gribbon, Fitzmaurice. Now he discovered that Ormsby-Gore was intensely interested in Zionism. Aaronsohn reports hours of discussion with him and with another officer, also a Member of Parliament, Lieutenant Everard Feilding, on agricultural prospects in the various zones of the country.

As with Gribbon in London, there was instant rapport with these officers. In London he had passed on very relevant information on Turkish dispositions. Emphasizing his conviction that a successful offensive in Palestine could, and should, be launched from the sea, he had produced a list, based on a physical survey he had made in July 1916, showing the fragility of the Turkish coastal defenses. Now, already in his first conversation with Lieutenant Feilding, he offered information on other Turkish weak spots: the railway between Ramle and Jenin, and the stations of Tulkarm and Ras-el-Ain (Rosh Ha'ayin) — all desirable targets for aerial bombing.

Not miraculously, three weeks after their first meeting (February 7), High Commissioner Sir Reginald Wingate[3] sent to Arthur J. Balfour, the foreign secretary, a memorandum prepared by the Arab Bureau on "agriculture and supplies in Palestine." In his covering note he added that "the information contained in the memorandum was obtained by Captain Ormsby-Gore mainly from Aaron Aaronsohn, director of the Agricultural Experiment Station at Zichron Ya'akov."

---

2. In his memoirs, *Wanderer between Two Worlds: An Autobiography* (London: Kegan Paul, Trench, Trubner and Co., 1941), Bentwich writes that Edmonds asked him to keep a check on Aaronsohn.
3. The effective governor of Egypt as a British protectorate.

The memorandum provided a comprehensive description, from the agricultural point of view, of several zones: Jerusalem-Jaffa, Samaria, the Galilee and Transjordan, the various crops and their harvests, the geology, the roads, the climate, the inhabitants.[4]

Meantime, on January 29, a further attempt was made to reach Athlit. Now Aaronsohn brought with him a new emissary, chosen by Aboulafia. He was Leibl Bernstein, a young man of proven courage and resource. He, too, was a Zion Mule Corps veteran of the Gallipoli campaign. Again, however, this time from the very start, the winds proved too fierce, and the waves too high for the *Chaveau*, a vessel smaller even than the *Goeland*, and so, defeated once more, they turned back to Port Said, and Aaronsohn — frustrated beyond words — returned that night to Cairo.

It seems that of the three officers with whom he worked those first days, it was with Feilding that he developed the strongest chemistry. On January 25, he spent the whole morning with him and Ormsby-Gore. In the afternoon he went out with an old Zichron friend, Peretz Pascal, for his regular bicycle outing — an essential exercise in his never-ending efforts to slim his heavy body. He went back to his hotel to keep a five-o'clock tea appointment with Feilding. But in the lobby he was met by Edmonds, "looking mysterious." He had been searching for Aaronsohn all day, and told him he must travel to Port Said immediately. "One of your people has arrived through the desert."

It was nearly midnight when, in great apprehension, he arrived at Port Said. In the Hotel de la Poste he found Yosef Lishansky, Avshalom's friend, who had worked so hard to secure Avshalom's release from jail in 1915. He was suffering from bullet wounds. He and Avshalom Feinberg had set out into Sinai in a new attempt to reach the British lines. They were attacked in the desert. Avshalom had been killed on the spot.

From Lishansky on his sick-bed, later from Sarah and from his own and

4. PRO/FO 371/3049/41442. It was the information he gleaned from Aaronsohn on the high prospect of a successful agriculture and the renaissance of a Jewish farmer class that turned Ormsby-Gore — who later gained high office in the government Lloyd George had formed in December 1916 — into a strong supporter of Zionism.

Liova Schneierson's recollections Aaron could piece together the sequence of relevant events after he had parted from Avshalom in Damascus six months earlier.

He had calculated that he would be back at Athlit by the end of October. In September from Denmark he had written to Avshalom informing him that he would be receiving three thousand dollars from the trustees in America. Then he had cabled Liova in Constantinople instructing him to return at once to Athlit — presaging his own early return. Liova himself was unable to leave Constantinople but on October 5 he conveyed the message to Avshalom. October however went by without a word from Aaron, and not a single dollar from the United States.

Days and weeks of frustration followed, and only in mid-November did Avshalom get a further telegram from Liova. This time he conveyed the news that Aaron had left, or was just leaving, England for Egypt. In fact he sailed from London for Egypt on the 24th. Ironically, on the *Karmala* he wrote in his diary on December 8: "What a surprise it would be if I found Avshalom there!"

This was when communication broke down. A letter that Aaron sent Avshalom on November 17 from England — through Denmark to Tsilla in Berlin, to Athlit — never reached Avshalom. In that letter Aaron informed Avshalom that (as he himself had just learned from Thomson and Gribbon) Woolley was not in Egypt, but in a prisoner-of-war camp at Kistamuna in Turkey.

Again Avshalom waited. Meantime his financial problems went from bad to worse. He was reduced to seeking loans to cover the day-to-day expenses at the station and to pay at least part of the wages of the workers he had not dismissed — and even the sources for loans were drying up.

Already in October Avshalom had begun to feel most uneasy. He had been left in charge of the station with all its responsibilities. On December 16 from Athlit he sent a note to Sarah at Zichron:

> Everybody tells me that Aaron is coming back soon; Tsilla, Haim [Avraham], Liova, etc. I wish it were so, but what can I do? — I don't believe it. By my calculation he should have been here a month ago — and more — and we haven't a penny. The situation is so terrible that I

do not want to talk about it even to the closest people lest it discourage them.

He decided to ask the American Consul Glazebrook to communicate, through the US embassy in Constantinople, with the trustees of the experiment station, and ask them "when they calculate I might expect a cabled reply from them, and [tell them] that if I don't receive instructions by that date I shall resign."

Evidently it was when no cable came at all that he decided once more to make his way to Egypt — through Sinai.

He first visited Jaffa and Jerusalem, and sent a note to Sarah. Its contents were inexplicably optimistic: "With patience and energy we can achieve everything, and I hope I shall still see you during February and at least send you good news...." It cannot be doubted that the optimistic tone of his letter derived from his certainty that in Egypt he would find Woolley.

On the eve of his departure Sarah pleaded with him not to take the risk once more. He knew better than anybody else from bitter experience, she reminded him, the hazards of venturing into Sinai, and how in 1915 he had been saved from dire consequences only by a miracle (or, more precisely, by the bribing of officials). Moreover, Sinai, now a live war zone, had become even more dangerous.

He did not listen.

Lishansky bought the camels and sought out a Bedouin who agreed to serve as their guide in the desert. On Saturday, January 13, Avshalom came to Yosef's house in the southern village of Ekron. They donned Bedouin clothes and set out on their camels. In contrast to Avshalom's route in December 1915 they skirted the coastal towns and villages, so as to avoid Turkish patrols. They traveled mostly by night and tried to hide during the day.

The journey, with many lengthy stops, lasted a week. When they came beyond the Turkish lines into No Man's Land at Sheikh Zuwaid near El Arish (then already in British hands) they did not know in which direction to continue. (It was evidently at this point that their Bedouin guide disappeared.) They moved around in the sand all night, and at morning light they found that they had been moving in circles. As the day dawned they were attacked by rifle fire from thirty or forty Bedouin.

First Yosef was hit in the leg and fell. The fall evidently saved him. Then

Avshalom was hit in the body. Yosef managed to reach him, but Avshalom could not speak. With his hand he raised the edge of the abaya and pointed; Yosef understood that he wanted him to get away. He began running, but he was hit again, by a bullet in his right shoulder. He fell and lost consciousness. He was picked up by an Australian patrol and brought to their base.[5]

Denied to Aaron was the solace of public mourning. He dared not even hint at the tragedy that had befallen him, his family, his work, the threat to all his plans. The many exiles from Palestine with whom he had regularly been meeting in Cairo or Alexandria must not be given an inkling. No sign of Avshalom's lonely death in the desert dared be carried back to Palestine. Sarah and father Fishel would have to be told as soon as possible and, through Alex, somehow the news should be broken to Rivka. Nobody else could yet be told, not even Avshalom's own family; there must be no murmur of sorrow in the streets of Zichron Ya'akov or Avshalom's village of Hadera. And he himself in stoic persistence must carry on, as though nothing had happened.[6]

His British collaborators had to be told. Part of the story they already knew through Lishansky's arrival; the rest he would have to fill in. Moreover, he needed their immediate help in taking care of Lishansky. He turned to a man whom he had met only two days earlier — Major Wyndham Deedes, who had but recently arrived to take charge of the intelligence services. At their meeting Aaron had sensed an instant empathy. To Deedes he now poured out his heart. He did not understand (so he writes in his diary) why he chose to speak to this "dry, hard" man. Yet he not only spoke. He could not restrain himself: he wept; and Deedes, conscious of the thousands of young men — the flower of British youth — dying in their hundreds and thousands

---

5. Eliezer Livneh, Yosef Nedava, and Yoram Efrati, *Nili: Toldoteha shel he-aza medinit* [Nili: A story of political daring] (Tel Aviv: Shocken, 1961), pp 121-22. In his diary on June 7, Aaron records that the British had arrested an Arab on suspicion of having murdered Avshalom. He was later released for lack of evidence.
6. He had to make a few exceptions — an old friend from Zichron, Peretz Pascal, Dr. Weitz and Rafael Aboulafia. One other fellow Palestinian knew the whole story: Charles Boutagy, the Christian friend of the family who worked for British intelligence; it was to him at Port Said the Australians had brought the wounded Lishansky.

in the fields of Flanders (just as Avshalom was, surely, of the flower of the youth of Palestine) heard him out and "he comforted me, telling me that what I was suffering was being suffered by so many faithful sons of Albion."

Aaronsohn, in his grief, blamed the British who, because of their suspicions and their delays, had brought about the tragedy. Deedes assured him that he knew of the shortcomings of British organization (he did not mention that he had been sent to solve that very problem) which in Aaronsohn's case had been compounded by mistrust. "With him, Deedes promised me, there would be no insults, no suspicions."

Deedes at once arranged hospital treatment for Yosef, the best possible — "first class as for officers." He telephoned to Edmonds and to Smith. "He is active," wrote Aaron, "and knows how to give orders."

Then, two days later, eight days after Avshalom had died, the first successful mission to Athlit was accomplished. Precisely that week it had been decided to make the new attempt. Aaronsohn, doubly conscious of the need to behave normally in everything he did, hastened the next morning, after visiting Lishansky in the hospital, to board an express train to Port Said. On his way out from the hospital, he met Deedes with Edmonds on their way in to see Lishansky. He arrived on time to board the vessel — a French torpedo boat named *Arabalite*, together with Smith and Bernstein and Boutagy.

With the setting of the moon that night the vessel, after the usual maneuvers, arrived opposite Athlit. The sea was calm; the boat was lowered with Bernstein, Boutagy, and Abdullah with his two sons. Twenty-five minutes later they signalled that Bernstein had swum safely ashore. Shortly afterwards, Aaronsohn and Smith saw the flickering lights of torches and then, unexpectedly, there was shouting. Whoever it was that had greeted Bernstein could not restrain his excitement. It was not, as it happened, Sarah who had greeted them, but two other members of the group, Baruch Raab and Yehuda Zeldin.

Evidently at Smith's instructions Abdullah this time kept the rowboat waiting. Bernstein was at the station for an hour and twenty minutes. In the meantime a strong wind had risen, high waves were beating at the shore and Bernstein, starting out to swim back, found himself in difficulties. Abdullah's sons jumped into the water to help him, but they too found the waves too difficult and turned back. Bernstein was left alone in the water. Strong swimmer though he was, he turned back to the shore.

Aaronsohn did not hide his chagrin at having to return to Port Said without Bernstein (and manifestly without intelligence reports) but there was nothing he could do about it. Another emissary would have to be found for the next attempt. The contact, however, for which Aaron had set out, had been made. It had taken six precious months; and Avshalom was dead.

Aaron did not know then — nor perhaps did he ever learn — of the mini-drama that was enacted that night at Athlit. It was preserved in the personal diary of Liova Schneierson, of whom sight had been lost for half a year of this narrative.[7] He was to have traveled as Aaronsohn's assistant all the way to England and Egypt, but was denied a permit to leave Turkey. Aaronsohn therefore asked him to remain in Constantinople as a contact man, to receive and carry messages to Athlit which might reach him from Aaronsohn direct or through Tsilla Feinberg in Berlin — whom Aaron hoped to enlist.

When Aaronsohn at last arrived in London in October he hoped to establish contact with Tsilla in Germany and Liova through neutral Denmark, but the person he had in mind declined to cooperate. There are no further references to the subject in his diary, and he remained effectively cut off from home until the first successful landing at Athlit. Liova obediently remained in Constantinople, under his false name (Hayim Cohen) and his correspondingly false papers. Until Aaron left neutral Denmark, Liova could receive messages, but from then on he was completely cut off just like Aaronsohn at the Egyptian end. Aaron was surely aware of the equivocal situation thus created for Liova, who had no contacts of his own in the Turkish capital. As Aaron however assumed that he would be returning to Zichron within a month or so, Liova's isolation should soon come to an end. Liova shared this belief.

As the weeks passed Liova's troubles mounted. The money he had brought with him, from his savings at home and from what Aaron had left him, was giving out. He had to maintain the secrecy of his extended presence in Constantinople. It was out of the question to make any contact with the Turkish authorities in order to obtain a permit for exit to Palestine — there were too many officials to overcome — nor could he feel it safe to seek out

---

7. The narrative henceforth, to the end of this chapter, is derived from Liova's diary, which was published many years after these events (in Hebrew) as *Miyomano shel ish Nili* [From the diary of a man of Nili] (Haifa: Renaissance Publishers, 1967).

Jewish institutions or personalities. He was not unknown in the Jewish community in Palestine, some of whose members, including deportees, might well be encountered in the streets of Constantinople. Among them there was, also, more than enough dislike of the Aaronsohns.

One chance encounter in the street however turned out to be not unfriendly. A voice said, "Shalom, Mr. Schneierson." He turned and saw it was Dr. Arthur Ruppin, who knew him well, but he answered at once, "My name is Hayim Cohen!" Equally speedy was Ruppin's response: "Shalom, Mr. Cohen." They stood chatting for a moment, and went their ways. Dr. Ruppin, an agronomist by profession, who was the head of the Zionist Office in Jaffa (representing the World Zionist Organization) and had cooperated with Aaronsohn in distributing relief money, had earlier been deported, for no specific reason, to Constantinople.

More weeks went by; no word came from Aaronsohn, nor from Tsilla, and Liova was reduced to a starvation diet. Now he remembered Ruppin. Abashedly no doubt, he went to see him to ask for assistance. He did not tell him why he had come to Constantinople nor with whom. Ruppin, as it happened however, needed some clerical assistance — copying of a manuscript. The pay was low, but it kept Liova afloat for a couple of weeks. Then, once more, he resumed the struggle for survival. His laconic diary entries reflect an imposed self-denial bordering on near-starvation. He managed to maintain himself by selling matches on the streets — albeit, as he writes, at two hundred percent profit.

In desperation he took the plunge. He turned once more to Ruppin. How much detail he now revealed to Ruppin he did not record, but manifestly enough for Ruppin to ask a shrewd question: "Are you going over to the British?" Liova (whether surprised or not) answered without hesitation: "Yes!" Ruppin asked him no more questions but told him to come back in two days' time.[8]

The miracle happened. When Liova came back two days later, Ruppin had a complete plan ready for him. He had persuaded a German officer, Major Klein, to take Schneierson with him to Palestine where he had been ordered to conduct a survey of forestry. He was told that Liova was regularly

---

8. Ruppin subsequently became the chief architect of Zionist agricultural policy in Palestine.

employed at the experiment station at Athlit and was a forestry expert. This does not appear to be a particularly persuasive argument in wartime, and there were no doubt other "arguments" Ruppin used to persuade the officer. They are not recorded in Liova's diary. However Hayim Cohen, traveling under Klein's wing, reached Damascus.

There he evaded Klein, and with his official travel permit as assistant to the major he boarded a train to Affula. A carriage brought him to Athlit and there he met Sarah.

She told him the painful story of the endless waiting for word from Aaron. She had had to take charge of the experiment station and also of the intelligence group. In the months that had passed since Aaron's departure, some members had left, but the others continued piling up information that could be relevant. But he asked the crucial question: where was Avshalom — Avshalom, his bosom friend, who was like a brother to him? She did not hide her own concern. Avshalom had been gone a month.

Liova returned to Hadera — to the relief and joy of his parents — and there was still no communication from Egypt, nor from Aaron, who should have been in Egypt weeks earlier. In Hadera, Liova was almost arrested by the Turks. They chose the night of Purim, when the community was celebrating, to carry out a search for deserters. His name was actually called out at the party by the searchers, but he managed to hide in the Feinberg house — which was empty except for a nervous housekeeper. There he lay down in Avshalom's room, dreaming and wondering what could have happened to Avshalom — Avshalom who used to enjoy Liova's reading to him from the Russian poets (Liova was born in Russia), and once repaid him by writing a poem dedicated "to Liova."

Then however he returned to Athlit and spent most of the time with Sarah at the station, "helping around" — and waiting. It was then, as he writes, that he learned "how strong and how brave" a personality was this, Aaron's young sister.

Suddenly, after only some days, the smoke of a vessel was espied on the horizon, and was soon seen sailing in their direction. Surely, surely, it must be the boat they were waiting for. Sarah, with several of the men working at the station, prepared to receive whatever visitors from Egypt the boat would deliver. Other visitors — professional people who came to see the station's plants on show — were offered an appropriate apology and were politely put off for that day. To keep the watchdog "Azmavet" out of mischief he was taken in charge by one of the watchmen. Reuven Schwartz (a cousin of the Aaronsohns) and Yitzhak Halperin arrived from Zichron to reinforce the welcoming party.

The boat turned northward and sailed out of sight — which was the correct procedure for the daytime — while the watchers, half unbelieving, impatiently awaited the darkness. At ten o'clock — the correct hour — they saw her brief signal as she anchored.

Two groups of watchers were already on shore. Schwartz, Halperin and Menashe Bronstein at one point, Baruch Raab and Yehuda Zeldin at another. Sarah and Liova remained in the building. One nervewracking hour passed, two hours... Heavy steps sounded on the wooden stairs. Liova jumped to the door, opened it — and fell back in shock. Raab and Zeldin rushed in, holding "a creature with bulging, frightened eyes, dressed in rags." The fellow, confused and half-crazed, looked around fearfully and asked in a low voice: "Who is this here?" but could not get any more words out. Liova yelled at him: "Speak, man, speak!"

He was obviously drunk, but finally mumbled: "Aaronsohn... boat... they must come... Reuven... Where is Hayim Cohen?... They must come..."

He took out a medallion from some pocket and gave it to Sarah. Sarah recognized it. It was a token Aaronsohn had left with her for just such an occasion.

Meantime Zeldin had made tea for the stranger, who got a grip on himself and talked more coherently. The British officers had given him whiskey to drink before swimming from the rowboat. He was Leibl Bernstein, he said, who used to work as a driver for Mr. Halperin of Petah Tikva — and suddenly Liova and Baruch Raab both recognized him. He had driven each of them by carriage from Petah Tikva. "So," Liova exclaimed, "this is the courier of good deeds, the renowned Reb Leibl Bernstein."

Thus properly welcomed, Leibl opened up, and told them how difficult the swim had been, and how on shore he had wandered about a while till he found the gate where they picked him up shivering with cold. By now he was completely relaxed, and he went on chattering. Liova and Reuven, taking leave of Sarah in enforced haste, caught snatches of his story — Gallipoli... Jabotinsky... living conditions in Egypt. There was not much to take with them: "No luggage, only intelligence reports." Sarah had seen to it that there should be no neglect of those sacred duties. The reports were sewn into a bag — but she, it emerged from Leibl's message, had been forbidden by Aaronsohn to go down to the boat. Distressed as she was, "discipline," wrote Liova, "is discipline."

Baruch Raab was accompanying them to the shore. "If we meet a Turkish patrol," he promised, "I'll fire a shot and cry out 'Rahat el bat (the duck got away).'" For the rest, they walked in silence, except for Leibl who went on telling Liova about the ship *Managem* and about Rafael Aboulafia, who was on the boat and whom he knew from Gallipoli.

At the shore, they found the two Arab seamen from the *Managem* — in a hurry to get back to the rowboat. Leibl would swim with them. But how would Liova and Reuven do it? While they walked the wind had risen and the waves were growing fiercer. Reuven refused flatly to move: "I don't intend to get drowned." Liova favored being carried on the backs of the Arab seamen, a task they had expected, but expert Leibl vetoed it. Liova's clothes, and presumably Reuven's as well, were too heavy.

Meanwhile the Arabs kept urging poor Leibl, "*Yallah, yallah*, Leibl, let's go." So, Leibl jumped in with the seamen and swam off; and Liova with Reuven and Baruch with his shotgun made their slow, silent way back to the station.

Liova knocked at Sarah's door:

> She is astonished to see me among the returnees. What could we have done? The sea doesn't take orders from us. We continue talking until a very late hour. All abashed, concerned for Aaron — and his frustration — and, and... what about Avshalom?
>
> Suddenly — it is 3 AM — a stone hits the window-blind. I jump out to the terrace. Somebody is whistling at the front door. "Wait a moment," I say to Sarah, "I'll go and see."
>
> But she doesn't let me go alone, and we go down together.... There, confronting us is a figure, all white, naked as on the day he was born. His teeth are chattering, and he mumbles out of fear and from cold, "I'm Leibl."[9]

Baruch and Reuven, who had long gone to sleep, were mobilized. They

---

9. Schneierson, *Miyomano shel ish Nili*.

brought some covering for Leibl, made him comfortable, and he told his story. He couldn't reach the boat, the seas were too heavy, and he nearly drowned. He lost the two Arab seamen and didn't know whether they reached the boat. The waves were terribly high and it was a miracle that he got back. They gave him something to drink and a rubdown with alcohol and put him to bed in the room at the top.

"Fortunately we hadn't given him the intelligence reports [to take to Egypt]," wrote Liova. "They would surely have been lost."

They furnished him with clothes, and he remained in that room for a few days. Nobody not directly involved that night was told of his presence. Then he was moved to Zichron where father Fishel took care of him until the *Managem* came again.

It was not until three weeks later that the boat was able, in a renewed attempt, to anchor off Athlit. By this time Yosef Lishansky in Cairo had recovered from his wounds, Aaron had had long conversations with him and — as he records — he inducted him into the range of the work of the group. It is evident that Aaron was sufficiently impressed with him as a practical executive to envisage his taking a leading part in the organization. He thus traveled with Aaron on the *Managem*'s second attempt.

This time all went smoothly. The weather was balmy, the sea was placid, and the two Arab seamen carried Liova and Reuven Schwartz onto the rowboat. There Aaron was waiting for them. The seamen took Yosef's luggage off and returned to the shore. Aaron started chatting to Schwartz, but Liova could not contain himself. "What about Avshalom? Where is he?" Aaron replied brusquely: "In Cairo, in Cairo," and went on talking to Schwartz.

Only the next morning, when the boat was well on its way to Famagusta in Cyprus, did Aaron tell him the bitter truth, and then only tersely: "Avshalom was killed"; and Liova was on the deck, devastated, speechless, only half conscious of his surroundings...

> Suddenly I hear Aaron and a British officer talking as they approach
> me. Then Aaron says to me, "Liova, maybe you know a suitable name
> for our undertaking?"
> For a moment I didn't realize what he was talking about.
> "You know," he said, "but it must be brief and sound good!"

My head is heavy. I'm not used to the swaying of the boat. I sit down on the deck-chair and try to think. I shut my eyes. They are tired too. Avshalom... Avshalom doesn't leave me. Suddenly a flash in my mind. Why not try the little Bible in the pocket of my coat. Whenever I am troubled by a problem, I take the Bible, stick my finger in among the pages, count down seven lines from my finger, and the next line gives me the answer.

That is what he did, with the small Bible Avshalom had given him as a gift with his photograph in it. He opened it, placed his finger on the opened page, counted seven lines, and on the eighth line, there sprang out at him: *Netzach Yisrael lo yeshaker* (the eternity of Israel will not lie).[10]

Wonderful! Just what we all feel, with all our hearts and souls! But it must be short. Maybe only "*Netzach Yisrael*"? Too long. Maybe the initial letters. What will it sound like? NYLY, Nili! That's it!

He jumped from the chair, went up to Aaron and the officer at the rail and burst into their conversation: "Aaron, I've found the name in the Bible!"

"In the Bible?" He seemed incredulous.
"See! *Netzach Yisrael Lo Yeshaker.* The initial letters — NYLY!"
"Not bad — not bad!" he said slowly. He turned to the officer. "Our Mr. Schneierson has found the slogan: 'Nili'!"
"Oh, how nice!" exclaimed the officer. "She must be a nice girl, this Nilly!"[11]

---

10. I Samuel 15:29.
11. Schneierson, *Miyomano shel ish Nili.*

Baron Edmond d Rothschild

Colonel Sir Mark Sykes

Jewish Agricultural Experiment Station
trustee Supreme Court Judge
Louis D. Brandeis

Aaron's mentor, Botany professor
Otto Warburg

Jewish Agricultural Experiment
Station trustee Judge Felix Frankfurter

Henrietta Szold, secretary of trustees committee
for the Jewish Agricultural Experiment Station

Aaronsohn's friend and later lifelong
enemy Zichron community
physician Dr. Hillel Joffe

Aaron's collaborator, Zionist scientist
Dr. Selig (Evgeny) Soskin

Zionist political activist
Chaim Weizmann

Commander-in-Chief
General Edmund Allenby

Jewish Legion founder
Ze'ev Jabotinsky

Aaron Aaronson

Seated at front: the
Aaronsohn family
patriarch, Efraim
Fishel Aaronsohn,
and the girls Sarah
(in the center) and
Rivka (on the left)
Seated at center:
Sarah's husband
Haim Avraham,
Shmuel Aaronsohn
(in the center) and
Alexander Aaronsohn
(on the left)
Standing at the back:
Aaron Aaronsohn

The *Managem*, the British ship through which Cairo GHQ maintained contact with Nili at Athlit

The Jewish Agricultural Experiment Station at Athlit

Sarah

Sarah on a visit to Cairo with central Nili figures Yosef Lishansky (right)
and Levi Yitzhak (Liova) Schneierson

Sarah and the co-founder of Nili, Avshalom Feinberg

Members of Nili

Sarah cleaning the coop of the pigeon that strayed

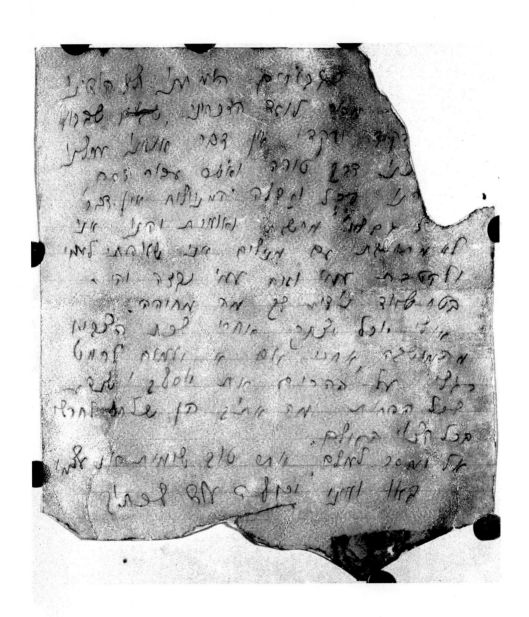

Sarah's last letter

The bathroom in which
Sarah committed suicide

שרה

Sarah's grave

Yosef Lishansky and Naaman Belkind, executed in Damascus,
December 16, 1917

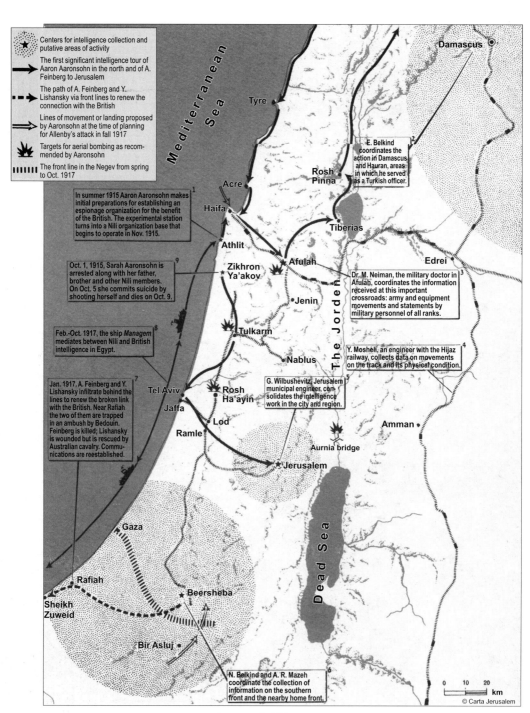

Legend:

Centers for intelligence collection and putative areas of activity

The first significant intelligence tour of Aaron Aaronsohn in the north and of A. Feinberg to Jerusalem

The path of A. Feinberg and Y. Lishansky via front lines to renew the connection with the British

Lines of movement or landing proposed by Aaronsohn at the time of planning for Allenby's attack in fall 1917

Targets for aerial bombing as recommended by Aaronsohn

The front line in the Negev from spring to Oct. 1917

Map labels and annotations:

Mediterranean Sea

Damascus

E. Belkind coordinates the action in Damascus and Hauran, areas in which he served as a Turkish officer.

Tyre

Rosh Pinna

Acre

Haifa

In summer 1915 Aaron Aaronsohn makes initial preparations for establishing an espionage organization for the benefit of the British. The experimental station turns into a Nili organization base that begins to operate in Nov. 1915.

Athlit

Tiberias

Zikhron Ya'akov

Afulah

Edrei

Oct. 1, 1915, Sarah Aaronsohn is arrested along with her father, brother and other Nili members. On Oct. 5 she commits suicide by shooting herself and dies on Oct. 9.

Dr. M. Neiman, the military doctor in Afulah, coordinates the information received at this important crossroads: army and equipment movements and statements by military personnel of all ranks.

Jenin

The Jordan

Feb.-Oct. 1917, the ship *Managem* mediates between Nili and British intelligence in Egypt.

Tulkarm

Nablus

Y. Mosheli, an engineer with the Hijaz railway, collects data on movements on the track and its physical condition.

Jan. 1917, A. Feinberg and Y. Lishansky infiltrate behind the lines to renew the broken link with the British. Near Rafiah the two of them are trapped in an ambush by Bedouin. Feinberg is killed; Lishansky is wounded but is rescued by Australian cavalry. Communications are reestablished.

Tel Aviv

Rosh Ha'ayin

G. Wilbushevitz, Jerusalem municipal engineer, consolidates the intelligence work in the city and region.

Jaffa

Lod

Amman

Ramle

Aurnia bridge

Jerusalem

Gaza

Dead Sea

Rafiah

Beersheba

Sheikh Zuweid

Bir Asluj

N. Belkind and A. R. Mazeh coordinate the collection of information on the southern front and the nearby home front.

0   10   20
km

© Carta Jerusalem

Scope of Nili's Activities

CHAPTER 11

"Aaronsohn Is Running GHQ"

Only from time to time does Aaronsohn in his diary hint at the devastating impact of Avshalom's death. Never does he refer to the complete disruption of his plans for the future operations of the Athlit group. By that plan Avshalom was to assume the liaison with the British headquarters in Egypt; political contacts in England would be entrusted to Alex, and he himself, on some moonless night, would land at Athlit to take over the reins of leadership.

In London, in light of the swift empathy that developed between him and Gribbon, the War Office chiefs had hoped that Gribbon would succeed in persuading him to accept the suggestion that he remain in London, and from there the operation would be conducted. It was a highly impractical, indeed preposterous, proposition. The only purpose it could in fact serve was to enable the EEF in Cairo to take over direct control of the Athlit group. Its members would then presumably be expected to operate completely under British army orders and discipline. But the members of the organization had not enlisted in the British army, and there was no likelihood that they would do so. The officials in the War Office ignored the motivation — explained to them by Aaronsohn — for the creation of the Athlit group: that it was not only the need to get rid of the Turkish regime, but ultimately to stake a claim for the restoration of the Jewish people in its historic homeland.

It was clearly because the British government had not decided to come out in favor of that restoration that Aaronsohn's valuable but Zionist wings were to be clipped. True, with Lloyd George's assumption of office as prime minister in December 1916, both Weizmann in his campaign for a pro-Zionist declaration by Britain, and Jabotinsky, in his campaign for the creation of a Jewish Legion, found themselves sailing in the mainstream of British war policy; a unit composed of members of the disbanded Zion Mule Corps had by now been accepted into the British army in Britain (and Jabotinsky had even joined them as a private) but neither the War Office nor the Foreign Office was yet attuned to the Zionist idea sufficiently for giving it even indirect recognition. Also, in London the Athlit group was almost certainly underrated. Aaronsohn had proved how valuable he was, indeed how invaluable, but London, and General Headquarters in Egypt for that matter, had little idea of the capacities of his followers. However, they realized that at General Headquarters in Egypt Aaronsohn was badly needed, so they had had to let him go to Egypt.

Aaronsohn was evidently wrong in believing that the reason for their refusal to allow him to land at Athlit when contact was established was that they did not trust him. A measure of mistrust may still have lingered, but when Edmonds told Aaron that the reason was that he was "too valuable," this was perfectly true and understandable. It need not have taken long for him to realize that if he were captured at any stage of the operation, he would be hanged as a spy — if, that is, he survived the inevitable torture. What then of his comrades? What then would happen to the task they had undertaken?

His experience in Egypt from the moment that he met with the more sophisticated officers in the military administration leaves no room for doubt that he was found to be indispensable. The role he began to play, stated in the strictest pragmatic sense, was no doubt due partly to the great uncertainty that had prevailed up to the end of December — when Lloyd George took office — as to whether there would be any campaign at all for the liberation of Palestine. The new premier, having struggled in vain for so long for the opening of an Eastern Front, and watching the gruesome, never-ending trench warfare of the Western Front, was more eager than ever to see that Eastern Front opened — with the immediate prospect of drawing off German troops from the west. By this time too it had become clear that very little succor, if any, could be expected from the figment called the Arab revolt.

It was thus at a most crucial juncture that Aaronsohn arrived on the scene — a classical deus ex machina. In Cairo the staff had had some grounding in Aaronsohn's memoranda, which had reached them from the War Office in London. They covered a broad swathe of his unique expertise in relevant issues. Pouncing on him now in Egypt they could not but discern that this man knew everything that was needed for an intelligent launch of the offensive. He had the answers to all their questions and he had the answers to the questions that he knew would yet arise — all in all a many-faceted curriculum which normally would occupy a team of experts. In the rare case when his knowledge was lacking he told them where to look. Thus in a single entry in his diary, on March 2, 1917, he disposes of two questions put to him by Lieutenant Taylor, about the road from Jerusalem to Jericho, and whether a supply service for cavalry could be organized between Beersheba and Hebron. Called in by Captain Graves, he was asked what diseases might be expected during the campaign. Naturally every layman knew of the threat of malaria, but for specifics he referred Graves to Dr. Naftali Weitz, one of the exiles from Zichron Ya'akov, an expert in the field.

The next day, however, he warns Graves of the dangers of fighting in the summer, and advises him on the means of overcoming them; he gives warning of swampy areas, some ranging even as far as Acre. In a later session he gives a Captain McRury details of a specific swampy area near the village of Jamama (the Hebrew Ruhama). The very next day, told that a raid by cavalry in the Hebron-Beersheba area is projected, he advises postponing it till the end of March or the beginning of April, "by which time the corn will have approached maturity." He produces another paper for the cavalry — warning of the incidence of "horse poisoning through new barley." When Captain Seymour Jones asks him for information on "animal-power and (agricultural) mechanization in southern Palestine" he gives him details, then adds advice on acquiring spare parts for the machines. He had earlier, on February 7, prepared a memorandum on "agriculture and supplies in Palestine" — the memorandum sent to Foreign Secretary Lord Balfour by Ormsby-Gore. He had already supplied General Headquarters with a list of current food prices in the country.

Barely six weeks after his first meeting with Graves he was called in to "work with him on a corrected edition of the (strictly secret) military handbook for southern Palestine." In the following days he worked on his own on the handbook. His diary does not reveal details about his contribution, except that he introduced "material prepared by Avshalom Feinberg."

Some days later, in a restaurant, Colonel Deedes, espying Aaronsohn, went across to his table and asked him if he was now satisfied with the progress of events — that is, evidently, with the behavior of Edmonds and Smith. He added, "I thank you for your valuable assistance in drawing up the handbook. I had no idea of this valuable assistance you have given us." Three days later Aaron, meeting Captain Crosthwaite, heard from him of the good impression he had made in his contribution to the handbook. "Everybody at GHQ" said Crosthwaite "is talking about it."

"This is evidently true," wrote Aaronsohn (March 20) "for today Edmonds told me that from every side reports are coming in emphasizing satisfaction with my participation."

Meantime Aaronsohn was engaged with Captain Crosthwaite on another most significant project. Together they went over the proofs of new maps that had been prepared. Evidently the existing maps were of similar vintage to those with which the War Office had provided General Ian Hamilton when he took over command of the forces in Gallipoli. Aaronsohn tersely described the old map — based on the Kitchener-Condor survey of 1878 — as "wrong."

However, while brimming over with appreciation of Aaronsohn, the men at General Headquarters gave no indication that they were prepared to make any move towards his objective beyond their specifically military requirements. He had proposed drawing up a statistical breakdown of the Palestine refugees in Egypt, analyzing the capacity of each one of them for potential war service. As he had told just about all the officers at General Headquarters of his hope that a Jewish military unit would be raised, they could be in no doubt of the Zionist purpose of his proposal nor indeed of his driving motivation.

It was Captain Feilding who brought him the response to his proposal: London had turned it down. They were afraid, he said, that it would "take them much further than they would like." Aaronsohn, he added, should perhaps organize such a "census" on his own. Though his idea was impractical, Feilding surely meant to be helpful. Indeed, some weeks earlier he had demonstrated a surprising identification with Aaronsohn. In introducing Aaronsohn to the admiral responsible for all the ports under British control in the east, he not only described Aaron as "a mine of information" but went on to speak of the Athlit project. "I wish," he said, "that I were a Jew and could participate in it"!

A more specific statement on British policy in those months of 1917 was penned by Sir Ronald Graham, under-secretary of state for foreign affairs. He had been a firm friend of the legion idea ever since the day in 1915 when in

Cairo he first heard Jabotinsky on the subject. In a persuasive letter to the Army Council urging the case for the legion, he nevertheless emphasized that it would be important for the government "not to identify themselves too closely with the political objects of a Zionist nature which underlie the proposal since by so doing they would be committing themselves to a definite course in a matter upon which the most representative Jews of the world are utterly divided."[1]

As the day of the offensive came closer and the work of the intelligence unit became all the more intensive, Aaronsohn stood out as a kind of universal oracle dispensing advice and knowledge to a variety of officers of all relevant ranks. Much of the work was inevitably devoted to roads. By now, the queries on roads, ranging beyond the south, reached well into the north of the country and even into Syria. After covering the area south of Nazareth he dealt with the area between Nazareth and Damascus. Throughout the country most of the roads were to some degree primitive.

The problem of water, most of which was piped from Egypt, was even more acute. Aaronsohn repeatedly urged that it should be sought by drilling. Machines and filters should be made available, as well as piping for bringing the water to Jerusalem. Jerusalem's water problem was at the center of his concerns — for the health both of soldiers and the civilian population. Not to mention the desirability of presenting to the world a livable Holy City as soon as possible after its liberation. An adequate water supply would moreover provide a moral boost to the inhabitants after the gloom and suffering in the dismal years of Turkish rule.

His repeated emphasis on the water problem, which he discussed with various officers at General Headquarters, was reflected in his paper "Some Physical Features of Southern Palestine," which was devoted to the geology and the water sources in the Beersheba-Gaza zone; and he discussed the

---

1. PRO/FO 319/657670. Graham remained a perceptive and a most active proponent of Zionism to the end of his career. As, however, every student of the period reveals, those "most representative Jews" were a fiction, though they were energetically promoted by the assimilated Jews in Britain. One of them, Edwin Montagu, led the battle against Zionism from within the British Cabinet. It took some time for the truth to penetrate the British establishment that the only claim to influence of these "representative" Jews was their wealth. That said, the Jewish people as a whole was divided in its views and feelings like every other body of people.

hydrography of the coastal plain and the Sharon with the chief engineer at General Headquarters, Major General Wright.

No special unit on the water problem had been created in the army, but now an executive officer, Major Neville, was appointed to work with Aaronsohn — who raised with him the possibilities of wells in the south. A second officer, Dawson, brought Aaronsohn the results of two spells of drilling, and complained that Wright did not understand that choosing targets for drilling should not be done on a hit-or-miss basis but must be scientifically guided by geology. Aaronsohn, now wearing the hat of an expert in geology (recalling his comprehensive surveys with Blanckenhorn) explained to Dawson that only at a depth of six to eight meters below sea level could one find the sheet of water as a source for subartesian wells.

Drilling was indeed carried out under Aaronsohn's direction but the results are not recorded in his diary. There is, however, revealing testimony on the application of Aaronsohn's theory — using not only geology but also history as a guide in digging for water. It comes from the report of a conversation he had with Sir Basil Thomson, deputy chief at Scotland Yard, soon after his arrival in London in the fall of 1916. This is what Thomson wrote years later:

> In the middle of a statement Aaron interrupted himself to ask: "Why do you bring water for the army from Egypt? It slows up your progress. There is water right there in the desert, three hundred feet down. All you have to do is to drill for it."
>
> "How do you know that?"
>
> "The rocks indicate it," Aaron replied, "and Josephus Flavius corroborates it. He wrote [in the first century CE] that he could walk for a whole day south from Caesarea, and never leave flourishing gardens. Today the desert sands reach to the walls of Caesarea. Where there were gardens there must have been water. Where is that water now?
>
> "I had the chance to explore the geology of Palestine, and from the rock strata I learned that there is sufficient water there at a depth of three hundred feet. Even the whole of the Sinai Peninsula could be turned into flourishing fields of wheat by means of irrigation. There is water there, only waiting for the pipes to bring it to the surface."
>
> "And what can you do?" Sir Basil inquired.

"If I were with the British army," Aaron answered, "I could show the engineers where to drill. I guarantee that they would find enough water for the army without having to bring a single drop from Cairo."

Aaronsohn did not find a receptive ear to his suggestions about drilling in the ground on the strength of evidence given by Josephus, but his great obstinacy overcame all obstacles. And eventually, at a depth of three hundred feet *enough fresh water was found for the needs of the army*.[2] (Emphasis added.)

While most of Aaronsohn's work with the officers at General Headquarters was directly concerned with the infrastructure for the offensive planned by General Murray, he did not turn his back on his own strategic vision, which had evolved from the early days of Turkey's participation in the war. He was certain that the country could be taken without great difficulty by a determined attack from the sea at some point in northern Palestine or in Syria. His was not a great discovery; it was in fact dictated by elementary strategic principle.

He knew, who better than he, of Turkey's internal moral weaknesses, its corruption and its incompetence. Turkey, as the nineteenth century's "sick man of Europe" had not yet changed substantially in the twentieth century despite the Young Turks revolution.

Unbeknown to him, the same idea for an attack on the Syrian coast at Alexandretta had been examined in London early in the war. Major Deedes, already then seen as an expert on the East, had supported the idea. It had however been dropped in favor of an attack on the Dardanelles.[3]

Aaronsohn had not wavered from that view. That was why, on setting out on his odyssey in July 1916, he had made his tour along the coast of Palestine and discovered that strong Turkish coastal defenses were simply nonexistent.[4]

2. Memoirs of Sir Basil Thomson, published in *English Life*, quoted by Anita Engle, *The Nili Spies* (London: The Hogarth Press, 1959), p. 72.
3. Livneh, *Aaron Aaronsohn*, p. 241 — quoting a memo in Deedes's private papers.
4. The official view was that the Turkish coastal defenses were too strong. The only rational explanation for this view was grievous misinformation, and, no doubt, CIGS Robertson's well-known personal opposition to any eastern campaign.

The opening of the British offensive in Sinai and the early capture of Rafa (Rafiah) had not changed his view. Nor did he relent when, after some delay, Prime Minister Lloyd George advised Murray to go ahead and "capture Jerusalem." With Murray planning continuation of his offensive from the south, Aaronsohn's idea had not lost its force. A landing from the sea behind the Turkish lines would create a "pincer" situation highly dangerous and possibly fatal to the Turks. He pinpointed Haifa as a preferred target. On February 6 he wrote in his diary: "I work with Feilding on the list (of personalities) in Haifa and its environs"; then he reports that Feilding introduced him to an admiral — the admiral in charge of all the ports between Crete and Singapore — with whom he could discuss his plan. Two months later (April 2) he was introduced by Simpson to a lieutenant-commander in the Royal Navy and "we examine the possibility of a landing at Athlit, Tantura, etc." He adds that "they borrowed my map of the Carmel."

There were more reasons for his persistence. A landing on the coast, where the Turkish defenses were so weak, would make possible the speedy liberation of the Jewish towns and villages in the coastal area; and not for a moment was he free of fears for the members of Nili. He saw them all as in constant danger of capture or exposure. How long would they be able to hold out? And Sarah was now the most exposed of them all. The other reason flowed from the fact that he knew his history. On April 6 he explained to Clayton that Jerusalem had never been captured from the south. He analyzed — no doubt to Clayton's astonishment — the battles of Roman Emperors Vespasian and Titus in the sixties of the first century CE (which led to the destruction of the Second Temple and the fall of the Jewish state), as well as the campaign of Napoleon Bonaparte and of the Egyptian Ibrahim Pasha in 1831. The crucial battle, after a landing in the Haifa area, should be fought in the Jezreel Valley. Then a speedy attack from the north would have all the advantages: tactical, strategic and moral. Clayton was obviously impressed and Aaronsohn, taking advantage of a further invitation, saw him again the next day — when they "talked about a landing and capturing the Carmel."

That Aaron's advocacy was not dismissed out of hand is demonstrated by the consequent internal British correspondence. Two weeks after these talks with Clayton, High Commissioner Wingate sent off a message to Ronald Graham at the Foreign Office in London suggesting consideration of "a

Franco-British landing at Alexandretta or some other spot on the Syrian coast."

Indeed Aaronsohn's views and ideas had by this time won so high a measure of respect throughout the military establishment that, as Edmonds wrote to Bentwich, the idea had spread that "Aaronsohn is running G.H.Q."[5] But British strategy was not changed.

The long-awaited offensive was opened by General Murray on March 26 by a frontal attack on Gaza — and was repulsed. The defeat was followed by a strange misunderstanding arising out of Murray's reports on the battle to the General Staff and through them to the War Cabinet. The circumstances are described in the British official history of the war:

> There is no doubt that these reports, the first of which resulted in congratulatory messages from H.M. the King, the War Cabinet, Lord Derby, the French General Neville, with personal telegrams from Sir W. Robertson and Sir John Cowans, created in their minds the impression that the result of the battle had been more favorable, and that the enemy had been harder hit, than was actually the case. This appears to have been one of those occasions in which a commander in the field, hoping immediately to improve his situation after what has appeared to him to be only a temporary set-back, has unconsciously understated the extent of that set-back in his reports to those in ultimate authority. He may by such action avoid creating needless despondency, but he may also give rise to exaggerated hopes, deprive himself of support which a fuller representation of the case would have ensured, and finally be forced to demand it after a further check to his plans.
>
> At the same time, even had Sir A. Murray's messages been framed in less sanguine terms, neither the C.I.G.S. [Chief of the Imperial General Staff] nor the War Cabinet would have been likely to admit that his offensive power had vanished as a result of one indecisive

---

5. For support by Winston Churchill for the strategy proposed by Aaronsohn of a landing on the coast, see Appendix 3.

action. It was, after all, an action which, judged by the standards of the Western Front, was small and far from costly.... Though the renewed British offensive, preparations for which were known to be in train, might have been less confidently urged, it does not seem probable that it would in any case have been cancelled.[6]

The offensive was indeed renewed in mid-April, and resulted in a second defeat for the British forces. The Turks remained entrenched on their Gaza-Beersheba line; and six months passed before the third battle for Palestine was fought.

The inhabitants of Palestine were probably not aware even that a battle had taken place. On March 28, in any case long before any news of the battle could have reached them, Djemal Pasha, out of the blue on a bright spring day, dropped a bombshell of his own. The townspeople of Jaffa were called to a meeting, and there it was announced in Djemal Pasha's name that all the residents of Jaffa must leave the town. The order was to include the surrounding area, from Tel Aviv as far as the village of Petah Tikva. Where were they to go? Djemal's order excluded Haifa and Jerusalem as places of refuge — they were the only two towns of any size that could somehow accommodate a serious number of exiles. Outside these two towns, Djemal explained, the wealthy would surely manage to find a place. The poor would be provided with accommodation — in Syria — somewhere in the area between Damascus and Aleppo. Some categories would be exempt — for example agricultural workers (but not their employers), and citizens of countries allied to Turkey — Austria, Germany, Bulgaria.

When, in the following days, a number of amendments to the order were announced, it was discovered that only the Jews would be compelled to leave, even if they were citizens of Austria, Germany and Bulgaria. The sick were not to be exempted.

As the festival of Passover was imminent, Djemal graciously agreed that the expulsion would be postponed for a week. Protests by delegations to Djemal were dismissed on the grounds that a British attack on Jaffa was to be expected. It was thus for the sake of the population that they must evacuate.

---

6. Captain Cyril Falls and Sir George MacMunn, *Military Operations: Egypt and Palestine*. Vol. 1, *From the Outbreak of the War with Germany to June 1917* (London: HM Stationary Office, 1928), p. 320.

Djemal did not explain why the agricultural workers and the Christian Austrians, the Germans and the Bulgarians were to remain exposed to those dangers. Djemal found it timely, however, to proclaim that he was "not an antisemite, only an anti-Zionist."

The leaders of the Jewish community took advantage of the week's reprieve to tackle the immediate problems arising from the barbaric orders — which they were warned would be enforced. Nine thousand Jews would need transport to reach their various destinations. The government (whether deliberately preemptive or not) had some weeks earlier confiscated all horses, camels and mules in the neighborhood. The communal leaders consequently set about combing all possible Jewish villages for carts and horses. On the whole, the villages responded promptly, though in some trepidation, for they themselves might soon be subjected to a similar expulsion order. All possible carts and carriages and their drivers were mobilized.

The operation was carried out in two phases. Nearly half the exiles from Jaffa and Tel Aviv were brought to Petah Tikva. A small number found lodging; others were "lodged" in the open. The weather was fortunately temperate, but the doctors in the community warned of the dangers of disease.

The respite of some days beyond the date originally announced by Djemal was seized by the exiles who had come to Petah Tikva as a means of stopping there. The remainder were taken much further afield, and most of them were lodged in villages in the Galilee, the vast majority sleeping in the open or in as many tents as could be procured. Some of the wealthier minority stole "illegally" into Haifa.

The ordeal of the bulk of the exiles lasted until the end of the year, after the British liberated southern Palestine.[7]

Had it not been for Nili, the outside world (given the Turkish censorship) might not have learned of the outrage for weeks or maybe even months. But the news reached Aaron ten days after the expulsion took effect. On April 19, Sarah arrived in Egypt on the *Managem* and told him all she knew about it. A written report — undated — compiled by the group's agent in the south, Na'aman Belkind, evidently arrived at the same time.

---

7. The day-to-day story of the exile is recorded in the diary — published years later — of Mordechai Ben-Hillel Hacohen, one of the leaders of the community: *Milhemet ha-amim*, p. 527 et seq.

To Aaron the news bore a special and ominous significance. He had learned already in 1915, and had had it confirmed to him by German sources during his stay in Berlin the previous year, that Djemal had in mind the expulsion of the Jewish inhabitants of all the towns on the coast.

Two urgent tasks stared out of the reports: to have the barbaric operation brought to the attention of the world, and to appeal to the Jewish communities abroad to come financially to the aid of the refugees. Aaron at once passed the information on at General Headquarters and a combined campaign was decided on to spread the news of the Jaffa "evacuation" as widely as possible. Aaron prepared telegrams to the Zionist leaders Weizmann and Sokolow in London, to his friends in the United States and to Baron Rothschild in Paris. In order not to wait for replies to the appeal for funds, bearing in mind the delays in international money transfers, Aaronsohn asked at GHQ for a loan of two thousand pounds sterling — to be sent on to Palestine as soon as possible! This constituted a breach of Britain's economic embargo — but the request was granted immediately. (The loan was later repaid.)

Sykes — who, like Aaronsohn, grasped the importance of the expulsion for British propaganda against Turkey and Germany — saw to it that the Foreign Office was fully informed, and High Commissioner Wingate also cabled details to Graham for the War Cabinet. Aaronsohn at once prepared a memorandum entitled "Evacuation of Jaffa" before the Turks and the Germans were able to disseminate their own inevitably mendacious version. Reuters News Agency spread the grim details throughout the world — using Aaronsohn's text; protest meetings were organized by the local Zionist organizations.

By all accounts the German government was stunned by the revelation of Djemal's brutality. A Socialist member of the Reichstag, Oskar Cohn, posed a question: "Is the Reichskanzler prepared to bring influence to bear on the Turkish government to prevent with all vigor repetition of the Armenian horrors in Palestine?" Whatever plans Djemal had had for carrying out further expulsions — and in Jerusalem the Jewish population had heard persistent rumors that they were next on the list — they were not implemented. Energetic intervention by the German government was a prime factor in staying Djemal's hand. Meantime Djemal, faced by the unexpected flood of early reactions of shock and outrage, issued denials of any evil intent even towards the Jews of Jaffa. To give point to his denials he called in a delegation from the Jewish community to support them. Obediently, and expediently, a group of the Jewish communal leaders published such a supportive denial.

Sarah was to remain in Egypt only three days. The siblings had not seen each other for nine months. And what nine months! Both their driven lives had been revolutionized.

Aaron — catapulted into a position of crucial importance in the war against Turkey; Sarah — suddenly transformed into undreamed-of leadership in the field over a group of men and women engaged in a most daring enterprise. Both had changed unbelievably. Iron threads of anger animated them — for the death of Avshalom, and of determination to accomplish the object for which he had lived and given his life. Now they met not only as sister-with-an-idolized-elder-brother but as a commander with his second-in-command.

Yet before they were able to converse as brother and sister, Aaron was shocked into uncontrolled anger at the arrival with Sarah of Yosef Lishansky. After his arrival in Athlit in late February following his convalescence in Cairo, he had carried out faithfully Aaron's instructions, grasped easily the essentials of the work at the station and worked with Sarah in admirable cooperation as her lieutenant. How then, when Sarah had to travel to Egypt, could he leave the group leaderless instead of remaining at his post! He was certainly not needed in Egypt — and Aaronsohn flew at him in furious reproach. In his diary he only hints at his anger, and evidently a full-blown quarrel was only postponed for a while.

Aaron and Sarah talked for many hours — interrupted however by the need to decipher the reports she had brought with her. They were, he confided to the diary, excellent. It was here indeed that Aaronsohn confirmed the order of command which had developed so naturally — with Sarah taking his place at the "front line" at Athlit. That evening, after the day's work, Aaron and Sarah, with their friend from Zichron, Peretz Pascal, were having tea at Gruppi's, a well-known cafe. Unnoticed by Aaron, Captain McRury and other colleagues (as McRury later confessed) were taking a peep at Sarah. It's

a pleasure, notes Aaron, to look at a heroine. Sarah continued to attract attention — and praise. Deedes himself unbent to congratulate him on having
"such a plucky sister," and he added, "Also, you know that we have never
received such fine reports as those sent in by your organization."

Accompanying Sarah and Yosef on to the *Managem* at Port Said for their
return journey, it was while waiting for the boat to sail for Athlit that Aaron
had a truly heated argument with Yosef. He knew that he had before him a
sorely troubled, complex young man. In his history was a childhood background of great deprivation. He was orphaned of both his parents — his
mother dying, and his father disappearing mysteriously soon afterwards. It
was not unnatural that he should develop compensatory qualities, even
eccentric behavior. However, this did not rule out his being gifted with a
practical mind.

A practical mind indeed had served him well when he worked for a trial
period as a candidate for membership of Hashomer (the Masonic-type organization that took care of the security of the independent villages). They
watched over those, mainly in the north, that had grown out of the First
Aliyah (1881–1905). He shone at the work; he was known, indeed famous for
his physical courage and for his capacity to make friends in the Arab and
Druze communities. He did not, however, achieve popularity with his Jewish
peers. He was not an accommodating personality, and they did not like his
assumption, real or imagined, of an air of social superiority. Irksome to a
rough-and-ready generation, and to this particularly rough-and-ready organization was, for example, his penchant for fine clothes. He also expressed
unorthodox views on attitudes to marauding Arabs: he believed in retalia-
tion; and when during an Arab attack on the village of Menahemiya, a
Hashomer member named Yehezkel Hankin shot and killed one of the
attackers, Yosef's comrades cozily accused him of the killing — though he
had not even been on the scene. He applied nevertheless for full membership
in the movement — and was rejected.

Deeply offended, he had set up a security organization of his own —
Hamagen. It seems to have been moderately successful. Though it operated
only in the south — where Hashomer did not operate — it provoked in many
members of Hashomer an undying hatred for Yosef Lishansky.

His life took on a new direction at the end of 1915, when, through his
contacts with Turkish officers, he helped Avshalom Feinberg, languishing in

jail at Beersheba as a suspected spy. He proved to be a friend indeed. He made contact with Avshalom, served, through Na'aman Belkind in Rishon Lezion, as a go-between with Aaronsohn and with the jailers, until Avshalom was transferred to Jerusalem — and later freed, albeit with further bribing. It was after that episode that Yosef joined the Nili organization. When, at the end of 1916, Avshalom decided to try once more to reach the British by way of Sinai, he found it natural to call on Lishansky — who had shown himself brave, loyal and resourceful — to accompany him. Aaronsohn later suggested to him that he should have tried to dissuade Avshalom. It is not likely that he did try, but if he did he would have had no hope of succeeding where Sarah herself had failed.

Aaronsohn had not had much direct contact with him until be was called to his bedside in Port Said after the death of Avshalom. When Yosef returned to Palestine, it soon became evident however that he was the indispensable aide to the leader of the organization.

Now at Port Said, waiting for the *Managem* to sail, he replied vigorously to Aaron's reprimands. Throughout the community — a small community where rumor and gossip ran rife — there was much speculation about the circumstances surrounding the disappearance of Avshalom. Somehow, questions about his whereabouts swirled around the fact that he had last been seen in Lishansky's company. In the community at large he had become the preferred focus of hostility towards the Aaronsohns; and not to be ignored was the long-standing hatred of Hashomer towards him.

He thus had reason for his discontent at home; and now in Egypt how was he being treated? Aaron, he said, did not appreciate him, had given him no tasks to perform, had not even introduced him to the British officers with whom he was working.

The *Managem* sailed with that crisis unresolved, but Aaron noted well that despite his "wild" behavior Yosef was kept in line by Sarah. Having Sarah "by his side," Aaron was confident that the necessary work would be done. Indeed it was Sarah herself who was Aaron's chief worry. He had asked her to come to Egypt in order primarily to persuade her not to go back to Athlit. The danger was too great. The organization's work was running smoothly. The agents dotted over the country were producing reports of outstanding excellence, satisfying the most stringent demands and evoking the highest praise of the British intelligence community. The reports brought personally to

Egypt by her and Yosef had delighted the British officers as they awaited tensely General Murray's renewed offensive at the gates of Gaza. It was Sarah as the leader who had done most to accomplish the miracle and, Aaron pleaded, she had done enough.

Sarah however had agreed to come to Egypt only "on condition" — she had used the phrase in her letter — that he would let her go back. Now, in all determination, she refused to bend. She had to go back, she insisted; her place was there, not in Egypt. After hours of discussion over two days he writes on April 20: "I see myself compelled to accept Sarah's sacrifice." He sees his Sarah with new eyes. "How brave she is, and how composed!"

Nevertheless he tries again the next day. She is adamant. Again and again she repeats, "It is my duty to go back, to the danger." He is overcome by wonderment. He tells his diary: "She is so simple in her greatness. She does not guess how noble is her spirit."

Aware of the struggle between them, the British officers who have the opportunity try to help. They urge her to stay in Egypt. She gives her reply with quiet dignity. Finally, Edmonds comes to take leave. An officer of great experience, writes Aaron, "tell Sarah and Yosef that their intelligence reports have never been excelled."

There was of course an intrinsic flaw in Aaron's assessment — a flaw of which he was evidently unconscious. Yosef was needed in the field to carry out executive tasks with which Sarah could not cope, but Yosef could not function at all without her leadership; and Sarah understood the nature of the problem.

Again their voyage was not successful. With high seas at Athlit, the boat sailed on to Cyprus. Conditions were not better on their turning back, and so, six days after their talk at Port Said, they, with Liova Schneierson — who now regularly represented Aaron on the boat — were greeted once again by Aaronsohn at the Cairo train station. That very evening after dinner Yosef came together with Liova, to talk to Aaronsohn in his room at the Savoy Hotel.

There was no joy in their conversation; Lishansky was in his worst possible mood. He threw an unprovoked tantrum, no less. "He reveals his true colors," wrote Aaron. "Our organization is not an organization [worthy of the name] and all the usual demagogic theories. I send him to the devil." Indeed Liova records in his diary that Aaron was so angry that he brought his fist down on the table, breaking the glass on his wristwatch. That, however, did not solve the problem.

The next attempt with the *Managem* was set for two weeks ahead, in the middle of May. At the last moment there was, in Aaron's words, a "theatrical explosion." Yosef announced that he was not returning to Athlit. The reason: he was not being accorded the respect and trust due to him; and Aaron writes: "A strike, and the threat of a scandal into the bargain. He has found a means of complicating my life. I leave him and go to inform R [British Intelligence Headquarters] that as Yosef has stopped accepting discipline I shall travel in his place." There was consternation in the office, but the boat had to leave, so they could not but accept Aaron's proposal; the hour of departure was fixed for that evening.

Many years later, one Yosef Alhadeff, of the village of Yesud Hama'alah in the Galilee, who was in Egypt at the time and in the confidence of the Nili group, testified that he had encountered Yosef and Sarah that evening in the Continental Hotel. "It seems to me that Sarah had been crying. She was very distressed; they were having a harsh conversation. 'I don't know what's come over him,' she said, and left us.

"But Yosef said, 'I know that this time I'm going to my death. I shall never return.' I argued with him, encouraged him… I reminded him of all he had done, the importance of his role, the significance of his work. He did not deny what I was saying, but at that moment he preferred arrest and trial in Egypt to the death he feared awaited him at the hands of the Turks. Yet…he did go back to meet his fate."[8]

"Yosef, who seemed to have lost his balance," wrote Aaron in his diary, "retracted and came to his senses. When he saw that it was intended seriously to leave him here until he calmed down, he became logical again and turned up with his luggage."

Never again did Yosef repeat his mutinous behavior. There were subjects on which he differed with Aaron, but they did not affect his absolute loyalty to Aaron — and Sarah — and the cause they were serving.

As it turned out, given repeated bouts of bad weather, *Managem's* next successful visit to Athlit was accomplished only on June 13. During the wait,

---

8. Letter to Dr. Yaacov Harozen on April 10, 1943, quoted in Livneh, Nedava and Efrati, *Nili*, p. 145.

Yosef was appeased by permission from General Headquarters to visit the area (which had meantime been liberated) of the attack on him and Avshalom, and to seek out Avshalom's grave. He reported back that he believed he had located the area, but the ground there had been levelled and the grave could not be pinpointed.

Soon afterwards Aaron was given an opportunity to help restore Yosef's troubled spirit. Captain George Lloyd of GHQ proposed the blowing up of bridges and arms dumps. Somebody would have to be trained for these tasks. Schneierson arranged for Yosef to go through a course of training in the use of explosives. Three weeks later Aaron submitted to Deedes a detailed plan for blowing up bridges at Tulkarm and Delhamiyeh. The first bridge, however, which Yosef, back in Palestine, was asked to dispose of was at El Jama'a, at the point where the railway from Beit She'an (Beisan) to Tsemah crossed the River Jordan.

Yosef himself however had doubts about this plan and consulted Nahum Wilbushevitz (a member of Nili who was an engineer in the service of the Turkish government at Damascus). Wilbushevitz rejected the proposal out of hand. Such an operation, he declared, would call down the wrath of the Turks on the Jewish villages in the nearby Galilee who would be suspected immediately. They were the only people in that region sufficiently sophisticated to carry out such an operation. Sarah took the same view. Aaron was therefore advised to propose to the British authorities that they carry out instead an attack on the bridge by a low-flying aircraft.

During his course of training the officer-in-charge told Lishansky that if he succeeded in blowing up the bridge at El Jama'a, he would be given a prize of one hundred pounds sterling. Liova Schneierson, accompanying Yosef (who knew no English) as interpreter, reported that Yosef reacted angrily. "Tell the officer that he doesn't know whom he's talking to. He thinks apparently that it's for money that we're doing what we're doing!"

CHAPTER 12

Who Was Who — and How — in Nili

During the crucial period of its activity — following the *Managem*'s first successful approach to Athlit in February, and the first physical contact there — the core of Nili consisted of some thirty members working full time. In the circumstances of its birth and build-up about half of that number were part of, or related to, or close personal friends of the two families, the Aaronsohns and the Feinbergs. Nili had no military-style hierarchy or chain of command, except at the peak: Aaronsohn sent instructions, requests and advice to Sarah. These were passed on usually by Lishansky, who served as executive officer, to the agents concerned. Being in the field, on the spot, each agent might have information or reservations or alternative proposals. Some of Aaronsohn's instructions originated in requests by General Headquarters for information; others originated in Aaronsohn's ideas. Among his standard instructions was the obligation to report on the condition of the Jewish community. In Egypt, no member of the organization accepted any substantive request from a British officer except with permission from Aaronsohn.

It is difficult to calculate how many part-time agents helped the organization — that is, people pursuing their own regular occupations, but available for specific tasks or, more pointedly, conveying to Athlit relevant information gleaned at their workplaces. Manifestly, answers to many of the questions that came down from Aaronsohn required information directly from those workplaces — the most relevant being the Turkish army and administration. In sum the operation of the group embraced a cross section of the whole community. There were farmers and doctors, engineers, businessmen and clerical workers. There were carters and watchmen. There were some public workers. There were two Christian Arabs: the brothers Ghanem, Nasser and Elias.

Nasser, the older, was the longtime driver of the carriage, who had served Aaronsohn for years.

In Egypt, fully in Aaron's confidence were two old friends, Dr. Naftali Weitz whom Aaron had met when both were studying in France and who subsequently worked in Zichron, and Peretz Pascal, a businessman also originally from Zichron. Rafael Aboulafia was recruited by Avshalom during his stay in Egypt; Leibl Bernstein was recruited by Aboulafia and both served at the very heart of the operation.

An illustration of the nature and scope of the work of Nili emerges from the experiences recorded by Moshe Neiman. A Jerusalem-born thirty-two-year-old physician in the Turkish army, he was appointed to a small military hospital adjacent to the railway station in Affula. His duties were specific and very special. Affula was the most important junction in the country, and through it came all Turkish troops and other military personnel on their way to or from the battlefields in the south. It was Neiman's duty to subject them all to a medical check-up, with special reference to possible contagious diseases. From Affula Dr. Neiman sent daily reports to Zichron Ya'akov — but they did not deal with medical subjects.

In his first report — as he recalls in postwar memoirs — he included a geographical description of Affula and its environs, pinpointing military installations, the number of railway engines and warehouses. He added a survey of earlier significant events at the station. The initial report he handed to his older brother, Mendel, who rode off with it to Zichron. He followed this procedure until the end of his stint at Affula. "In between medical examinations," he wrote:

> I would take a seat in the officers' compartment on the train. I would invite them to a glass of wine. Meantime my brother would be making a count of the train's cars and their load of ammunition. When there were too many soldiers to be examined, not leaving me free to chat to individual officers...I declared one or two of them to

be ill. I would hospitalize them and then I had the opportunity to cross-examine them. The fact that I had the rank of an officer helped to loosen their tongues.

At my request the Turkish authorities sent me a daily schedule of the trains, so that I should know in advance at what hour of the night I would have to get up to conduct examinations. This information I would send to Zichron together with my reports. During the days of the great military traffic towards Gaza and Beersheba, I noted in my report the names of all the Turkish divisions coming from Constantinople, Salonica and the Caucasus, together with details of the numbers of soldiers, their past activities and their countries of origin.

Patients arriving from Medina gave me details about the Hedjaz front. I discovered the identification numbers of units which had escaped the notice of the British intelligence. I paid special attention to German officers and pilots, who were drawn to me because I spoke German.

I served as interpreter between them and the Railway Control Officer at the station. The pilots explained to me the structure of the planes; submarine officers told me of their adventures.

None of them imagined that every word they uttered was being taken down and would soon be the subject of conferences at British Intelligence Headquarters in Cairo.

Famous generals like Enver Pasha, Djemal Pasha and Falkenhayn (Inspector-General of the German forces in Turkey) also underwent my medical examination, and I was able to send advance information on their comings and goings.... British prisoners-of-war who came through Affula found a faithful friend in me. With the permission of the Turkish commander, the British officers would be invited to take a meal at my home. As I had command of English, I regularly sent the names of these officers to Zichron Ya'akov. Djemal was impressed by my diligence, and gave me fifteen days' leave in Jerusalem.... I visited him there. Every word of what he told me I passed on.[1]

In June 1917 Neiman was transferred to the military hospital at Ramle:

---

1. Dr. Moshe Neiman, *Mi-Petah Tikva le'emek akhor* [From Petah Tikva to a gloomy valley], privately published in the 1940s.

I continued writing my diary and reported on military movements at the railway station. I also recorded what was happening at the German airfield, where I substituted for a German doctor who had gone on leave.... I made a tour with my friend (Yosef Lishansky) and showed him all the important sites, the airfield, the radio station, ammunition dumps, the hospital, etc.

Thereafter, in August, Neiman was again transferred, but this time out of the army to Petah Tikva, where he treated exiles from Jaffa and Tel Aviv. His activity here for Nili was limited to answering specific questions. For example, he was asked to point out on a map of Nazareth "every public building and its purpose, ammunition dump, military hospital, etc."

It was in Petah Tikva that Dr. Neiman was later arrested.

An extract from Neiman's daily reports in one week of March 1917 illustrates the style and detail of his contribution. He did not spurn a touch of humor. On the 20th he writes:

> The train from Damascus carried one motorcar; four cannons belonging to division No. 53; two cars of benzine; two cars of food; seventy soldiers for the 53rd division; one complete plane accompanied by a pilot and two German mechanics. They explained to me that the plane was named Fokker after its inventor; it could attain a very high speed; it was armed with a machine gun which could emit seven hundred bullets a minute.... The machine gun could be adjusted to fire in all directions, upwards, downwards, left, right.... It was forbidden to fly the Fokker across the enemy lines, to prevent any inspection by the enemy if it was brought down. Its purpose — defensive.

On the 24th he adds:

> Mr. Kowalsky, a Jew, the conductor of the 23rd division orchestra [stationed] at Nazareth came here to ask for a train "whistle" to add to the instrumentation of "Die Bahn [the train]" which they have been playing for a month and which is popular with the officers. He mentioned that battalion 137 had arrived from Lebanon. All the men were weak, all were short of stature, and all dressed alike — that is,

barefoot — except for one who is wearing shoes, and he upsets the uniformity....

Four days later, he reports:

> Towards nightfall four Germans came through here; General von Lante, Dr. Baron von Maltzen and two officers. They are attached to the military commission sent from Germany at the request of Enver Pasha to inspect the front. Cheered by wine at my home, they told me that the greater part of the army was at Tarsus, Taurus, as far as Aleppo. The general is satisfied with their condition.... Djemal Pasha is leaving Damascus tomorrow for Ma'an and then Jerusalem. Divisions Nos. 3, 16 and 53 are at Beersheba.... They are bringing up Nos. 4 and 5.[2]

Nili had a new agent at Affula, David Sokolovitz — another cousin, through marriage to Paulette Glatzano, a niece of Malka Aaronsohn. A farmer, he was reporting for Nili in the Galilee and the Jezreel Valley. At Sarah's request, after Neiman's transfer, he consented to change his occupation. He became a shopkeeper, managing a buffet near the railway station at Affula. Having a perfect command of Turkish, Arabic and French he was able to converse with many of the Turkish and German officers. From them he learned of the composition of the units passing through Affula. Officers gave him detailed descriptions of the German and Turkish forces at various sectors of the front — Gaza; Ruhama; Tel Shariya between Gaza and Beersheba — where the forthcoming battle must be fought. These reports included details of planes, big guns and machine guns.

From the south of the country at Rishon Lezion came a chapter of intelligence on many facets of the Turkish forces. It was supplied by Na'aman Belkind, who had a number of assistants. Na'aman himself had many acquaintances among the senior Turkish officers whom he met frequently, and they casually gave him information. They told him on March 17 (shortly before the first battle of Gaza) of "a meeting chaired by the general commanding the 20th army corps, Abdel Rahim Pasha. Among those present were German staff officers and engineers. They discussed the digging of

---

2. Ibid.

defense trenches, and preparing posts for gun batteries. Eleven mountain guns had arrived."[3]

Two days later, he reported, eight of the mountain guns were sent south to the Gaza front, and three north to Tel Aviv. Here Na'aman sent the plan for the placement of the guns. The same day he reported that a German officer named Tiller and his staff had been killed in an aerial bombardment at Gaza.

Another dispatch (this time on August 14) contained a report of special significance. General Kress von Kressenstein complained that the Turkish officers were deserting. Desertions and disease were making serious inroads into the army. Battalions had been reduced to little more than half their normal strength. "It must be assumed," wrote Na'aman, "that there are no more than thirty thousand Turkish soldiers fit for battle on this front."

The special significance of this brief report lay in two facts. On the one hand the British persisted in overrating enemy strength. On the other, Aaronsohn had consistently been telling his British interlocutors that the Turks were much weaker than they thought.

Like Na'aman Belkind, Moshe Neiman's brother Mendel had his own personal acquaintances or friends, in his case among the German officers who chatted too casually about their secrets. He paid special attention to their air force. He was able to send information on the reports of their raids, where planes were stationed, comments on pilots' training, their regular flight plans, orders for special flights, and travels by air of senior officers.

In the summer disturbing reports reached General Headquarters of ominous sightings of German submarines off the coast of Palestine.

Their base was at Beirut in Lebanon. Aaronsohn asked Athlit to report what they knew about the issue, and Reuven Schwartz — whose regular job was as security officer of the experiment station — went out to Beirut. On his way he carried out a survey of Turkish coastal defenses similar to Aaronsohn's survey a year earlier. His findings were similar, too. There were no serious defenses on the coast.

At Beirut, he reports that he visited Mrs. Emmy Haas, who held a post at the college. "Visiting her was a Miss Schubert who had friends among submarine officers and had herself, by invitation, visited a submarine — number 63. I learnt from her that there were six submarines in the Mediterranean, two

---

3. Livneh, Nedava and Efrati, *Nili*, p. 222.

large and four small. The small vessels brought ammunition to the large ones..."[4]

Of number 63 she told him the names of the officers, and the number of men, no less than thirty. The officers had explained to her that "they do not fire at small ships, because every torpedo costs thirty thousand marks.... Consequently they sought out only big ships.... The central store for their ammunition in the Mediterranean is at Constantinople. For the submarines based at Beirut the ammunition is stored at Rayak on the road to Damascus. The size of submarine number 63 is approximately fifteen meters."[5] The obliging Miss Schubert presented Schwartz with a photograph of submarine 63 which was duly sent off to Cairo.

Schwartz's sortie in the north was not an isolated operation outside Palestine. Working there for Nili was Eitan Belkind, Na'aman's younger brother, who had been recruited into the Turkish army. He was nineteen years old when he was transferred to Damascus in the spring of 1917. There he reported on military targets "worthy" of being bombed from the air, like a factory producing oil used by the Turks as fuel. He sent also detailed information on the German radio station close to Damascus — including the code it used.

One of the Turkish army officers working at this station, reported Eitan, was a pal of his, a graduate of the Herzlia Gymnasia (high school) in Tel Aviv named Eliezer Lipson, who was able to enlighten him. The station was two-way, he reported, connecting the Middle East with Damascus and with Naian in Germany. There were two kinds of transmission: open — mainly for news, and in code — for military orders and instructions.

Lipson served at the station as a translator from Turkish and German, but when required he also handled encoded messages. "One day," wrote Eitan,

> I told him I'd like to visit the station and see how a message was received from Naian and then was transmitted to the southern front. He didn't dream that I was a member of a spy organization, for after all I wore a Turkish uniform and was one of the first three Palestinians who in 1911 had traveled to Constantinople to study at a

---

4. Reuven Schwartz, letter to Aaronsohn, July 7, 1917.
5. Ibid.

military college. I thus came to the station one night and was ordered
not to reveal anything of what I saw.

In his room I saw a sheet of paper sticking out of a tube, and that
contained the code. My friend explained that the Germans habitually
changed the code from time to time…and so when he left the room
for a moment I withdrew the paper from the tube and slipped it into
my pocket. That night I made a copy and had it sent as soon as possible to Athlit. The next day my friend called me in agitated tones: the
code was lost. I told him I'd help him look for it; and so, pretty quickly
I found it among the papers in one of his drawers.

Not always did agents have a ready means of sending their reports safely to
Athlit or Zichron. Reports were thus often collected at their source. Most
often it was Lishansky who made a tour of the agents' posts. There were also
obviously potentially useful people whom it was thought desirable to recruit.
Sarah and Lishansky had made such a tour after his return from Egypt. It was
then that they visited Affula and succeeded in enlisting Dr. Neiman. Later,
Sarah on her travels took with her her bosom friend Tova Gelberg. On
another occasion Tova was entrusted with documents to take to Damascus.
"It wasn't easy," wrote Tova. "The trains were choc-a-bloc. I was alone, without an escort…. I had dressed like an Arab dancer, in a white dress and wearing many bracelets. Somehow I was given a seat. Throughout the journey I
didn't say a word, for I didn't speak Turkish. Luckily nobody bothered me,
and I returned safely to Athlit."

On another occasion Nahum Wilbushevitz's wife, Shoshana, was sent
urgently from Constantinople. She carried his report and drawings to Athlit
in a shoe box. Shoshana was Avshalom Feinberg's sister.

One letter from Aaron to Sarah,[6] on July 10, 1917, provides a glimpse of the
considerable scope and variety of intelligence encompassed by Nili. It
contains a lengthy list of requirements and questions to which, given his

6. Not many of his letters to Sarah at Zichron or Athlit survived, but clearly the questions noted here were intended for Lishansky as well.

knowledge of her resources — and of Lishansky's — he had reason to expect compliance or satisfactory explanations.

He refers her to earlier questions to which he has not yet had a reply. "What have you learned about Frank and Hugo Wilner?" (These were two dangerous agents working for both Turkey and Germany.) He had asked for details of a 125mm gun. "What have you learned?" Now he goes over to a new question: "Turkish ammunition — where is it stored? And food? And fodder? Where? In caves?" He asks for substantive information about train movements. This was at the time that Neiman had been transferred by the Turks to the medical post at Ramle. The question had thus to be answered by David Sokolovitz. He lacked Neiman's advantages, especially the authority to order Turkish or German officers to bed with an imaginary illness so as to question them at his leisure; but somehow he managed to coax information from transient customers at his shop.

The questions Aaronsohn asked (obviously at the request of General Headquarters) went beyond the projected operations in western Palestine. What was the weight of railway traffic — not only that passing through Affula to Ramle and Beersheba, but also to Der'a across the Jordan, and from Dera'a to Medina in Hedjaz? Or roads — were any being built or projected, particularly north-south; and were any railway extensions being planned? Where were new bridges being built? How accurate were British aerial attacks proving? He wanted to know changes in Turkish and German personnel — complete with biographical detail. An update was needed also on the state of the coastal defenses. And — were any Turkish units being trained for night attacks, or in the use of flame throwers, or of gas?[7] What did the Turks know or believe about British intentions? Were the Germans planning acts of deception?

He urged upon them to keep sentiments out of their reports. He wanted no "how wonderfuls" or "how terribles" to which evidently Sarah was prone. He did want them to include in their reports descriptions of the state and spirit of the Jewish community. How many Jews remained after the expulsion from Jaffa in April — and where were all the refugees? He stressed the importance of reports on the Jewish community in Jerusalem. He reminded them

---

7. Gas was being used by the Germans in Europe on the Western Front.

that every reference to Jerusalem had its impact on the hearts and minds of
Jews the world over.

In another letter he complains about a fault unrelated to their immediate
task, but disturbing to his vibrant scientific soul.

> The report I received of the journey... of R.S.[8] and his companion...
> made me very angry. The objective was undoubtedly desirable, and
> because of this, many thanks to them. But are our people blind?
> People from the experiment station go out on a long journey and
> make no notes on any worthwhile scientific subject? How is this
> possible? Experiments cannot be carried out at the station. All that is
> left is work done on scientific journeys — and so they go and write
> sloppy reports. Our workers must sharpen their scientific sights and
> their scientific logic. They must train themselves. They must train
> themselves to make a habit of the open eye and the recording hand.
> Let nothing be unimportant to them and do not say 'this is known' or
> 'this is not worth writing down.' Do not judge. Their journey had
> therefore been fruitless from a scientific point of view!
>
> The few lines on the state of the crops and the fields are very
> interesting. Give more. From workers at the station I would expect to
> receive at least meteorological reports and information on the state of
> the crops...

Infinitely more serious than such aberrations was the crisis that developed
precisely when the Nili operation approached its political climax, at the end
of June, between Aaronsohn and the EMSIB group — Major Malcolm,
Captain Edmonds and, most prominently, Captain Smith. The *Managem*,
with Liova Schneierson aboard, had just docked at Port Said when Liova
reported to Aaron that the voyage had been "handled badly." It was a new
chapter in the old story of Smith's rude behavior towards the members of Nili.
Indeed, Schneierson had reported on several recent occasions that Smith's
behavior was insufferable, and Aaronsohn now decided not to tolerate it any

---

8. Reuven Schwartz's visit to Beirut.

longer. Accordingly the next morning he raised the matter with Major Malcolm. Malcolm promised his urgent attention, but Aaron was evidently not convinced by his promise, and spoke to Deedes.

Deedes promised to take up the issue with Smith the next day when Smith was due to return to Cairo. Smith inexplicably did not arrive the next day. Aaronsohn, feeling that he was being given the runaround, spoke to Edmonds. Edmonds took a stand. He claimed there was too much "fuss" over the matter. Aaron retorted sharply. He reminded him that the work of the people at Athlit was difficult and dangerous in the extreme, and they should not be subjected to the additional burden of humiliations. Harshness and arrogance, he said, might seem natural in dealing with Englishmen (who were Smith's subordinates) but were most insulting to his Nili people. They, he added, were intellectuals who had volunteered to serve the British cause in the war (moreover performing duties which were most unpleasant) because they believed that the cause was identical to their own nation's cause. Edmonds did not respond.

Two days later the conflict reached new levels. Aaronsohn was told by Deedes that Malcolm and his colleagues wanted to talk to him. At the EMSIB office Malcolm ripped into him. The problem for them, it seems, was not only Aaronsohn but ongoing internal resentments and jealousies. Malcolm said flatly that if Aaron wanted him to "take an interest" in his (Aaron's) work, he should not "drag" Deedes into it. It was Smith however who lost control of himself. He burst out with astounding counter-allegations. The Nili people were false, he claimed, and their work was worthless. It could be done more efficiently by other people.

Aaronsohn kept his cool. If indeed they believed that there were others who could do the job better, he said, he would withdraw and hand the operation over to them. He would be happy "not to have to continue exposing my friends and our undertaking to danger." Accordingly he announced, "I am leaving the game."

Edmonds intervened, trying to cool the atmosphere, but made no concessions. "It seems to me," wrote Aaronsohn in his diary, "that he realized that Smith had gone too far." Indeed he was well pleased with the situation: now there would have to be a showdown. "Either the situation will be clarified and accepted, without evasions, without dependence on the whims of this or that captain, or the vagaries of the weather, or we shall exchange farewells." When he told Graves what had happened, Graves "expressed doubts as to Smith's having mysterious agents with whom to threaten me."

That afternoon, in a tranquil mood, he went off to a literary event, conducted in Hebrew, and was gratified to find the hall filled to capacity with Palestinian deportees.

The next day Edmonds, pretending that nothing untoward had happened, asked him for his views on a subject that had been under discussion for some time — the possibility of making contact overland with Athlit. Aaronsohn declined to answer. Instead he pointed out to Edmonds that "having been informed by Smith in your and Major Malcolm's presence, that is by EMSIB officially, that there are other people who could do my work, I have no right to endanger my friends any longer."

That day, manifestly distressed by the possible consequences of Smith's egregious blunder, Captain Graves presented a memorandum to his superior, Colonel Nugent. There he wrote bluntly that Aaronsohn's reports were most important from the military point of view, and that every effort should be made to ensure that they were received "speedily and regularly." He added, to make himself quite clear, that this should be done "even if we are compelled to abandon other sources from which we receive reports," and he informed Aaronson of what he had done.[9]

It is surely inconceivable that the political wing of the intelligence unit was unaware of the dubious quality of the information supplied by those "other sources" employed in EMSIB by Smith and his colleagues. Esprit de corps, however, blistered by internal jealousies, had inhibited Graves and his peers from bringing matters to a head. Now that Smith had deliberately opened up the issue, Graves — no doubt in consultation with his colleagues — decided to take advantage of the quarrel and of Aaronsohn's stand to try to free the intelligence unit from those sources.

Meantime however there was deadlock. The next morning Deedes, who had been away briefly in Alexandria, returned to Cairo. Aaronsohn, in order to give him an opportunity to learn from others what had happened in his absence, went to see him later in the day and asked for a meeting with the three EMSIB officers. Deedes called them together the next morning, and (with Edmonds absent) a "stormy" discussion took place. To Aaronsohn's

9. PRO/WO 157/722, August 8, 1917.

amazement, Smith and Malcolm did not try to justify, or explain, or apologize for Smith's attacks. They simply denied that they had ever said a word about there being "other people," and insisted that they obviously had not said that other people would do Nili's job better.

Deedes evaded the issue, tried to be "even-handed" by blaming "both sides," and the meeting ended inconclusively; but Graves, with George Lloyd and Feilding, worked hard the next day to exert pressure on the EMSIB group, and arranged a further meeting. This time only Malcolm was there from EMSIB. The increasing gravity with which the incident was regarded at General Headquarters is evidenced by the presence of Deedes as well as Graves and George Lloyd. Lloyd had assured Aaronsohn in advance that there would be a showdown, and Aaronsohn agreed to a "cease-fire." This meeting — for which it is evident an agreed conclusion had been reached in advance — was peaceful. Malcolm explained that Aaron had "misunderstood" them. Aaronsohn, for his part, assured everybody that he had no personal feelings against Smith, but insisted that "Smith must be taught what our aims are, and that he treat my people with proper respect." The meeting then continued with a discussion of practical matters that needed attention, as though there had been no crisis.

The status quo was thus formally restored on the surface, but the matter was not allowed to end there. Smith had endangered more than he seemed to understand. By his intemperate wild accusations he had awakened certain sleeping dogs in the intelligence organization, and so provoked a "clarification" for which the "politicals" had surely been waiting.[10] One month later it came to a head. It was established by GHQ intelligence that Nili was the one reliable source of intelligence. In the secret war intelligence file for August 1917 there is a report on the 8th of the month worded with great care and signed by Deedes:

> Conference at Port Said with Smith to consider closing down some of the agencies along the coast. The information furnished by these agencies is not of a very high order and as a rule arrives too late to be of any value, and their maintenance costs a substantial sum. It was finally decided that in spite of this we should not be justified in

---

10. Aaronsohn, *Diary*, pp. 302–308.

closing them down since, if anything happened to our other and better sources of information (the very reliable and [sic] A[aronsohn] organization), we should have nothing else to fall back on.[11]

Aaronsohn was not invited to this professional "conference." He would however have quietly torn his hair at the decision of a responsible and intelligent group of intelligence officers to be prepared "to fall back on" agencies whose information was "not of very high order," and as a rule arrived "too late to be of any value"!

---

11. PRO/WO 157/722, August 8, 1917.

CHAPTER 13

General Allenby Takes Advice

April 27 was a black day for Aaronsohn. He met Mark Sykes, who had come from London a few days earlier; and he brought Aaron the latest secret news from the Palestine front. General Murray had launched his second attack on Gaza, and had been defeated once more. Sykes was distraught; and what news he had brought from London was also bad. The atmosphere there was dominated by pessimism, generated largely by reports from Russia of widespread propaganda for ending the war. A complete Russian collapse seemed to be just over the horizon — with disastrous implications. The Germans would undoubtedly be strengthened in their efforts to break the deathly deadlock on the Western Front; and they could free forces in Eastern Europe for reinforcing their front in Palestine. All in all, British fortunes in the spring of 1917 were at their lowest ebb since war broke out in August 1914.

In return for Sykes's bad news, Aaronsohn gave Sykes his bad news — of Djemal's brutal evacuation of the Jews of Jaffa — which had reached Aaron days earlier on Sarah's arrival in Egypt. Sykes responded with extreme emotion. He feared that a manifestly triumphant Djemal would now feel free to deal with the Jews as the Armenians had been dealt with, and he came to some astonishing conclusions.

If there was to be no further advance in Palestine, he wrote to the Foreign Office, he foresaw that the consequences for the Jews would be horrendous. Therefore it would be essential to halt all Zionist projects and even to stop all Zionist propaganda in Britain and America. The "Jabotinsky Project" (for a Jewish Legion) should also not be proceeded with.

Aaronsohn was no less shaken than Sykes by the new defeat at Gaza, but he was not surprised. Before the first battle at Gaza he had warned of the difficulties of the terrain in a frontal attack from the south. He had then proposed to Captain Graves that an outflanking movement to the east should be carried out — provided a thorough examination of the soil were made, to determine whether it could sustain the movements of an army. Here was another outline of the strategic rethinking which he was later to bring to complete articulation. General Murray rejected this advice.

It was believed in some quarters that already in April Aaronsohn submitted for General Murray's attention a complete alternative plan for the second battle of Gaza. There is no hard evidence of this, and Aaronsohn met with General Murray himself, evidently for the first time, only three weeks *after* Gaza Two, on May 22. The purpose of this meeting, as reported in his diary, was to press the desirability of forming a Jewish Legion; and Murray in the friendliest fashion gave the idea short shrift. During that year the additional manpower — a contingent to be trained and fed — would be a hindrance, not a help. He graphically enumerated for Aaron all the troubles and incongruities he had to contend with: "Turkish defenses and infantry, German machine guns and Austrian artillery, and faithless Russians at their back." As for a Jewish division, it "would be able to serve at the front only in a year's time at the earliest." "With my single railway line," Murray added, "I have to maintain every man and every animal."[1]

The harassed general was in truth expected to win battles, not to make political decisions, and his reply to Aaronsohn was eminently reasonable from a military point of view. When the first Jewish battalion was finally set up in England, even though it included a nucleus of battle-tried soldiers who had served in Gallipoli as well as a number of regular British officers who had been transferred from existing units, it took months before it set sail for Palestine.

It is difficult to understand why the officers in Cairo to whom Aaronsohn broached the idea of a Jewish Legion failed to tell him that by this time the idea had made considerable progress in London. Jabotinsky had won influential support not only in the British press, but inside the government. Particularly active in its cause were Leopold Amery, now a member of the prime minister's inner secretariat, and Ronald Graham, who had been

---

1. Isaiah Friedman, *The Question of Palestine 1914-1918: A Study of British-Jewish-Arab Relations* (London: Routledge and Kegan Paul, 1973), p. 183.

brought back from Egypt to serve in the upper echelons of the Foreign Office. In that month of April, Jabotinsky together with Captain Yosef Trumpeldor who, under Colonel Patterson, had commanded the Zion Mule Corps at Gallipoli, sent a memorandum directly to Lloyd George, and it was being seriously studied.

Some sixty men demobilized from the Zion Mule Corps had been formed into "Platoon No. 16," which Amery envisaged would be the nucleus of the first Jewish battalion. Jabotinsky himself had joined that platoon while continuing to pursue his diplomatic campaign. It was thus indeed that he was invited to call on the war minister, Lord Derby, to discuss problems arising out of the plan to set up a Jewish force. This meeting (to which Jabotinsky in the uniform of a full sergeant brought Captain Yosef Trumpeldor in the equally full uniform of a Russian captain) was surely one of the most bizarre episodes of the war.[2]

Indeed, in Whitehall there was no sign of support for Sykes's impetuous burst of defeatism, but Aaronsohn had also reacted to the news of the defeat at Gaza with much trepidation. "This is terrible. We are in danger of a second Gallipoli," he wrote, but he did not ever repeat the idea. Sykes, for his part, was soon able to discern that the officials at his own level in the government in London were quite solidly opposed to his conclusion. Indeed Djemal's excesses strengthened the hands of the promoters of specific Jewish participation in the war. Sir Ronald Graham expressed his view succintly. In a letter to the Army Council, formally in the name of his chief, Lord Robert Cecil, he wrote:

> The objection previously urged, namely that the raising of a Jewish battalion for use in Palestine would produce massacres in that country, has now fallen to the ground because such massacres appear to have already begun; and the second consideration is that the raising of a Jewish legion, if accompanied by assurances from His Majesty's government of their sympathy with the desire of any Jews to settle in Palestine and build up a community there, might produce a most beneficial effect in encouraging the Jews of the United States and

2. See my *Lone Wolf: A Biography of Vladimir (Ze'ev) Jabotinsky* (New York: Barricade Books, 1996), vol. 1, pp. 257–60. Trumpeldor, the only Jewish officer in the Tsar's army, won fame for bravery under fire in the Russo-Japanese War of 1905.

Russia to lend their wholehearted support in the form of carrying the war through to a successful conclusion.[3]

Aaron did not elaborate on his reference to Gallipoli; but he surely remembered the reasons for the Gallipoli disaster — the egregious blunders, the absence of knowledge of the terrain and the failure of intelligence. His own view, which had been reinforced from Turkish sources before he left Palestine, was that the British had overestimated Turkish strength. Given adequate and accurate information, the Gallipoli campaign could have been turned into a victory. He could not but recall his own dismayed reactions — to which he gave expression in his diary during his stay in England and then in Egypt — to British slowness and what he saw as sloppiness or incompetence. And this, with an initial infrastructure of honest ignorance. Even the recent capture of Baghdad by General Maude served to recall the earlier failure and ignominious surrender at Kut el Amara. He consequently did not have to explain to himself the recurrence of this phenomenon in the defeat at Gaza.

But his considered conclusion was entirely contrary to Sykes's: "to take every possible measure to ensure our success."[4] Sykes, fortunately, soon recovered his composure. As for Ormsby-Gore who, too, had been appointed to Lloyd George's inner secretariat, he was more blunt as to what should be done in response to Djemal's brutality. He urged "the use of the pogroms in Palestine as propaganda."[5]

Certainly Prime Minister Lloyd George was not going to deepen the woes of his people by raising a white flag in Palestine. He made two decisions: General Murray would be replaced by Sir Edmund Allenby, a cavalry general from the Western Front; and a new offensive would be launched for the conquest of Palestine. Before appointing Allenby, however, Lloyd George had offered the command to the South African General Smuts. Smuts was prepared to accept the appointment, but only on condition of a change in the

---

3. PRO/WO 81775/W50 Graham to War Council, May 8, 1917. The report that had reached London that there had been violent deaths accompanying or following the expulsion was untrue.
4. His first idea was to suggest to Deedes that Djemal should be offered a heavy bribe. This was not entirely far-fetched. Earlier in the war, there had been rumors suggesting that Djemal would be amenable.
5. The Sledmere (Sykes) Papers, Ormsby-Gore to Sykes, May 8, 1917, quoted by Friedman, *The Question of Palestine*.

strategy. Instead of a frontal assault on Gaza, he believed that the Turks should be attacked from the rear. His plan was very similar to the proposal repeatedly voiced by Aaronsohn to the officers at GHQ in Cairo. Aaronsohn had outlined the idea early in May to Colonel Deedes: to withdraw the British troops from Salonica, execute a surprise landing in the Haifa-Acre Bay, capture the Carmel ridges and the Jezreel Valley, and then make a lightning assault on Jerusalem.

He then put the idea to General Clayton who, after discussing it with General Murray, sent it to the government in London. There it was rejected. Put by Smuts it suffered the same fate, and he rejected the offer of the command. Mark Sykes later revealed to Aaronsohn that the government had rejected the idea because of the debacle at Gallipoli; they were loath to attempt another landing from the sea.[6]

General Allenby arrived in Cairo to take over command of the Egyptian Expeditionary Force at the end of June 1917. A fortnight later, on July 12, he already telegraphed his plan for the capture of Gaza — based on a frontal attack on the town.

Notably, at this time the strategic plan offered separately by Aaronsohn and Smuts was being put forward to Prime Minister Lloyd George also by Winston Churchill, who had been restored to Cabinet office.

Writing to Lloyd George on July 22, 1917, and after criticizing the pressure by General Robertson, the Chief of the Imperial General Staff (CIGS), to launch a new offensive in the west (which Churchill, like the prime minister, feared would merely prolong the mutual slaughter — as it did), he goes on to give his advice on the east:

> The truth is staring us in the face. An army of six divisions, British or Franco-British, should be taken from the Salonica front *and put in behind Djemal's army. This will force that army to surrender, and all the Allied troops* in Syria and Palestine, including Allenby's, will be free by the spring of 1918 for action in Italy or France.[7] (Emphasis added.)

---

6. Ibid.
7. Winston S. Churchill, *The World Crisis* (London: Odhams Press, 1938), p. 1208.

Lloyd George had told Allenby that he wanted him to capture Jerusalem by Christmas. It must consequently have been a considerable shock to the new commander to receive the "commentary" on his proposal of July 12, which was sent on July 19 to the Cabinet in London by CIGS Robertson.

There the CIGS painted a very gloomy picture overall. It reflected the Western Allies' most difficult days of 1917 on the Western Front, as well as the still persistent fear of a Russian dropout from the war. On the military prospect in Palestine, too, he outlined a chilling prospect. According to his analysis of the facts on the ground Allenby would certainly not be able to deliver "Jerusalem by Christmas." "It is quite clear," wrote Sir William, "that the campaign will be a far greater undertaking than it appeared when considered at the beginning of the year."

The Turks had reinforced the Gaza front. Indeed Allenby himself found that their fortifications of the Gaza lines were such that his heavy artillery requirements would be on the same scale as obtained in France.

What Allenby needed in the way of additional forces (in effect, one division), wrote Robertson, could be sent to him only in November. Once advanced to the Jaffa-Jerusalem line (that is, after overcoming Gaza and fighting his way to that line) he might require a considerable further addition to his strength. He would certainly need those reinforcements for an advance beyond that line.

Robertson now described a peculiar complication. On the one hand, the railway system leading from Egypt needed to be expanded; on the other hand, an adequate supply of water had to be assured for running the railway.

Because of the overall shortage of water, a new pipeline had to be laid from Egypt in addition to the existing pipeline. For this purpose more pipes were needed. These could be obtained only from the United States. This, he wrote, was being investigated. Building the new railway line, Robertson estimated, would need more than six months; to bring the pipes, five ships would be needed, and the time required to bring the pipes would be seven months. Taking into account the water factor and assuming that the order sent to America for pipes would be promptly and safely executed, the campaign could reasonably be opened only by about March 1918.

Robertson dealt in greater detail with the shipping problem:

Once General Allenby is launched into a campaign for the conquest of Palestine it is impossible to say exactly how many troops he will need, and it is necessary that the shipping controller should guarantee that shipping will be available not only to move the reinforcements and to maintain the force asked for, but there must also be available a considerable surplus to meet possible further requirements for holding the Jaffa-Jerusalem line, and for going beyond if required. If the shipping is not assured we may at the end of the year find ourselves hanging on to our line with great difficulty, and unable either to retire or to advance, and the force generally *immobilised until the end of the war.* (Emphasis added.)

Moreover, in light of the expected developing war situation later in the year, the CIGS found he had to examine the shipping problem as a whole on all the fronts. From this problem Palestine could not be divorced. Thus he continued:

The shipping situation may be much more difficult than now, and we must bear in mind the necessity of adequately supplying coal, etc., to France and Italy so as to avoid shortage and consequent trouble in these countries during the coming winter. The French army will certainly be weaker than it is now, and American assistance to counter-balance this depends upon the doubtful shipping factor. Our present dispositions are already the reverse of good, and we need to consider very carefully the greater necessity which may later arise for collecting our troops.

Before all these considerations could come into play, however, the major battle at Gaza had still to be fought. On this he added a grim prospect: "As regards the plan itself [prepared by Allenby], it is clear that the attack on the Gaza position will mean heavy casualties. We are already in great difficulties in keeping Egypt up to strength in drafts. These difficulties will increase with the growth in the forces and with more intense fighting, and it would not be safe to calculate on having less than *forty thousand casualties by the time we reach the Jaffa-Jerusalem line.* (Emphasis added.)

In light of all these sober facts and assessments Robertson put forward his alternative:

It is for the War Cabinet to say whether the political advantages to be gained by the occupation of Jerusalem and southern Palestine are such as to justify our undertaking at this stage of the war a new and great campaign with the consequent strain on our shipping and all other resources. It is my present opinion that the purely military advantages to be gained would not justify the expenditure of force required and the risks incurred, though I do not say that this opinion may not be modified later.

In other words, he jousted head-on with the wishes of the prime minister; and he went on:

My proposal therefore is that we should at once proceed with doubling the railway, subject to what may be ascertained in regard to the water pipes; make General Allenby's present force up to strength in all possible respects; withdraw a certain number of guns from Salonika at once; and decide later on *whether the campaign can be undertaken or not.* In the meantime General Allenby should take any advantage offered of pressing the Turk.[8] (Emphasis added.)

It is true that Robertson had consistently upheld the conviction of the Kitchener school — that the war would have to be fought and won exclusively in the west. Perhaps his drastic proposal, to postpone and perhaps even forego the conquest of Palestine, was colored to some extent by that prejudgment. However he was not overstating the difficult, even grim circumstances facing Allenby, which would at best make the launching of an offensive at Gaza feasible only by March 1918.

Yet, by December 1917, Allenby had not only captured Gaza, but had fought his way, as Lloyd George had "commanded," to "Jerusalem by Christmas." On December 9 he made his ceremonial entry into the city.

How had this dramatic transformation taken place?

That was indeed the question to which the Director of Military Intelligence (of all the British forces) General George MacDonogh addressed himself in a lecture he delivered after the war on November 15, 1921, at the Royal Military Academy at Woolwich:

You will remember Lord Allenby's great campaign in Palestine in that year and you may have wondered at the audacity of his operations. It

---

8. PRO/WO 106/721 (July 19, 1917).

is true that in war you cannot expect a truly great success unless you are prepared to take risks, but these risks must be reasonable ones. To the uninitiated it may sometimes have appeared that Lord Allenby's were not reasonable. That however was not the case, because Lord Allenby knew from his Intelligence every disposition and movement of the enemy. Every one of his opponents' cards was known to him, and he was consequently able to play his own hand with the most perfect assurance. In those circumstances victory was certain.[9]

A later comment from Allenby's entourage pinpointed this assessment further. Captain Raymond Savage, deputy military secretary to Allenby (and Allenby's biographer) said:

It was very largely the daring work of young spies, most of them natives of Palestine, which enabled the brilliant Field Marshal to accomplish this undertaking so effectively. The leader of the spy ring was a young Jewess, Miss [sic] Sarah Aaronson.[10]

Lord Allenby himself (in his condolence letter of July 19, 1919, on Aaronsohn's death, to Dr. David Eder), wrote that "Aaron Aaronsohn...was mainly responsible for the formation of my field intelligence organisation behind the Turkish lines."

Disappointed but not daunted by the rejection of the plan for a landing in the rear, and having a good idea of the defenses which had twice defeated General Murray at Gaza, Aaronsohn returned to an idea that he had already considered, when he asked GHQ to examine the strength of the terrain towards Beersheba. The replies were evidently positive, and he began to propagate a change of strategy: the main offensive should be at Beersheba with a feint or sideshow at Gaza.

The same idea had been broached by a senior British general (later field marshal), Philip Chetwode. Such a plan however could reasonably be

---

9. *New York World*, December 4, 1921.
10. Quoted by Anita Engle (author of *The Nili Spies*) in the *Times Literary Supplement* (May 7, 1993).

adopted only if field intelligence showed that Beersheba was a less formidable target than the bastion, twice unbeaten, at Gaza. Soon after the second Gaza defeat Aaronsohn, whose knowledge of the area was unique, evidently sent detailed instructions to Nili. From them he received the essential up-to-date military information they had amassed in the field. He was now able to present the case to Allenby for a major change in his strategy. Providentially it came at the right moment.

It was brought by Schneierson on the *Managem*, which was delayed by rough seas, but effected a safe anchorage at Port Said on or about July 10. The report, dated July 3, was written by Nili's chief agent in the south, Na'aman Belkind — and it demonstrated the depth to which Nili had penetrated the German-Turkish establishment. Belkind points out that no new Turkish divisions had appeared, but the Turks were not resting on the laurels won by their two victories at Gaza, and so existing divisions had all been brought up to full strength. There had been a change of commanders, Turkish and German, and Belkind named the current commanding officers of the units spread out at the bases along the front between Gaza and Beersheba. The list showed a preponderance of strength at Gaza and the proximate bases on its left. What was perhaps Belkind's most important titbit: he had learned of the strategic decisions of the German High Command. If the British did not attack by October, they would open an offensive themselves from the Gaza sector.

This was the sector, his German informant had told him, which they believed they could defend successfully. True, they were afraid of a possible British attack on Beersheba, but their trump card was to be the successful defense of Gaza. All in all, Belkind's report contained sufficient detail for showing Allenby the high strategic feasibility of Aaronsohn's plan.

By this time the water problem had been solved. The wells in the neighborhood of Beersheba had been found untouched. The Turks and Germans had evidently not expected an attack from that direction. Now Aaronsohn's friends at GHQ took a hand. They immediately arranged for Allenby to meet Aaronsohn — and on July 17, General Lyndon-Bell, the chief of staff, ushered Aaronsohn in to the office of the commander in chief. Allenby had certainly been primed both from the Headquarter Staff and from the government in London on Aaronsohn's extraordinary abilities — and the high, if unofficial, status that he enjoyed.[11] They had a long talk. Allenby asked many questions on a variety of subjects about people, viewpoints, the different communities' agricultural problems. Some questions were raised by Aaronsohn, which Allenby left for the HQ officers. Nowhere, however, is there a single mention in Aaronsohn's diary of the burning subject of the forthcoming battle. This seems to have been a distinctive feature of his behavior throughout the war years. It was no doubt a salutary habit but disconcerting to his biographer.

At the end of his diary entry on his meeting with Allenby, he writes laconically, "he tells me he will be calling me frequently."[12]

This turned out to be a huge understatement. In the circumstances they then created, they must have been in constant touch during the next few months. On September 13 Aaronsohn left for London, returning (to Palestine, rather than Egypt) only in March 1918, well after Allenby had captured Jerusalem — sixteen days before Christmas. Yet Allenby, in his letter after Aaronsohn's death to Dr. Eder, points to a close working and even personal relationship that could have been established only in those eight weeks after July 17, 1917: "The death of Aaron Aaronsohn deprived me of a valued friend and of a staff officer difficult to replace."

But the consequences of that first meeting were stupendous, even historic. Viewed under the searchlight of Robertson's analysis of the prospects of Allenby's plan — the eight months' further expected delay (to March 1918) before launching the attack, the likelihood of the loss of forty thousand dead and the possibility of its frustration altogether by a preemptive German-Turkish offensive — what was the realistic chance of victory and conquest in Palestine? And what of Syria? Allenby did not take long to make up his mind. On July 26, nine days after meeting Aaronsohn, he sent a telegram informing Robertson that he intended to encourage the Germans to believe that it was Gaza that was going to be attacked. He thus ignored the analysis and the "advice" of the CIGS, jettisoned his own plan, and almost overnight embraced the strategy of the civilian Aaronsohn.

He must certainly have received backing from London, and thence acquiescence from Robertson — but he did not escape Robertson's criticism. Well after the battle, indeed just before the capture of Jerusalem, on December 9, 1917, he wrote to the secretary of war. "No General Staff and no General would have been justified in basing a plan of campaign upon chances of this

---

11. Friedman, *The Question of Palestine*, p. 273.
12. Aaron Aaronsohn, *Diary*, p. 315.

nature. Had they done so, and had the campaign failed, they would have been justly condemned."[13]

Indeed the moments of greatest tension at GHQ came after Allenby made his decision — to undertake the task of "persuading the enemy" that Gaza continued to be the projected British target in the next round. Responsibility for this crucial, most sensitive, sophisticated and often dangerous operation fell on the shoulders of a comparatively new arrival in Egypt, head of intelligence at GHQ, Colonel Richard Meinertzhagen.

Aaron flung himself wholeheartedly into the operation. From the terms in which Meinertzhagen wrote of Aaronsohn's significant contributions, which could have been made only the during the few weeks between Allenby's decision of July 26 and Aaronsohn's departure for London on September 13, it is clear that he played an important role in the planning and execution of some of the specific acts of camouflage, such as feints at Gaza, phantom military camps and landings from the sea. Given Aaron's complete silence and Meinertzhagen's expressed fear of divulging the facts, one can only guess at their exact nature and scope.

More forthcoming than Aaron was nevertheless Meinertzhagen himself: "My best agent was a Jew," he writes in his memoirs, "a man who feared nothing and had an immense intellect. This remarkable man was the most daring and unassuming agent.... I am not at liberty to divulge many of his exploits as it would publicize matters better left secret."[14]

Some of Meinertzhagen's personal exploits achieved fame in the annals of war, notably the so-called "Haversack Plan." It was worked out some time in August or early September. On September 12 an officer, Captain A. C. B. Neale, was sent into No Man's Land. As he rode his horse, he dropped his haversack (which contained documents pointing clearly to a renewed frontal attack on Gaza) on the assumption that it would be found by a Turkish patrol. The Turks however did not see the haversack. A second officer, this time an Australian, was sent on October 1 — again with no result. Whereupon Meinertzhagen himself made the attempt. He was fired at, and retired in seeming flight to the British lines. But he dropped his haversack, which

13. PRO/WO 106/727, Robertson to Secretary of War, December 9, 1917.
14. Richard Meinertzhagen, *Middle East Diary 1917–1956* (New York: Thomas Yoseloff, 1960).

contained his notes, maps, and lunch. From a distance he saw the Turks pick up the haversack and his rifle. It was stained with blood — which he had obtained by inflicting a small wound on his horse.

The enemy, naturally suspicious when they picked up the haversack with its tell-tale blood, nevertheless decided in favor of the assumption that this was not a trick, but a collection of genuine documents. The documents even included a letter by an officer who expressed disagreement with the plan of attack on Gaza. What followed was complete success for the ruse. The Germans swallowed the plan.

The German Commander Kress von Kressenstein claimed in his memoirs that he had tended to change his mind about Gaza but, weighing advantages and disadvantages of the two objectives, he concluded that militarily he was justified in deciding on the strengthened defense of Gaza. He may well have been right, but the trouble was that his strengthened defenses were aiming southwards and in the end Gaza was taken from the east.[15]

As though to give history's smile of recognition of Nili's significant contribution to the nullification of those Gaza defenses comes the story of Avshalom Fein.[16]

Late in August, young twenty-four-year-old Avshalom Fein was entrusted with the task of making an updated survey of the Turkish Gaza-Beersheba front line. A request had come from Aaron, emphasizing in particular the need for information on the Turkish guns. It was Na'aman Belkind who acquired the means to make the survey possible. There was a German businessman name Suss under contract with the Turkish army to deliver supplies to the soldiers at the bases between Beersheba and Gaza. Na'aman arranged with Suss to serve as his "subcontractor" and for Fein to serve as his assistant. Lishansky procured a wagon with two mules for Fein and all was ready. Na'aman went off on a project of his own, Fein found lodging in the nearby

---

15. Britain had a similar devastating experience of her own twenty-five years later in World War II. The defenses at Singapore were regarded as invincible. They were however pointing seaward, and the Japanese, overcoming intimidating obstacles in the terrain (February 1942), unexpectedly attacked by land from the rear.
16. No relation to Avshalom Feinberg.

Arab village of Hodj, and he was provided with a Turkish army free pass to enter all the bases with supplies.

Moving freely in and out of the bases, Fein made careful notes of the caliber and location of each gun and, through casual conversation, the number and distribution of men at each base and the names of their officers. The evenings he spent convivially with Turkish officers. Adopting the aplomb of a businessman, he never failed to bring along a bottle of wine or cognac to heighten the spirits of the evening, and to help him guide the conversation in the right direction. He sometimes "lost his way" in the field (after all he was only a civilian businessman) and when he was questioned he had his bottles of wine or cognac with him, whereupon all would repair to an officer's tent to celebrate.

In his report, along with specifics, he related how at one of these evenings he met an officer who had come from the Salonika front. When they parted from the others for a stroll, the officer revealed that he was a Jew and that he bore the Turks no love. Repeating the common talk among his fellow officers, he assured Fein that "the British would never break through at Gaza unless they first captured Beersheba."

Fein reports laconically: "At [adjacent] Ruhama, I succeeded in meeting a man who had all the plans and maps and locations of water. I made friends with him and finally succeeded in stealing from him the documents and maps."[17]

Fein brought his bulky report to Liova Schneierson, who was at Zichron awaiting the imminent departure of the *Managem*. The boat was to sail first to Famagusta in Cyprus and then to Port Said. Rafael Aboulafia was on board, and he would translate Fein's notes, so that the essence of his report could be sent by telegraph to Egypt.

Reading the report, Liova realized — though as he writes in his diary he "knew nothing about strategy" — that it contained intelligence of the greatest importance. He handed it over immediately to Captain Louis B. Waldon, the intelligence agent on the ship, who also recognized its special importance.

Waldon was indeed so excited that, Aaronsohn being absent from Egypt (and already on his way to London), he did not send the report to his superiors in Cairo, but direct to field headquarters. "For this," wrote Liova, "he was

---

17. Livneh, Nedava and Efrati, *Nili*, p. 326.

a) reprimanded for breach of discipline (going over the heads of his superiors) and b) awarded promotion from Captain to Major for providing a report of such significance." And Liova adds in his diary: "What about us?"

Here by contrast is the official British brief summing-up of the third battle for Gaza:

> Allenby's plan was to encircle and capture Beersheba, and then roll up the Turkish front. The Turks defended the wells stoutly and they had not sense enough to destroy them before they were driven out of Beersheba. German General von Falkenhayn [head of the German Military Mission to the Orient who had overriding authority] had ordered the abandonment of Gaza. Allenby's manoeuvre had succeeded in driving the Turks, some units in panic, off the whole Gaza-Beersheba front. He had routed the Turks and captured a great proportion of their artillery and other material.[18]

---

18. Captain Cyril Falls, *The First World War* (London: Longman, 1960), p. 307. See also Friedman, *The Question of Palestine*, pp. 120-22.

CHAPTER 14

A Myriad of Problems

Why was Aaron absent from Egypt in September when Fein's report was delivered? True, the main burden of Nili's work and of his own remarkable contribution to all the branches of the British Intelligence Service for the impending crucial battle — and beyond — had been accomplished. He was well satisfied with the standing he and Nili had achieved with the British establishment. His euphoric feelings were reflected in a letter written on September 17 to Rivka from the *SS Kaiser-i-Hind*, which was taking him to London.

There was still, in truth, some unfinished business, but on September 4 — nine days before Aaron left Egypt — Liova, who had just arrived from Athlit, was able to report to him of the remarkable project, still in progress, of Avshalom Fein with his cart and two mules, coolly operating from the heart of the Turkish lines, building up what was likely to be Nili's final intimate report on the disposition of Turkish men and armor on the Beersheba-Gaza front.

From Liova he heard also of Sarah's report on difficulties and hazards that had arisen in communication with Damascus — whence Nili was supplying early intelligence in aid of Allenby's prospective attack in Syria and further operations in Mesopotamia.[1] Urgent need had evidently arisen for a change in couriers, and Sarah had had to send Tova Gelberg — her bosom friend — on her long, unpleasant journey to bring the latest intelligence for General Headquarters from Damascus.

Perhaps the most cheering part of Aaron's letter to Rivka was the news of a

---

1. Colonel W. B. Gribbon memoirs (unpublished), Aaronsohn House Museum, Zichron Ya'akov.

breach in the wall of disavowal and hostility set up by the communal leaders in Palestine against the Aaronsohns and their comrades in Nili. It is possible that the change was due to Nili's new role — delivering the golden aid for the victims of the April evacuation. That gold was delivered physically in bags to the community's relief committee after being carried on the *Managem*, loaded onto the rowboat to the shore, and finally carried by toiling Nili members to the experiment station.

It would be understandable if the communal leaders softened their attitude to Nili only because of Nili's emergence as a ministering angel to the stricken community and as a sign of its significant influence on the British. There was, however, also another positive influence at work — in the personality of Meir Dizengoff, the head of the relief committee. Dizengoff was a man of higher caliber and broader perspective than his colleagues, and he sensed the direction and the thrust of Aaronsohn's creation. Fourteen years earlier he had shown his mettle while a businessman in Odessa. In defiance of the Tsarist regime he had gone out to raise funds for arms for what was evidently the first Jewish self-defense group in modern history. It was with him that in June Nili (through Lishansky) reached an agreement. The gold would be delivered to him (no questions asked) and he (with his committee members) would be responsible for the distribution of aid among the needy evacuees, as well as among the needy in the community at large.

Then in July a request had come to Zichron Ya'akov for a meeting with two named delegates from the community. Aaron was informed, and the proposal was brought to High Commissioner Wingate — who promptly promised to extend the necessary facilities for a meeting in Cyprus. Aaronsohn expected the meeting to take place in September.

To Aaronsohn, the breakthrough signified a great victory. "Today I can say," he wrote in his diary on July 26, "that the mission I imposed on myself has succeeded." The news certainly presaged a change in the internal relations in the country, a tremendous psychological relief to the members of Nili. At last the communal leaders, it seemed, had recognized the value and great importance of his devoted band; and the nightmare of being hated and ostracized would come to an end. However, because of the urgency, as he saw it, of his journey to London, where he hoped to persuade Weizmann to accord Zionist recognition to Nili, he had sent a message to Athlit, postponing the Cyprus meeting.

As for practical arrangements for the period of his absence, which he calculated should not last more than a month, he had made them all. Alex had arrived in London from America and according to intelligence at General Headquarters, had left for Egypt on August 27. He would substitute for Aaron in relations with the British at GHQ; they had been informed. Until Alex's arrival, there was Pascal, who was known to the British, as were Liova and Rafael Aboulafia and Leibl Bernstein — all knew their parts for the *Managem*'s visits to Athlit.

For all the euphoria that Aaron conveyed to Rivka, it was not for a relaxed vacation that he was traveling to London. Very much to the contrary. He had become involved in a dispute which began in Egypt but, it transpired, could be resolved only in London.

Its first symptoms had appeared early in his stay in Egypt. He had soon had to give up any idea of remaining incognito. From almost his first days, whether in Cairo or Alexandria, he was bumping into Palestinian friends and acquaintances in the street. It was an unavoidable risk, but at least he did not fall into the trap of asking that they tell nobody of the encounter. After all, that warning would only double the danger that most of them would rush to report the encounter to all their relations and friends. It is a remarkable fact that though the Turks were reputed to have many spies in Egypt, there is no sign of their having any idea that Aaronsohn was there too.

There was certainly speculation among the Palestinians about Aaronsohn's sudden appearance in Egypt; and there were a few who went beyond speculation. These were active in the affairs of the deportees, and at least one of them was a man who saw himself as a kind of representative or communal leader. This was Ze'ev Gluskin, who was indeed the contact man for the ad hoc Zionist leadership group set up by Chaim Weizmann in London, and he enjoyed the personal friendship of Nahum Sokolow. Whatever the reason for Aaronsohn's arrival in Egypt, Gluskin felt it only natural that Aaronsohn should have called on him to tell him what he was doing there, and that he should have invited Gluskin's cooperation and advice.

To Aaronsohn, then, came Gluskin accompanied by his friend and business colleague David Yudelewitz — also a deportee with whom, as it happened, Aaronsohn was on friendly and mutually respectful terms. Gluskin, not having an inkling of what Aaronsohn was doing but certain that it was something important, offered his (and Yudelewitz's) help. Aaronsohn who, after all, could not even tell them why he could not tell them what they wanted to know, answered in glacial, even brusque terms. He was doing what he was doing, he said, because it had to be done. He had not asked for their help. If a need for their help were to arise he would call on them. They would then, he added, have to carry out his instructions. Yudelewitz retorted that unless he was told what it was all about he could not simply take orders from anybody. This, no doubt, well suited Aaronsohn's purpose, and there the matter was left.

Aaronsohn however had to call on them much sooner than he expected. Circumstances had changed drastically. The Jews of Jaffa had been evacuated. Aaronsohn, with the eager aid of the British, disseminating the news of the outrage throughout the world, had also launched an appeal for funds. America's breaking off relations with Turkey effectively closed the doors of Palestine to the flow of regular relief funds that had been coming directly from the American Jewish community. Now came the burden of the grim addition of the needs of the homeless from Jaffa, many of them even pauperized. Overnight the condition of the community had become desperate.

Aaronsohn reacted swiftly and boldly. He demanded help from the British military authorities. They must relax their blockade to allow funds to flow into Palestine.

For lifting the blockade a major policy decision was needed; but evidently the British cut all corners: within hours permission was granted, and Aaronsohn even received from General Headquarters a loan of two thousands pounds sterling to start with.

It was not proper however that incoming funds should be handled by a single individual. Aaron consequently, on April 30, 1917, formed the Special Committee for Aid to the Deportees. He would be in charge of the physical transfer by way of the *Managem*, but his name would not appear. He appointed the committee's members: banker Jacques Mosseri, a leader of the Egyptian community and of its Zionist Federation, and Aaron's old friends Dr. Naftali Weitz and Peretz Pascal, together with Gluskin, Yudelewitz and two others, Margolius and Kahanov.

The committee did not last a week, and there were weighty reasons for its dissolution. Gluskin was a vintner, head of the well-known firm of Carmel Mizrahi, with Yudelewitz in charge of his office in Alexandria. The proceeds of their export of wines had customarily been received by direct transfers from the United States to Palestine. Now, with the breaking off of relations between the United States and Turkey this channel was blocked.

Aaronsohn having revealed that he had made an arrangement with the British for sending relief money directly into the country, Gluskin asked Aaronsohn to obtain permission to add the private business funds from his customers abroad to the funds sent from Egypt. Aaronsohn agreed, and it was arranged with Gluskin that Aaronsohn would not have to sign any documents. He would receive Gluskin's check, endorse it and hand it over to Major Malcolm at General Headquarters, who would issue a receipt. That was as much as Gluskin had to know. Malcolm himself would handle the transaction up to the point where the funds (in gold) were brought aboard the *Managem*.

At the last moment, when the *Managem* was about to sail for Athlit, Gluskin and Yudelewitz, instead of bringing a check, asked for a receipt from Aaronsohn and other documents recording the transfer. Aaronsohn lost his temper. He accused them of being interested only in retaining a record to make sure sure that Gluskin's name should be associated with the relief fund. It is not clear whether the *Managem* was delayed because of this quarrel; but when three days later, Gluskin brought his cheque, Aaronsohn refused to accept it. What is more, he dissolved the committee, and reestablished it, appointing only his friends Weitz and Pascal and adding a well-known Cairo lawyer, Alexander.

Yudelewitz, deeply distressed by behavior that he found insulting, explained to Aaronsohn that the rules of their firm did not allow the firm's money to be mixed with other monies; and Gluskin had thus had to obtain the consent of other directors of the company. Hence the delay. Lame though the excuse was, Aaronsohn might well have relented, but for an even more serious circumstance: two misdemeanors by Gluskin.

Gluskin had written a report of one of their meetings which contained a blatant falsehood. Then, he had held on to a document containing minutes of a meeting which Aaronsohn, in his diary, describes as "secret" and which, in an unusual gesture, he had shown to the members of the committee. Gluskin had failed to return it. For Aaron this was the last straw. He would not, he asserted, in any circumstances work with Gluskin.

Gluskin sought an alternative to Aaronsohn's arrangement with the British. He turned to Edgar Suarez, a well-known banker and a declared anti-Zionist, who had however also started raising funds for the Jaffa evacuees. Together they set up a committee of their own, based in Alexandria, where they both lived. Suarez, who had excellent relations with the British administration, applied for a permit — just as, he assumed, Aaronsohn had done — to send money into Palestine; and High Commissioner Reginald Wingate naturally refused.

Gluskin at once gave up the struggle. He asked Suarez to send Aaronsohn any money he had raised, and informed Aaronsohn that he had called on Chaim Weizmann and Sokolow in London to do likewise. This should have ended the dispute; but now Weizmann and Sokolow got involved. Weizmann was in the throes of negotiation with the British government in the effort to obtain an official British declaration of support for Zionist aspirations. He had no official status in the Zionist Organization — which had declared itself neutral in the war — but he had decided, like Jabotinsky and Aaronsohn (each from his own independent angle) that the fate of Palestine would be decided by an Anglo-French victory. In the committee of like-thinking people which Weizmann called together, Sokolow — who did have status as a member high in the Zionist hierarchy — served as vice-chairman. Thus a touch of official acquiescence was added to the committee's breach of Zionist neutrality.

Now, having received from various quarters relief funds (at this moment some twenty-eight thousand pounds sterling) in response to Aaronsohn's appeal — in which he had used Weizmann's address for contributions — Weizmann and Sokolow decided to send money not to Aaronsohn's committee for whom it was intended, but to keep the money under their own control, and send it piecemeal to Gluskin.

Letters and telegrams sent by Jacques Mosseri on behalf of Aaronsohn's committee, calling for the dispatch of what they regarded as their committee's funds, met with no direct response. Weizmann and Sokolow now insisted that Gluskin must be a member of the committee, indeed of any committee formed to handle those funds. Using the British Foreign Office channel of communication they issued an ultimatum whose message may be simplified into "No Gluskin, no money," and sent a demand that a new committee be formed, consisting of Gluskin and a nominee, Wexler, together with Weitz and Mosseri (thus excluding Aaronsohn's colleagues Pascal and Advocate Alexander). Aaronsohn, they wrote, should be executive secretary.

Flabbergasted and outraged by this highjacking of funds that he had generated (and which he alone was able to bring into Palestine), Aaronsohn refused to knuckle under and even refused to receive from Gluskin three thousand pounds which Weizmann and Sokolow had defiantly withheld from Aaronsohn and sent to Gluskin. He wrote two lengthy, very angry letters to Weizmann (on August 15 and 25).

Weizmann and Sokolow having been granted communication facilities by the British Foreign Office, that office became, in effect, an advocate of pressure on Aaronsohn. Thus a lively discussion was now also activated between Ronald Graham at the Foreign Office and High Commissioner Sir Reginald Wingate — who was expected by London to exert pressure on Aaronsohn.

But Wingate, well informed on the whole Aaronsohn phenomenon, came out unreservedly on Aaronsohn's side. He did not mince words. He urged support emphatically for Aaronsohn. He warned Graham of the danger of alienating him: "There may be reasons not known to me for your not finding it desirable to support Aaronsohn, but from my experience and that of the military authorities he has proved himself honest and reliable. If you wish to continue using his organization I propose that he receive the support he is asking for."[2] Understandably unwilling to commit to writing how great was the debt Britain owed to Aaronsohn, he repeatedly reminded Graham of the support of the "military authorities" for Aaronsohn.

Indeed the military authorities were going out of their way to assure Aaronsohn of their belief in the justice of his case. Deedes too, who had been angry at Aaronsohn for refusing to take the money Gluskin had received from Weizmann, recanted when he learned from Aaron the full story of Gluskin's behavior, and told Aaronsohn: "We're with you, but we can't take sides."

Aaronsohn did (on August 12) encounter one British officer who proved to be a glaring exception in the so-friendly group in Egypt. It was Captain

---

2. PRO/FO 371/3053/159351.

Thomas Edward Lawrence (otherwise known as Lawrence of Arabia). He was strictly speaking not stationed at General Headquarters — though a member of the Arab Bureau and ultimately involved in whatever was going on in the Hedjaz. He had begun to gain fame for that series of exploits with the Hedjaz Arabs which, in the main, never took place.[3]

Aaron had met Lawrence six months earlier. He did not record their conversation at that meeting. He had merely described Lawrence in one word: arrogant. The description in his diary now of this second meeting was much more comprehensive and enlightening:

> This morning I had a talk with Captain Lawrence (an interview without a scintilla of friendliness). Lawrence has enjoyed too much success at too young an age. Has a high opinion of himself. He gives me a lesson on our settlements, on the spirit of the people, on the feelings of the Arabs, and why we shall be doing the right thing if we assimilate among them, among the Arabs, etc. Listening to his words I had the feeling that I was present at a lecture by a Prussian scientific antisemite who expresses himself in the English language. I fear that in the ranks of the archaeologists and the priests a good deal of the spirit of the "Boche" has penetrated....
>
> Lawrence, with the means available to him, intends to carry out a survey for himself of the feelings among the Jews in the Galilee villages. If they favor the Arabs — they will survive. If not — they will be slaughtered.
>
> He hates us openly. Fundamentally he is of a missionary breed.

Weizmann and Sokolow refused to be softened. In a telegram couched in deceptively friendly language they urged him to agree to their proposal which would involve him, as executive secretary, in collective responsibility (that is, with Gluskin). This, they wrote, would ensure their "every support." He was left speechless.

Two evenings later, taking his regular bicycle exercise, he made up his

---

3. Aldington, *Lawrence of Arabia*.

mind. "The quarrel with Sokolow and Weizmann," he wrote, "is insoluble.... Why not travel to London?" The next day he put it to Deedes and Edmonds and to Pascal; all agreed that this was the only feasible way out of the impasse.

Throughout those summer weeks Wingate was kept aware of a much deeper cause for Aaronsohn's unease. In his close relationship with senior officers at General Headquarters, Aaronsohn did not hide his impatience and his nagging fear at the continued silence from London about making public a declaration in favor of Jewish aspirations in Palestine. For months Weizmann and his friends had been negotiating, and negotiating, and negotiating...

The content of the declaration being discussed by the British Cabinet was not intended as an act of altruism towards the Jewish people, but a political undertaking aimed at turning the sympathies of Russian and American Jews (many of them neutral or even pro-German) towards the Allies. It was needed moreover as a preemptive coup in view of a possible pro-Zionist declaration from Germany... The German government, though hobbled by their alliance with Turkey, was known to be searching for a pro-Jewish formula.

Moreover, even Jabotinsky after his long struggle, parallel to that of Weizmann, had already achieved British acceptance of his plan for a Jewish Legion to fight for the liberation of Palestine from the Turks. Why, Aaronsohn agonized — why the delay?

Wingate, fully aware of what the Nili organization had already wrought, at what price and in face of what dangers, took seriously Aaronsohn's suspicion that in the end the service and the sacrifice might well be in vain, that Nili's reward might be not the redemption of Palestine or even the recognition of Nili as an ally, but some form of lip-service, or some personal medal to some member or members. What, then, would prevent Aaron from taking a desperate step — taking his comrades and followers out of danger and thus dismantling British intelligence behind the Turkish lines in Palestine and beyond?

Wingate, after all, was not merely an official servant of His Majesty. He had a vision — of the dismantling of the Turkish Empire — which he had defined earlier in the war: to build a confederation of Arab states, under the tutelage — yes, most importantly under the tutelage of Great Britain. First, however, the Turks must be defeated. At this moment, the approximate zone of battle for that consummation was the Palestine campaign. Most immediately it was the capture of Beersheba and Gaza — by the strategy evolved by Aaronsohn; and that strategy hinged on the crucial intelligence provided exclusively by Nili. Needless to add, according to the philosophy of the "Easterners" school, it was through victory over Turkey that the road would lie open to victory in Europe.

At this moment, with the battle for Gaza lying still some weeks ahead — it was planned for October 31 — nobody could be sure of victory. Indeed the German commander, General Kress von Kressenstein, did not immediately swallow the strategic bait being prepared for him by the British; he waffled for a while. He might still spring a surprise by strengthening Beersheba, and the outcome of Gaza Three might be the same as Gaza One and Gaza Two. Who, in that case, could tell that, if even Gaza remained unconquered, the Nili contribution would continue in all its vitality to further operations as it had done in the past?

Wingate, it so happens, knew from Graham that already in July the Zionists in London had been given a general undertaking by the government. But nobody placed much value on general declarations. Indeed Wingate himself, referring to that general declaration, wrote to Graham:

> I gather however...that the matter is by no means decided and that you wish me to keep Aaronsohn satisfied without telling him anything very definite. This has been done, though it would of course be convenient both to him and to myself to know rather more clearly how we stand...[4]

It was consequently with a sense of great relief that he learned from Graham towards the end of August that a final text for a declaration was close. Indeed the Zionists in London believed that finality would be reached at a Cabinet meeting on September 3. A further delay did follow but, like most of the obstacles in those months, it emanated from the vigorous and virulent opposition of Jews — Jewish assimilationists. They fought tooth and nail against the very concept of a Jewish nation. They claimed there was no such thing, only a Jewish religion, and they regarded with undisguised horror the notion that they personally might be treated as anything but true-blue "Englishmen of the Jewish faith" — described by a percipient Christian wag

---

4. PRO/FO 371/3983/5359, July 23, 1917.

as "Englishmen of the Jewish face." However, for all the harm they were doing through a vigorous and unscrupulous representative inside the British Cabinet — Edwin Montagu, the secretary for India — the die was cast. A pro-Zionist declaration was to be issued on November 2.

Aaron's meeting with Wingate on September 2 was most friendly. Wingate reminded him that, after all, Britain did not yet have Palestine in her hands — but she would support Zionist aspirations energetically. In a special gesture in anticipation of Aaron's visit to London, he volunteered the information that he had decided to correct a wrong impression about Aaron that might exist in London. Lest they assume that Aaronsohn was just a thinker but not a "doer," "we have taken the trouble," he said, "to provide the Foreign Office at length with the information on the service provided by Mr. Aaronsohn to the military section, and we are convinced that he is capable not only of planning but also of execution."

Aaronsohn, heartened by the conversation, was congratulated two days later by Deedes on the impression he had made on Wingate. Deedes, himself an outspoken man, said he had described Aaron to Wingate "as a man who hated compromises, a fellow who crossed his t's and dotted his i's."

Aaronsohn's euphoria was somewhat dimmed that day by a visit from Gluskin who came, as he said, "to have a little chat." He seemed to want to apologize for withholding the document about which Aaronsohn had been so angry. He himself, he confessed, did not understand politics or diplomacy, so he had misunderstood the document's purpose; and he would gladly return it. Beyond that, he wanted to make clear that Aaronsohn was wrong in attributing to him any underhand or hostile intention. He revealed that he had had a letter from London reporting that the Weizmann committee were "very appreciative of Aaronsohn's work," but insisted that he should co-opt "experienced veterans like Gluskin"!

Aaron however did not allow their dispute or the rather silly message from London to lessen his willingness to help Gluskin, if he could, in solving his personal business problem. Three days later he urged Deedes to agree to the transfer of Gluskin's business money together with the relief funds, even though this would constitute "trading with the enemy." Deedes brought the request to Clayton — but Clayton, two days later, turned it down for fear of creating a precedent.

Suarez, a few days later, had better luck. After all, however, the money he had raised was not private like Gluskin's but was intended for the evacuees' relief. This time he did not apply for a permit to transfer. He simply asked Wingate whether the authorities would handle the transfer for him. On Aaronsohn's advice Deedes informed Suarez that the British authorities would certainly fulfill this request — at the first opportunity. Aaronsohn insisted that his "special committee," which, after all, was the only channel through which Deedes would keep his promise, should not be mentioned lest Suarez be distressed.

There followed a hectic week for Aaronsohn; it was eased by a valuable gift — a British passport, its validity albeit limited to "one journey only." It was issued "on special instructions from H.M. High Commissioner in Egypt." Almost simultaneously he was cheered by the news that a carrier pigeon from Zichron had arrived — one of seven dispatched — though the message it brought was not important.

Aaron had for a long time feared that a British military success would trigger a further evacuation by Djemal of Jews northward along the coast, and so he now repeated to Deedes his request that in that eventuality, the people at Zichron and Athlit be taken off by sea, out of the reach of the Turks. Deedes acquiesced, but referred him to General Clayton to work out details — of organization, size of groups, how many people in each group. He also discussed with Clayton a plan of his for the agricultural development of Palestine under a postwar British administration, one of several of his ideas for the flowering of the Jewish state-to-come.

He had been told by General Headquarters that Alex sailed from London on August 27, but the boat, which reached Port Said on September 10, arrived without him. He consequently introduced Pascal formally to Edmonds to represent him temporarily; other matters, beyond Edmonds' sphere, he passed on to Deedes — evoking signs of resentment from Edmonds — a sign that the British "family" conflict had not abated.

Somewhat uneasy about Alex's non-arrival, he nevertheless hoped that when the *Kaiser-i-Hind*, with him aboard, sailed on September 13 from Port Said, he would meet Alex at Valetta in Malta where the next boat from London would have to put in. That miracle actually occurred. Soon after the *Kaiser-i-Hind* anchored in Valetta harbor, a smaller boat came sailing in, and "impertinently" — as Aaron described the scene in his letter to Rivka — anchored ahead of the *Kaiser*. It was no easy matter to get permission to visit the other boat — but when he did, sure enough, there was Alex on the deck.

They had not seen each other for two and a half years. They now talked through the night, so that Alex had a complete picture of Aaron's nine months in Egypt. Now, Alex in Cairo would be able to replace him in dealing with the British officers and officials, and handle with Liova and Rafael whatever reports would be coming from Athlit.

It was in his letter to Rivka that Aaron described the meeting with Alex. His diary had gone silent on the eve of his departure from Egypt, and he did not resume writing for more than two months. What has survived relating to the period before his arrival in London is some correspondence with Henrietta Szold, and it contains a rarely intimate look into the heart and mind of that remarkable woman on the sensitive question of "Jewish spies."

For a long time there had been no correspondence of a personal nature between them. Through her he had sent several requests for money from the station's trustees; she after all was the secretary (though unpaid) of the trustees' committee. Most of his requests, usually telegraphed, had remained unanswered, or had been followed by a statement in the name of the committee that Aaron must satisfy them about the exact use to which the money would be put. In one case he had suddenly received five thousand dollars. All this she had done as part of her duties.

In a letter in a personal vein written to Aaron in Egypt (on May 5) she had expressed deep annoyance at the fact that Judge Julian Mack (and later Alex) had not taken her into the confidence of Aaron's "confession" from Copenhagen.[5]

Now that she knew the truth, however — and Aaron had expressed the hope that his course had her approval — she conveyed a friendly, warmhearted but philosophically precise song of praise, not for what he was doing but for the personality of the man who was doing it. Conscious of the way

5. See chapter 7 above.

some of her colleagues on the trustees' committee (notably the wealthy members) had in effect turned their backs on him, she wrote:

> Happy the man who, in these circumstances, may act, and act in accordance with his convictions. His personality remains whole, one and undivided, no matter what may happen to him otherwise, no matter what this one or that one of his friends may think, no matter what the issue may be. And that is the way the personality of some individual has triumphed in the midst of turmoil, and has been saved in spite of every disrupting sacrifice it has made....
>
> Have I made you understand that what you have done and are doing is way above approval? To most of us who know you, it is just you, the you whom we need and prize according to your great ability to meet our need. Unfortunately we — some of us at least — have not had it in our power to give you support in your need. So much the worse for us. Do you understand now? What I feel and what I should like to tell you, goes way beyond approval — has nothing to do with approval. And I believe I am expressing, however haltingly, the sentiments of your closest friends over here....
>
> Only one thing more — do as you must, your friends remain your friends.

Her letter was addressed "Dear Mr. Aaronsohn."

Four months later (September 8), after she had meantime received personal letters from Aaron, she addressed him as "My dear friend."

Here she conveyed a little more enlightenment about his American friends. She painted a balanced picture. It seems that the one charge against him that they all still shared was that he had neglected his duties at the station, to which he was committed by their agreement. Beyond that, only one of them — Julius Rosenwald — remained so angry with Aaron that it was no use talking to him — so much so that she had withheld an admonitory letter Aaron had sent her to pass on to him. He had asked her to read it before passing it on to Rosenwald — who was even intending to resign as a trustee. She emphasized however that Magnes and Mack and Frankfurter remained his friends.

Reverting to herself in her letter, she complains again that his friends, as well as Alex and his brother Sam who had been staying in America, do not understand her.

> They, misunderstanding my nature, will represent it as my colorlessness. At all events, they will make you understand that my attitude towards the great catastrophe [Avshalom's death] does not coincide with yours. But I wonder whether they will tell you that though my brain works differently, my heart responds to your actions with a sympathy as keen as admiration for your powers, and devotion to the end you have in view, can make it. My feelings are somewhat like Rivka's — I envy those who are winning their souls by losing them. I wrote to you before of the happy individuals whose personality remains whole in these tumultuous times. You will properly infer now that I do not enjoy this happiness. My spiritual struggles have perhaps been as acute as yours. I feel as though I were now living my sturm und drang period, and, to quote myself as you have quoted me in one of your August letters, after forty — one should have "arrived," materially and spiritually as well. Storm and stress when one is gray-haired is unproductive. Little action can be expected to follow from such spiritual struggles.
>
> I really did not intend the excursus on myself to be so lengthy. It was entered into only to make you understand…that my heart comprehends and admires and appreciates what my brain could not originate. That indicates in another way a divided personality, which in this case at least has the advantage of being able to extend the hand of fellowship and the word of encouragement to you across seas and across differences of opinion.

It was perhaps in consequence of this letter that Aaronsohn wrote her on October 5 — this time from London. Though remaining true to the warmth of their correspondence, he had a bitter message for the trustees in America. The work of the experiment station had continued throughout nearly three years of war with its wartime restrictions and the ever-hovering dangers from the Turkish authorities. Reports up to July 1917 had been sent to the trustees.

He found their behavior reprehensible. Though the work of the station had been hampered by the war conditions, and some of the personnel had indeed left, those who remained were employees of the trustees' committee and stayed at their posts, out of devotion to the institution and out of Jewish self-respect; they did not deserve being left to starve. There were of course, as Henrietta had pointed out, two views on Aaronsohn's own absence from Athlit — but this did not absolve them of their human obligation to the workers at the station. If it were argued that it was illegal to send money (because of the blockade), "I have destroyed the pretext." The British authorities had lifted that corner of the blockade, at his request.

In London, he revealed to her, a suggestion had that very morning been made that he proceed on an important mission to the United States. But he would not travel to the United States, where he would be expected to meet the trustees of the station, if they persisted in their attitude. "Rather than break with them," he wrote, "I prefer not to have to meet them again." Indeed he appealed to her to "sound out the ground" and telegraph him, as this would probably determine whether he would accept the mission.

He had reached London only on October 1, and there, as he confided to Miss Szold, a most disagreeable confrontation awaited him with the Zionist leaders.

CHAPTER 15

Weizmann's
London Political Committee

A less propitious moment for Aaronsohn's encounter with Weizmann's Zionist Political Committee in London can hardly be imagined. Interestingly enough it was a senior Foreign Office official, George Kidston, who wrote a concise summary of Aaron's problems in a minute on an internal office report. "Mr. Aaronsohn," he wrote,

> would appear to profess Zionism in its extreme form and to be in difficulties with the Jews in Palestine and in Egypt as well as with the Committee here. The internal feuds in Jewry are too complicated for the mere Gentile to follow, but there is little doubt that there are very highly placed Jews here who would be glad to wreck his Palestine schemes and the London Committee may not be altogether immune from this influence.[1]

Aaronsohn himself could not know that during the weeks before his arrival a long-simmering dispute with Weizmann's committee had come to a head. The issue was the Jewish Legion.

In Weizmann's negotiations with the British government at its top level — Prime Minister Lloyd George and Foreign Secretary Arthur James Balfour — he enjoyed generally the full support of the members of his committee. Their very presence on the committee signified readiness to contribute to victory for Britain and her allies. They were thus perpetrating a clear violation of the

---

1. FO document, handwritten comment.

neutrality decided upon by the World Zionist leadership operating from neutral Denmark.

There was one member of the committee, effectively Weizmann's deputy, Nahum Sokolow, who held an official position in the world Zionist hierarchy. He was an elected member of the Smaller Actions Committee, the inter-Congress legislative body of the World Zionist Organization, and he had secured the consent of its vice-chairman, Yehiel Tchlenov, for the obviously dissident conduct of the Political Committee in London.

It would surely seem then that propaganda for a Jewish Legion to help Britain was a natural corollary of the Political Committee's own raison d'être. Yet its members, with two or three exceptions, had balked at the very notion and confronted its every manifestation with a fierce hostility. Weizmann himself was a strong supporter of the campaign for the Legion, and had indeed cooperated with Jabotinsky from the very outset in early 1915 — though always from behind the scenes. When he founded the Political Committee he maintained the secret. By this time, however, the nucleus of the legion had already been created and, at the same time, Weizmann's own negotiations for a pro-Zionist declaration were well advanced.

A concatenation of circumstances in the summer made it clear that Weizmann's involvement with Jabotinsky could be kept secret no longer.[2] His angered colleagues urged him to issue a statement that while he personally was in favor of a legion, the Zionist Organization as a whole was neutral. Weizmann's response stunned the committee: he announced his resignation. Without the legion, he declared, he could not negotiate with the British.

The committee members had evidently not grasped that the relationship Weizmann and Jabotinsky were trying to forge with the British was founded in a perceived mutual interest. Enabling Jews to fight as Jews to liberate Palestine — and issuing a declaration in favor of Zionist aspirations — would surely bring about a surge of support for hard-pressed Britain in the influential Jewish communities in the United States and in Russia.

Over and above this reasoning, there was the potential moral effect in Britain itself of Jews fighting, and fighting in a Jewish unit. Already in the spring Lloyd George had pointed out to Weizmann: "It would have the most unfortunate effect on public opinion in regard to the Jewish demands on

2. See my *Lone Wolf*, vol. 1, pp. 314-19.

Palestine if it turned out that they were not prepared to fight for it." And Weizmann could not forbear replying: "They will fight, and they will fight well!"

Present at that meeting with the prime minister was Charles P. Scott, the legendary editor of the *Manchester Guardian*.[3] Weizmann, more in sorrow than in anger, penned a bitter comment on the dispute within his committee — a comment that went to the very root of the "Jewish problem." Only thirteen years had passed since the death of Herzl and twenty years since he had startled the Jewish people, and the world, with his revolutionary proposal for a Jewish national state; and it seems that its implications had yet to be completely assimilated into the Jewish consciousness. It manifestly called not only for a territorial solution to the Jewish problem, and not only for the essential reworking of the structure of Jewish society, but for a transformation of the Jewish soul, the honing of the sense of national will, an urge to master fate and, not least, putting an end to the submissiveness engendered by centuries of life in a hostile environment. What the war with Turkey had done was to illuminate the immediacy of the need for that transformation.

There is an element of the near-miraculous in the fact that in three separate fields of endeavor which were needed at that historic moment a leader had emerged who stood out to meet the challenge.

They were almost exact contemporaries: Weizmann in mid-1917 was forty-two, Aaronsohn was forty-one, Jabotinsky thirty-six. On August 21, Weizmann wrote to Shmuel Tolkowsky, a member of the Political Committee who had long and vigorously opposed the legion idea and its progenitor:[4]

> Believe me, dear friend, that the "Jewish Legion" is only a specific instance emerging from the spiritual state and mood of our Zionists, and of the nation as a whole. After three years of very hard work I must admit that we have all the time been working for an anonymous people, which is not yet ready to give support to the great struggle that will be essential for creating the Jewish national society. The war came too soon for us.

---

3. Charles Prestwich Scott, *The Political Diaries of C. P. Scott, 1911-1928*, ed. Trevor Wilson (London: Collins, 1970), April 3, 1917.
4. Chaim Weizmann, *The Letters and Papers of Chaim Weizmann*, ed. Meyer W. Weisgal (London: Oxford University Press, 1968-1979), vol. 7, no. 481.

Weizmann did finally withdraw his resignation from the committee. He did try to cool the dispute by claiming, untruthfully, that he had not discussed the legion with the British. Events however were moving fast, the infant legion was growing — and its opponents were ineluctably falling into line.

Even while the legion crisis was at its height, however, the Political Committee was startled by another intolerable discovery. Not only was this man Jabotinsky planning in London for Jewish boys to become Jewish soldiers, but that man Aaron Aaronsohn in Palestine had already turned a number of Jewish boys — and girls, heaven forfend — into spies. It was however, in all fairness, long before they learnt of this awesome fact, that Aaronsohn's name had become anathema to most of them. The origin of this emotion was within his own Palestine community. He had very few well-wishers among its leaders. Over the years before the war he had succeeded in quarreling with, or alienating, some of the leading members of the community and, no less, some of the prominent Zionist personalities abroad.

He had a sense, only too well grounded, of intellectual superiority, and a unique record of important scientific achievements, but he did not wear these crowns lightly. He displayed towards most of the Palestine personalities a manner abrasive and contemptuous. In private agricultural projects in which he had engaged before the war, sometimes as advisor, sometimes as participant, he had been accused of being high-handed and overbearing. He had a dispute, over his fees for services rendered, with Dr. Arthur Ruppin, the agronomist head of the Palestine Office of the World Zionist Organization, whom he managed to insult (though in fact he respected him).

Perhaps most hurtful to his name had been his treatment of Dr. Hillel Joffe, whom he passed over for the head of the Health Bureau funded by Nathan Strauss. There, on the face of it, his decision was justified professionally; but his brusque rejection of appeals on behalf of the highly esteemed Dr. Joffe — notably that of Russian Zionist leader Yehiel Tchlenov — earned him enemies throughout the Zionist establishment. Even some of his close friends, like the warmhearted, understanding Dr. Naftali Weitz, were cooled for a while.[5] And after war broke out what excuse could there be for his humiliating outburst against the group of communal leaders who turned to

5. See chapter 5 above.

him for advice in their hope of meeting Djemal Pasha and trying to influence him to alleviate his behavior towards the Jewish community?[6]

Over the years these impressions lingered. It is consequently not to be wondered at that when the Political Committee was informed of the dispute between him and Gluskin and the action taken by Weizmann and Sokolow, they lined up against him at once. Weizmann was not present at the meeting (on August 11, 1917) where Sokolow made it clear that it was only the fact that Aaronsohn was held in high esteem by Sir Mark Sykes, an esteem which, as he said, "we do not share," that he and his colleagues were prepared to deal with Aaronsohn at all. It was now that Sokolow revealed that a letter had arrived weeks earlier from Gluskin "complaining about certain activities of Aaronsohn, something that reinforces our attitude. It seems that he is engaged in certain activities connected with intelligence services."[7]

Aaronsohn's reaction to Gluskin's behavior during the brief period of their cooperation is thus shown to be justified. It was no secret, after all, that he was in constant touch with British General Headquarters. It was also no secret that the British aim was to liberate Palestine from the Turks. Examining the dates, it must have been in July already that Gluskin had become aware of the special element of "intelligence" in Aaronsohn's cooperation with the British military, and he at once rushed to tell on him in writing. Sokolow's revelation also throws light on Gluskin's visit in pretended friendship to Aaron that took place in late August, long after he had sent his complaint to Sokolow.

Not irrelevant in this context is an earlier incident involving Gluskin in Egypt. In December 1914 when the first appeal was made (by Jabotinsky and Trumpeldor) for volunteers to serve in the British army, fifty-five-year-old Gluskin rushed forward insisting that precisely his signature should head the list of volunteers for military service which was to be submitted to the British General Maxwell!

As for the horror expressed by most of the members of the Zionist Political Committee in London — all sophisticated men of the world — at the idea of a Jew being a "spy" — there is a rational explanation. The Jewish Diaspora after all had no military tradition, and there the term *spy* bore the pejorative

---

6. See chapter 6 above.
7. Tolkowsky, *Yoman Tsiyoni medini*.

connotation of "informer." It had nothing to do with military affairs. It related to the behavior of traitors who, spying on their fellow Jews, informed on them — whether guilty or innocent of some misdemeanor — to the Gentile authorities. Certainly Sokolow and most of his colleagues without much thought simply borrowed this traditional attitude, and applied it to Aaronsohn.

Moreover, suffering as they were from complete ignorance, the committee members engaged in some cynical speculation on Aaronsohn's proposed use of the money. Indeed it was only two months later, after Aaronsohn had arrived in London, that the whole issue of the relief money was cleared up. Sokolow then, in Aaronsohn's presence, told the committee that "the situation is slightly different from what we assumed." Aaronsohn, he said, was "not the problem." The problem lay with the British, who had laid out seven thousand pounds sterling, which had to be repaid.[8]

In fact, Aaronsohn in his letters of August 15 and 25, which had reached Weizmann in the first half of September, had conveyed the gist of the story of Nili and his own activities. Arriving himself in London on October 1, he immediately had a conversation of several hours with Weizmann, who was thus now substantially enlightened on Aaronsohn's tremendous contribution and the unique role of Nili in the campaign for the liberation of Palestine.

Thus at long last came an official Zionist expression of recognition and admiration. On October 6 Weizmann sent a telegram to Alex, deputizing for Aaron in Egypt.[9]

> We are doing our utmost to secure a Jewish Palestine under British auspices. Your heroic sufferings are greatest incentive of our difficult work. Our hopes are great. Chazak Ve-ematz until Eretz Israel liberated. Weizmann.

Those were the final weeks before the long-awaited declaration, which Balfour issued on November 2. At his meeting with Weizmann — the debate

---

8. The account of the proceedings of Weizmann's Political Committee is from the diary of Shmuel Tolkowsky (a member of the committee), *Yoman Tsiyoni medini.*
9. Weizmann, *Letters and Papers,* vol. 7, no. 515.

in the government over the text was still in progress — Aaron agreed, in effect, to join Weizmann's "team," pressing for an adequate undertaking towards the Jewish people. Aaronsohn, then, spent much time with the friends he had made in the British establishment — notably the voluble Mark Sykes (officially deputy secretary of the War Cabinet); Walter Harold Gribbon and his chief, General MacDonogh, the Director of Military Intelligence; and Ormsby-Gore, now on Lloyd George's intimate secretariat — and only Weizmann knew that each of these important British officials had been brought around to enthusiastic support for the Zionist cause by Aaron Aaronsohn.

Thus the "few days" he had expected to spend in England turned into weeks. Then the Balfour Declaration came, bringing with it the imperative of new Zionist endeavor, to help the British government reap the fruits of its pro-Zionist policy. The weeks seemed to be turning into months; and still Aaron knew nothing of the devastating events that had convulsed the Jews of Palestine after he had left Egypt. He did not know — and throughout his stay in London he did not learn — that on the very day he reached London Nili had been destroyed; and Sarah was dead.

CHAPTER 16

Sarah — The Leader of Nili

The first knell of Nili's doom had sounded on the day that Avshalom Feinberg died. The shadow of the tragedy that hung over the group can be traced as it grew and spread day by day until eight months later when October dawned and the Turkish blows descended. Yet it was precisely in those excruciating months that Nili made its major contribution to British victory in the campaign for the liberation of Palestine from Ottoman rule.

Sarah learned of Avshalom's death only at the beginning of March. The news was brought to her by Yosef Lishansky, who arrived at Athlit on the *Managem*'s first successful voyage. In his report to Aaron, Yosef did not hide how, in abysmal agony of spirit, he had for several days postponed the telling. He and Sarah hardly knew each other; he had not been a member of the group. He had visited Athlit once, or perhaps twice, as a friend of Avshalom's, and he might, or might not, have exchanged a few words with her, but nothing more. It was as a friend, indeed a close friend, of Avshalom's that after Avshalom's arrest in 1915 he sweated to achieve his transfer from the Beersheba prison to the less dangerous Jerusalem jail — and from there to freedom. It was as a close friend that Avshalom had asked him to accompany him to the Sinai desert — from the outset a most hazardous venture. But it was as an almost complete stranger to Sarah that he now had to tell her of the unspeakable tragedy in her life — and the part he had played in it.

When he told her all that had happened in the desert, the reaction he might have expected did not come. Sarah did not weep. Sarah was strong, he wrote to Aaron. Certainly she kept her tears for her solitary moments with herself. Even in the letter she then wrote to her own brother-and-mentor there were no tears.

As it happened, she had prepared a letter for sending to Aaron before

Lishansky's arrival, together with a pile of intelligence material. There she
admitted that she would like to visit Aaron in Egypt, and to see how
Avshalom (to whom she refers affectionately as "our crazy") was getting on.
Yet, in manifest foreboding she asked Aaron to persuade Avshalom himself to
write her "a few lines." Now, after Lishansky's revelation, she wrote:

> Enclosed here you'll find the letter I wrote when I still knew nothing;
> today I already know about our horrible disaster. But it is with a brave
> heart, filled with feelings of revenge that I want to continue his work.
> The disaster is too overwhelming to make comfort possible. But with
> courage God will let us live so that we may carry on. Nobody else
> here knows…

In a letter a few weeks later she bursts out, not in tears, but in fierce, even cold,
determination:

> It's hard for me to put down on paper what I feel…. It's terrible, terri-
> ble and there's no comfort. But I must tell you: I'm stronger than iron
> and very cool. I would never have believed that I could find such
> strength in myself. There are times when I feel as though I'm dead or
> a worthless vessel; for how is it possible that I'm able to restrain
> myself in the face of such an awful sacrifice? Maybe it's the work
> allotted to me, the debt I owe: to continue the work our dear one
> began. Yes, I want only to continue. And revenge.

It was only four months later, on July 14, 1917, that Sarah wrote about
Avshalom to Rivka and Alex for the first time. "Even if we succeed in our
work and the redemption of Israel will have been achieved by such a sacrifice," she wrote, "I would not wish for the sacrifice. However much we talk
and however many tears we shed our hearts will not be lightened…. But why
should I pour salt on the wound. You, Rivka, are miserable and suffering
more than any of us…."

She added words surely designed to give some comfort to Rivka:[1]

---

1. An examination of the dates suggests that Aaron had written to Magnes very much
earlier of Avshalom's death — with the idea that he should personally tell Rivka and
Alex. Magnes evidently misunderstood, and it was only early in May that the news
reached them from Henrietta Szold. Then Rivka wrote to Aaron and he replied in a
detailed letter on June 25. Sarah's letter was evidently a follow-up to Aaron's.

You have no idea how far your loved one and I became close to each other.... I was the only to whom he could come to pour out his heart, his thoughts and his hopes, and I helped him very much. I encouraged him and raised his spirits. My suffering is great.... But to whom can we complain? Our work, which continues, will always be a memorial named after our dear founder, Avshalom...

Forced on her was the understanding that the mantle of leadership had fallen on her shoulders. It was when it became clear that Aaron was not coming back, and would not be able to come back before the British army, nerve-wrackingly tardy, liberated the country. The letter Yosef Lishansky had brought from Aaron informed her, in due formality, that Yosef was to be her deputy. In it Aaron had listed what range and quantity of intelligence the British lacked, and what Aaron thought they needed in addition. It had to do with heavy arms; with identification of Turkish army units and their bases at the front; with units on their way to, or being withdrawn from, the front, and which trains were going where — through Affula and Ramle, and Dera'a across the Jordan, and Damascus in Syria. And never, never, must she omit to devote a page in her report to the state of the Jewish community.

Lishansky from the first moment demonstrated how suited he was to the task Aaron had assigned to him. Sarah soon assured herself that he was intelligent and practical-minded. Indubitably his previous organizational experience in Hashomer and Hamagen stood him in good stead. In a letter to Aaron written days after Yosef's arrival (March 6, 1917) she wrote: "As far as work is concerned, rest assured that everything will be done properly. Tuvion [the code name for Yosef] is a hard worker, brave and optimistic.... I try to help him as much as possible." Nor was he ever troubled by his status as deputy to a woman; and Sarah in a later letter assured Aaron that Lishansky "does not make a move without consulting me." In this respect an absolute bond of mutual trust was established between them.

Henceforth her decisions were made in consultation with Yosef — sometimes on his advice or even at his initiative, sometimes in disagreement. There was never any doubt: she was the natural leader — Lishansky was not alone in his grasp of this truth. Recognition of Sarah's rare quality had long lodged in the hearts and minds of the men and women, all of them her own age, who had been serving and suffering with her in the long months of wait-ing.

Throughout those months Sarah had been a frequent watcher on the dark moonless nights when several members went down to the shore — to carry supplies, brought on the *Managem* for the Community Relief Fund. A vignette by Menashe Bronstein, also a regular participant in the vigils, recalled many years later a particular night when he and another young man had accompanied Sarah.

It was about midnight when one of them on the shore, looking out to the east, espied lights at the station, which should not at that hour have been lit up. Clearly something had happened, and so "we all thought that we must find out what it was, and that somebody must go back to the station."

"My companion and I waited for Sarah to give one of us the order to do so. The order was not given. We only heard Sarah say, as though speaking to herself: 'You'll stay here, I'm going' and she was about to start off."

The distance was about three kilometers and the terrain was uneven and wild, rocks abounded, and hillocks and trees and bushes were everywhere. Every shadow might be an Arab villager out on some nocturnal mission, such as searching for an animal missing from the flock or the herd. The area was cut through by the Doustra Wadi (a dry riverbed) and by the road to Haifa, where one might encounter a Turkish military patrol.

> I couldn't agree to anything of the sort [recalled Bronstein] — to let her go alone on a pitch-black night on such a dangerous venture, most dangerous for a woman, and a woman alone! I started talking to her, explaining and describing the dangers from several angles. Here were two men; one of them could and should do the job. At least — at least! — if Sarah must go, one of us should go with her for reasons of security. All in vain! Sarah rejected the idea and said, in the tones of a commanding officer: 'I'm going alone. You must wait for the boat.'
>
> Nothing helped. Sarah left us and went. Our eyes followed her until the darkness enveloped her....
>
> Sarah often took upon herself responsible and dangerous tasks.
> Fears she dismissed with contempt, and dangerous tasks she

chose to carry out herself. That night as always. That was what her conscience told her. Such was Sarah![2]

When Lishansky took over the operational work of Nili he forbade Sarah, surely on Aaron's instructions, to participate in the vigils on the shore; but — as she revealed in a letter to Liova — she would take advantage of his absences from Athlit to steal down with the others. There was a touch of the tomboy in Sarah.

But there were limits. It was surely one of those nights that Yehuda Zeldin, another frequent participant in the vigils, described in a memoir. The ship had brought carrier pigeons and gold. Zeldin threw a bag of the coins over his shoulder and, with help from Aboulafia who had come on the ship, carried the cage with the birds. Sarah carried a second bag of coins. Halfway to the station it proved to be too much for her and poor Zeldin had to manage the second bag as well.[3]

When she took over the leadership Sarah had lost no time in preparing a program of action. Nasser Raghem, the Aaronsohn's veteran driver (and a member of Nili) harnessed the horse to the station carriage, and Sarah with Yosef went out on their first tour to brief the Nili agents throughout the country. Some of them did not know Yosef; all of them had to be told that he was henceforth the man in charge of the daily operations, appointed by Aaron. Subsequently he could do the rounds himself, collecting reports and conveying instructions. Of all the Nili members, his being seen traveling all around the country drew the least attention. Traveling was part of the work he had been doing for Hashomer and then for his own Hamagen. He was as ubiquitous as any commercial traveler.

They were able on this tour to bring the long-awaited tidings that the connection with the British in Egypt had been firmly reestablished, and that Aaron was in Cairo working with them. Intelligence reports delivered to

2. From the memorial volume *Yosef, ish Nili: Aharit davar* [Yosef, a man of Nili: An epilogue], ed. Yosef Nedava (Jerusalem: Agudat Hashmonai, Merkaz le-hinukh ule-tarbut, 1986).
3. Livneh, Nedava and Efrati, *Nili*, p. 167.

Sarah or Yosef would be sent by the boat, and after evaluation by Aaron would reach the British General Headquarters. Requirements of the British would be transmitted by Aaron to Athlit. With their sense of mission refreshed, the men and women of Nili went to work.

It was on this tour that Sarah achieved a scoop of great importance. At Affula she succeeded in enlisting Moshe Neiman, the medical officer in the Turkish army who was to perform wonders in reporting on the movement of trains, of arms and men, to and from the Turks' Beersheba-Gaza front, and who, with his large quiver of languages,[4] established friendly relations with a host of talkative Turkish and German officers — and with British prisoners-of-war. From that tour Nili made another significant gain.

A friend of Yosef's from his days in Hashomer, Yitzhak Rosenberg, had been appointed the mukhtar (headman) of the Jewish community in Haifa. On their arrival in the town, Yosef called on him, and they spoke without reserve about Nili. To Aaron he reported that Rosenberg "offered me his services in our work, as much as I would ask of him and as much as he could perform." Rosenberg's authority seems to have included that of a notary public. He could issue a certificate for a release from military service, for employment of a civilian worker by the army, for attestation of citizenship of a foreign nation. But it was even more important for Nili at the time simply to have Rosenberg as a friend, for he was a member of the executive committee of Hashomer.[5]

Yosef did not have to reveal the secret of Nili's existence to Rosenberg. It had already been the subject of discussion in Hashomer and elsewhere in the Zionist establishment. Rosenberg was not the only member harboring sympathy for Nili, but he was manifestly in a small minority. The dominant element in the movement had already become extremely hostile to Nili. Two of its leaders, Yisrael Giladi and Shmuel Hafter, demanded action from the community to "root out the evil." They noted signs of support for Nili among their own members, whom they warned consequently not to come into contact with the Aaronsohn-Feinberg group. Moreover a public warning, though worded cautiously, was published in a resolution by the executive

---

4. Apart from Hebrew, Yiddish and Arabic — English, French, Turkish and German.
5. Livneh, Nedava and Efrati, *Nili*, p. 176.

committee of the Labor movement — which contained many members of Hashomer — in its organ *Hapoel Hatza'ir*:

> Our realistic policy in the present situation is one of absolute civic loyalty, and any action outside of these limits must be seen as an attack on the existence of the community.[6]

Another encounter, in itself less notable, yet casting light on the elusive element of personality, took place during that tour of Nili's field of operation. At Na'aman Belkind's house at Rishon Lezion Na'aman introduced twenty-three-year-old Avshalom Fein to Sarah, and Fein was overwhelmed. "I was trembling," he wrote. "I saw a blonde woman, pretty, tall, gentle. Belkind introduced me as 'one of the boys prepared to make sacrifices. He can be depended upon.' She answered with a sweet smile: 'Good, we'll made him work hard.'"

Writing to Aaron some days after his arrival in the country, Lishansky referred to the rumors circulating in the community. Each person had his own speculation about the group; but its work, he wrote, was proceeding in orderly fashion, "and we do not fear betrayal to the authorities."

It was in this spirit that Sarah, later in March, accepted Aaron's invitation to visit Egypt. She did not however take the first opportunity of doing so. She insisted on an assurance by Aaron that after fifteen days she would be enabled to return home. It was thus that only on April 19 was Aaron able to record in his diary his welcoming her at Port Said. "Sarah," he wrote, "is pale and weak."

She traveled to Egypt with mixed feelings. Her mood was gloomy to start with. For good reason: she was deeply in love with a man who, she believed, loved her no longer and now even regarded her with a jaundiced eye. When the *Kosseir* sailed from Larnaca in Cyprus[7] she started writing a letter to Liova Schneierson, who was on the boat.

She went on writing — that is, she wrote, then tore up, began again and

6. Quoted in *Sefer toldot ha-haganah* [A history of the Haganah], vol. 3, *Mi ma'avak le-milhama* [From struggle to war], ed. Yehuda Slutzky (Tel Aviv: Am Oved, 1978), vol. 1, p. 365.
7. EMSIB headquarters were at Famagusta in Cyprus. Sometimes the *Managem* would call at a Cyprus port before returning to Port Said.

tore up (as is a habit not exclusive to girls in love) until she reached a final text.

She gave frank expression to her feelings in the very first sentence: "I think of you all the time." She did add flippantly — "from nine o'clock after breakfast"; but the burden of her letter is a desperate effort to understand — and at the same time to interpret — the change in his attitude to her. After all, when Liova had come from Constantinople in the winter they had spent many, many hours, sometimes whole days together at Athlit or Hadera. What had they talked about all those hours? There were enough problems and issues related to Nili but, evidently in shared felicity, they had also lighted on a subject of more personal interest: themselves.

Liova, who loved Russian romantic literature, himself wrote poetry, and on his arrival from Port Said at Athlit on the morning of April 16 he had given her a little notebook containing a poem (or maybe more than one). She recalls in her letter that it was precisely that day at Athlit that she sensed a change in his attitude. She had read the notebook, she would "think about it, and read it again and a second and maybe a third time, because I want to understand you well, the reasons for your finding in me such despair and disillusion; and why you have decided not to tell me about your own agonizing, everything, as you used to do. On every page you mention that I don't understand you."

Here she provides the most self-revealing part of her letter. "You know very well that I understand you thoroughly, and there are not many who understand you as I do. However, if you've made up your mind, so be it. Maybe one day you'll admit your mistake. My feeling is that we are fated to understand one another."

This, however, is not the end of the argument. She goes on to a more significant analysis:

> It is not in my nature to boast.... I"m forever criticizing myself...and I don't like to listen to others singing my praises. But lately I've learned that I must appreciate myself and put "myself" in its rightful place.
>
> Liova, I understand many things and sense and feel even more, but God has not given me the writer's talent of finding the right expressions. That is why many beautiful things and thoughts are

buried deep in the recesses of my heart — and nobody knows and nobody understands. Not many are left of those who did understand. The dearest one, who understood, is no longer with us... But you, Liova — there was a time when you did understand me, when you poured out your heart and read me your writings — surely a sign that I understood you and was worthy...

Now suddenly you've become a different person. I assure you: you are to blame, not I. For the "me" you saw, for what you saw in me in the first moments, has remained the same. It's only your poetic spirit, your broad and lonely soul.... You have wandered far away, distancing yourself from me, rising ever upward, and now from the heights you look down on me and see me small.

You loved me for my greatness of spirit, and built towers and poems about me — and they are all buildings in the air. That's why they soon came to an end. That is what always happens. And I warned you.

For I am strong. I have a clear and simple mind. I don't get excited about anything, and that is why the flame is not speedily extinguished. I regarded you coolly, and what I was able to understand I drew out of you.

That's how I've remained with the same view of you to this day. Now, my friend, look at yourself, see how you have forgotten everything. You built everything on fantasies and visions. I am alive; you need dreams in the air, you need beautiful girls, pure as crystal, as you imagine them and who don't exist anywhere in the whole world, and you won't find them. The world is one big lie. You may be happy in your world but I, sad to say, must live with life as it is...

Liova's own laconic diary account of their meeting, when he had arrived late at night, reinforces this conclusion:

Here's the station. Light in the windows. On the veranda I see Yosef! Sarah! And Sarah comes running down the steps — and a warm meeting with kisses and embraces, etc., etc.

The next day, however, when Sarah continued her letter, her mood had changed drastically. Liova had handed her a letter, but she had been seasick and in bed most of the day, and so had not read it. Now, overnight, she did read it and "I searched for the lines of your song of hatred" — the hatred she thought she had seen in his eyes — "and I was surprised. I didn't find what I was looking for."

She is shaken. "Liova," she writes, "I sensed that you had been overtaken by melancholy — and then I realized that I am to blame, that it was I who brought it about." She does not explain this self-accusation; presumably all she had written the day before was a mistake. But she concludes her letter with a sudden cry. "Understand me, Liova. Why has God cursed me, why do I see everything in black?"

It is pretty certain that she did not show this letter to Liova. But the sources of her agony remained.

How could she not be melancholy? A catalog of her experience sounds devastating. Five years earlier, when she was twenty-one, her mother had died suddenly; and her sorrow had been compounded by the household responsibilities then thrust upon her. Her marriage was undertaken in order to open the way for Rivka to get married, but the move to the alien and unlovable Constantinople was a stifling daily ordeal. War broke out, and its constraints deepened her sense of isolation from her family and her homeland. Then she was shocked to learn that Rivka, for whom she had made the sacrifice, was going off to America with brother Alex. Whatever the reason for that decision, it did not change the fact that Rivka was still not married and Heaven alone knew when and where she and Avshalom would meet again. Sarah could not even contemplate Rivka's marrying anyone else.

Sarah had freed herself from the daily sorrows of her existence in Constantinople, but not of its legal bonds. She came home. And now she remained Mrs. Haim Avraham, her well-loved sister was thousands of kilometers away, brother Alex was there too; and brother Aaron, whom she worshiped, was with her only for a while. However, she plunged into the great patriotic adventure in which Avshalom and Aaron were engaged. When Aaron left on his odyssey, she helped Avshalom whom she loved as a brother and who, working with her, lightened her burden tremendously. Then he went — and was lost forever. Now she was in love, the path of love was not smooth, and even if it turned out to be requited love, she was still Mrs. Avraham, and Rivka was still unmarried…

Imagining this recurring cycle of introspection, who would not be overcharged with melancholy? Why indeed did God so load her with tribulation after tribulation?

When they arrived in Egypt, Sarah and Liova behaved like two normally good friends. Liova mentions in his diary several long conversations between them — though not a word about their contents. Indeed throughout his diary (published many years later), Liova never once gives any indication of anything between them more than friendship; not a word about love letters, of poems. It is not conceivable that this romantic soul did not confide in his diary. Mentions of Sarah in his diary were surely edited out later. Not a single one of his letters to her survives. Sarah probably burned them.

There was another very serious reason for Sarah's gloom on the voyage. She writes, also in that letter from Larnaca: "We are approaching Port Said. My heart is beating, beating strongly, for who knows what awaits me there?... I have a feeling that something unpleasant is about to happen between us and Aaron." She well knew the reason: it had to do with Lishansky. He had not been invited, indeed had been asked not to come but to take charge of Nili affairs during Sarah's absence; but he came nevertheless.

To Liova he explained that he simply must go to Egypt: there were things that he alone could give to Aaron. Liova argued with him, but to his surprise Sarah sided with Yosef; and he was left with no option but to acquiesce, to let Yosef come on board. There was nobody to whom to give the money he had brought for the general relief fund of the community; so he had to take it back to Egypt with him.

Sarah's dilemma is clear. Of her own volition she would not have proposed Yosef's leaving Athlit even for the two or three weeks she expected to be absent. She realized the potential dangers in leaving Athlit without leadership. But the moment Yosef proposed, and insisted, and demanded — his whole problem came alive. She had conveyed to Aaron high praise of Yosef's efficiency, his diligence and his devotion to the cause, and how easy it was to work with him. She could not forget his courage in answering Avshalom's call to join him in his dangerous venture in the desert. But she knew very well of the hatred which his erstwhile comrades in Hashomer had disseminated against him in the community, and how he had become a stalking-horse for their fierce opposition to the Nili venture. To none of this was he impervious, and it was too much to demand, against his will, that he be left alone to face what might befall as a result. For Sarah had learnt his life history, and at such moments she saw before her the child who had remained orphaned and abandoned. Maybe she did not quite find words for it, but for all his ability and his courage, it was she who was sustaining him, the maternal shield and comforter.

She had then to choose between two evils — facing Aaron's wrath on the one hand, and a severe reaction by Yosef if he stayed behind at Athlit — a situation which might seriously affect his work and their cooperation in the future. She must have seen this as the greater evil.

She could not foresee the degree of Aaron's anger when he found that Yosef had arrived, nor the depths of Yosef's misery at the tongue-lashing he had suffered from Aaron. Did she not say to Yosef Alhadeff who witnessed their quarrel in the Cairo hotel: "I don't know what's come over him."

Egypt was not a happy springtime for Sarah. The emotion-laden reunion with Aaron was scarred at once by Aaron's outburst at Yosef for having left his post at Athlit. Aaron's diary does not record any reaction from Sarah to his attack. Obviously an explanation was due from her as well — but understandably she would wish to talk to Aaron in private. There she would be able to illumine the sensitivity of Yosef's case — precisely because she understood the complexity of this inherently strong character who was so dependent on her psychologically.

It turned out that there was something she did not understand. From Yosef's conversation with Alhadeff after his quarrel with Aaron it emerged that he was haunted by fear — the fear that because of the atmosphere created about him by his former Hashomer comrades, he would be caught by the Turks. Hence his announcement that he would not be returning to Athlit. And Sarah cried out: "I don't know what's happened to him." She evidently had never heard him speak of fear.

It is likely that the reason — or one reason — for his soon reversing himself was his realization of the plight he would be forcing upon Sarah if she was left alone to face all the dangers. Certainly from that moment his loyalty to her and to Aaron never faltered. True, Sarah did retain at the back of her mind the possibility of another breakdown (she hints at it in a later letter to

Aaron), but the reality of Yosef's dedication and devotion, of her solicitude and their mutual trust was maintained to the end.

With the Lishansky crisis behind them, Cairo could have been a tolerable place for two or three weeks, but no more. There is a fine snapshot of a fashionably dressed Sarah walking down a Cairo street, perhaps on a shopping excursion, flanked by Liova and Yosef. Part of the irksomeness of her stay was surely lightened by the attention of the two cavaliers and, needless to say, by the several long talks tête-à-tête with Liova which solidified the close relationship between them. Then there was Aaron, albeit busy at intelligence headquarters, contributing to her relaxation and entertainment — the theatre, a museum, a lecture. Sarah recalls a social evening in Alexandria with a crowd of friends and acquaintances from Palestine. It was pleasant; "Nobody," she wrote, "asked any questions. They no doubt understand that there is something."

She did not like Cairo, however, just as she had not liked Oriental Constantinople. But then she did not like cities at all. She was a farmer's daughter after all, and she was a part of the open spaces, of the land with its seasons, just as they were a part of her, as with her father and her big brother.

The enforced visit to Cyprus, when the *Managem* was unable to anchor at Athlit, did little to assuage her frustrations. She had reckoned on being absent from Athlit in the period between two voyages of *Managem* — theoretically about three weeks; but she and Yosef were absent almost two months.

In the end, indeed long before the end, her health was undermined. She fell ill again and again. The references to her bouts do not indicate what the troubles were except for a bout of malaria in Cyprus. What is certain is that when she landed at Athlit late in June, she was pale and wan. She had been told in Cairo by Naftali Weitz, who had been her doctor ever since childhood, that she must rest and not engage in any activity.

This, from Weitz, who knew what her "activities" were, was a serious, indeed, unpalatable, instruction. She, however, went straight back to work. Indeed at her very landing at Athlit — as she reports proudly to Cairo — she helped the welcoming group carry the luggage and the numerous parcels to the station. And after a couple of weeks she was restored to perfect health.

She brought back from Cairo however a disquieting revelation. Shortly before her return, Rafael Aboulafia sent her a note: Pnina Levontin had received from her friend Rivka Aaronsohn a letter telling the story of how Avshalom Feinberg had tried to reach the British lines in Sinai and had been killed by Bedouin.[8]

---

8. It seems that Pnina — no doubt warned by Aboulafia — did not disseminate what she had heard from Rivka.

CHAPTER 17

The Pigeon Errant and the Blunder Human

Again Sarah lost no time in getting down to work. Activities, though reduced, had not ceased during her absence and a quantity of intelligence material had piled up. She went to Dr. Neiman, who was now stationed at Ramle, and he presented her with a many-faceted report for the previous several weeks. From the end of May onwards there had been a lively movement — of troops, big guns, explosives and food — to the front in the south. There were also marching units — apparently the Turks were suffering from a shortage of automobiles and railway engines.

"They say," wrote Neiman, "that all the soldiers on the Caucasus front are being sent to Palestine." One day six railcars of explosives went down to Gaza, and when they arrived there every railway official was awarded fifteen pounds in appreciation of the speedy execution of the operation. In that period, too, some of the Turkish bigwigs had passed through — also on their way to the front: Djemal, Falkenhayn, the great Enver himself and others whose names Neiman did not know. A regiment of Austrian infantry had passed through. They were tired of the war and despaired of enjoying an early peace.

The health of the soldiers was generally good, except for a high proportion of sufferers from sexual diseases. Neiman was impressed with the Turks' system of medical examination and reporting. Every trainload of passengers passing through was examined at four centers: Dera'a (across the Jordan), Ramle, Affula and Wadi-Sarar.

British airplanes had carried out two attacks at Ramle and Tulkarm (where sixty people were injured at a wedding). There were three air bases at

Ramle — one outside the town limits with fifteen planes, of which only six were serviceable; a second was on the Jerusalem road, near the railway, with twenty planes. A third was at Jaffa, but he had not yet discovered exactly where. The planes were guarded by units of Turkish infantry.

The German air contingent numbered two hundred fifty, of whom one hundred twenty had syphilis. But they were well paid and well fed.

A German officer, of course in strict confidentiality, had revealed a special secret to Neiman. A certain German private soldier, working day and night, had earned promotion to colonel, because of remarkable work he had done breaking the keys to the English codes. The English now had no secrets from the Germans — who now knew everything! The English (the officer said) had better find for their codes a language the Germans did not know. Neiman, tongue in check, added in his report: "They should try Hebrew."[1]

This and much more was Sarah able to send on the *Managem's* next voyage. She added a brief report of her own, of a British air raid on Tulkarm which had followed information supplied by Nili. She went to Tulkarm later that day to see for herself what damage had been done and found a number of craters in an open field.

Nili's workforce was on track doing its job for the British, but within days of her return from Egypt with Lishansky she discovered that in the quality of their lives there had been a great deterioration: "Our people, our helpers and our families are consumed with fear; they would like to see us already gone from here."

The change in spirit had not come about through any action by the Turks; it reflected the pressures of the community. After her and Lishansky's departure for Egypt the Zichron Ya'akov community council, acting together with the Hadera council, had called her brother Zvi and questioned him. "He must tell them," Sarah quoted, "what we are up to, and where, and whither we had disappeared. They claimed that (in any case) they knew everything, and they could not consent to play with the fate of the whole Jewish community."

What had inevitably made things worse was the long absence of Sarah and Yosef, the absence week after week that was inexplicable to everybody. This affected the Nili people no less than the community at large, where one

---

1. The gullible German officer was naturally unaware of the tremendous British successes in the opposite direction. See Tuchman, *The Zimmermann Telegram.*

rumor had it that they had "run away." Neither Zvi nor anybody else could answer these questions. Everybody was talking about them in the streets, wrote Sarah on June 25, "even infants in their cradles." The fear grew that word of all this would reach the government.

Indeed, she warned Liova that the local community leaders had their eye on three of them — Liova, Lishansky and Nissan Rothman, Avshalom's friend, whose regular job was as steward on the Feinberg farm. Rothman had just gotten engaged to Tova Gelber, Sarah's bosom friend, when the Hadera community council ordered him out of the town. As for Liova himself, she believed he was threatened by specific dangers from both Turks and the Hadera council, and she warned him that he must not enter the country when next he came on the *Managem*. She forbade it! As his task at Athlit was to pick up the intelligence reports, he could receive them all on the boat.

In her letter to Liova she explained further: "We ourselves have not yet settled down; we are watched by a thousand eyes. Every step of ours is followed, and we don't know what's going to happen to us. In a few weeks' time if all is quiet, Liovka, then 'Welcome!'" Forbidding Liova to visit her at the station, and Aaron's veto on her coming down to the shore to meet the *Managem*, thus cut her off completely from him. They could send notes to each other whenever the boat came but that was small comfort — and she had learned that discipline was discipline.

Precisely now however it became possible to hope for improvement in relations with the community. A new fact had materialized: money. Sarah and Liova had brought gold for the relief fund of the Jaffa evacuees, and Yosef had gone to Haifa, met Meir Dizengoff and handed him the bags of coins. It was not unreasonable to expect that as soon as it became known that Nili, through British cooperation, was providing the communal leaders with the means to carry out their most important task — of sustaining the thousands of Jews, homeless and helpless, whom Djemal had driven out of Jaffa-Tel Aviv — those leaders would seriously reconsider their attitude.

Three weeks passed before *Managem* came to Athlit again. There was not much information waiting for dispatch to Cairo, but what there was, was manifestly of tremendous importance. It was in those weeks that Na'aman Belkind put together (on July 3) his comprehensive and masterful report. It was surely the single most important intelligence dispatch received at General Headquarters up to that crucial point in the Palestine campaign.

What was no less important than its detailed description of Turkish and German dispositions in the south, was that the report demonstrated to the newly arrived Commander-in-Chief Allenby the unique caliber of this small group of dedicated Jews. There can hardly be any doubt that that first report, giving Aaron the basic data to reinforce the advice he was to give Allenby and his staff, for breaking the deadlock at Gaza, opened Allenby's mind to the strategy with which he was to win the battle. Not least significant in the history of Nili was the manner — free-and-easy with the officers at the nearby base — in which Belkind acquired his information.

Together with the intelligence report Sarah wrote a letter (July 14), which reflected more shadows than light. In the first place circumstances in the field had changed, making Nili's work more difficult. New Turkish regulations provided for travel passes in the north. More serious was the impending retirement of Dr. Neiman after his stint at Ramle; and Sarah was still struggling to accommodate Neiman's successor at Affula.

It was not likely that her tactic of opening a canteen at the Affula railway station could produce as rich a harvest as the inimitable bedside manner of Neiman; but Sokolovitz, who took Neiman's place as the chief agent at Affula, had gained investigative experience working for Nili in the north of the country; and, provided by Sarah with an assistant, he did produce results. The problems were irksome, but Sarah kept her cool; she assured Aaron that they would be solved.

She had other more oppressive concerns. The hostility to Nili in the community did indeed cool, but its impact had sharpened; it had become organized, and now Sarah was not only subjected to criticism, but was faced by demands.

Hashomer representatives had joined the communal leaders and, it appeared, had forged a united front against Nili. Yitzhak Rosenberg was their messenger. Their central demand was to "dismiss" Lishansky. Their grounds were blatantly presumptuous: he was, they claimed, suspected by the Turks — and therefore dangerous; he could not possibly be efficient because he had no experience as an organizer. He must leave the country. Let him go to Egypt. They, then, would appoint a successor.

Sarah, in her letter to Aaron, expressed the belief that the motivation for the demand was naked envy. They saw that Yosef, for whom the Hashomer people harbored a visceral hatred, was now playing an important role, working with Aaron himself in his relations with the mighty British Empire. Also he must be doing well: see how well dressed he was.

Be that as it may, the authors of that demand did not grasp how absurd and transparent it was. If, as they claimed, Nili's very existence was placing the whole Yishuv in mortal danger, how could they propose a candidate of their own for leadership in the organization except as a Trojan horse to bring about its termination? Their purpose then was obvious: to render Nili innocuous. With Yosef gone Sarah would be thwarted and hindered at every turn until she was paralyzed completely. Her immediate reply to Rosenberg was that, as he knew, the leader was Aaronsohn, and she would convey a report for Aaron to decide.

To her report of this conversation she added a renewed and very positive appraisal of Yosef: his personal loyalty, his dedication, his diligence. But she asked for a formal reply and, again, a letter from Aaron direct to Yosef, which could be shown to prove that Yosef was working strictly according to orders from Aaron.

She had another urgent request. Aaron must also write to their father and Zvi to calm them down. They were making her life a misery. They were a conductor of all the fears and phobias of the village.

They identified themselves at once with Hashomer's demand for the removal of Yosef, whom Zvi, through envy and overall resentment, had grown to hate. Indeed Zvi, at best an irascible man, bore a heavy load of grievance. It was a load that had grown ever since Aaron and Alex with Avshalom had decided in 1915, without consulting him, to launch the intelligence group. It had grown when Aaron, about to leave on his long journey in 1916, had appointed Sarah — and not Zvi — to work with Avshalom. Then Avshalom disappeared — and Sarah still refrained from consulting him. His resentment reached boiling point when Sarah and Yosef went to Egypt, leaving him in charge of the station but excluding him once more from the direction of Nili. It exploded now in strange conjunction with the concentrated attack by the communal council.

There were fierce quarrels whenever they met at the family home in Zichron. Zvi raved and ranted, demanding that Nili desist from its activities. "They are terrified of the slightest triviality, a falling leaf frightens them," wrote Sarah. "Some Jew has said such-and-such and they are panic-stricken:

the work, they say, must be stopped at once and we must bury ourselves alive without delay."

But she concludes: "Of course we must listen and thus understand what must be done" — and consequently she had turned down all the demands to stop the work by a simple "No!" "Let them talk, the work will go on; and they will get used to the idea that that is how it's going to be."

An enraged Zvi however lost control of himself, and shouted that they must let him go to Egypt or he would "show them," and he would interfere with their work.

He followed up with two specific demands in a letter to Aaron: that both Sarah and Lishansky should be removed from Palestine and he, Zvi, should take over the leadership of Nili. He now openly accused Lishansky of having murdered Avshalom, in order to take over the Nili leadership; and he plucked out of the air a love affair between Sarah and Avshalom, with Lishansky in the role of the jealous supplanter in Sarah's affections.

Yosef himself wrote a frankly unhappy letter to Aaron: "I am suffering very much from your family, that is from Zvi. You'd be amazed at what he's saying about me. I don't reply to his curses and pretend not to understand.... Believe me, I"m sick to death. If it were not for your sister who, in her great wisdom, knows how to quieten them and to influence your father, more or less, I would run away to the ends of the earth. Do please write to your father that it is your wish that Sarah and I should be in charge of the work...and tell him that he should make friends with me."

Aaron did write to the old man in this spirit, but Zvi did not desist from his slanders against Yosef. On the contrary, he evidently repeated them in the community; and again Sarah was asked the same questions by their close associates: "Where is Avshalom? If he's alive, why doesn't he write? If he's dead, why don't you tell us?" And Na'aman Belkind was becoming more and more agitated — and suggesting that he be enabled to go to Egypt to find out.

In desperation Sarah and Yosef suggested to Aaron that he fabricate a letter, as though coming from Avshalom in London (where, they had been telling people, Avshalom was training to be an air pilot). He should explain that he (in the guise of Avshalom) had to write in English because of censorship; and that he would soon be returning to Egypt to join the front there. Aaronsohn replied patiently (August 3) that he could not do as they asked.

He could not even imitate Avshi's handwriting, and the whole idea was blasphemous. He added:

> Please, Sarah, not this, my dear. If you can't help yourself, tell the truth, the whole bitter truth. You will understand me, Sarah, and don't be angry. In many ways I am a woman, as you, my dear, are in many ways a man, a strong man, whom we can be proud of.

Sarah, replying on August 23, admitted it was wrong to have made such a suggestion; but she declined to act on Aaron's permission. If she were to tell the truth to the family and others close to Avshalom — and they constituted the core of the group — it was possible that they might leave Nili in despair. The whole community would soon learn, and the leaders would find in it new ammunition for vilifying the whole Nili venture. Not to be forgotten is the fact that there was considerable doubt in the community about Britain's ability to liberate the country. British failure to attack from the sea had from the start sown such doubts; and how could the two defeats at Gaza not strengthen misgivings? Add to all that the sacrifice, for the sake of the British, of the young, widely beloved Avshalom... There was no alternative: the secret had to be kept.

The community leaders came back to the attack. On June 19 the chairman of the Zichron Ya'akov council, Albert Alter (whose son-in-law, Reuven Schwartz, a cousin to the Aaronsohns, was an active member of Nili) came to Sarah and Yosef in the name of several village councils. Now the demand for Yosef's leaving the country was modified slightly. He could stay in the country but keep away from Zichron Ya'akov, and give up his work for Nili.

Yosef's answer was "Nothing doing!"[2] Whereupon Alter threatened that they would send "their people" into Athlit and prevent the work physically.

"At this," wrote Sarah to Aaron two days later, "we both burst out laughing. Yosef said, 'You're talking nonsense. Can you interfere in a private business, especially as Athlit doesn't belong to Mr. Aaronsohn, still less to me? The station at Athlit is American. If the government couldn't take it, how do you think you will?'" Alter however had an answer: "We'll take it by force in the name of the whole community."

---

2. Sarah, in her report to Aaron, rendered the reply in Yiddish vernacular: "Nain mit a spodek!"

In cooler tones Alter raised a more persuasive argument. Who had given them the right to do this work? Did they have the agreement of the leading Zionists abroad? Did those leaders at least know what was going on?

Sarah could of course have explained that underground or revolutionary movements most often conducted their struggles despite or even against established authority, though there was usually a grassroots element in their genesis and their growth.

Indeed precisely at this time Nili's grassroots element had increased perceptibly: there were many indications of sympathy particularly among the youth. A philosophical reply from Sarah to Alter's questions however was not likely to appease the honest agonizing of the local leaders. What was more, she believed that Aaron should be able to obtain statements of approval from prominent leading Zionists in London; and so she and Yosef agreed to a compromise.

Yosef would not appear in Zichron. This was not a difficult undertaking, for Yosef spent practically all his time at Athlit anyhow, and he and Sarah had decided that Sarah would live most of the time at Athlit. Second, they would give Alter a reply in forty days' time.

"What will happen," Alter asked, "if you won't be able to give it to us? Will you then stop work?"

"Why should we talk now," Sarah replied, "about what will happen in forty days' time?"

Appealing to Aaron for a reply, she suggested that he might approach Gluskin! Even a letter from Gluskin would satisfy them. There were other signatures too that would be adequate: veteran Zichronite Dr. Weitz, for example. And, she asked, what about Dr. Weizmann?

Meantime, however, another kind of gesture had come from the community. There existed a "political committee," headed by Dizengoff, which enjoyed a sort of recognition by the Turks. On the 4th of July, Yitzhak Rosenberg had come from a meeting of the political committee with a letter for Aaronsohn. It was couched in fraternal terms — of one group of Jews working for the Jewish people to another with the same objective at a critical stage in the nation's history. It proposed that Nili (the name was not spelt out) should enable the committee to send two representatives to meet with him and his colleagues in Egypt. "They might, together with you, survey the situation and discuss what cannot be put in writing, and they should bring to us, who are cut off from the whole world, the views of the Jewish nation, so that we should know what we have to do. Failing this, we shall be unable to decide on our future steps."

The letter added that their emissaries would discuss the issues that needed clarification, and would be able (through Nili) to establish frequent contact with Zionists abroad. Rosenberg had said that they hoped their emissaries would be able to go to the United States to attend a projected Jewish congress. The letter was initialled by Yitzhak Rosenberg and Mendel Hankin on behalf of their principals: Dr. Yaakov Thon, Bezalel Joffe,[3] Meir Dizengoff and the manager of the Anglo-Palestine Bank, Eliezer Hoofien.[4]

There was, however, an addendum conveyed by Rosenberg by word of mouth. The idea of the committee was that their emissaries — Rosenberg himself and Hankin, a member of a most respected family in the country — would be accompanied by Yosef to Cairo. There, after learning the nature of Nili's work — provided that they approved of it — they would return and replace Yosef, who would remain in Cairo. Rosenberg urged once more that Yosef had to be dispensed with because he was too well known to be able to engage in illegal activities in the country.

Yosef was not overwhelmed by the proposal or by the prominent personalities behind it. His criticism was pertinent and demonstrated a keen sense of protocol. If these people were really serious, he argued, they would send to Egypt a national personality like Dizengoff. He was a man capable of grasping all the implications of what Aaron and Nili were doing and the role they were playing in the British plans for the obviously impending offensive. But, Yosef pointed out, they did not propose to send Dizengoff. Why not? Because it was not intended by the committee that Dizengoff should be the one to replace him. Their replacement would be a Hashomer person — who would then proceed to destroy Nili from within.

Fearing that Aaron, out of euphoria at the idea of a peaceful solution, might accept the conditions, Yosef (who would, as he wrote to Aaron, obey

3. Not Dr. Hillel Joffe.
4. See Livneh, Nedava and Efrati, *Nili*, pp. 180–81.

orders) urged an alternative reply which, while not rejecting the plan, would prevent interference. Aaron should reveal what it was safe to reveal about Cairo and about Athlit. As for establishing contact with America, that could be achieved by their handing letters in at Athlit that would be forwarded to Cairo for dispatch.

Sarah, for her part, pleased though she was at the turn of events, rejected any notion of a drastic change at Athlit. Her message to Aaron was unequivocal: to drive out Yosef was unthinkable.

Aaron's reaction, when he received Yosef's letter informing him of the proposal, was diametrically different from that of Yosef. He was delighted. Here he was being asked by the leaders of the community — most of whom were but yesterday identified with the treatment of Nili as a dangerous pariah — to negotiate, to confer, to reach an agreement, to find a way to cooperation. Whatever the outcome might be, this was a tremendous victory for Nili, a vindication of the concept, and of the methods for its implementation, that he and his colleagues had laid down in the spring of 1915. In his diary he wrote on July 26: "Today I can say that the mission I imposed on myself has prospered."

He made his assessment clear in the reply he sent to Yosef. He saw the prospect of a broadened program of action, in the name — in practice — of the whole Jewish community. The signature of two members of the committee (Dizengoff and Thon, who ran the Zionist representative office in Jaffa) gave Aaron additional assurance of the seriousness of the act of recognition of Nili.

He urged Yosef to put aside his fears and suspicions of the Hashomer people who, it was true, had embittered his life. Instead he could take pride in the achievement. People like Dr. Thon, who had cursed and incited against them and called them crazy, were now forced to confess their error by jumping on the bandwagon.

"Nobody," he wrote, "will be able to rob us of the spiritual joy that we on our own, with our own strength, did what had to be done, and others could not and did not do. True, we must know whom to encourage and from whom to keep our distance, but on no account should we pelt them with stones."

What was more, it did not matter to the nation whose name would be commended for Nili's activities.

"And if you will say, this is undue modesty — on the contrary, with me it comes from arrogance. I see myself and all my helpers as lighting a candle from which others light a second candle. It can happen that the second candle shines more brightly, but our light will not thereby be diminished."

Aaron, having dismissed Yosef's objections and suspicions, did not lose sight of the enormity of the demand to oust Yosef and put a Hashomer member in his place. Indeed he reiterated (in his letter to Sarah on August 3) how much agony they and Yosef had suffered before they had gotten used to each other. "How can we tell what kind of person his replacement would be?" In any case he would be a man totally inexperienced in this kind of work. "To go the way of nihilism, to destroy without building — No! Do reassure Yosef on this score. Any troubles he encounters in his work, and how to defend him, will be my concern. That is [the duty of] a chief."

The aura of leadership which surrounded Sarah was described graphically by Aaron in his letter (of September 17) to Rivka from the ship carrying him to London: "Without her we have no leader."

Learning from Sarah that the local Zichron committee did not accept the new relationship to which the national political committee was agreeing, he urged Sarah to go as far as possible in appeasing them, even giving them a larger share of the money. He also proposed however, that Sarah, if need be, should hint at a threat. She and Yosef had been told that a list of one hundred alleged supporters of Nili had been drawn up to be submitted to the Turkish authorities if a crisis arose. She should make it clear, wrote Aaron, that if such a list was prepared, another list could also be drawn up. (Aaron should have understood, as he probably did, that the Zichron committee would not dare to submit such a list. Whoever did so would be the first to be tortured and hanged by the Turks — for not submitting it earlier.) "Sarah," he wrote, "would know how to make the threat." Recalling that their mother had been a most outspoken person, he added, "You after all, have inherited our mother's qualities."[5]

In the midst of the turn of events that promised at least tolerable relations

---

5. Quoted in Alexander Aaronsohn's *Sarah, shalhevet Nili* [Sarah, the flame of Nili] (Jerusalem, 1943).

with the community, Sarah took the time to attend, with some outside help, to long-neglected chores in Aaron's rooms in the family grounds. "We have begun to rearrange the herbarium and the general library..." She assured Aaron that all those books, as well as those in his personal library, would be returned to their proper places.

It was not that she had much free time. On the contrary, as she explained to Aaron, "Since my return [from Egypt], I've worked hard and it's good I came back when I did. I'm busy all the time. I don't notice the time passing and that's better than brooding and recalling our great disaster. Without all this, I wouldn't exist."

Yet in replying once more to Aaron's renewed urging that she go to Egypt, she wrote — surprisingly:

> It is really difficult for me to decide to leave. I shall wait a while. We'll see how the work progresses. We are waiting for your advice and replies to a number of our questions. If the voyage were really short — to meet and return — I would willingly go, kiss you and come back.
>
> But I know what delays may occur. I have had the experience, and I know how difficult it was to untie all the knots you tied around me.

Clearly she did not dismiss the idea outright. She explained what seemed now to be the prime obstacle to her leaving Athlit. She described her role there, and — certainly unwittingly — she was describing the role of a leader. "I really would be very much missed. I help to maintain the relations among all of them. I cannot do otherwise. I am fortunate in that they all believe in me. Maybe they are mistaken, but that's how it is."

To these relations there was of course one serious exception: Zvi. Indeed contacts with him had been broken off completely. She informed Aaron that she had stopped talking to him. He had written her a horribly insulting letter.

Aaron's response (on August 3) was fiercely sympathetic. "I am not surprised. I long ago distanced him from my work because I could not rely on him. But I never dreamed that he would be so foolish as to torure you so cruelly."

He confirmed to Sarah that he had asked Efraim Fishel again to take Zvi seriously to task and warn him to put a stop to his behavior "if he wants us ever again to talk to him in peace." Zvi's whole life, he wrote, "is not worth to me one drop of your pure blood."

The *Managem* came on August 14 with Liova aboard, and he brought with him Aaron's reply to the political committee. It was very positive. He welcomed the proposal of a meeting with two emissaries, and hoped that they would be representative personalities who could speak in the name of the whole community. Arranging the meetings however would take a while until formal, technical and other difficulties were ironed out.

Yosef dutifully passed this reply on to Rosenberg, and added, as he reported to Aaron, that "we would gladly let them participate, and any tasks that they can carry out we shall gladly assign to them." At the same time he impressed on Aaron that he was not happy with Aaron's evident welcoming of the Hashomer members.

> Who knows them as I do — I who invested most of my life and my energies with them? I don't oppose letting them participate in the work — but only when all the youngsters in Zichron are allowed to. I know them well. They want everything to be credited to them. This wouldn't bother me…but I'm afraid of the demoralization they'll bring into our ranks with their "principles." We do need more manpower, but this I can find among the youth of the country with whom I'm sure we won't fail.[6]

Yosef knew something about Hashomer that Aaron was not aware of, but which was widely recognized in the community. "Hashomer is too old to create something new," he wrote. "Our youngsters, who up to now have done nothing [for the nation] are more easily influenced and this is where our salvation will come from."

He and Sarah had in fact begun looking for new blood among the youngsters; and indeed several groups had come to them competing with each other. "We shall reject nobody," he wrote. "On the contrary, we shall accept each one, but under our organization and our discipline." In practice, they were more cautious. Sarah wrote to Aaron that you could not just pluck

---

6. Yosef Lishansky to Aaron Aaronsohn, August 15, 1917. Quoted in *Yosef Lishansky, Ish Nili: Ketavim mikhtavim divre zikhronot* [Yosef Lishanky, a man of Nili: Writings, letters and memorials], ed. Yosef Nedava (Tel Aviv, 1977).

anybody out of his present occupation without arousing attention. A feasible solution would have to be found in every individual case. However, with thought and care, she claimed, this could be achieved.

Sarah wrote Aaron on August 23 a long letter which reflected a measure of tranquilization in her mood. She opened with an amused rendering of a telegram and a letter she had received from — of all people — her husband, Haim Avraham. He had moved from Germany where he had spent nearly two years and was now living in the Hague in Holland, whence it was apparently easier to communicate with Constantinople. He informed her that he had donated one thousand German marks for the Jaffa deportees, and to her he was sending a gift of twenty pounds sterling. If necessary, he wrote, she could use five for the Zichron community.

> What do you say to his generosity? she asked. How it amused me. If the poor man knew how many thousands of pounds pass through my hands, and how many thousands of francs I spend, what would he say? He also…writes that he has lost a lot of weight in the latest German fashion. He works hard and suffers from our being separated. He tells me how much he would like us to meet again; he has a lot of work to do and I would be able to help at night by [doing some] writing for him, etc.
>
> I am surprised at him, a man who has had a German education, and moreover has spent two years in Germany…. The man will maybe save money, and when the time comes to enjoy it, he won't have the strength and the youthfulness. What do you think?

Learning with glee from Aaron's letter of the satisfactory end of his showdown with Captain Smith, whom he had taken down a peg or two, she recalled Smith's belittlement of the Nili workers which had brought the conflict with him to a head.

> I should like to see him in our situation…. If only he knew our roads, to see me from a distance through his binoculars riding in a carriage from Petah Tikva to Rishon Lezion in the burning heat, and the wheel breaking; our tying it with ropes till reaching Zichron…. What would he say then? Would he then still say we were being lazy?… Then after a journey of twenty-four hours there and back, [and we]

not in good condition, for there are no rest-rooms in the hotels at the best of times and certainly not now, and when we reach the hotel to drink barley water instead of tea, and all this at terrible prices — a journey from Zichron to Rishon costs no less than sixty francs, apart from the mule and the carter...

"But," Sarah interrupted herself in her diatribe, "my intention is not, heaven forfend, to complain that the work is too difficult or to ask for a raise in wages...."

> For two weeks we ran around in Haifa trying to get a vasika [travel pass] to Constantinople only to find that even if we were to cover the Turks in gold, it's impossible to get a pass for a man, so we had to give the task to women; believe me, trips to Constantinople in our trains are not very interesting. To show you how responsive and devoted everyone is — here you have Shoshana [Wilbushevitz] who is no Sarah, a fancy dresser, and not strong physically[7] — and she brought us reports from Constantinople, and she'll be going back there. If we need this once again, believe me I would be the first to go, and so would they all.

"Even in your time things were hard, now they're worse and," suddenly Sarah, momentarily forgetting Smith, adjusts her sights and feistily directs a little dig at Aaron and his co-workers in Egypt, "if you'd begin to understand this...you wouldn't be nagging us about expenses or occasional delays in our reports."

Aaron, in the comparatively luxurious conditions of life and travel and work in the Savoy Hotel in Cairo, did apparently sometimes forget his own experience of Turkish backwardness and its daily hardships and frustration.

Now she took Aaron to task for sending gifts of groceries which materialized as a huge nuisance by the time they reached Athlit.

Menashe Bronstein had to carry the heavy parcels off the *Managem* onto the rowboat, and then across the three kilometers of hard going in order to discover a complete mess at the station. Chocolates were ground to dust and

---

7. Shoshana (sister to Avshalom Feinberg) was about ten years older than Sarah. She was the wife of Nahum Wilbushevitz, a senior engineer in the service of the government, and privy to information most useful for the coming Syrian phase of the British campaign.

mixed in with Sunlight soap (a British brand), safety matches were damp, sugar and salt mixed together, candy amidst broken glass. Sarah scolded:

> Please — and it's not pleasant to complain — please send us only what we ask for. And please — send arms. We lack arms in the country. The office [of the community] has been sending emissaries from city to city, from village to village, to buy arms. Obviously for organizing defense…. Bronstein wouldn't object at all if you sent arms even it it were to leave him with a humpback….

In this wide-ranging letter, she raises another troublesome subject. She is ever conscious of Yosef's troubles, and she is worried about his two children, Ivriah aged six and Tuvia aged two. What would happen to them if they were orphaned? She had been talking to insurance agent Avraham Ludvipol about them. "Why should Yosef's children suffer because their father was a great idealist, who gave his head and his body and everything else…"

The promise of a smooth passage for inaugurating friendly relations with the community was not fulfilled. It was precisely at this juncture that Aaron had come to the conclusion that he must hasten to London to straighten out the relationship with Weizmann — which should include recognition of Nili. This would automatically repair the schism within the community in Palestine. He expected (so he wrote to Sarah) to be absent no longer than four or five weeks, and the delay in the projected meeting with the committee's emissaries would be worthwhile for both sides.

Now obstacles had arisen in the community as well. There had been no consensus as to who the emissaries to Egypt should be. Dizengoff, who was a unanimous choice, declined because — contrary to Yosef's suspicions — he feared his absence would be noticed by the Turks. Several names were discussed, until finally the choice fell on Rosenberg. But this was not all. Probably at the prompting of the Hashomer members, a new train of thought had begun to move the committee. On September 3 two members, Avraham Ludvipol and Mendel Hankin, acting for Dizengoff, had brought a message to Yosef. They thought, reported Yosef, that Aaron had (wrongly) taken the right to work in his own name. They wanted to know in whose name the work was being carried out and what other personalities were working with Aaron.

Further, they calculated that as part of the money from abroad was allocated to Nili, the rest should be placed in a sealed envelope (in Egypt) and delivered unopened to the committee.

Yosef, again restraining himself, told them that all these demands could be met, but he made a condition. The method of sending messengers was not the best way for negotiating. The committee must agree to arrange a meeting face-to-face. Maybe there Dizengoff would be able to come with a cut-and-dried proposal for Aaron's meeting with Rosenberg and the other emissary. Ludvipol and Hankin promised that the committee would be holding another meeting on September 8 and then would give Sarah and Yosef a final reply. Yosef declared that he would travel to Haifa the next day, there meet Dizengoff, and thrash out the whole issue.

He did not see Dizengoff the next day. He did set out for Haifa, but on the way he was stopped by an agitated, indeed panic-stricken Rosenberg, who begged him to destroy every document in which he and other communal personalities were mentioned. That day the whole edifice of negotiations had blown apart; and Nili had suffered a severe shock — all through the unpredictable behavior of a carrier pigeon.

Early in Aaron's sojourn in Egypt, when he had experienced for a month or more the frustration of the failure of the EMSIB ships to make the first contact with Athlit — he had discussed with Edmonds and other officers the possibility of working out some other system to replace or complement the *Managem*. The discussion went on for months. First they investigated the possibility of wireless telegraphy — and Liova, after all, was even sent to Alexandria to learn how to operate it — until it was found that the danger of the discovery of the transmitting instruments was too great. Aaron proposed a complex plan of cable laying at Athlit — part on land, part under water — but this was found unworkable and insecure.

After Allenby's advent, the British suggested that Jewish refugees who had come to Egypt from Gaza might be recruited to establish a contact overland; but Aaron rejected the idea for fear that such agents, even if they knew the terrain, would not be strong enough, if caught, to withstand Turkish torture. Then came a proposal to land planes at selected spots. But where? This idea was also dropped. Somebody suggested using planes that would simply drop mail, to be picked up by an agent from Athlit. This, at best, however would solve only half the problem. Finally, in June, the proposal to use carrier pigeons was discussed seriously. There were divided counsels among the

British. Deedes recalled that in a previous war the effort had been a complete failure. Nevertheless it was decided to try; and Edmonds, after a number of pigeons had been trained, sent them out on a trial flight.

As the birds all returned to base, the trial was adjudged successful.

A number were then sent to Zichron. But this trial ended in almost complete failure. Of seven pigeons sent out from Zichron only one reached its destination in Egypt. Now suddenly on September 3 a pigeon with a message tied to its leg came to rest among a cluster of pigeons at the home of a Turkish official at Caesarea. It had obviously lost its way. Going out to feed his own birds he recognized a stranger. He found the note on its leg, tried to read it, failed to decipher the text, which was coded in Latin characters; and by the next morning the news had spread: there were spies in the land.

The story of the pigeon reached Athlit on the morrow. That night Menashe Bronstein slaughtered and buried at Zichron all but three of the pigeons. He spared the three in order to send them to Cairo with news just received from a usually reliable informant that between the 10th and 15th of September the Turks would launch an offensive in the south. (Two of the pigeons reached Cairo with an additional message: "Please come on September 20.")

That night Sarah and Yosef disposed of a number of documents, apparently also by burial, and so were prepared for searches and interrogations. Nothing of the sort happened. The guilty pigeon was brought to a hotel in the village and there displayed for all to see. The Turks probably believed that the sight of the bird would evoke some automatic response. They were disappointed. Many people came to see, but simply stared stolidly at the bird.

At Athlit they heard that there had been searches at Hadera and Caesaria. At Zichron there were more soldiers to be seen in the streets, but there were no searches either there or at Athlit. Sarah believed that this was a feint, that in fact the Turk's central target was Zichron, and they were being lulled.

However days passed, the Turks' only step was to reinforce their patrols on the coast, and the feeling persisted that the immediate crisis had passed.

Meantime two other problems were thrust upon her. Aaron had persuaded the British authorities to permit the entry into Egypt of Sam, the third Aaronsohn brother, who had been away in America, as well as his wife Miriam who was in Zichron with their little boy Yedidiah. Aaron intended to hand over to Sam the role of liaison with EMSIB at Port Said. It is not clear why he needed this when Liova, sometimes accompanied by Aboulafia, had been regularly sailing on the boat, and knew the ins-and-outs at both ends. Sarah, close friend though she was to Miriam, was not happy at the prospect of Miriam's leaving Zichron. Her departure could not be kept secret. The village would be buzzing once more, this time with the news of her "flight." What Nili needed least was renewed rumors about its personnel.

What was more, and worse from Sarah's point of view, was the likely resentment that would be aroused among the Nili workers themselves. Among them there were men who also had wives and children. Why, they might well want to know, precisely Miriam and Yedidiah? They might not say a word to Sarah, but this discrimination could well affect their work. She consequently wrote to Aaron (on September 10): "What is better, to endanger the work or to endanger Miriam?" Two days later, writing to Liova, she was still undecided.

Then there was the case of Baha-eddin, an Albanian officer in the Ottoman army, who wanted to desert and had asked Na'aman Belkind to help him. Na'aman came to Athlit to propose that Baha-eddin be moved to Egypt on the *Managem*. He also wrote to Aaron in glowing terms of Baha-eddin's importance as a political figure opposed to the Young Turks regime. More important, however, he was on the staff of Division 51 stationed at Gaza and served as secretary to the commander, General Fakhri-eddin. He had recently accompanied Fakhri on a tour of the Gaza-Beersheba front.

Neither Sarah nor Yosef welcomed the idea, which had its manifest dangers. Even Na'aman's relentless pressure to get them to agree might not have sufficed to persuade them. It became clear however that Na'aman had revealed to Baha-eddin the secret of the *Managem*'s voyages, and so they consented, hoping that at least the military information he would supply should be helpful. They met the man, found him intelligent, and urged him to pass on his information to Aaron immediately on arrival in Egypt. Aaron would do his utmost to dissuade General Headquarters from treating Baha-eddin as a prisoner of war.

Execution of the plan was simple on the face of it. Baha-eddin was entitled to four days' leave-of-absence from his unit. He would take that leave to coincide with the expected date of *Managem*'s next arrival — due on August 23.

Managem however did not arrive on August 23. His four days went by. He would soon be sought by the Turkish military police — and now Nili was saddled with a deserter as well. He had to be hidden; he was brought to the Schneierson home in Hadera, there to await the next *Managem* date — September 10. But the ship again failed to arrive, and the man was moved to Haifa. Sarah and Yosef, contending with the problem of Miriam, now had an unexploded bomb threatening them from Haifa.

Nothing could be more eloquent of the tension besetting Sarah than the outburst in her letter of September 14, in angry criticism of Aaron and the whole setup in Egypt for the failure of *Managem* to come to Athlit for five whole weeks. Again Sarah described the ordeal, night after night, of the watchers who after five hours returned in the early hours of the morning, dispirited and with empty hands, to the station.

It was an astonishing performance by Sarah, to which Yosef made his contribution in a separate letter. He was no less harsh in his criticism. It was manifestly their nervous mood that made him and Sarah forget... Had they not had their own experience of shuttling for a month and more between Port Said and Cyprus because of *Managem's* not being able to anchor at Athlit?

Their experience was indeed being repeated exactly. On each occasion *Managem* had met with heavy seas off the coast. On two nights in succession in each case Liova had begged to be allowed to land. He knew how much had to be reported from and to Cairo. And the money — a lifeline to the community, and to Nili... On each of these nights a consultation between the ship's captain and friendly senior intelligence officer Captain Waldon had resulted in the verdict: "Too risky."

Another indication of Sarah's troubled mood was the reply she gave on the subject, raised once more, of her going to Egypt. She weighed up the dilemma as she wrote.

The work at Athlit, she assessed, was progressing well and quietly. From that point of view, Yosef could manage without her and she had accommodated herself to the idea of leaving. But — "I don't know," she writes, "whether I have a right to do it." Yet her life had become tortured, the strains were taking their toll, the ugliness of the pressures in the community made life distasteful; and depression was deepened mightily by the disillusion with the British. Was it not shameful that a major power could not overcome so weak and so hungry a nation as the Turks?

Nevertheless, all she could consider was a short visit to Cairo with her three brothers. There was no question of her leaving for good. "It is precisely at the point of danger," she wrote, "that I want to be."

Moreover, apart from danger, Yosef might at any moment be faced at Athlit with a serious situation requiring a lot of work. "I will not leave the work and the workers." If there was a decision to evacuate women, "I shall be one of them, but the last one, not the first."

When she wrote, the "serious situation" had already arisen. On September 17 a message reached her in Zichron. Na'aman Belkind, who had decided to carry out his oft-repeated threat to get to Egypt through Sinai, had been captured by Bedouin four days earlier and was now in Turkish hands as a suspected spy.

CHAPTER 18

The Death of Sarah

Sarah revealed to Aaron (in a letter on September 21) that Na'aman had given her and Yosef no rest, insisting that he be taken on the *Managem* to Egypt.

> He must see Avshalom, he has to know whether he is alive, and only when he knows will he know what he has to do. The way things are he cannot work or live. However much we explained to him how foolish this was, and how difficult it was to take him across without your permission! Wait [we told him], let us first ask Aaron and after getting his reply, we'll answer you yes or no.
>
> He would not budge. If we wouldn't give him a promise immediately, he would go to the desert. How brave he is, after all, we know, and so we thought that he would not dare, and that he wanted simply to frighten us — the way Mendel Schneierson did, and Eitan [Belkind] and our brother Zvi.
>
> Then Yosef met him in Petah Tikva and he agreed that he would cooperate in the work, and all was well.... He wrote us a letter and also a short report which you'll see. He writes that he is traveling to Hodj to collect material, and will send us a large amount. He also wrote that he was with friends and they were delaying him, so that he will be away for a while.

Manifestly Na'aman had worked out his plan of operation with caution and intelligence — evidenced by his behavior at the meeting with Yosef at Petah Tikva. There he acceded to Yosef's pleadings to continue working — only after Yosef had promised that he would urge Aaron to agree to his visiting Egypt. He pretended to believe him. He then asked Yosef to help pay his pressing debts. Some of them had been incurred on behalf of Nili. There was nothing untoward about the request, and Yosef gave him the money.

It was evidently at the meeting in Petah Tikva that he reported to Yosef on his arrangement with the German Edouard Suss which would grant him — and Avshalom Fein — free access into the Turkish bases on the Gaza-Beersheba front. It was then that Yosef gave him the money to buy the mules and the cart. He delegated the project (which turned out to be one of the great intelligence coups of the war) to young Avshalom Fein. It was Fein who settled down at Hodj, while Na'aman went off — without explaining — on his Sinai adventure.

As it turned out, he had confided in his brother-in-law Shepka Gintsburg — who bought a horse for him and negotiated with the Bedouin who was to serve as his guide in Sinai. When his young brother Eitan heard (whether from him or from Sarah) of his intention to get to Egypt through Sinai, he begged him not to do it.

From all the reports received subsequently, mainly from Arab sources, it remains unclear whether the guide actually led Na'aman into the hands of the Bedouin patrol, or whether he simply decamped. What was established was that when Na'aman was captured his guide had disappeared.

Na'aman was brought to Beersheba. The German commander Kress von Kressenstein was in the town and was at once informed of the capture. He passed sentence at once. The man was to be hanged, though only after being tortured. The torture at Beersheba went on for three days. Na'aman however held firm, opened up only to ask his captors to allow him to see his wife and his child before he was executed.

As soon as the news reached his family at Rishon Lezion, they sent a messenger named Rosen to inform Sarah at Zichron, and began looking for means of buying off any official who could possibly help to bring about Na'aman's release.

"The great obstacle," wrote Eitan many years later,

> was that Na'aman had made the mistake of taking with him documents which he sewed into his clothes. They were discovered [when he was searched] and were handed over to Atif Effendi, the secretary to Bhagat Bey, Commander of the Desert Zone. Atif summoned Eliahu Mizrahi, an agronomist working for the government, and

advised him to get in touch with the family and to tell them that he, Atif, was prepared to return the spy documents in return for five hundred pounds, a considerable sum in those days.[1]

Yosef, alerted by Sarah from Zichron, had already arrived in the south together with Yitzhak Halperin and Nissan Rothman. He gave Eitan the three hundred pounds which was all he had found in the cash box at Athlit.

"At Yosef's recommendation," recalled Eitan,

> I went to Menashe Meirowitz [a prominent member of the community] and asked him to lend me two hundred pounds, which would be repaid from the money the *Managem* would be bringing on its next voyage, but Meirowitz refused. With difficulty I scraped together the two hundred pounds from friends of the family. I traveled to Rehovot, gave the money to Mizrahi, and urged him to take it by carriage to Beersheba.[2]

The next afternoon Mizrahi informed Eitan that he had received the documents from Atif. When however Eitan asked him to hand them over, Mizrahi claimed that he had burned them.[3]

Meantime the German businessman, Edouard Suss, whom Yosef had called upon for help, was mobilizing assistance. He had made the deal with Na'aman which enabled Avshalom Fein to carry out his free-ranging visits to the forward Turkish bases. Now he sent a message to the authorities, complaining that the arrest of Na'aman was damaging to his business, and he was sure that Na'aman had done nothing wrong.

Yosef organized a meeting at the village of Gedera with Halperin, Rothman, Avshalom Fein, Eitan, and a friend of Yosef's from Hashomer, David Fisch. The only proposal they discussed was how to free Na'aman by force. "Force," of course, meant first of all bribery for guards. There was no money — and so the idea was dropped.

The Turks announced a postponement of the hanging and continued with their interrogation; no indication of its progress reached the community. It was at this juncture, on the night of September 21, that the *Managem*

---

1. Livneh, Nedava and Efrati, *Nili,* p. 252.
2. Ibid.
3. H. V. F. Winstone, *The Illicit Adventure* (London: Jonathan Cape, 1982), p. 252.

made its appearance with Liova, Rafael and Leibl Bernstein on board. Liova, who knew nothing of what had gone on at Athlit during the past five weeks, decided to reconnoiter the ground before taking the parcels and the gold to the station.

On the shore he had taken only a few steps when he was stopped by the password "Nili, Nili." Zeldin, Bronstein and Belinkov were there waiting, and they launched at once into a narration of the woes that had befallen; and there had been no money for the essential bribery. Yosef had gone to the south, and Sarah was alone in the station.

Liova turned back to the boat with the group and asked Rafael to remain on board, while he would go back and stay at the station till the next day. The packages and the gold were then taken to the station, and the boat distanced itself from Athlit. It would return the next night.

At the station, Liova reports laconically, Sarah was warm in her greeting, though she soon taxed him with the unreliability of their timetable. But, replied Liova, what could they do? They were controlled by the sea, which did not take orders from anybody.

On Baha-eddin, Liova agreed to take the responsibility for getting him to Egypt. He should be brought the next day from Haifa to Athlit, where he could board the *Managem* together with Liova the next night.

The talk with Sarah went on almost till daybreak; then a cart was sent to Haifa to fetch Beha-eddin from his hiding place at the home of the driver Nasser.

Later that morning Liova and Sarah were going through bookkeeping accounts and checking the intelligence reports that had accumulated for dispatch when suddenly a carriage arrived with Yosef on board. Ill and pale, he had been down with fever for three days. His temperature was now 105.8 (forty-one degrees Celsius). They put him to bed, applied ice packs to his head, and in the afternoon he felt better. He was however still very ill, and Sarah was preoccupied taking care of him. In the evening, Liova records: "Yosef's temperature has gone up; one can't talk to him."

Liova, with Beha-eddin in train, prepared to return to the *Managem*. He promised that the boat would come back once more two days later and bring as much money as was needed.

Back on the boat, Liova explained to Captain Waldon Nili's complicated and dangerous plight. Consequently, instead of making for Egypt, Waldon ordered a return once more to Famagusta, where Beha-eddin would be transferred to the *Kosseir* and debriefed. There, Waldon would be able to obtain from Captain Smith a supply of money for Nili, and make arrangements for a mass evacuation of Nili personnel to Egypt. On the way to Famagusta, Waldon received a radio telegram from Cairo, with the news that a certain "Kintzberg" of Petah Tikva had been arrested by the Turks. "Kintzberg" was obviously Gintsburg, Na'aman's brother-in-law, who had supplied Na'aman with the horse and the guide.

At Famagusta on September 23 Liova was able to enlighten Smith on the imminent dangers arising from the capture of Na'aman. Smith acted at once. He telegraphed Cairo, and received permission to mobilize a second intelligence boat, then lying at Famagusta. It would accompany the *Managem*, and on the night of the 25th take off sixty or more people, who would be waiting near the shore.

The plan was not executed. Its postponement was never fully explained. The *Managem*, with the second vessel nearby, arrived on time on the 25th. Liova landed, this time with Leibl. They were met by Yitzhak Halperin and Menashe Bronstein who told them simply that there would be no mass evacuation by the boats. Bronstein brought Liova a letter from Sarah, who had remained at the station.

She wrote that they would not send a report about Na'aman because Yosef was still ill, too ill to write. Moreover, she wrote, "we hope to be there [in Egypt] soon, and will write a full report about everything. And now for our present situation. It's going from bad to worse. Yet we can't flee at this moment, because by sudden flight we shall be doing harm to the whole community, especially those close to us."

And would a departure at any other moment not be a "sudden flight"? Altogether it was not a very coherent letter. With such a myriad of troubles on her mind this is not surprising. Yet what does emerge is that, in all probability, if Yosef had been freed of the fever, they would have organized some measure of evacuation. For Sarah's final request was that the boat should return two nights later, on September 27, for such an evacuation. She had not yet decided how many people would be gathered on that night. For with the money that *Managem* brought (a respectable total of over three hundred pounds in gold) and with their weapons reinforced by five Mausers and five thousand rounds of ammunition, the needs of those remaining behind could be assured for at least a while. The contact with Cairo, she added, would of course be maintained.

But the 27th was too late for the *Managem* to come. A full moon was only three days ahead. By midnight on the 27th, which would be on the eleventh day of Tishrei (the lunar month), the sky would be too well lit. The 25th was the last free night.

Liova thus asked Menashe to report to Sarah that the *Managem* could return only at the next new moon — on October 12. The only evacuees that night then were Miriam, Sam's wife, and little Yedidiah; and the only bright light on that sad night emanated from Yedidiah. While Liova and Leibl were talking to Menashe and Yitzhak, three other Nili men were waiting behind the rock in the bushes with Miriam and the boy. Captain Waldon relates that Yedidiah was whimpering, but was silenced by his mother: he must not make a sound, she told him. She and the boy were carried on to the rowboat, and then hauled on to the ship; there Yedidiah asked his mother: "May I cry now?"[4]

Sarah in her letter to Liova had written, "If you have time to come to talk to us for half an hour, this would be fine. If not — may God be with you. God willing, if we are not caught by midnight on the day after tomorrow, we shall still meet again..."

A few days earlier, before the boat came, she had felt the need to express her feelings for him. She wrote, "I want to travel a long way together with you." And in signing her name she had repeated "who wants to travel a long way together with you." They never met again.

One can only speculate about the contradictions in the note brought to Liova from Sarah. Why did she change her mind? The vessels were ready to take off at least sixty people, and the danger was imminent. Why the delay of two days? The only feasible explanation is that on the 25th Yosef, in high fever, would have to be left behind — on his own — and he would be a prime target for Turkish vengeance. Evidently she calculated, from common knowledge about the progress of fever, that two days later he would be fit enough, with a little help, to walk the three kilometers to the sea.

They had received no signs that Na'aman had broken down under torture. On what day precisely in the last week of September he was transferred to a

4. Louis B. Waldon, *Hard Lying, Eastern Mediterranean 1914-1919* (London: Herbert Jenkins [undated]), p. 194.

Damascus jail was not disclosed by the Turkish authorities. Moreover, by the 25th all Nili's secret sources of information on Na'aman's plight appear to have dried up. Perhaps this was because Yosef was immobilized by his illness, or perhaps because there was no money left even for buying information. Be that as it may, a pall of silence descended on the Zichron scene. Even the rumormongers had gone to sleep; and a muted fear was the ruling passion in the whole community.

Though Liova, in his final message, had made it clear that the *Managem* would not return on the 27th, Sarah may have hoped — as who would not — that the British officers in Cairo, who thought so highly of Nili, might be persuaded by Liova's report to take the risk of sending the boat. When the 27th came and went, Sarah knew that she must expect the worst. Several weeks earlier she had explained to Avshalom Fein what she saw as "the worst":

> Avshalom, you're doing good work and you're quick. Keep going that way. Who knows whether our days are not numbered. After all, they will catch us and hang us. So let's go on working without losing a moment.

Now she made it clear to herself that she would face her fate alone, and would have to try to persuade the Turks that she alone was responsible for whatever Na'aman had told them.

Two or three days later Yosef had indeed recovered sufficiently to travel. On the evening of the 30th they drove up to Zichron. It was the eve of the Succot festival and it was inconceivable to Sarah that Efraim Fishel should be left to celebrate alone. As for Yosef, he had recently brought his wife Rivka and the two tots, Ivriah and Tuvia, to live in Zichron. Thus he was able, as he always insisted, to celebrate the festival with them.

Late that night he and Sarah met and held a council of war. Sarah laid it down that Yosef must leave Zichron at once. It was most important that one of them should be mobile and have freedom of action. That was the only way to ensure a future for Nili if any future was still conceivable. The other would remain to face the Turks when they came — as they might at any moment; and to that end she would remain at home in Zichron while Yosef took to the mountains. She presented him with a Mauser pistol which she had long kept in her room.

Yosef, preparing to leave, conveyed the order to two other members,

Yitzhak Halperin and Menashe Bronstein, who set out with him for the Samarian mountains. Menashe however soon came back to Zichron. He calculated that if the Turks were to look for him and did not find him, it would go hard with his family. It was still dark when he stole into his home — and went to bed.

Yosef himself also did not get far. He felt he must keep in touch and informed of what was happening in Zichron; and so he sent Halperin to find out. The journey was not without its hazards. Halperin had to evade Turkish patrols, but he angled himself through — and met Sarah in her courtyard. She was taken aback by his report. He must go back, she told him, and tell Yosef she insisted on his doing what they had decided. He must distance himself at once from Zichron. She went into the house and brought out a loaf of bread to be taken to Yosef. Halperin went off, did as he was told, gave Yosef the bread, but in case Sarah should need help he should be on hand — and he went back to the village. That night, at the start of the second night of Succot, a unit of the Turkish army, headed by the Kaimakam (the local governor) of Haifa, surrounded Zichron on four sides.

Several hours before they came Sarah had been given authentic warning that the Turks were on the way. Elias Ghanem, brother of Nasser Ghanem, the Maronite driver of the Aaronsohns, had obtained inside information of the Turkish move. He rushed to Athlit, alerted Zeldin, and Zeldin went off in the carriage to warn Sarah.

Zeldin had in fact taken over the management of the station, and Sarah had urged him to stay at his post and keep with him there as many of the workers as possible. The only protection for all those who could plausibly plead innocence was by eschewing any semblance of flight.

When Zeldin left her she went through the rooms to check that there was nothing there that could help the enemy. Then, one of her friends who lived opposite saw her sitting on a bench outside the house. She joined her and they sat quietly chatting a while.

When the Turkish soldiers began the operation in the evening, it soon became apparent that this was not to be a general attack on the village. They worked by a prepared list of suspects. There were, no doubt, some Nili members and sources that Na'aman did not know, but judging by the people who were interrogated by the Turks he had given them enough and more for their purpose.

They did err in some cases as to the relative importance of the suspect. One such case was that of Reuven Schwartz. The Turks appeared to believe that he was a leader together with Yosef and Sarah, and they started searching for him immediately. His father-in-law, Albert Alter, had taken the early precaution of approaching an Arab friend, Abu Arishi, to hide Reuven in his large house outside the village. Not finding him, and as Alter claimed that he did not know where Reuven was, the Turks arrested Alter and beat him up. They then led him through the streets, and he called out "Reuven, Reuven, where are you?" Reuven did not appear. The next morning they resumed their work on Alter — by torture; then they arrested Reuven's father and gave him the same treatment. By this time Abu Arishi heard what was happening to them. He told Reuven, and Reuven went down into the village and gave himself up.

Meanwhile the search and the interrogations went on. The operation at the Aaronsohn home had been given pride of place. They had found Sarah and her father without difficulty.

What was done at Zichron that day and the days that followed was done largely in the public gaze, certainly in public earshot — in one or another of several houses in the village. Little could be hidden.

Nor did they have any inhibitions. Torture was an acknowledged procedure of Turkish justice.

Dr. Hillel Joffe, the physician of the village who evidently made notes at the time, wrote in his diary, later published in his memoirs:

> On Tuesday, October 2, I was brought to old Aaronsohn's house. He had been beaten mercilessly. His legs were swollen and blue, he breathed with difficulty, but he was holding out bravely. Sarah showed me the marks of whipping on her legs and her waist.... I reported this to the Kaimakam and he explained that he had already punished the officer who beat her, and it would not happen again for, after all, it was not the Turkish way to beat women. But he threatened to continue to lash the old man if his daughter refused to reveal Lishansky's hiding place.[5]

---

5. *Dor ma'apilim* [Generation of brave pioneers] (Tel Aviv, 1939), p. 587.

At noon that day they moved the father, his son (Zvi) and his daughter to the Hershkowitz house and from there to a new torture center at the outskirts of the village — the home of Yitzhak Rivniker. In one of the rooms the master of lashings, Osman Bey, had installed himself, and his men had distributed all the prisoners throughout the house. Among them was also Rivka, Lishansky's wife, and their two little children, Ivriah and Tuvia.

Rivka had never had any contact with Sarah. From the beginning she had not liked the Nili operation and, at least at first, she believed that it was Sarah who had inveigled Yosef into it. Indeed, as appears from a memoir she wrote many years later, she was sure that they were having an affair. Now the Turks brought Rivka and Sarah together in the house of torture.

"There," Rivka recalled, "I discovered her nobility of spirit. She told me she was taking all the blame, and that she would tell her torturers that I knew nothing. And that is what happened. The Turks didn't torture me at all. I believe that Sarah saved my life in those terrible days."

But there was no mercy for Sarah. She suffered the more — for they forced her to see her father tortured. She tried to strengthen his spirit. From time to time she called to him, "Father, say nothing" — and screamed to Osman: "My father is innocent." But they paid no attention.

Then they started in seriously on Sarah. Osman Bey, holding his whip, would order her to reveal Yosef's hiding place, and then would lash her body. After a while he varied the procedure: he and his assistant tweaked her flesh with tongs, they pressed hot boiled eggs into her armpits and behind her knees, they crushed her fingers; her body became a mass of black and blue stripes.

She told them nothing of what they wanted to hear. What they did hear were statements — in French, in Arabic and in Yiddish — repeated again and again. She shouted that she would tell them nothing; they should not delude themselves that because she was a woman she would beg for mercy; she had had no partners in her activities. She spelt out Turkey's fate. "Your end is nigh, you will fall into the pit that I have dug for you. You are murderers, bloodthirsty wild animals. I, a weak woman, decided to defend my people lest you do to us what you did to the Armenians." She never forgot the horrendous sights she had seen from the train in 1916. "I have hated you, heroes of the falaka and the baksheesh.... Osman, you hangman, what a hero you are, beating up women!"[6]

On the third day, October 4, the Kaimakam, as director of the operation, called together the Zichron Jewish community committee and other prominent men to deliver a message. As some did not understand French, the talk was translated into Yiddish. A spy ring had been discovered, he said, and it was headed by Yosef Lishansky, whose code name was Tubin. He had to be found at all costs. "When the Fatherland is in danger," he said, "I am prepared to punish a hundred innocents in order to find the one guilty man.... See how powerful is this organization." He gave an example: Yehuda Zeldin had been severely tortured, yet he persisted in his statement that it was he who usually traveled with Sarah Aaronsohn, when in fact he, the Kaimakam himself, had seen Sarah in the company of Lishansky. He recalled for his listeners his personal achievement in the massacre of the Armenians. He had killed a number of them with his own hands; and his men had killed them in their thousands. Now he gave the elders of the village twenty-four hours to produce Lishansky. If they did not give him up every house in Zichron would be destroyed.

A meeting of the committee took place immediately, and it was decided to call a mass meeting in the synagogue. The emergency meeting took place — evidently the same day — and all present swore on the Torah that whoever found Lishansky would hand him over to the Turks. Delegations would be sent south to Judea and north to the Galilee to search for Lishansky, and the Turkish authorities would be asked for an extension of time.

That day the order came to Zichron to transfer all the prisoners to Nazareth. Sarah's reaction was swift. She asked for permission to go to her house to change her clothes.[7] Permission granted, she made her way home.

It is evident that that was when she decided to write the last letter of her

---

6. The testimony of Dr. Joffe was amplified by people in the house of torture including, strangely enough, Yosef's little daughter Ivriah, who wandered freely around the room. Ivriah's memoir, like other memoirs about Yosef, were collected years later by historian Professor Yosef Nedava, and published as *Yosef, ish Nili: Aharit davar* [Yosef, a man of Nili: An epilogue]. Ivriah writes that Sarah even told her mother (Rivka) how to answer the Turks' questions.

7. According to Rivka Lishansky's memoir it was she, Rivka, who asked the Turks on Sarah's behalf.

life. At her own home, while she was supposed to be washing and changing, with the door locked, she could write freely. While still at the Rivniker house she must have spoken to her little nephew Avner, son of Zvi who, like all the little children, was allowed to walk about freely in the house of horror — and told him to go along later, play around the back of the Aaronsohn house, pick up a letter which he would find on the ground and to whom to give it.

With soldiers guarding her, she slowly made her way home. Though her legs were swollen, she walked erect. At the gate of her house she paused, and looked around for a moment at the rolling hills. Inside the house the soldiers took up positions at the doors.

She went in and made straight for the bathroom. Paper and pen must have been in one of the Nili hiding places, and she sat down to write.

After a minute or two she turned on the faucet full volume, and then went on with her letter. She broke off writing when she heard "them" coming, threw the letter out of the window, picked up the revolver from its hiding place, and shot herself through the mouth.[8]

One of the soldiers burst open the door, saw her on the floor and a small revolver by her side.[9] He rushed out of the house, calling, "Doctor, doctor!"

Dr. Joffe recorded for October 5:

> I was called urgently in the morning. Neiderman, the mukhtar, was shouting, "Sarah has committed suicide, hurry, save her!" I took some instruments and rode to the scene. I found Sarah lying unconscious on the floor of the bathroom. Next to her was a small revolver. Her pulse was faint. Blood was coming out of her mouth. I gave her a caffeine injection and her consciousness returned. She recognized me, and pleaded: "For heaven's sake, put an end to my life. I beg you, kill me... I can't suffer any longer..." I carried her out to a bed. I examined her and found that her hands and feet were completely paralyzed. The bullet had passed through her mouth...and had lodged in the spine. In her agony she didn't stop begging me to give her poison. She cursed the military commander, the civil authority

---

8. Sarah's letter is reproduced in full in Appendix 1.
9. She had borrowed it some time earlier from her friend Tova Gelberg. It was probably her own Mauser that she gave Yosef when he left.

and most of all the police officer Osman Bey who had tortured her. When I wanted to rinse her mouth she wouldn't let me.

The next morning she was examined by the army surgeon from Nazareth, Adel Bey. When he discovered that Sarah was paralyzed, he called for two nurses to be sent from the German hospital at Haifa. "Sunday October 7," writes Dr. Joffe:

> Sarah's temperature has gone up, but her pains are slightly weaker. She is completely lucid. Her right leg has improved slightly (especially the movement of the big toe), but her left leg and both arms are completely paralyzed. She keeps begging for an end to be put to her life. The military commander swears that if she recovers she will not be tortured again… temperature still rising… she is quieter now and asks for a morphine injection. Tonight the German nurses have arrived…

There were others who took turns to care for her. Three young girls — her cousin Haya-Rivka Aaronsohn, Ahuva (Reuven Schwartz's sister) and Freda Schwartz — and her own sister-in-law (Zvi's wife) Sarah-Hinda, and three neighbors, Esther-Leah Berkowitz, Dvora Hornstein and Miriam Lidano. Yosef Levi, a Yemenite laborer, who had been ordered by the Turkish army commander to do some work in the courtyard, would steal into her room to console her, reciting Psalms and praying for her recovery.

Dr. Joffe continued in his diary:

> Monday October 8: Sarah's condition worse. Last night I came to examine her three times…. She continues to ask for death…. Her temperature 39.5–40 [103–104 Fahrenheit]. Completely lucid, infrequent hallucinating. At 3AM she expressed fear that she might lose her mind.

Then Tuesday, October 9, Dr. Joffe recorded at seven o'clock in the morning:

> Sarah's pulse has weakened considerably despite injections of camphor and caffeine. She asks to say good-bye to her father, and says farewell to all the friends who came to her room. She asks them all to look after her old father, repeats for the last time her appeal that he be released. She says she is dying. She lifts herself up for a moment

and falls back on the bed. At eight-thirty she gives up her soul without having revealed a thing to the Turks.

I write a death certificate, Adel Bey and I both sign. I also sign, together with the two German nurses, a declaration affirming Sarah's last request: that her father be freed.

A large gathering accompanied her on her last journey. The Turkish military commander relaxed his restriction on movement; and the people came out of their houses to join the funeral procession.

When they reached the cemetery,[10] the grave — next to that of her mother Malka — had not yet been dug, and in that rocky ground it took two hours of digging. All the while the gathering stood silent around the coffin. Through the cotton netting her face was seen clearly. It was, they were to tell afterwards, wondrously beautiful.

In the end, overhead, as the body was being laid to rest and covered with the soil, the sky grew overcast and the first rains of the year came pouring down.

---

10. Today opposite Zichron's central bus station.

CHAPTER 19

Hangings in Damascus

Not the least remarkable of the developments in the aftermath of Sarah's death was the survival of her father (then sixty-nine years old). All the prisoners taken at Zichron (members of Nili) and the hostages (the community council members) were moved to Nazareth while Sarah was yet alive, on October 6.

They were housed in an abandoned monastery, where a spacious room was set up as the torture chamber. It was presided over by one Hassan Bek, a man in his forties who, even in that barbaric service, had won renown throughout northern Palestine for his brutality. Much of the torture he applied personally without assistants. Having been briefed that Efraim Fishel Aaronsohn was probably in possession of a good deal of information, he devoted himself personally to softening the old man.

Efraim Fishel having undergone three days of Osman's work at Zichron, now with the transfer to Nazareth evidently found a means of steeling his spirit. Hassan delivered the traditional falakas to the soles of Fishel's feet with his leather whip, kicked him, and tore his hair out. Efraim Fishel advised his cell-mate to raise his voice while he was being lashed: shouting, he said, reduced the pain. He himself followed this pattern: he reacted to the blows by calling out Sh'ma Yisrael. Indeed from the number of times the prisoners on the lower floor heard the Lord's name called out, they were able to tell how many lashes the soles of his feet had been given. His only response to Hassan's questions was to recite a Psalm. When he was being taken back to his cell, he was humming a well-known passage from the daily prayers.

What saved his life was undoubtedly the Turks' belief that he was dying. He was moved to a hospital in Nazareth where a Christian nurse devotedly cared for him. But as his condition seemed to be deteriorating, he was moved back to his house in Zichron. There, slowly, in a room in his own house — the rest of the house was occupied by soldiers — he recovered and went back to work on his land; and at night he would creep up to the loft where Sarah had hidden Aaron's herbarium, and there tended to the plants. He died twenty-two years later.

A special fate was reserved for Reuven Schwartz. His torture sessions lasted seven nights. He was put in a cell with eighteen other prisoners. Among them was Elias Ghanem, who was tortured so badly that there were days when he could not speak or eat. Reuven was taken out of his cell each midnight and brought back at dawn. He was by then unable to walk and so was dragged by the soldiers. His father was in the same cell, and recited Psalms to himself.

"One morning," wrote one of his cell-mates, Eliezer Lubrani, "I was awakened by soldiers kicking me; and there we saw Reuven hanging above the window."

None of his cell-mates knew what had been done to Reuven that night. They had stopped their ears against the cries coming from the torture chamber below them. The Turks claimed that Reuven had committed suicide — but it was generally believed that he had died under the lash, and that the hanging body was a cover-up.[1]

An ironic contrapuntal theme accompanies the narration of Yosef's flight from Zichron. It opens necessarily with the arrival on September 21 of the *Managem* — which brought the long-awaited load of gold. The greater part, designed for the communal relief fund, was delivered immediately to Yitzhak Rosenberg for Dizengoff's political committee. The committee, however, having decided after the capture of Na'aman Belkind to cut off relations with Nili, now decided also to refuse the money. Rosenberg thus passed the money

---

1. When, the next year, British troops liberated northern Palestine, Alexander Aaronsohn (who served with them) prepared a list of the Turkish torturers at Zichron and Nazareth. Hassan Bek was the only one who was traced — by one of his victims. He was discovered in Aleppo, Syria, and was put on trial in Haifa; but the British prosecutors could not prove him guilty of murder. He was sent to jail for ten years' hard labor.

on to the treasurer of the labor movement, Efraim Blumenfeld in Petah Tikva, for safekeeping and return to Nili. Blumenfeld in a letter (on September 23) to Rosenberg, proposed that it be returned at once to Nili.

The Hashomer leaders, learning of this intention, decided to confiscate the gold for Hashomer's own purposes. Yosef Nahmani sent two of his colleagues, Shmuel Hefter and Zvi Nadav, to Blumenfeld, and they persuaded him, over some scepticism on his part, that Rosenberg had authorized them to receive the money and to return it to Nili.

He delivered the bags of gold coins to them. They piled them onto a cart, and invited a Jewish officer in the Ottoman army, one Pinhas Riklis, who happened to be in the vicinity, to join them. He was in any case on the way to rejoining his unit in the north. This impromptu touch helped to create the impression of an official mission under armed escort.

Their destination was the village of Tel Adashim in the Jezreel Valley, a Hashomer stronghold, but they decided to make a short stop on the way, at the village of Karkur. That decision, by the two Hashomer members, cost Yosef his life.

When they arrived at Karkur, evidently on September 23 or 24, they were told by a member of the village commune, Ya'akov Fichman, that Yosef — who had arrived at Karkur some hours earlier — was in hiding in the village. The people there, said Fichman, were not happy to have him, and he suggested to Nadav and Hefter that they give Yosef a ride and bring him to the Galilee.

Yosef added his own appeal. After some discussion between the two, they agreed to take him, and set off. Yosef was so much absorbed in his troubles that he did not notice the bags in the cart — containing the money, in gold coins, designated for relief of the community and for which he and his friends had labored and suffered.

Arriving at Tel Adashim, he was not received with even a semblance of open arms. On the contrary, the community was in a panic — and not only because of the dangers Yosef brought with him. Hashomer itself was very careful not to do anything to hint at a contact with Nili, and nobody there relished the prospect of any visit by Turkish soldiers.

Meantime he was allowed to stay. More to the point, he was prevented from leaving. They made him change his clothes so that he now looked like a farm laborer. They took away his watch and most of his money — he was essentially a prisoner.

On October 4, the Hashomer leaders held an emergency meeting at the village of Yavne'el to determine what to do with Yosef. They decided not to kill him, but to help him reach the northern border at Hamara, near Metulla. There, after moving him from place to place, they put him under guard in a tent. His guards were Shabtai (Shepsel) Ehrlich and Meir Kozlovsky.

At this juncture two emissaries from Zichron Ya'akov arrived in the Galilee, came to Yosef Nahmani (the leading Hashomer member in the region), and demanded that he hand over Yosef, so that he could be delivered to the Turks. This, they claimed, would bring about the release of fifteen elders of the Zichron community whom the Turks were holding as hostages. Nahmani did not hand Yosef over. Instead he sent another Hashomer member, Pinhas Schneierson,[2] to Hamara, with the order to have Yosef killed.

Schneierson came, conveyed Nahmani's orders to the guards, and then told Yosef to go out and wait at a point nearby for a vehicle which, in a little while, would take him across the border. Yosef had made this request with the idea that once across the border, he would make his way to the coast, and somehow make contact with a British vessel — like the *Managem*. The idea was not put to the test. When he left the tent, followed by Ehrlich and Kozlovsky, he was shot from behind by Ehrlich. He fell into a pit, and there was left for dead.

Meantime, Nahmani got in touch with the Arab chief of police at Tiberias, Fuad Nashashibi, with whom he was evidently on friendly terms — and made a deal with him. He reported that he could now hand over the body of Lishansky; Fuad should come, view the body, take it away, and then claim the prize money the government had offered for the capture of Lishansky. His smooth cover story would be that this group of Jewish Ottoman patriots had captured Lishansky, and immediately called Fuad to the scene, that he had taken Lishansky into custody, but Yosef had tried to escape, and so Fuad shot him.

Fuad, then, with two policemen, accompanied by Nahmani and two Hashomer members, Menachem Horowitz and Zvi Nissanov, made their way to Hamara to view the body. But the body was not there to be viewed.

---

2. As far as is known — not a relative of Liova.

Ehrlich's bullet had not killed Yosef. It had wounded him in the left shoulder. With that wound, Yosef had fled the scene.

Another version of what happened suggests that the deal with Nashashibi was made earlier, as soon as Yosef was brought to Hamara; that the Hashomer decision at Yavne'el on October 4 was in fact to eliminate Yosef, but in such a way as to avert the suspicion that it was Hashomer members who killed him.

Thus began the third stage of Yosef's flight. Not much is known of his movements during the next several days. He continued to seek shelter in the Galilee. At Metulla, in a house where relatives of his lived, two Hashomer searchers had forestalled him and were actually sleeping in the house when he arrived. In another he was given food but the householder would not risk having him in the house. At Yissud Hama'alah, he was enabled to sleep in a barn and food was brought to him.

He decided to go south. He revealed to Dr. Neiman, later his neighbor in the jail in Damascus, how he had made his way towards his destination — at Petah Tikva where he had friends — walking by night and sleeping during the day. When he reached Karkur he used the little money he had left to buy a horse, and rode off to Petah Tikva, directly to the house of Peretz Pascal. (This was the Pascal, Aaron's friend and confidant in Cairo, who had found asylum there from the Turkish authorities.) It was about eleven o'clock at night when Yosef arrived. He knew the house well, and in fact had recently, together with Sarah, visited Peretz's wife Miriam, to whom he had brought gifts from Cairo.

He unsaddled his horse and led him round to the almond orchard near the house. Two of the three Pascal daughters, Batya and Lorette, were chatting together in the living room when they heard a light knock at the window and a voice that said, "Don't be afraid. It's Lishansky."

They took him in. He was weary beyond measure. His shoulder was in bad shape. They bandaged his wound and prepared a meal. He told them his story, and heard their account of the horrendous plight of Petah Tikva. The Turks were carrying out searches incessantly, a number of arrests had been carried out, and a general air of panic pervaded the town: their house was in particular danger, rumors had been spread that they were connected with the spies, because their father was…and so on and so forth.

The girls awakened their mother, Miriam, and she, strongly backed by a young man of seventeen, Binyamin Orel, who was staying in the house — perhaps a deserter — wanted to send Yosef away. The elder daughter, Lorette, however, declared that this was out of the question. She threatened that if he were "expelled" she would go too. She had her way.

Still, it was a terrible risk they were taking. They decided consequently to find him a hiding place outside the house proper.

They lodged him temporarily in an unused stable. He had brought his saddle with him and Lorette and Binyamin buried it — a fortunate precaution.

Some hours later a watchman employed by the community found the horse and brought it to the council office. There no chances were taken, and the horse was suitably hidden away. Meantime Miriam, caught in a brutal dilemma, pondered hard. Yosef — and the family — would not be able to stay safe for long. In order to escape he would need a good deal of money. She, like everybody else by this time, knew that for several months the relief funds brought by Nili had saved the community from mass starvation; and Meir Dizengoff had been the channel for distribution. He was living nearby, and she went to see him. She revealed what had happened and appealed to him to provide the money needed for an attempt to save Yosef from certain execution.

To her surprise and dismay, Dizengoff denied ever having received money from Yosef. He would not give her any money to help him, and he assured her that he did not care in the least what happened to him. In a new family consultation at the house, they decided that the stable was no place for human habitation; but the Pascals owned an empty packing shed a little over a mile from the house. Miriam traveled to Tel Aviv, bought clothes to disguise Yosef as an Arab woman and, with Lorette, she brought him to the shed. There they had fitted out a rough-and-ready corner where he could sleep in comfort. For meals, Miriam rode out on her horse and brought him food. She dismissed an Arab worker who worked on the family grounds. The middle daughter, Batya, and the youngest were sent off to Jerusalem "out of harm's way."

The arrangement did not succeed. Yosef, evidently not careful enough, was sighted by a Jewish worker, who warned Miriam of the danger. Miriam now felt she had no alternative, and she, together with Binyamin, explained to Yosef that he had to go; otherwise not only he, not only the Pascal family, but the entire Petah Tikva community — in any case under obvious suspicion — would be in danger. In unconcealed trepidation Yosef accepted the inevitable.

Miriam paid a further visit to Jaffa, and bought some typical Bedouin attire; Binyamin — who was an art student — made Yosef up as a Bedouin, and escorted him out of the village. Miriam had given him whatever money she could spare; and there was Yosef on his way again.

Now he went southwest — on foot. He chose the Rehovot neighborhood for his goal. He had friends there among the Bedouin, and with luck he would find one who would give him shelter until the British came,[3] or he might be able to reach the British lines.

But the British did not come, nor did he reach their lines. He reached Rehovot and was given shelter for a night by a friend, Nakdimon Altshuler. The next day, resuming his flight, he saw in a field at nearby Nebi Rubin an unattended camel. Added to his Bedouin attire and artificial coloring, a camel could be a godsend for evading the hunters. He started mounting the camel, but was seen by children playing nearby. They alerted their elders, who speedily surrounded him. Some of them recognized him. They remembered him from his days as a watchman in that very neighborhood. As it happened, they were not friends, they were all in the service of the Turks; and they took him to Ramle. The district governor communicated at once with his superior officer, the governor of Jerusalem. The governor, in all haste, traveled down to Ramle in person to bring him to Jerusalem.

Except for a few blows casually administered for the fun of it, Yosef was not subjected to physical violence during his ten days' stay in Jerusalem. His capture, when it became known, caused considerable concern among all those who had been in touch with him — but there is no indication that he gave away anything or anybody. There was, perhaps, one exception: Shepsel Ehrlich, who had tried to kill him. For the Turks did later search for Ehrlich. Even that is not certain: it may have been Nahmani, in negotiating with Fuad Nashashibi, who mentioned Ehrlich's name.

Yosef was almost the last member of Nili captured. All the denizens of the prison in Damascus were there before Yosef arrived. There was perhaps among his jailors a tinge of inverse respect — for his heroic role, the immensity of the tension and turmoil his flight and evasion had caused. One of the jailers recounted to him some of the information received in Jerusalem. Thus

---

3. Lishansky, from all the intelligence that had passed through his hands, surely had reason to believe that the British offensive could not be long delayed.

Yosef learned for the first time how many people had been incriminated by
Na'aman Belkind. Later Dizengoff, who had treated him so scurvily, and who,
even years later in his memoirs, persisted in the prevarication that he had
never received money at Yosef's hands, paid tribute to him for having kept
silent about him.

There was certainly no restraint in the organization of his transfer from
Jerusalem to Damascus. A vivid picture is drawn by fellow prisoner Yaacov
Kantrowitz, a censor in the government service — and no member of Nili. He
was already seated in the train, he wrote, when

> considerable military movement developed on the station, now filled
> with armed soldiers, high military officials, and even the governor of
> Jerusalem himself. The whole tremendous operation was performed
> for the "reception" of one person, of medium height, broad shoul-
> ders, with shaven head — walking in chains — which had formerly
> served as part of the anchor of a ship that had sunk off the coast.
>
> Fear and trembling was our reaction to the sight of the captive,
> whose face showed weariness, suffering, vengeance — and fear. The
> soldiers formed a circle and through it the man was pushed into a
> freight car, which was then locked and sealed by the governor
> himself. Four armed soldiers were posted on the roof of the freight
> car.... The "awful person" was Yosef Lishansky.

It was a slow train. It reached Damascus only on the fourth day. There they
were given a welcome comparable to the farewell party in Jerusalem. All the
prisoners on the train were taken to the army headquarters where a mass of
officials "crowded round us so as to view [the man] with their own eyes."

Then the prisoners were lodged in the Khan el Basha "politicals" prison.
Kantrowitz and a colleague from the censorship, Ronya Maziya (who was a
member of Nili) were able to bribe their way to quarters on the top floor.

In the cell opposite theirs was a well-known Arab newspaper editor,
Naguib Nasser, who was in opposition to the government but virulently anti-
Jewish. They discovered that like most of the Jewish prisoners he was being
provided with food from outside by the committee which Dizengoff had
formed for prisoners' relief. This food constituted an essential supplement to
the grossly inadequate fare provided by the prison authorities. Nasser was so
grateful for the spontaneous humane treatment by the Jews that he openly

expressed regret for the anti-Zionist and antisemitic articles he had been writing in his paper *Karmel*, and promised that he would turn over a new leaf. When, later, in return for a series of articles flattering Djemal Pasha, he was released from jail, he concentrated all his talents on reviling the Jews and the Zionists. When Dizengoff later was taunted with this story, he defended himself bravely. He had no regrets, he said, for his humane treatment of the enemy. His humanity however did not extend to Yosef Lishansky and Na'aman Belkind. They were given neither supplementary food nor other humane aid in the shape of beds, pillows, blankets supplied to the other prisoners. They slept on the stone floor.

The success of Dizengoff and his colleagues in obtaining these concessions from the prison authorities was naturally by way of bribery, and the money for bribery at that time obviously came almost entirely from the only source of charity funds in the country: the gold brought by Nili from Egypt.

Dr. Neiman,[4] who was one of the fortunate recipients of three meals a day, arranged with a jailer to make a collection among the prisoners and thus a small amount of money was raised for the sustenance of Yosef and Na'aman.

Suddenly on the 8th of November, Dizengoff and two of his colleagues, Abraham Brill and Nahum Kalverisky (who were not in jail), were summoned to Djemal's office, for no other apparent purpose than to be given a drubbing. However, the meeting with Djemal contained a new element: he spoke of Aaron Aaronsohn. Dizengoff in his memoirs described the encounter:

> When he saw me, he jumped from his seat in anger, gave me a fierce and penetrating look and emitted a lion-like roar: "Who can tell me that this man standing in front of me isn't a second Aaronsohn.... All my friends warned me, don't trust the Jews, and I treated them well.... See how Aaronsohn showed me his honesty and his trustworthiness. I allowed him to travel to Berlin for his alleged scientific purpose — and he escaped to the British and organized spying against me...." He flew at Kalverisky: "You are the one who sends information to the ICA [Jewish Colonization Association] in Paris about what is going on here! If the European press gets to know of the

---

4. Neiman's memoirs, quoted in Livneh, Nedava and Efrati, *Nili*, p. 299 et seq.

> interrogation of the spies and the actions of the authorities against
> the Jews — you will be hanged at your Rosh Pinna."

Dizengoff and his colleagues, surprised at the outburst, did not know what Djemal Pasha had known for several days: the British breakthrough at Gaza and Beersheba had come at last, Gaza had fallen without a shot fired, and the battle at Beersheba had been a military walkover.

It was sheer frustration, and the realization that somehow Aaronsohn and his followers had played a part in the British victory, that provoked Djemal's outburst which — unwilling to admit that he had been outwitted by Aaronsohn — he must have kept bottled up. Frustration was perhaps also the reason why in his memoirs Djemal Pasha wrote not a single word about Aaron Aaronsohn.[5]

Communication among the prisoners in solitary confinement was strictly forbidden, a prohibition which of course was soon nullified by the prisoners. There were three known methods. The most sophisticated was to deliver the message loudly in the singsong intonation for reciting Psalms. Most of the young Jews of that era knew their prayers. A second method, for longer conversation, was the common lavatory. It goes without saying that, for anybody who could afford it, there was bribery.

Dr. Neiman was able financially to use this, the best method of all. He and Yosef were lodged in neighboring cells and an accommodating jailer left their cell doors open at night. They talked face to face for hours. There Neiman learned a good deal about Yosef's life history, but something especially striking emerged from this freewheeling conversation: Yosef's thoughts were not concentrated only on his own plight. It was the ruling passion of his life that dominated his thinking even in that menacing, malodorous jail. "We Jews," he said,

> hope to achieve through the British the rights of a nation, like the
> Poles and the Armenians. They have shed blood and taken part in the
> war as a people, but what have we done, what account will we be able
> to present at the Peace Conference that will give us the right to
> demand national rights? Seeing that we cannot shed our blood on the

5. Ahmed Djemal Pasha, *Memories of a Turkish Statesman, 1913-1919* (London: Hutchinson, 1922).

battlefield we have to help the Allies in the field of spying — and not
as private citizens.[6]

While the Hashomer people held him at Tel Adashim, he told Neiman, they
had pressed him to reveal "the hiding place of the gold Nili received from
Egypt."[7]

Djemal was thinking on the same lines. He had Yosef brought to him
from his cell and pressed him to explain how the gold was brought from
Egypt. He even undertook, in return for this information, to set Yosef free.

At this revelation Neiman exclaimed to Yosef: "Don't give away information about the community's activities in order to save yourself!" But Yosef had
an original reply for Djemal: "Do you really believe the English would allow
money to reach the country of the enemy?" To Neiman's appeal Yosef replied
with some hauteur: "I had not the slightest intention of bringing down disaster on anybody. I only wanted you to know that I had an opportunity to save
my life but I chose to be a victim in their [the communal leaders'] place."

Djemal, in his conversations with Yosef, appears to have treated him with
a certain respect. Whether on his initiative or at Yosef's instigation, Yosef
gave him a lengthy dissertation on British plans for the conquest of Palestine
and Syria; and he assured Neiman that there was not a word of truth in any of
it. "On the entrance to hell I'll lead them astray — so that I may die with the
Philistines."[8]

Neiman wrote with wonder at Yosef's changes of mood. In the daytime he
seemed cheerful and carefree, often singing, but at night he shed this pretense
of nonchalance — and often Neiman heard him sobbing in his cell.

"From my conversations with Yosef in the prison," wrote Neiman, "it
became clear to me that he knew he was going to die." But he hoped against
hope that somehow he would be saved — perhaps by an exchange of prisoners; and one of the older Arab prisoners, a friendly character named Shukri el
Ayoubi, was spreading the rumor that the Turks were going to announce a
general amnesty. "Of course," Neiman recalled, "he told me that he was thinking of ways to escape. Once he told me that he had actually decided to get
away. But he needed money for bribing jailers as well as for his subsistence

6. Yosef Nedava, ed., *Yosef Lishansky, Ish Nili*, p. 336.
7. Ibid.
8. Quoting Samson. See Judges 16:30.

outside, and for a place to hide until things quietened down…. He asked me to help him financially, claiming that for twenty gold pounds the jailers would open the gate. But he did not succeed in raising even five pounds among the prisoners."[9]

He was most angry with Rosenberg, who had been imprisoned as a member of Hashomer. They talked in the lavatory. Lishansky said: "You got all that gold from me! And now you refuse me the few pounds for saving my life." Rosenberg, like Dizengoff, refused to lift a finger.

Formal trials took place, in groups of four or five prisoners. The Nili prisoners' turn came on December 1. Neiman, being an officer in the army, was given a chair to sit on. His companions, kept standing, were Yosef, Na'aman, Zvi Aaronsohn and Yitzhak Halperin. Judgment was not actually delivered, but, Neiman writes, "we left the courthouse under the impression that Yosef would be sentenced to death and Na'aman would go free." After the examination of the accused, Yosef had addressed the judges in tones of resignation: "Before you decide, remember that I am a father of two small children."

Na'aman however had much more to say to the judges: "I gave you a complete thing, I held back nothing of all that I knew, whether about persons or about the whole [community]. I delivered all the spies, and everybody who had been in touch with me and with Yosef Lishansky. Now it's for you to carry out what you promised me."[10]

The success that Djemal had enjoyed for a while in the spring, keeping the world in the dark about the expulsion of the Jews of Jaffa — until it was revealed and effectively exploited by Aaronsohn — was not repeated in the autumn. Hardly a week had passed when the news of the exposure of Nili and the violent reaction by the Turks was brought to the attention of the German government. It came from a German source: in an appeal from the Technion (the technical college in Haifa which was supported by funds from Germany) that it should not be touched. It was indeed spared, nor was any other Jewish institution troubled.

The news struck a most sensitive nerve in Berlin. On the 15th of October the German government instructed the ambassador in Constantinople, Bernstorrf, to press upon the Turkish authorities to refrain from acts of

9. Livneh, Nedava and Efrati, *Nili*, pp. 302–303.
10. Ibid.

revenge on the Jewish community. Specifically Bernstorrf (in talks with Prime Minister Talaat Pasha) urged him not to carry out Djemal's threat to expel a second time the Jaffa Jews who had meanwhile found shelter, mainly in the coastal villages. Talaat was asked moreover to refrain from any anti-Zionist actions whatever.

The Germans did not hide their bitter recollections of the worldwide uproar against Germany over the original brutal expulsion from Jaffa. They wanted no repetition of that kind of propaganda which would surely follow news of renewed Turkish excesses. They were, on the contrary, engaged at that very time in trying to improve relations with the Jewish community in Germany, and indeed to encourage the quite substantial pro-German feelings still harbored by many Jews (and Gentiles as well) throughout the world.

Their policy in the weeks that followed was to persuade the Turks to treat the spying phenomenon as just an episode involving a small minority of the Jewish community.

For a moment this policy was endangered in a threat emanating from the governor of Jerusalem — a most virulent antisemite — to carry out massive expulsions of Jews from the city. He had delivered a violent speech on October 19 at Ramle against the Jews, and for this the German consul general at Jerusalem now took him severely to task. In a telegram to Berlin, he reports that he called upon the governor to "prevent anything that will anger the Jews as a community and provide our enemies with ammunition for more 'horror-propaganda.'"

With the Germans repeatedly reminding Constantinople of the certain danger to Germany if they did not moderate their behavior towards the Jewish population, the Turks conceived the idea of letting the Germans handle the cases of the spies. The idea was supported by the German Zionists, and was conveyed in messages from Ruppin to colleagues in Berlin. The rationale of this intervention was clear: German officers sitting in judgment on Jewish prisoners would certainly not sentence them to death. Na'aman would possibly be spared punishment because of the deal he had struck with the Turks; but even Yosef would certainly have been sentenced only to imprisonment, albeit longterm. But Berlin, while keeping a close eye on developments, refused to undertake any public involvement in court trials. Thus the fate of Yosef and Na'aman was sealed.

The two were nearly joined by a third: Eitan Belkind. There is every indication that he revealed nothing to the Germans about his reports from Syria (on Turkish transport and troop movements towards Mesopotamia). He was saved by his age, about which the Turkish authorities had some doubts. He was in his twentieth year — the youngest of all the Nili members.[11]

On the morning of Friday, December 14, Shukri el Ayoubi passed on the information that Lishansky and Belkind would be executed in the early hours of Sunday morning. The prisoners in the know did not tell the condemned men, but that night, which was the sixth of Hannukah, when the candles were lit, there was no singing. On the Saturday night when the prisoners were locked in and candles extinguished, Eitan Belkind was called out into the corridor and there was old Shukri waiting for him. "I promised," he said, "that I would arrange for you to meet your brother." Eitan had not seen Na'aman since the day when he begged him not to take the road to Sinai.

"Has his time come?" asked Eitan; but Shukri said he did not know. "It's always good for brothers to meet," he added. Though they spoke softly, it was evidently loudly enough for nearby Lishansky to overhear. He called through the door: "Eitan! Where are they taking you? Do they mean to hang you before me?"

"No," replied Eitan, "I bribed the guard and he's taking me to talk to Na'aman."

"Thank God!" exclaimed Yosef, as though the order in which executions were carried out was a matter of protocol. "Say hello to him from me."

"In Na'aman's cell," wrote Eitan later, "we sat on the floor next to each other, and his words came pouring out. He asked about his little boy, about his wife and the other members of the family, and how they looked. Had they suffered much? Then he said: 'The reason they've let you visit me is that this is my last night.'"

Ayoubi interrupted. He came with three cups of coffee and began chatting about the wonderful future of the common homeland after the war, free of Turks. He kissed them both on the forehead, and went away. They remained alone, but in a little while the guard came back and took Eitan to his cell.

"I couldn't fall asleep," he wrote later. "How the good-looking young man

---

11. Ibid., p. 304 et seq.

had changed! His eyes squinted. His beard was white and wild. He was broken in body and spirit. The signs of hunger stared out of his whole body."

A collective restlessness pervaded the prison. Suddenly Lishansky's voice was heard. "Shalom, my friends. I'm about to die!" He had been taken from his cell, but the warder assured him that he was being transferred to Aleppo. "Stop your nonsense!" Lishansky retorted, "do you take me for a woman?"

Now Eitan was listening, and he understood the hour had come. He banged on the door of his cell, and called to be allowed to see his brother. Yosef too began shouting. Eitan's door was opened, and he went down to the ground floor. He rushed up to Na'aman and embraced him. "Na'aman kissed me and said, 'I'm glad that it's I, and not you, who's going to the gallows. Give my love to the whole family. Be a father to my boy. Teach him to be a good Jew. If it becomes possible bring my remains home to Rishon.'"

Then Na'aman turned to Yosef. They had not spoken to each other in the jail. Now they shook hands, and Yosef, his whole body shaking, embraced Na'aman. Then he said to Na'aman: "We must steel ourselves to die like heroes, so that our enemies should not rejoice at our misfortune."

Yosef and Na'aman were hanged that morning. But not before Yosef had his say. When he was brought to the central square, Marj — to which the population had been invited to view the executions — the workmen had not yet completed setting up the gallows. Yosef mocked them. "You are even incapable of putting up gallows in time."

But he went further. The rabbi whom the chief rabbi of Damascus had appointed to attend the execution, Netanel Hacohen Taarav, later related how Lishansky boldly denounced the Turkish regime. Speaking loudly in Arabic, he declared:

> We are not traitors, for treason must be preceded by love. Only a lover can betray his beloved. But we never loved the homeland of the falaka and the baksheesh, the homeland of the hangman of the Armenian people. We hated her, hated her so deeply. We didn't betray her, but she disgusted us. We have been digging her grave with all our might so that she should get out of our dear homeland....
>
> We, members of Nili, headed by the great Jew Aaron Aaronsohn, have dug you a big grave, contemptible Ottomania. We made contact with the English army which has come to liberate our country and to

hand it over to us. And while you are preparing to hang us, Great Britain's army is entering our Holy City Jerusalem — and your armies are fleeing the city without resistance.

He did not finish what he had to say. His words (in Arabic) were being translated into Turkish and at this point he was silenced. The order was given to a trumpeter to drown out his words.

That afternoon a Jewish soldier in the Austrian army (Daniel Auster, half a century later mayor of Jerusalem) photographed the two bodies. It was six days later that Allenby entered Jerusalem.

After the executions in Damascus, tensions relaxed throughout the country. No new arrests were carried out; and in Khan el Basha conditions were eased. The prisoners could, it seems, communicate freely with each other. Energetic intervention by the German government resulted in Turkish acceptance of the proposal for the handling of the Nili episode as altogether a minor phenomenon promoted by a tiny group within the Jewish community. Only against that group would Berlin approve punitive action, and even that should not be excessive.

Aaronsohn would have been gratified to learn that in their communications to Constantinople the Germans did not fail to recall the damage caused to their own good name throughout the world by the exposure of the barbaric expulsion of the Jews of Jaffa the previous spring. Nili's report and Aaronsohn's swift initiative, with British help, in disseminating the news throughout the world, had achieved a permanent curb on the Turks. There is no doubt that the Jewish community was thereafter spared unutterable further suffering.

The Germans however did not suggest sparing the rod towards those who could be charged with direct action or subversive intentions against the state. Those prisoners who had been sentenced by the court, nearly all Nili members, were left to serve their sentences. Two who, after the court trials, were given to understand that they would be hanged (Zvi Aaronsohn and Eitan Belkind) were reprieved. No explanation was offered for Zvi's case; but in Eitan's case there arose, first of all, the disagreement about his age. Was he below the legal age? But the presiding judge solved the problem by ruling: "It would be wrong for a mother to lose both her sons!" It is possible that a similar touch of humanity moved the judge in the case of Zvi — as the brother of Sarah.

Sentenced to two years' imprisonment was Nissan Rothman, and his fiancée Tova Gelber was given six months. Yehuda Zeldin, Menashe Bronstein and Yitzhak Halperin got twelve months. Astonishingly, thirty-two-year-old Dr. Neiman, despite his being a Turkish army officer, was let off lightly — twelve months. Farida Lulu, the young housekeeper at the station (and a member of Nili) was also subjected to torture and imprisoned. After her release she took charge of the house at Zichron for some time, and was able to take care of Fishel.

Among the prisoners were a handful of Hashomer members, suspected of harboring revolutionary ideas about Ottoman rule. One of them was the ubiquitous Yitzhak Rosenberg. Then there were some, of unknown affiliations, if any, and the friendly old Arab Shukri el Ayoubi. As for Avner Ehrlich, even when the Turks were persuaded by Yosef Lishansky that he was not Shabtai Ehrlich who had tried to kill Yosef, he was kept in prison for twelve months.

The prisoners were packed into trains of unheated freight cars, and moved by stages through Aleppo and Adana to Constantinople — and given no food. Writing to his wife, Zvi Aaronsohn asserted that they were saved from starvation by Jews — and at one point by a convert to Christianity — in the towns through which they passed. The sick, some genuinely ill, others successful malingerers holding certificates from cooperative doctors, were placed in Constantinople hospitals. There they remained until they were taken over by the victorious British in October 1918.

Forty of the hundred-odd prisoners taken at the time are estimated to have died of disease or malnutrition during that period.[12]

Ultimately, the survivors were brought back to Palestine by the British army aboard a French boat — flying the Zionist flag.

Throughout his stay in London, Aaron heard nothing from Alex as to what had happened and what was happening between Cairo and Athlit. In a letter

---

12. Slutzky, *Sefer toldot ha-haganah*, vol. 1.

on November 17, seven weeks after his arrival in London, Aaron upbraided his younger brother: "I have not received a single letter from you since you arrived in Cairo on September 22. I don't need to tell you that no explanation can excuse this.... Try to get rid of your torpor when there is writing to be done."

Alex's behavior was not merely inexcusable; it was incomprehensible. A description of his "torpor" reached Aaron in a letter from his brother Sam a few weeks later. After Alex had left for the war front, Sam wrote, a number of unposted letters had been found "lying around" in his quarters...!

That Alex had joined up, Aaron had no doubt learned from his British sources, and in that letter of November 17, he added, always indulgent, "I learned yesterday that you have gone to serve where service is needed. I wish you well."

It follows from Aaron's casual acceptance of Alex's enlisting in the British army that he had learned earlier — obviously not from Alex, but from General Headquarters in Cairo — that Nili had been destroyed, and he had probably recovered from the first shock. (He made no diary entries during the crucial period from mid-September till November 16.)

The fate of Nili became known to General Headquarters in mid-October, and his friends there had certainly informed him. Thus a month had passed before he wrote his letter to Alex.

As Liova had made plain to Sarah it was only at the new moon on October 12 that *Managem* could be expected at Athlit.

That undertaking was implemented. On the night of October 12 the *Managem*, accompanied by the fishing boat *Versis* and escorted by a destroyer, anchored opposite the station, all in preparation for taking off sixty persons. On board with Captain Waldon were Alex, Liova, Leibl Bernstein and Rafael Aboulafia. Liova and Leibl were rowed out to the shore while the others waited in a second boat nearby.

It did not take them long to grasp what had happened: there was nobody waiting for them. Nevertheless, in vain hope, they waited, reconnoitered the area and found no sign of life; no light showed from the station. Disconsolately, after two hours they returned to the *Managem*, which sailed away to the north.

The next night they returned on the *Managem*, now escorted only by the destroyer. This time all but Waldon went ashore. There they debated whether to go up to the darkened station but decided that it would only be a futile and dangerous exercise; and the *Managem* sailed back to Port Said.

After their return to Cairo, Alex proposed that a further effort should be made, but the officers at General Headquarters turned down the idea: it would indeed be futile and dangerous. The fog surrounding the fate of Sarah, and of Yosef and all their comrades, did not lift; and so Alex and Liova decided to volunteer for the British army, now beyond Gaza, fighting its way to Jerusalem. Alex was granted an immediate captaincy in the intelligence service, Liova was given officer's rank and was to be attached to Alex.

Owing to a severe illness, which Liova records in his diary, he did not accompany Alex to the front. He was inducted into the army only on November 22. On that day he was kept busy being fitted out as a soldier of His Majesty. Just as he was preparing to leave for the desert front he received from General Headquarters the report of an interrogation of a Jewish prisoner of war, a medical officer named Benyamini, who described what had happened at Zichron in the first days of October. Not every detail was correct (he reported that Efraim Fishel had been killed) but the essence was there.

Thus it was that Liova first learned of the martyrdom of Sarah — lying in a bunk in a military camp in the heart of the desert. That night he did not sleep. The image of Sarah flitted through his mind again and again.

"I tossed and turned," he wrote in his diary. "I was haunted by visions and nightmares: Sarah! Here she is, laughing, here she is — weeping, here she comes towards me, her pale, dainty hands stretched out in greeting. Here she is — among the rocks at Athlit, in a carriage in Cairo, at a concert, she is laughing again, and then again sad. Ah, Sarah, Sarah!"

For thirty-six hours he carried the lonely pain in his heart — he could share it with nobody — until he finally caught up with Alex; and then once he had with difficulty uttered Sarah's name, a great silence fell on both of them.

CHAPTER 20

Avshalom and Yosef — Postmortem

The story of Yosef Lishansky could not be allowed to end with his death, thus reasoned an erudite Israeli police officer named Shlomo Ben-Elkanah nearly half a century later. Ben-Elkanah, it so happened, had made a study of the Bedouin tribes of the Negev, and had made friends with Bedouin precisely in the neighborhood of Rafiah. Somewhere nearby Avshalom Feinberg had been murdered in January 1917.

In 1960 Ben-Elkanah decided to try to find Feinberg's grave, and thus made possible, once and for all, the elucidation of the manner of his death. From a scientific examination of his remains it should be possible to put an end to the monstrous charge that he had been killed by Yosef Lishansky. Ben-Elkanah discovered that on March 20, 1931, a Haifa railway engineer, Binyamin Rann, had declared that he had discovered where Feinberg was buried. It was revealed to him by a Bedouin named Yussuf Abu Safra of the Rumeilat tribe. Yussuf had described the spot as being on the southern side of the Rafiah railway station and it could be reached by a "path running eastward."

Given the clue, Ben-Elkanah started studying maps and documents of the period, went down to the Negev, and found members of the "irregular" Bedouin unit of the Turkish army. He came to the conclusion that there was a chance, with the help of Bedouin from that tribe, of finding the grave.

Being subject to police discipline he was prevented from pursuing this personal objective, which his chiefs did not see as a proper subject for police investigation. (It is not impossible that he was regarded as a crank.) His chance came however after the Six-Day War, when he was transferred to the

Israel Defense Forces and obtained permission to go ahead from his commanding officer Colonel (later Chief of Staff) Mordechai Goor.

Ben-Elkanah was wary of tackling members of the Rumeilat tribe directly, lest their fears be aroused that some descendant of Feinberg might still want (in keeping with Muslim custom) to avenge his death. He consequently approached a friend from another tribe — Sheikh Frayah Farhan el Masdar of the Nasayrat tribe — one of the most respected and influential Bedouin leaders in the Gaza and northern Sinai districts. He asked him to find out from Abu Safra and others about the spot called "The Jew's Grave" and how the Jew came to be buried there.

It took some time, but his request was fulfilled. This is the story as told in October 1967 to Ben-Elkanah by the Sheikh:[1]

Shortly before the British captured Rafiah, two Turkish soldiers (or perhaps policemen) at the Rumeilat tribe's headquarters in Sanana were sitting in the tent of Sheikh Salameh Abu Safra, when a Bedouin came running and shouting, "*Juassis, juassis* (spies, spies)." Two strangers, dressed as Bedouin, had been seen going in the direction of the British lines. A number of Turks and Bedouin rushed out and caught up with the two men. There was an exchange of fire. One of the strangers was wounded and fell to the ground; the other managed to run away.

The wounded man, fighting for his life, shot one of the Turks in the hand but finally was overcome. The Turks shot him in the head, and he died on the spot. The Turks said that the man was a Jew, and ordered his burial. A year later the Bedouin were surprised by the sight of a wild palm tree growing out of the grave. They decided that he must have been a man of virtue and thenceforth called the spot "The Jew's Grave."

Sheikh Frayah gave Ben-Elkanah the names of several Bedouin eyewitnesses of the event who were still alive.

"On October 25, 1967," wrote Ben-Elkanah,

> I set out, together with Sheikh Frayah, Sheikh Shakhta Za'arub and Abdel-Hamid el Kashta — the mayor of Rafiah — his deputy and Bedouin Sheikhs Hassan and Hamad Abu Rabaya, as well as others,

---

1. Shlomo Ben-Elkanah, "My Work in Finding the Grave of Avshalom Feinberg," in *Yosef Lishansky, Ish Nili*, ed. Yosef Nedava (Tel Aviv, 1977). Yosef and Na'aman had been buried in October 1919 in a common grave.

to see what the grave contained. Among them was also Haj Muhammad Salameh Abu Safra, who at first had been afraid (of possible vengeance), but now admitted to me that it was he who had told a railway worker 'Mr. Binyamin' the story of the 'Jew's Grave.'

Ben-Elkanah in his memoir describes the careful, painstaking work of the Bedouin who with him dug up the remains. From the position of the roots of the palm tree they come to the conclusion that it grew out of the dates that Avshalom had brought with him to eat on the way. The Bedouin had evidently searched the body, eaten the dates, and spat out the stones into the open grave. They dug out the whole tree and Ben-Elkanah subsequently gave it to Eitan Belkind (Avshalom's cousin).

Ben-Elkanah brought the remains, covered in a sheet, to Tel Aviv, and delivered them to Professor H. Karpelus, of the Institute of Forensic Medicine, for the identification of the body. The findings were conclusive. The measurements were normal.

Two incidents in Avshalom's life, recalled by his sister Tsilla, added a final touch of authenticity. He had once broken a tooth cracking a nut and the dentist had inserted a filling; and there was a second sign — on a bone in his finger — recalling the occasion when Avshalom had accidentally shot himself in the hand.

Thus on November 7, 1967, Professor Karpelus reported that the skeleton found by Ben-Elkanah at "The Grave of the Jew" was that of Avshalom Feinberg. What was not made clear, adds Ben-Elkanah wryly, was whether Avshalom was shot by the Turks or by the Bedouin, or by both.

On November 29, 1967, Avshalom Feinberg was accorded a state funeral with full military honors, on Mount Herzl. The speaker of the Knesset, Kadish Luz, delivered the eulogy, and in the name of the government and the Knesset, asked for Avshalom's forgiveness and that of his comrades for "the tragic misunderstanding, and the failure to recognize their great achievement." Five months later, on May 2, 1968, Israel's Independence Day, the act of contrition and reconciliation was given completion by the president of the state. He conferred on all the surviving members of Nili the Military Medal.[2]

In concluding his account, Ben-Elkanah expressed his gratification at

2. This account is taken from Ben-Elkanah, "My Work in Finding the Grave of Avshalom Feinberg."

having been enabled not only to give this national hero a Jewish burial, but to clear the name and the memory of Yosef Lishansky, he too a Nili hero, who had been falsely accused of the murder of Avshalom.

A full decade was yet to go by before the injustice to Yosef Lishansky, kept alive for sixty years after his death, was publicly and officially eradicated. The magic wand waved by Shlomo Ben-Elkanah in 1967 to reveal the truth about Feinberg's death had not touched the problem of Yosef. It left him buried, as he had been in 1919, in Na'aman Belkind's hometown of Rishon Lezion — a town with which he had no special relationship.

The hatred and vilification that had been his lifetime lot were visited in brutal measure after his death on his wife Rivka and the two children. All the old slanders spread about him by his bitter enemies in Hashomer and the supposedly more responsible leaders of the community — compounded moreover by the "sins" of Nili — found their way into the warp and woof of the communal fabric. Rivka was ostracized socially and economically, rescued only with help from the meager resources of her family. The children were taunted mercilessly at school. Their father, they were told, was a traitor. They, vulnerable and perpetually unhappy as they were, remained unbowed. They knew the truth; their mother taught them. They grew up in the knowledge that their father was a hero, and they loved, nay, worshipped him. Ivriah had memories of him from her early childhood and endlessly she recounted them to Tuvia, who made them his own.

Life became intolerable for Rivka — and soon after the war, she took the children and made for the United States. Life there however she did not find congenial, and she soon returned to Palestine, finding refuge again with her parents.

Out of the blue she suddenly received a letter from Ze'ev Jabotinsky who, having heard of her plight, was able to arrange for financial assistance. It was however only a year later that she found a social foothold and some personal solace. She met a warm and caring man, Moshe Lifschitz, a former Jewish Legionnaire, who offered her marriage. Her children finally had a home of their own; and the old memories seemed to fade.

The drama of her life however was not ended. In 1937 suddenly she was given an opportunity to hit back at Yosef's detractors. A play (incidentally of dubious dramatic value) by one Ever Hadani about the Hashomer movement was presented by the premier theater Habimah. It depicted a cast of characters all of indomitable heroism — except for one, Yosef Lishansky, who was portrayed in the blackest of colors, an unmitigated scoundrel.

Rivka was in the audience. Her tolerance reached breaking point. She suddenly stood up and screamed: "Lies, this is all lies! Shame on you, Rovina! [Hannah Rovina, the famous Number One Lady of the Hebrew theater] Aren't you ashamed of yourself?"

She could not be silenced — and, wonderful to relate, the whole audience walked out of the theater. She did not relent. She went to see Rovina (who had come to Palestine only after the war) and told her story. Rovina burst into tears. The play was killed; but the stigma was not thereby erased. That had to wait for Shlomo Ben-Elkanah.

Soon after the ceremony of Avshalom Feinberg's burial on Mount Herzl, Rivka wrote to Prime Minister Levi Eshkol appealing to him to order the transfer of Yosef's body for burial near the grave of Feinberg on Mount Herzl. He refused. This was not a matter for the government, he wrote, but for determination by historians. It was then recalled that Eshkol, as a young man, had been a member of Hashomer.

The ultimate miracle, however, was not to be denied. But Rivka did not live to see it. Shortly after she died, the Labor government, now headed by Yitzhak Rabin, was defeated — and Menachem Begin came to power. It was now the children, Ivriah and Tuvia, who took up the struggle. They were joined by a committee of public figures, among them the great nationalist poet, Uri Zvi Greenberg; the historian Yosef Nedava who, in many writings over the years had kept the memory of Nili alive; and Shlomo Ben-Elkanah.

Begin, leader of the underground Irgun Zvai Leumi which, with the Lehi, had revolted against British rule and had seen themselves bearers of the Nili tradition, responded warmly to the appeal.

Thus the epic came full circle; and in 1978 Yosef joined Avshalom on Mount Herzl — so that in death they were not divided.

CHAPTER 21

Grandiose Plans

When Aaronsohn and Weizmann — in one nocturnal session — had put their differences behind them and the telegram of the "recognition" of Nili had been sent to Alex, they settled down to a survey of the political situation. When the story is told of the Zionists' struggle for a British declaration, a salient fact, often unrecognized, is that the Zionists had already, in July 1917, won a major battle — for recognition. The French government had then addressed such a statement to Nahum Sokolow. Now both Weizmann's diplomacy, and Jabotinsky's campaign for a Jewish Legion, were backed by the powerful advocacy of the most influential officials at the highest level of the British government. Mark Sykes, William Ormsby-Gore and Leopold Amery were all — providentially — members of the small intimate secretariat of the prime minister himself; and probably the most active of them all, Ronald Graham at the Foreign Office, maintained an alert and unrelenting pressure in every conceivable direction to promote and speed up the partnership with the Zionist movement.

The Zionists' first officially proposed draft for a declaration by Britain had been submitted to the government, in July, in a letter by Lord Rothschild — and this became the formal basis for negotiation.

It was precisely then that the efforts of the assimilationist Jews reached new heights. They were headed by a brilliantly articulate member of the Cabinet, Edwin Montagu, who wrote memorandum after memorandum denouncing Zionism as a false nationalist movement. The Jews, he claimed, were after all not a nation at all, but a religion. Unfortunately, most of the members of the British establishment, in whose social milieu many wealthy and titled Jews found a comfortable niche, believed that these wealthy Jews were representative of their community. Chaim Weizmann epitomized the conflict in sarcastic terms:

> The dark forces in Jewry have again been at work and this time they have mobilized their great champion who, although a great Hindu nationalist, now thought it his duty to combat Jewish nationalism. It is — I confess — inconceivable to me how British statesmen still attribute importance to the attitude of a few plutocratic Jews and allow their opinions to weigh against almost a unanimous expression of opinion of Jewish democracy. Here we are, after three years of hard work, after having enlisted the sympathies practically of everyone who matters in England, faced again by opposition on the part of a handful of 'Englishmen of the Jewish persuasion'.[1]

When in October Montagu, having been appointed secretary for India, left England on his official business, he had failed in his main objective, but succeeded in insinuating a degree of obfuscation into Anglo-Jewish relations for the next three decades.

With Montagu gone, there remained only one strong opponent of a pro-Zionist declaration in the Cabinet: Lord Curzon, who simply did not believe in the feasibility of Zionism. Though Aaronsohn, at Weizmann's request, tried to enlighten him — as he had succeeded in persuading Sykes and Ormsby-Gore and Meinertzhagen — that Palestine could be developed into a fruitful country, and that the Jewish people could produce a generation of farmers, Curzon (in a memorandum of October 26) did not budge from his negative stance. The concession he made was to accept the Balfour Declaration, issued a week later, as a fait accompli which he would not challenge.

Aaronsohn in those few weeks in October certainly could do little to help combat these negative influences. The great contribution he had made much earlier — in his "conversion" of some of the major British personalities in the inner core of the government — had long become a significant part together with those of Weizmann and Jabotinsky, of the collective Zionist achievement.

---

1. Weizmann, *Letters and Papers*, vol. 7, no. 489, September 16, 1917.

The Balfour Declaration once issued, the British lost no time in seeking ways and means to secure the Zionist quid pro quo — the mobilization of Jewish opinion, especially in the United States and in Russia, for the British cause.

Ronald Graham set about organizing the campaign. Before the declaration was published he conferred with Weizmann for the dispatch of delegations to the United States and Russia.

It was thereupon decided that Aaronsohn, as the expert on the situation in Palestine, would go to the United States, while Sokolow, Tchlenov and Jabotinsky would proceed to Russia immediately and start making propaganda. "I have no great faith," Graham wrote,

> in the capacity or usefulness of the first two gentlemen, although they carry weight in Russia from their position. Mr. Jabotinsky, on the other hand, is just the type of man required. He is an enthusiast to whose efforts the formation of the Jewish Regiment in our Army is principally due — he carried it through in the face of much opposition. He had a high position in Russian journalism and is known as an exceptionally good and moving speaker.[2]

The outbreak of the Russian Revolution put an end to the plan for a Zionist delegation — as indeed it put an end by stages to the Zionist movement altogether in Communist Russia. The plan for the United States went ahead however — and Aaronsohn sailed for America — but not before his enemies in the Zionist establishment had introduced a very sour note into his mission.

At the Zionist office, Weizmann handed him a letter containing a list of instructions upon which he and Weizmann had agreed. It was signed by both Weizmann and Sokolow. Rereading it later that day he was flabbergasted. Contrary to his prior arrangement with Weizmann, it forbade him to give interviews or make public speeches in the United States!

"I am really angry," he writes in his diary, "especially because of Weizmann's deviousness." Taxed with this, Weizmann explained that it was a decision by Sokolow and Tchlenov. Why then had he not told Aaronsohn at once? "Indeed," he writes in a pregnant comment, "every day brings more proof of Weizmann's lack of frankness..."

---

2. FO 371/3083/92964, to Hardinge November 3, 1917.

It was Mark Sykes who offered Aaron some balm to his wounds. If he were in Aaronsohn's place, he said, he would be only too happy to accept some restrictions. They would free him from the importunities of journalists and others.

Aaronsohn's anger was further assuaged by a gesture, friendly and useful, from the British authorities. They furnished him for his voyage to America with a new travel document. It was a British diplomatic passport.

His boat left Liverpool on November 18. While he was at sea two telegrams for him came from Cairo. They were forwarded to New York, and he received them soon after his arrival in New York on Saturday, December 1. One telegram informed him that his brother Sam had arrived in Cairo. The other, evidently from General Headquarters in Cairo or the War Office, read:

> 27 Nov 1917. We are in receipt of the following from Samuel to A.A. which we forward with our deepest sympathy. Several have been arrested including father, Hirsch, Sarah, Joseph, which fact has been ascertained from a prisoner.
>
> After torture Sarah died bravely by own hand. The shock killed father. Naaman has been executed. Liova and Alex are proceeding towards Palestine. Mary and child[3] are here and well. The fate of the others unknown.

The reaction he committed to his diary that day was terse. "The sacrifice has been completed. I knew that the greatest of tragedies awaited us. But the fear of impending evil cannot be compared to the certainty that it has already befallen, and that all hope has gone. Poor father, my poor Sarah. Her loss is surely the most cruel disaster."

It was no consolation to him that he had carried in his heart for months the foreboding of precisely this fate.

All he could do, all he had to do was bring the awful news to Rivka — and Rivka was in Chicago. He should no doubt have taken the first train to Chicago — yet that had to be postponed. He had evidently agreed to come that night to Washington for an urgent meeting. His diary records a rushed journey and "a long talk with Brandeis." It is probable that they needed to

---

3. Sam's wife Miriam and little boy Yedidiah.

confer on the fulfillment of a task Aaronsohn had undertaken at the request of Weizmann on the one hand, and the British War Office on the other — to prepare a list of leading figures in the American Jewish community who would be prepared to serve on a body which the British government had decided to set up. It was to be named the Zionist Commission, and its objective would be to start preparing the infrastructure for the Zionist upbuilding of Palestine. It was to be headed by Weizmann and would serve as the liaison with the British Occupation authority. Captain Ormsby-Gore would be the connecting link.

On the commission there would be Zionist representatives from Britain, and representatives from the other Allied countries — France, Italy and the United States. It appears from Aaronsohn's diary that it was the composition of the American delegation that he discussed that night with Brandeis.

He returned to New York, and thus reached Chicago only on the Monday morning. Though fate had left it to him to apprise Rivka of what he himself had learned only two days earlier, he gives no expression to emotion in his diary. "We reached Englewood after nine o'clock. There, tired but brave, was Rivka. Her heart tells her, without her wanting to admit to herself, of the disasters that have befallen us."

The offensive prohibitions dictated to him before he left London were ignored and soon forgotten. Aaronsohn appeared at numerous meetings and gave many interviews — as a propagandist for a Zionism entering the phase of practical response to the promise of the Balfour Declaration, and mobilizing Jewish support for a still heavily embattled Britain. The one known public reference to Nili was in a speech Aaronsohn delivered at the Zionist Conference in Baltimore, when he told the story of heroism and death of the "martyrs who had held the fort for the sake of the nation's future."

It so happened moreover that, in regard to the policies to be pursued immediately, he tended strongly on the one hand to the nationalization of land ownership in Palestine and, on the other to a free market economy — political philosophies which were being promoted enthusiastically by the leaders of the American Zionist movement. It established a new bond of political cooperation, so that in the months to come Brandeis and his colleagues came to see Aaronsohn as a spokesman for their views.

On this visit he succeeded in mending his remaining fences with the trustees. Julius Rosenwald, the most intractable of them all, finding himself now on the same side of the war, greeted him like a long-lost brother. However, looking into the future, it was the deepening friendship with Frankfurter, Mack and, perhaps above all, with Brandeis, that seemed to promise fruitful cooperation in the years of nation-building that lay ahead.

A serious snag however, which affected adversely the planned founding of the Zionist Commission, arose in Washington. The British hoped that President Woodrow Wilson would underwrite the Balfour Declaration. They had every reason to believe that he would indeed give it his official blessing. As late as September 27, 1917, Louis Brandeis, who was in constant touch with the president, assured the Zionist Committee in London that Wilson had assured him of his agreement. Now, after the declaration was published, he adopted an attitude of complete neutrality. What had happened?

The president could not act alone. The conduct of Foreign Affairs was in the hands of the State Department — and the Secretary of State, in his advice, came down emphatically against endorsement of the declaration.

It was a reasoned briefing. In the first place, Secretary Robert Lansing pointed out, the United States was not at war with Turkey, while the Balfour Declaration could be interpreted as promoting the severance of the Palestinian province from the body of the Ottoman Empire. Second, not all Jews were in favor of Zionism.

Wilson had no doubt foreseen these arguments and they could be answered effectively. Lansing however had a third argument, which came down hard on Wilson's liberal head. Many Christians, wrote Lansing, would resent the notion that the Christian holy places would be handed over to the race which was seen as responsible "for the death of our Lord."[4]

---

4. Quoted in Frank E. Manuel, *The Realities of American Palestine Relations* (Washington, DC: Public Affairs Press, 1949), p. 172.

Therefore, claiming that in the future peace negotiations it was essential for the United States to adopt a neutral stance between the belligerents — it would not be right for the United States to participate in a body committed to the British cause — Wilson made known his wish that no American citizen should be a member of the Zionist Commission.

From the outset, then, the commission was to have its wings clipped.

From virtually the beginning of the work of the Zionist Commission a state of tension arose between Aaronsohn and Weizmann. Weizmann's position was admittedly difficult. The members of the commission were after all formally appointed by the Zionist Organization — and there Aaronsohn was still regarded as a black sheep by some of its leading figures. Moreover, the leaders of the community in Palestine, whom the commission could certainly not ignore, had not forgotten or forgiven him. Weizmann however knew that for the tasks before them there was nobody as capable, knowledgeable, and professionally equipped as Aaronsohn; nor could his unequaled standing with the British be brushed aside. The result was a certain deviousness in Weizmann's behavior.

The crucial problem was significantly Aaronsohn's very status. While the commission was still on its way to Palestine (in Rome, March 10, 1918) he records in his diary: "The composition of the Commission is finally: Weizmann, Sieff, Cowen, Eder, Ormsby-Gore, Sylvan Levi, Levontin (unattached) [whatever that might mean], Rosenheck, Walter Meier and I. Jimmy [Rothschild]," he added, "is also with us."

Yet at their first meeting in Tel Aviv, on April 15, he confronted the members of the commission with the question: Am I a member or am I not? He went on to suggest, moreover, that if this question were not clarified he would be unable to continue. A hubbub ensued. He must not, everybody agreed, dream of resigning because of the idiocies of the communal leaders. Dr. Eder even declared that his resignation would be tantamout to treachery. Nevertheless Weizmann's ambivalence continued, and Aaronsohn's real status was reduced to that of an "expert adviser."

There was, behind Aaron's dissatisfaction, a fundamental bitterness. He could not free his mind of the past. He even gave vent to it in a talk with Ormsby-Gore. "The past is repeating itself. Yohanan of Gush-Halav died, an unknown hero, while Joseph Flavius, traitor and coward, lived on to write the history. My Sarah died at her post as a heroine, while the silly teenage girls in

Tel Aviv remain to write the history. Many generations will pass before Joseph stops being a saint, and the honor due to Yohanan is restored."[5]

The first task of the Zionist Commission, which arrived in Tel Aviv on April 4, 1918, was of course to repair the ravages wrought within the Jewish community by the Djemal Pasha regime. The horizons of the commission however were much broader. While its members were still in Cairo on their way to Palestine, Aaronsohn had proposed to British Headquarters a far-reaching plan of settlement on land long unworked, empty of inhabitants and landowners — in the area between Jaffa and Rafiah on the Egyptian border. He put forward the idea to an early meeting of the commission (April 7, 1918) in Jaffa.

The Military Administration, established by General Allenby after the liberation of southern Palestine, would be asked to grant the commission a concession for agricultural development of four hundred thousand acres (nearly two million dunams). Development would be by intensive mechanized methods.

Aaronsohn believed that at most a very small proportion of the area would involve absentee owners, and the solution to this problem would present no difficulties. The area as a whole would be controlled by the commission, and Aaronsohn — in two lectures — demonstrated that if the plan were taken in hand at once and the necessary funds made available in time, the next winter's harvest would be adequate for feeding the whole civilian population as well as the armed forces.

Weizmann reported to the commission that Generals Clayton and Money of the Military Administration had expressed approval of the scheme provided that the Military Administration were enabled to supervise its implementation. Responsibility for the actual execution, provision of machines, materials and manpower, would be in the hands of the commission. Two representatives of the commission — Aaronsohn and veteran agronomist Yitzhak Wilkansky (Volcani) — and two British officers spent eight days surveying the area, and on May 16 Aaronsohn reported to the

---

5. In the revolt against Rome.

commission. As had been foreseen eighty percent of the area was unworked; and the concept of "dry farming" would govern the development. In the first year the harvest would be moderately good; in the second year a bumper harvest could be expected.

Three more veteran agricultural experts joined Aaronsohn and Wilkansky in a further report, presenting a more detailed plan, now covering administrative costs and funding.

The work force required would be one thousand eight hundred skilled Jewish farm workers. There were not enough in Palestine and some would have to be brought from Egypt, where there were still refugees from the 1914 expulsion. Two thousand Arabs would be needed as well. Once again Aaronsohn emphasized the significance of employing Arab labor (as he had done when he established the experiment station in 1910): modern technology would best exploit ancient methods of the East — and those were the methods of the unskilled Arab workers.

Immersed in the constructive planning — and that precisely for work on the land — Aaron was yet being made conscious of the old hatreds in the community. It was while he was still in Cairo on the way to Palestine that it made itself felt. Here Aaron encountered an enemy he had not known. It was Eliezer Hoofien, the manager of the Anglo-Palestine Bank.

While Nili was functioning Hoofien had decided, as the senior banker in the country, that all the relief money coming in from Aaronsohn's Special Committee for Aid to the Deportees in Cairo should be handled by him and not by Dizengoff. With the capture of Jerusalem, he urged the headquarters of the bank in London to put this demand to the special committee in Cairo (now peacefully functioning — with Gluskin cooperating).

He went further, however. He dragged the issue into the British arena. He applied to the newly appointed military governor of Jerusalem, Ronald Storrs, asking to be permitted to visit Cairo — where, so he told Storrs, he would convince General Headquarters of the utter unsuitability of the Special Committee to handle funds. Not content with this, he wrote a private letter to Storrs, vilifying the Cairo committee — and Aaronsohn personally. He described Nili under Aaronsohn's leadership as a collection of talkative incompetents, led in Palestine by a person of ill repute, and stupid to boot. Similarly scathing was his criticism of the members of the Cairo committee, notably banker Mosseri, lawyer Alexander and even physician Naftali Weitz. Before sending the letters, however, he discovered that Gluskin had made peace with the Special Committee, and was intending to visit Palestine so as to enlighten the community of the new and tranquil order in the Cairo Committee's affairs. He therefore called on Gluskin not to come to Palestine but to await him, Hoofien, in Cairo.

Gluskin, who also was under no kind of obligation to Hoofien, ignored the demand. Whereupon, Hoofien wrote a further letter, this time to an aide of Storrs, Lieutenant Monckton. There he boldly accused Gluskin of mishandling a certain transfer of relief money!

Finally, after two months of effort, Hoofien was permitted by the British authorities to visit Egypt — and he arrived there almost simultaneously with the Zionist Commission. Calling on Aaronsohn, he at once launched into a virulent "statement." He, Hoofien announced, regarded Aaronsohn as a politician. He denounced his activities in the past, and warned Aaronsohn that unless he explained his objectives in the past and his present purposes, he would not be allowed to work in Palestine. Aaronsohn kept his cool, suggested that it was Hoofien who should be making explanations; and he concluded the conversation by proposing that they debate the issues in the presence of members of the commission.

Hoofien accepted the challenge. A record of that encounter was made by commission member Israel Sieff. Hoofien, though still blustering, and threatening even the commission with boycott, was reduced to near silence by Weizmann's forthright description of Aaronsohn's work for the community, his major contribution to the British military campaign and his importance to the Zionist cause.[6] Aaronsohn noted a very satisfying victory.

When however the commission arrived in Palestine, Aaron discovered that Hoofien's attitude, brutal as it was, did reflect broadly the feelings — and behavior — of the community towards the Aaronsohns and the memory of Nili. Indeed a letter reached him in his last week in Cairo giving him a foretaste of the climate in Jaffa.

It came from Alex and presented an ugly picture. On his arrival from

---

6. Aaron Aaronsohn, *Diary*, p. 382, March 31, 1918. See also Central Zionist Archives.

Egypt, he wrote, he had been treated with open hostility by the communal leaders. He named them: Betzalel Joffe, Mordechai Ben-Hillel HaCohen, Eliahu Berligne. His only companion and comfort in all those weeks had been Liova Schneierson. (Liova himself had suffered his share of contumely.) "For months," wrote Alex, "we were the loneliest people in the land. When we passed people in the street they stopped talking. They called us spies, scoundrels, traitors. They created a veritable boycott against us. Moreover not a single Nili member was spared by the community. They and their parents, and their children. Na'aman Belkind's father, with a famous record of pioneering patriotism, was not accepted in a single Jewish home. They could not find employment. Even Neiman, the physician, and who of the boycotters could guess how much of their present freedom they owed to him?" Even Weizmann's intervention did not help. "And the graves of our loved ones still fresh."

The only bright spots were in the villages and settlements, where the "ordinary" people lived. There the leadership's hatred had evidently not penetrated. There the people were not affected by the real phobia that revealed itself among the leaders of the community — their fear that Aaronsohn would want to take over the leadership of the community, precisely because he had the knowledge and the ability to do so. Moreover he had influence with the British Military Administration.

Their hatred and fear was so deep that they turned to Weizmann and appealed to him to prevent Aaronsohn from occupying any political position in the country. Weizmann, who was not interested in quarreling with these good Zionists, tried to introduce a measure of rationality to their attitude. In his reply to Mordechai Ben-Hillel HaCohen, he pointed out that Aaronsohn did not occupy a senior role in the Zionist hierarchy. He had come to London in October 1917, when the major effort for the Balfour Declaration had already been made. Then, on its publication he had been sent on a mission to the United States and had done a good job. There was every reason to exploit his capacities and his connections. He was a force "which we have no right to give up; and he has done tremendous service in disseminating among the British the Zionist idea in all its grandeur."

On what he himself experienced on his return to Palestine, Aaron wrote a sort of summing-up to Frankfurter:

My life's work has been destroyed. My collections have been scattered to the four winds, the library has been demolished. My books have been used to wrap butter in Damascus. And after all that has been done to us — not a single word of sympathy from the self-appointed leaders of the community — the Hoofiens, the Thons and the like who claim they cannot forgive me for the danger in which they might have found themselves because of me. A real boycott. A man who gave the British the aid I gave them is lost from a moral point of view, and there's no room for him in decent society.

Yet seen from a distance of nearly a century, it seems that the true depth of the continuing hatred towards the Aaronsohns was revealed from another source, unexpected and incredible.

With the fall of southern Palestine into British hands, there came to life the long suppressed desire among the Jewish youth to join in the battle for northern Palestine. It soon developed into a vibrant movement, headed by people who had had experience of public affairs, predominantly leaders of one of the Labor parties, Poalei Zion; and it was carried forward on a tremendous wave of enthusiasm. Jabotinsky later penned a graphic description of the phenomenon, as he saw it in spring of 1918,[7] when the British Military Administration had finally given its consent for recruiting.

I was approached by old mothers, young mothers, Sephardim and Ashkenazim, who complained that the doctors had "shamed" their sons — by not accepting them for service. "I daren't show myself in the street for shame," was their plaint. A sickly Jew, who looked like Methuselah's grandfather, came to protest that he had not been able to deceive the doctor: he had said that he was forty, but the doctor was most unkind.... As for the youngsters, there was nothing that could stop them. Yet I heard that what I saw in Jerusalem was as

---

7. In his *Story of the Jewish Legion*, also quoted in my *Lone Wolf.*

nothing compared to the excitement which raged in Jaffa and among the workers in the colonies.[8]

Both Colonel Patterson and Major Radcliffe Salaman, the medical officer of the Thirty-ninth Battalion, noted this phenomenon when the volunteers arrived in Egypt for training — of youths who added three or four years to their age and old men who deducted twenty from theirs.

How had the battalion come into being at all? Appeals to the Military Administration to create a third Jewish battalion out of the volunteers had at first been met by blank refusal. In fairness, on purely military grounds, the refusal could be justified (as had been the rejection of Aaronsohn's suggestion to Allenby's predecessor, General Murray). Moreover the request was given no support by the Zionist Commission (with the exception of Weizmann who tried to intervene with the British authorities and failed). Whereupon the group of leaders — Dov Hoz, Eliahu Golomb and David Sverdlov — turned to Jabotinsky. Could he not use his influence?

Jabotinsky, only too happy at the idea of another battalion, explained that as a mere lieutenant he had no influence. There was only one man, he said, who had influence with the British military authorities — Aaron Aaronsohn. Golomb and his colleagues, for their part, certainly realized that that was the answer. But to approach the hated creator of Nili — not to mention the employer of Arab labor! Impossible!

At that point, they even considered giving up the whole idea of a battalion — and turning their backs on the tremendous fervor of the people — if it could be brought about only through an approach to the hated Aaronsohn! Meanwhile Jabotinsky had spoken to Aaronsohn, who assured him that of course he sympathized strongly with the volunteer movement and believed that he could turn the scales with the British, but he certainly would not take any initiative to help his and his martyred sister's vilifiers.

Still unwilling to deal with Aaronsohn, Golomb and his colleagues sent another colleague, Rahel Yanait, who recalled the happy days she had spent at the experiment station, to talk to Aaronsohn. His reply was sharp. He himself, he informed her, had spoken and written in favor of a Jewish Legion, and of

---

8. Colonies — the term then used for the agricultural villages.

course he could help with the British. But — the attitude and behavior of the group she represented towards him and his family and his comrades had forced him into a position where he didn't feel any desire, nor indeed did he have any right to interfere in their affairs. "They pretend," he added, "that they are pure souls. Contact with us would therefore soil their nobility." He for his part, he told her, remembered the sentence of death by Hashomer on Lishansky and its execution — which still horrified him.

"This shakes her to the depth," he writes in his diary, "and her response is a pathetic apologia."

Thus, it was deadlock. Jabotinsky, however, did not let go. He spoke once more to Aaronsohn; and he brought to Golomb and his group Aaronsohn's last word. He would certainly meet with them, but they must come to him. What was more, he would not agree to cooperation if they intended to keep secret that they had made contact with him. Again Rahel came to Aaron but in vain. Now Jabotinsky intervened once more, and told them bluntly that they must overcome their hatred if they wanted a battalion. That finally convinced them.

Four of them came to Aaronsohn: Eliahu Golomb, Dov Hoz, David Sverdlov and Rahel. They even found a formula for keeping their hands clean. Nili was unacceptable. But, as they explained to Aaron, if a "regular" military unit came into existence, spying was of course a legitimate adjunct...

The outcome was dramatic. Aaronsohn went to work that very day. He explained to Deedes and Clayton and to General Money that setting up this battalion was a British interest. Only if a Jewish battalion was created would there be a possibility of creating an intelligence service behind the Turkish lines in the north! Three weeks later (on May 14, 1918) Allenby reversed himself. He sent a recommendation to London for the creation of a battalion of Palestine volunteers.

For procuring the funds and equipment for the big agricultural plan as well as for promoting enlistment in the new volunteer battalion (which, however, never saw battle as the war ended before it could enter the field), the Zionist Commission decided to send a delegation to the United States. Weizmann proposed going himself, but Ormsby-Gore insisted that he remain in

Palestine; and so again the choice fell on Aaronsohn. He visited London, Paris and the United States, and was able to experience at first hand the varying political winds blowing in the international arena in those last months of the war. Most important was the French pressure for a share of control in Palestine. On this subject he encountered a hostile attitude even from Baron Rothschild who expressed opposition to Weizmann's and Aaronsohn's pro-British policy. Aaronsohn believed this was a pretense because of Rothschild's need to exhibit a patriotic pro-French front. Aaronsohn learned of anti-Zionism among Americans — promoted by the Red Cross, which was campaigning against British colonialism.

Indeed a climate of anti-imperialism was spreading in America itself against Britain, with Zionism an inevitable target as being an alleged British tool. Aaronsohn consequently devoted considerable attention to putting the British case for the future control of Palestine, emphasizing that Britain, unlike another power he "could name," was displaying a caring attitude to the inhabitants and to the economy of the country. As he explained in a subsequent memorandum, advocacy coming from a small nation proposing British rule was obviously much more effective than advocacy by Britons themselves.

His hearers were made aware, moreover, of the burgeoning conflict between Britain and France over the northern border of Palestine — where France was pushing for a major part of the Galilee to be included in a Syria controlled or "protected" by France.

Not the least important effect of Aaron's visit to the United States was, again, his deepening relations with Brandeis. He saw in Brandeis his natural leader. "He is great, he is a statesman," he wrote to Alex. "On my first day here we spoke for fourteen hours, the next day for six. I was exhausted..." And Brandeis, for his part, recognized in Aaronsohn "character, good judgment, wisdom." The natural personal chemistry between the two men was enhanced by an unsentimental, pragmatic attitude on the economic system they wished to see adopted in Palestine, a system which in later years was to be dubbed "the free market."

But what of the great plan for settlement in the south which was to be the brightest jewel in the crown of the Zionist Commission and — more important — the opening of a glorious era of reconstruction in the Jewish homeland? The plan was never launched. Despite the expressed approval by the British military leaders in Palestine itself, despite Aaronsohn's very friendly relations and what had been his unassailable standing with the British authorities in London, despite his exciting advocacy of the plan, not only was it turned down by the British government, no explanation was ever published.

Aaronsohn's earlier biographer, Eliezer Livneh, writes laconically that the plan "evaporated together with many other Zionist hopes of that period."[9]

Even this bald assessment, written half a century later, is an understatement. The Middle East Committee of the British War Cabinet which had decided on January 26, 1918, on the creation of the Zionist Commission, noted the important political results that had already accrued to Britain from the Balfour Declaration — the tremendous pro-British Jewish demonstrations throughout Russia that had followed its publication, and a distinctly favorable change in Jewish public opinion, not only in the United States but even in enemy countries. And it explained the formation of the Zionist Commission itself by the need for putting the assurances given in the [Balfour] Declaration into practice!

In fact the Balfour Declaration was then — and for the next two years — not even published in Palestine. That meant simply that for the Palestine population it did not exist. The military administration ignored it completely and acted according to a code of its own, which was directed against any manifestation of Zionist development. It pretended to a strict adherence to the Turkish status quo — including the absence of the nine thousand Jews of Jaffa driven out by Djemal a year earlier. Even this claim of honoring international law was spurious. In Jaffa it nonsensically declared Arabic to be the only official language. The official language in the Turkish Empire had of course been Turkish. Thus an appointed municipal council for Jaffa — whence the Turks had driven the Jews out — contained seven Arabs and two Jews, ignoring the Jewish expellees; in Jerusalem where there had been a Jewish majority for sixty years, the mayor appointed was an Arab.

Protests, verbal and written, did not help. Ormsby-Gore lamely explained the situation by the fact that the British officers now in Palestine had all previously been serving in Arab populated countries, and did not know anything about Jews. And the government of Great Britain was powerless to enlighten them! Moreover, anti-Jewish incitement by Arabs was maintained at a high level with open British complaisance; and the government in

---

9. Livneh, *Aaron Aaronsohn*, p. 327.

London, where Lloyd George was still prime minister, refrained from any action. The net result was that Jews who had had experience of the pogrom-ridden antisemitism of Tsarist Russia claimed that British military antisemitism in Palestine was very similar. Weizmann wrote in precisely such terms to Ormsby-Gore, and Jabotinsky recalls in his memoir his own no less scathing description of British policy in a letter he had sent Weizmann.

When the war ended, Aaronsohn — at Weizmann's request — returned to England from America. They both knew that Zionism was about to be faced by a host of obstacles. It had yet to achieve international recognition of the Jewish people as a modern nation, and as such to be accorded recognition of its historic claim to Palestine. In the forthcoming peace conference the strug-gle for recognition might well have to be renewed. A new political climate was evolving in the aftermath of the war. Among the leaders of the victorious Allies new assessments of national interests would inevitably be made.

Nevertheless a failure of will overtook Weizmann. To Jabotinsky's appeals that the truth of the British retreat from the Balfour Declaration should be brought to the British public — which was still largely pro-Zionist — and that dangerous precedents were being created, Weizmann pleaded that British friendship had undergone no change, and that what was happening in Pales-tine was a temporary aberration. The future civil government, he insisted, would straighten everything out. Aaronsohn, who during the war had warned Rivka that the British might yet "betray us," reacted like Weizmann. Maybe, like Weizmann, he was misled by the warm personal relations he enjoyed with men like Deedes and Clayton. Yet he and Weizmann continued to express optimism in the face even of the strenuous protests by the British Colonel Patterson at blatantly unfair conduct of General Headquarters towards his men in the Jewish battalions of the British army.[10]

---

10. Within a year Weizmann admitted his blunder and now foresaw its grim conse-quences. In a report to the Zionist Organization Greater Actions Committee on January 7, 1920, he said: "It was wrong not to have fought this situation beforehand. Precedents are being created which can be very damaging in our dealings with the English, who are sticklers for precedent." The full story of that period has been told in many places. See Weizmann, *Letters and Papers*, vol. 8; Jehuda Reinharz, *Weizmann: The Making of a Statesman* (New York: Oxford University Press, 1993); Jabotinsky, *Story of the Jewish Legion*; J. H. Patterson, *With the Judeans in the Pales-tine Campaign* (London: Hutchinson & Co., 1922).

CHAPTER 22

Great Hopes

A new world was being born. After all, the great Germanic empires were being dismembered; the once glittering, and powerful, Turkish Empire which had sprawled over the Eurasian land mass had ended her last pitiful struggles in utter defeat. A greater jumble of problems could not be imagined; nor could so colorful a variety of solutions. A lively and inventive mind like that of Aaronsohn, when meeting some of the reputedly best brains in the world as the statesmen gathered in Europe at the end of the war, could not but get involved in discussions about the future picture of Europe and Asia Minor. His diary at the time reflects many of his interesting conversations and meetings on a variety of world issues — which in the end had no practical outcome.

One specific issue, relevant to his immediate concerns, in which Aaronsohn became deeply involved, was Armenia. On the sufferings of the Armenians, first revealed to him by Sarah on her return from Constantinople and later studied during his own visits to Turkey, he had written repeatedly.

Moreover he had developed a political thesis on the subject, partly, or maybe even largely, influenced by the dream of Mark Sykes, that three liberated nations in the Middle East should work together, and create a form of federation against a restoration of the influence and power of Turkey: the Jews in their state-to-be in Palestine; the Arabs in the broad territories they looked forward to in Syria, in Mesopotamia and in Hedjaz; and the Armenians in a state that the Western powers should establish. The potential interests of the Western nations in such a confederation seemed to be clear.

Aaronsohn worked tirelessly on behalf of the Armenians in cooperation with James Malcolm — the fervent Armenian pro-Zionist. However, despite unofficial promises from various quarters, despite even a resolution at the peace conference, the idea never got off the ground. It was given no Arab support. The recognized Arab spokesman, Feisal the son of Hussein, the ruler of Hedjaz, rejected it out of hand — despite the efforts of Weizmann and Malcolm to persuade him of the benefits for all three projected partners. The Americans were cold to it, the British ambivalent. No strong "diaspora" of Armenians rushed to its support. No Western governments came out demonstratively to express recognition of Armenian national rights, or to offer to help plan a future for the anguished Armenian people.[1]

There were signs that even the consummation of the promise contained in the Balfour Declaration was not guaranteed. Some of its traditional opponents, who had accommodated themselves to it because it had served British wartime interests at one of the most critical moments of the war, now felt free of any obligation to the Jewish people. Lord Curzon, Balfour's successor as foreign minister, had never owned to any emotional antagonism to Zionism, but did not budge from the unsentimental belief that Zionism was simply unachievable — and he was not alone. There were others equally pragmatic, at a high level in the establishment, who believed that a better deal could be made with the French by letting them "have" Palestine and gaining for Britain useful territory elsewhere in the defeated German and Turkish empires.

These were not empty fears, but derived from reliable sources. Clearly, then, Weizmann must not leave London but remain in close touch with the Foreign Affairs establishment. He consequently proposed to Aaronsohn to proceed to Paris, already overflowing with delegates preparing for the peace conference. There he should set up the Zionist campaign — which would include the demand that Britain be granted the trusteeship over Palestine, to oversee its development, pending the ultimate establishment of the Jewish national home.

True, the "permanent" representative of the Zionist leadership in relations with the French government was Nahum Sokolow; but Paris was rapidly becoming the capital of international politics. Sokolow did have to his credit a French pro-Zionist declaration, the first by a great power, in the summer of 1917. He had however had little experience with the British Foreign Office — where Weizmann was completely at home — and no

---

1. In the fall of 1920 Soviet Russian leader Lenin cooperated with the leader of the new Turkey, Kemal Ataturk, in dividing Armenia between their two countries.

American experience at all; and the Americans, under President Wilson's direction, expected (and were expected by many others) to occupy the center of the stage — and the backstage — in the Paris deliberations.

By absolute contrast, here was Aaronsohn, a household name both in the world of science and in the diplomatic world in the United States. In his several long visits there he had amassed a host of political and social connections and admirers. He possessed moreover an unusual insight into issues in American affairs — on which, one might say, he "spoke American like a native" — which served him to great advantage in all his contacts.

Now he developed excellent relations with members of President Wilson's entourage — primarily with his intimate advisers Colonel House and William C. Bullitt[2] (who was later to write that he believed that Aaronsohn was the greatest man he had ever met). It was through Bullitt that Aaronsohn arranged for Weizmann to meet with Colonel House (January 6, 1919) and, a week later, with the president himself.

As for the British delegation to the conference, its military section could at first sight have been handpicked by Aaronsohn. Whatever doubts were being debated in London about the merits and the future of the Balfour Declaration, their attitude was not affected. Here were all old friends, and now indeed colleagues: Sir Basil Thomson, Colonel Harold Gribbon and his chief, the Director of Military Intelligence General George MacDonogh. Here also was Mark Sykes. Their individual personal sympathies coincided with their official proclaimed objectives — to secure international support for the establishment under British guardianship of a Jewish National Home in Palestine. Moreover an important reinforcement came to Paris, in the person of Major Charles Webster, the liaison officer between the political and the military section of the delegation, headed by General Sir Henry Wilson, chief of the Imperial General Staff.

From this vantage point Webster was able to "see whole" the political panorama in Paris, and to keep Wilson informed with an authentic account and analysis of the Zionist potential for the promotion of the British interest. Between him and Aaronsohn a close collaboration developed. They exchanged information freely; and historian Sir Charles (as he became)

---

2. In later years US ambassador successively to Moscow and Paris.

revealed years later that Aaronsohn had had frequent personal meetings with Sir Henry Wilson.[3]

Significantly, in an article in 1942 Webster asserted that "it is quite clear that the supporters of the [Jewish] National Home would not have overcome the obstacles if this was not seen as essential to important British interests. Of particular influence was the effective support of the General Staff."[4]

It would seem natural that the Zionists — from Europe and Palestine — assembled in Paris should welcome Weizmann's choice of Aaronsohn to lead the Zionist campaign in Paris. There surely was not a single member of any of the delegations in Paris at this crucial stage in history even remotely approaching Aaronsohn's unique knowledge, persuasive capacity and opportunities in stating his nation's case.

Yet, at every step involving Aaronsohn, Weizmann had to contend with severe resistance from both Palestinian and European Zionists. The old prejudices and hatreds continued to play a dominant role in their attitudes. Even now Menachem Mendel Ussischkin, veteran leader of Russian Zionism, could say, "If you must, you make use of spies, but you don't shake hands with them."[5] The American Zionists, who continually pressed Weizmann to accord Aaronsohn an official position — and standing — in the Zionist establishment, and now in the peace conference, were still a minor player in the movement.

The result was a strange tug-of-war between Aaronsohn and Weizmann. Time after time, as revealed in the diary, seeing himself denied influence in the internal affairs of the Zionist Organization, Aaronsohn decided to retire from the arena, go back to Palestine and resume his scientific career. Time after time, Weizmann argued that Aaronsohn was indispensable and irreplaceable; that it was his patriotic duty to continue contributing his unique talents to the cause; and that his withdrawal would have a cataclysmic effect

3. Recorded by Eliezer Livneh, who interviewed Webster in London in 1960. Livneh, *Aaron Aaronsohn*, p. 378.
4. Philip W. Ireland, ed., *The Near East: Problems and Prospects* (Chicago: University of Chicago Press, 1942).
5. Livneh, *Aaron Aaronsohn*, p. 342.

in many quarters far beyond the delegation to the peace conference. In the end Aaronsohn had to admit to himself that he had no option but to succumb.

A sharp reflection of the problem by which both men were faced is provided by the way the Zionists handled their preparations for presenting their case to the Council of Ten — the "executive committee" of the peace conference. It is graphically described by Aaronsohn in his diary on January 27, 1919 (in London):

> At one o'clock this afternoon I go to the Carlton [hotel] at the invitation of De Haas and Flexner [of the American Zionist leadership]. They are very worried. Something has changed. At midnight they were told on the telephone that by Friday at the latest our proposals, including the boundaries [of Palestine] will be submitted together with the reasons justifying them. It is therefore essential that between now and this evening I must create a memorandum on the borders, and their rationale. I protest in the strongest terms against these working methods. For months I have been protesting to Chaim against these unheard-of methods. The task is assigned to (Harry) Sacher or to Leon Simon or Albert Haimson, and in the end, at the last moment, it transpires that nothing has been done — because they did not ask experts to do it. I haven't got even a miserable map...
>
> I go out at once to the War Office and to the Naval Intelligence and work with the help of Captain Mackindoe, Captain Buxton, Dr. Dixon, etc. I collect a number of maps and data and set to work.... I develop the rationale for our borders...

The British delegation to the conference had no difficulty in adopting most of the essentials of Aaronsohn's formulation; and its members undertook to seek acceptance by the prime minister. A week later, on February 3, Aaronsohn records in the diary:

> At ten o'clock Gribbon comes to call me. What is being discussed is the definition of the northern and northeastern borders of Palestine and to present them in a manner which will affect the imagination of Lloyd George and others. To this end we adopt the formula "the country of the Jordan and its affluents." Sir Henry Wilson approves.

Lloyd George is very keen on the Palestine problem, but he thinks
that the border is somewhere near the Sea of Galilee.

"The British friends," he writes the next day, "would defend the [proposal on]
the northern and north-eastern borders, but out of consideration for Feisal
they propose leaving the definition of the eastern border to negotiation
between Jews and Arabs."[6]

Indeed on this subject Weizmann and his Political Committee had earlier
reached agreement with representatives of the British government: the
border between Palestine and the Arab territory would be within
Transjordan. The Zionists had urged the inclusion in Palestine of the Hedjaz
railway, but the British had insisted — and had their way — that the Hedjaz
railway belonged to the Arabs. The border agreed upon thus would run just
west of the railway. What was needed now urgently was a much more detailed
presentation; and the thrust of Aaronsohn's memorandum and map was thus
a combined function of his scientific mind and his geopolitical vision.
Though the borders he drew reflected in essence the territory of Palestine in
traditional historical terms, they would also ensure the economic viability of
the ultimate Jewish state, and specifically its need of adequate water
resources. This required inclusion of the Litani and the Yarmuk Rivers.

That too had long been agreed upon in principle with the British. Even
twenty-two months after Aaronsohn's submissions, while negotiations with
the French were still in progress, Foreign Secretary Lord Curzon wrote to the
senior British negotiator Robert Vansittart:

> His Majesty's Government are not prepared to conclude any arrange-
> ment which does not contain due provision for the future utilization
> by Palestine of the waters of the Yarmuk and the Litani, which may
> well prove vital to the economic development of the country and the
> creation of the National Home for the Jews.[7]

What Curzon did not know and what Aaronsohn certainly could not know
was that already in December 1918, at the very outset of the talks with France,
Lloyd George, keeping his foreign minister in ignorance, and allowing the
Foreign Office officials to continue negotiations with their French opposite

---

6. See my *Lone Wolf*, chapter 37.
7. PRO/FO 13621/4164/44, November 9, 1920.

number on the basis of the British understanding with the Zionists, had accepted the restrictive terms laid down by President Clemenceau for the northern border of Palestine.

Lloyd George had his reasons. He was demanding for Britain certain oil and railway rights in Mesopotamia.[8]

Having completed drawing the historic map, Aaronsohn turned his thoughts once more to retirement from the political arena. He was being given no peace by Weizmann, who now insisted that Aaronsohn participate in a Zionist conference to be held in London on February 23, 1919. But this time, he writes in the diary, he did not give in: "I shall not travel to London, for I have nothing to do at their conference."

This seemed to show that his mind was finally made up to go back to his scientific work. It is conceivable that an additional component of his discomfort had developed: disappointment with Brandeis. Two months earlier, on December 25, he had written in the diary: "I should like to go to Washington. If he does not give up his post there and come to take the [Zionist] helm, he will be assuming a heavy responsibility to history."

He badly wanted Brandeis to come now to Europe; but Brandeis did not come. Precisely because he was able to observe several of Brandeis's important and able Zionist lieutenants — Felix Frankfurter, Stephen Wise, Bernard Flexner and Jacob De Haas — who were active in Paris and cooperating at close quarters with him in his diplomatic contacts, he was able to assess that without Brandeis they would not constitute a counterweight to the Europeans and the Palestinians in the internal affairs of the Zionist Organization.

Brandeis's own dilemma was surely manifest. It was no small achievement to be a judge in the highest court in the land, not to mention the special position of trust that he occupied as a friend of President Wilson, at the pinnacle of American affairs. On the other hand, he was developing the belief that with Britain becoming the effective ruler of Palestine, and thus the guardian of the projected Jewish National Home, the Zionist political struggle would be

---

8. British Foreign Policy Documents (BFPD), vol. 7, p. 865. For a detailed account of the Anglo-French negotiations, see my *Lone Wolf*, vol. 1, pp. 547-51 and 688-95.

ended; the British would fulfill their obligations and the Jews would be able to concentrate exclusively on the economic upbuilding of the country. To the upbuilding he would be able to contribute without giving up his seat in the Supreme Court.

Brandeis's belief in the British was deep-seated. In June 1919 he visited Palestine and he quarreled angrily with Jabotinsky, who described to him the hostile behavior of the military administration, and the consequent dangerous growth of anti-Jewish incitement among the Arabs; but he had talked to Allenby, representing the British Empire, and Allenby evidently reassured him. "I believe in British justice," he told Jabotinsky.[9]

Precisely then, amid the Zionists' preparations for the presentation at the peace conference, another shocking blow came down on Aaronsohn, indeed on the whole Zionist movement. Mark Sykes passed away. He was felled by the raging worldwide influenza epidemic — and two days later, on February 4, he died. From the time a year earlier, when he first made contact with the Zionists, he had developed into a devoted advocate for their cause within the British establishment. When the government decided on the final text of the Balfour Declaration, it was Sykes who came out of the Cabinet room and joyfully exclaimed to Weizmann: "It's a boy!"

For Aaronsohn he had been, next to Gribbon, his closest friend and confidant in Britain. Six days before his death they had met in Gribbon's office. He had returned a few days earlier from a brief visit to Palestine, and he presented a frank and disturbing report. Aaronsohn summarized it in his diary:

> The British officers in the Administration have friendly feelings for Islam and are opposed to the Jews. The Arabs are becoming more and more brazen. It seems, as Sykes himself admits, that Jabotinsky's interpretation [of the situation] is not mistaken at all.

And in that conversation, evidently their last, Sykes gave expression to another emotion which was moving him. He asked Aaronsohn whether he

---

9. See my *Lone Wolf*, vol. 1, pp. 510-14.

believed that the British government should set up a memorial to Sarah. Aaronsohn replied, "Yes, without a doubt!"[10]

On February 18 Aaronsohn received a message that Rivka was on her way from New York and would be in London on the 23rd — which was the day of the Zionist conference. He telephoned Weizmann immediately to tell him that he would come to London on the 23rd after all — not for the conference but in order to meet Rivka.

He had broken off his diary in the middle of a sentence on February 21 — obviously because of pressures of the preparations for the peace conference. When he met Rivka she told him she intended to continue on to Palestine in April. (She was about to receive a British travel document.) Aaron urged her to postpone her return for a month, and then they could travel home together. Rivka however was impatient, wanting to get back to her father; and she turned down his suggestion.

Four days later came the turn of the Zionists to make their statement before the Council of Ten. The ten represented the five victorious Allies — Britain, France, Italy, Japan and the United States. Arthur Balfour and Lord Milner represented Britain; Stephan Pichon, the French foreign minister, and Andre Tardieu represented France; the United States chief representative was Secretary of State Robert Lansing.

Sokolow spoke first, briefly and concisely. He demanded recognition of the historic claim of the Jewish people to the Land of Israel, and the creation of conditions in that country that would bring about the development of an autonomous Jewish commonwealth. He called for economic aid to bring in immigrants and for their settlement.

He was followed by Weizmann who, in the tradition of Herzl and Nordau at the first Zionist Congress, described the distressful condition of the Jews in Eastern Europe — indeed the communities were, at that very moment, passing through a wave of pogroms of unprecedented ferocity. The only solution, he declared, was Zionism.

He, like Sokolow, quoted from the official Zionist statement which, together with the map and commentary by Aaronsohn, was submitted to the conference.

---

10. But, as he explains bitterly in his diary, his reply was hesitant — because he believed that this should be done by the Jewish community. Nothing came of the idea.

Aaronsohn having been denied a place in the delegation at this historic event, and not having renewed his diary entries, his reactions are nowhere recorded.

There was, however, a reaction from another quarter. That evening, at a moment's notice, Shmuel Tolkowsky gave a dinner to some twenty guests. Present, in addition to the Zionist spokesmen at the conference, and other prominent Zionists, were three British officers. All had worked with Aaronsohn during the war: Gribbon — now a colonel — Meinertzhagen and Ormsby-Gore. There Gribbon made a loaded remark:

> The Jews must remember that no man has done more than Aaron to make the conquest of Palestine by the British possible.[11]

Aaron, for his part, failed to maintain his threat to leave the political arena; and he continued, as an adviser to the Zionist delegation, to travel to and from Paris. Indeed he had taken to flying. The Royal Air Force accommodated the delegates to the peace conference on their aircraft (with room for one or two passengers) and Aaron — whether to save time or because he enjoyed the exhilarating experience — preferred to take advantage of the RAF offer.

Several friends, as well as Rivka and Avshalom's sister Tsilla Feinberg, who was in London at the time, warned him of the dangers, but to no avail.

On May 11 Aaronsohn arrived in London by air from Paris. With the pilot of the plane, Jefferson, he arranged to be taken back to Paris a few days later. Vera Weizmann (Chaim's wife) asked to be allowed to join the flight. But official regulations did not allow women to do so.

Thus in the morning of Thursday, May 15, Aaronsohn called at the War Office for a talk with Colonel Gribbon, and then made his way to the airfield in a War Office car carrying mailbags destined for France. Tsilla accompanied him to the Kenley airfield.

With the mailbags loaded, the plane took off; but, as Tsilla later reported, it came back minutes later. A fault was discovered in a propellor. Tsilla took

---

11. Engle, *The Nili Spies*, p. 222. Gribbon in his memoirs (unfinished at his death in 1948) also declared that Aaron [by his strategic advice to Allenby] had saved the British forty thousand casualties. This had been the assessment by CIGS Robertson of the likely casualties if Allenby's original plan had been carried out. See chapter 13 above.

advantage of Aaron's return to urge him once more not to fly. He angrily accused her of cowardice. The plane, much delayed, took off a second time. Meantime, a fog was developing over the French side of the Channel. The plane never reached its destination. It fell into the water close to the French coast at Boulogne. All that was found were floating bags of mail.

Appendix 1:

Sarah's Last Letter (October 9, 1917)

After my departure please give the Zeldin family 105 francs, the Schwartz family 105 francs, and to Menashe 102 francs. As regards the laborers of the station[1] we do not yet know their fate. If they are released and allowed to go on working at the station, then they can live on the stores of wheat, and receive small sums of money, 30 francs a month; there are wheat and barley at the Station.

Should the government forbid the continuation of work at the station, and the workmen be discharged, please advance them 50 francs each and let them go and seek work. You should, however, wait a few more days to see what actually happens to us.

Tell Grad to pay out not one single sou without your permission. We wish to reserve the money for ourselves; we may perhaps help with money. It seems that they have made no use of our money, and have done nothing.[2]

According to what I heard,[3] the Mudir, in reporting to the Commandant, gave him the following three names: Appelbaum, Feitelson, and Madorsky of Hedera. It seems to me that these have given our work away; they have simply betrayed us.

Our situation is very bad, mine most of all because the whole blame falls on me. I was beaten murderously, and they bound me with ropes. Do remember, to describe all our suffering to those who shall come after we have passed away. I do not believe that we shall survive after having been betrayed, and

---

1. The Jewish Agricultural Experiment Station at Athlit.
2. The Zichron communal committee who, she believed, if they had tried, could have rescued her by bribing the officials.
3. Sarah, having lived in Constantinople for two years, had learned to understand Turkish.

the whole truth about us probably exposed. The news of victory must eventually come, and, as you will be seeing my brothers, tell them about our martyrdom, and let them know that Sarah has asked that each drop of her blood be avenged measure for measure; vengeance both upon our Jews and, especially, upon the rulers under whom we are living; that no mercy shall be shown, just as they have shown no mercy to us.

Believe me, I have no more strength left to endure, and I prefer to kill myself than to be tortured any more at their bloodstained hands.

They say they will send us away to Damascus; there they will surely hang me. I shall try to get hold of some small firearm or poison. I do not want them to maul my body.

My sorrow is the greater for seeing my father suffering in innocence. But there will come a day of reckoning; we have died as warriors, and have not given way.

Tell the Committee of Zichron that on the day of judgment they will be judged. No matter; we have striven, we have paved a road of happiness for the nation. Pearl and Adele;[4] the wicked ones, it matters not; I do not condemn even them, and I say let them flourish. I have striven for my people; and if my people be mean, so be it.

We still shall surely get news from Haifa. A day or two after the military have evacuated the village, Izhak could perhaps go out on to the mountains on foot in search of Yosef, so that we may at least learn of his whereabouts. Did they not send to comb out the country to find him? He must never give in, far better that he should kill himself.

They have come, and I can write no longer.[5]

---

4. Two Zichron women who, when the Turkish soldiers came, helped by directing them to the homes of Nili members.
5. Little Avner, who picked up the letter, delivered it to David Sternberg (not a member of Nili, but a relative of the family). Sarah had entrusted Sternberg, for emergencies, with one hundred gold pounds.

Appendix 2:

Turkish Defenses on Palestine Mediterranean Coast as Reported by Aaron Aaronsohn in July 1916

Place	Garrison	Remarks
Jaffa NNE of Jaffa Town	200 Mujahaddin Post of 12 coastguards	Near mouth of the Auja
Sidna Ali (Arsuf)	Post of 20 to 30 coastguards	
N. of Nahr-ul-Falik	2 posts of 8 to 10 coastguards each	Opposite wreck of Russian steamer on rocks 200 ft. high. Could be shelled easily from the sea.
W. of Mukhalid (Inland from Ain Tubah)	Post of 12 to 15 coastguards. Reserve of 30 to 40 men under a Yuzbashi [captain]	
Between Nahr, Askanderunah and Minet-abu-Zabura	Post of 12 coastguards	Usually
Near Birket-es-Safra (NE of Tel-el-Akdar)	Small post of coastguards	
Caesarea	Post of from 15 to 20 coastguards	

Place	Garrison	Remarks
Tanturah	Generally about 30 regulars	15 to 20 regulars on hill of Zum-Marin (Zicron Yaqub). Good carriage roads here from sea are protected by dynamite fougasses [mines]. Helio [small aircraft] communication with Dahlieh.
Athlit (Jewish village)	Post of 12 coastguards	Observation post in water tower.
Bir el Bedawish	Post of 12 coastguards	
Neuhartdhof	Post of 16 to 18 coastguards	The Germans sent their women away on arrival of Gendarmerie.
Tel es Sammaq	3 to 4 coastguards	
French convent	Observation post	Telephone connection to Haifa.

Appendix 3:

Churchill's Concurrence
on the Strategy Urged by Aaronsohn

In Winston Churchill's book, *The World Crisis*, published after the war, he refers to the fact that after General Murray's dismissal Lloyd George offered the command of the British forces in Palestine to General Smuts. "After deliberation Smuts replied that he was willing to accept the task on one condition, namely that he should be allowed to land an adequate army to cut the Turkish communications."

Further in his book Churchill, pouring the highest praise on Allenby for his victory, goes on to say that nevertheless

> It would have been far safer and far cheaper in life and resources to run a greater risk for a shorter time. The advantage of command of the sea should not have been neglected. If, while Allenby held the Turks at Gaza, a long-prepared descent had been made at Haifa or elsewhere on the sea coast behind them, and if the railway by which alone they could exist had been severed in September by a new army of six or eight divisions, the war in Syria would have been ended at a stroke.

By Churchill's calculation, with Syria conquered, the great bulk of the British force in Palestine would have been transferred to the west in good time to meet the Germans' spring offensive. In the critical circumstances of that spring indeed, sixty-one British battalions were incontinently snatched from Palestine to plug the hole of the 21st of March (1918). They were returned later to continue Allenby's offensive in Syria till the victory (October 14, 1918).

Churchill continued:

> It will be incredible to future generations that the strategists of an
> island people then blessed with the unique and sovereign attribute of
> Sea Power should...have failed so utterly to turn it to offensive
> profit.[6]

---

6. Churchill, *The World Crisis*, p.1208.

Appendix 4:

Colonel Richard Meinhertzhagen on T. E. Lawrence

No single one of (his admirers) had any first-hand knowledge of Lawrence's Arabian exploits, having gained their knowledge from Lawrence himself and from what he spread about, knowing it to be either false or exaggerated.... Lawrence never commanded anything but a looting rabble of murderous Arabs, he took part in no military operations and his desert exploits had not the slightest bearing on Allenby's campaign. In his own words his was a "side-show of a side-show"....

I probably knew Lawrence better than any living man.... I believe I was the only one of his friends to whom he confided that he was a complete fraud.[7]

---

7. Meinhertzhagen, *Middle East Diary*, pp 41–46. A comprehensive, meticulously documented debunking of Lawrence was written by Richard Aldington.

Appendix 5:

The Mysteries Surrounding Aaronsohn's Death

For many years a widely held belief persisted in Palestine that the British had brought about Aaronsohn's death. There were no known facts to justify such a belief. It was a surmise rationalized by the famous question *Cui bono?* (Who benefits?) The British, it was said, were too deeply indebted to Aaronsohn for his contribution (though few knew its true measure) to the British military victory. It was assumed that, had he lived, he would have been most determined in his demand for the fulfillment of the British wartime promises.

There were however some strange circumstances surrounding his death. The basic facts were that on a foggy day the RAF mail plane in which he was traveling fell into the sea off the French coast at Boulogne, and he and the pilot Captain E. B. Jefferson were drowned. The fatal accident was reported in the *London Times* five days later, accompanied by a biographical note on Aaronsohn and his contribution to the British campaign in Palestine.

An official War Office inquiry was held by the commander of Kenley air field, Lt. Col. Neil Primrose, from which the plane, No. 5894, took off. Its report contained the evidence of two eyewitnesses, fishing boat captain Henri Ramet and his son. The father saw the plane come down at a distance of about fifty meters from his boat. It was making a loud noise and he concluded that the engine was working. The son, amplifying, said he saw a body floating on the surface of the water, but it sank almost immediately. Some mail bags were recovered.

Only two local French newspapers, *Le Télégramme* and *France du Nord*, contained these details; but they reported one additional fact: on the same day, at about the same time, 3:30PM, another plane came down near the same spot.

The Harbor Master at Boulogne saw the plane foundering in the water, rushed a rescue team — and that pilot was saved.

No other newspaper, in France or in England, repeated this report.

There is no record of a War Office inquiry on the second plane, nor was its loss reported in any other newspaper. Nor is it mentioned in the RAF registry. Strangely enough, the RAF records are equally bare of any mention of Aaronsohn's plane — and the Primrose report is not there. It is to be found only in the archives at the Aaronsohn library and museum at Zichron Ya'akov.

More than sixty years later, the British writer H. V. F. Winstone made an investigation of his own, visited the Port of Boulogne and scrutinized the RAF files in London. It is in his book — *The Illicit Adventure* — that he revealed the additional facts: the complete silence about the existence and fate of the second plane, and the disappearance from the official archives of the Primrose report.[8] Winstone ends his account: "It is perhaps significant that a few months after the fatal accident the RAF Inspector of Accidents resigned."

---

8. Winstone, *The Illicit Adventure*, p. 355.

Appreciations

In the aftermath of Aaronsohn's death many of the personalities who had come to know him well wrote messages of appreciation to his brother Alex or his sister Rivka, or to Dr. David Eder, then the acting chairman of the Zionist Commission.

Among them also were officers with whom he had worked at General Headquarters in Cairo: Allenby, Clayton, Deedes, Ormsby-Gore and Meinertzhagen. All emphasized his contribution to the Palestine Campaign. Some of their remarks have been quoted in the body of this book. More than once, there occurs a reference to a quality of which there is no hint in his diary: physical bravery in the face of life-threatening danger.

Deedes, who emphasized Aaronsohn's outspokenness "to the point of bluntness, but he never said behind your back what he would not say to your face," declared that Aaronsohn had "placed unreservedly at the disposal of the military authorities his invaluable knowledge and experience and gave us most important assistance, often endangering his freedom and his life."

Henrietta Szold, in a passionate memoir written a year after his death, recalled all his great achievements in every field he touched, and knowing how important he was to his people, chided him: "Why did he have to fly!"[1]

Two other friends of his in America wrote in terms just short of idolatry. David Fairchild, in a letter to Frankfurter a week after Aaron died, wrote:

> I was accustomed to think of Aaronsohn as one of the eternal natural forces, and I cannot think of him as one of us.... Something tremendous has been snatched from the range of our interests with the death of Aaronsohn and his disappearance into the unseen world, which has not yet been studied scientifically.

---

1. *The Maccabeans*, June 1920.

More comprehensive was William C. Bullitt who wrote a year later (to Alex on April 9, 1920):

> He was, I believe, the greatest man I have known. He seemed a sort of giant of an elder day — like Prometheus. He was the quintessence of life: of life when it runs torrential, prodigal and joyous. Many men, no doubt, are as great as he was intellectually, though I have never known his peer, but if they are great intellectually, they are not also great emotionally, as he was; great in courage, in sympathy, in desire, in tenderness, in swift human understanding; great at once in dealing with statesmen and children, with scientists and artists, great at once in humor and constructive imagination.
>
> Aaron, to me, was not merely the flaming embodiment of the determination of the Jewish race to have a home and to be again a nation, but rather a captain in the foremost company of that small army of humanity which marches ever against ignorance, superstition and hatred.
>
> I remember him in Washington — how the diplomats sat open mouthed, astonished by his knowledge and his insight, and were warmed by his picture of the Zion that was to be. I remember him in Paris at the Peace Conference — how from the first he foresaw the end of that tragic drama, how unerringly he picked his way through a thousand diplomatic pitfalls, how wise he was in counsel and how strong in friendship. And withal how human.

Bibliography

English

Aaronsohn, Aaron. "Agricultural and Botanical Explorations in Palestine." US Dept. of Agriculture, *Bureau of Plant Industry Bulletin*, no. 180. Washington: Government Printing Office, 1910.

———. "Wild Dryland Wheat of Palestine and Some Other Promising Plants." *Dry Farming Congress Bulletin* 3, no. 190 (1910): 161–71.

Aaronsohn, Alexander. *With the Turks in Palestine*. Boston: Houghton Mifflin, 1916.

Aldington, Richard. *Lawrence of Arabia: A Biographical Inquiry*. London: Collins, 1955.

Antonius, George. *The Arab Awakening: The Story of the Arab National Movement*. London: H. Hamilton, 1938.

Bentwich, Norman. *Wanderer between Two Worlds: An Autobiography*. London: Kegan Paul, Trench, Trubner and Co., 1941.

Churchill, Winston S. *The World Crisis*. London: Odhams Press, 1938.

Djemal Pasha, Ahmed. *Memories of a Turkish Statesman, 1913–1919*. London: Hutchinson & Co., 1922.

Engle, Anita. *The Nili Spies*. London: The Hogarth Press, 1959.

Fairchild, David. *The World Was My Garden: Travels of a Plant Explorer*. New York and London: Charles Scribner's Sons, 1938.

Falls, Captain Cyril. *Military Operations: The Palestine Canpaig Pt. 1*. London, 1925.

Friedman, Isaiah. *Germany, Turkey and Zionism, 1897–1918*. London: Oxford University Press, 1977.

———. *The Question of Palestine 1914–1918: A Study of British-Jewish-Arab Relations*. London: Routledge and Kegan Paul, 1973.

Hardinge, Charles. *Old Diplomacy: The Reminiscences of Lord Hardinge of Penshurst*. London: John Murray, 1947.

Jabotinsky, Vladimir. *The Story of the Jewish Legion*. New York: Bernard Ackerman, 1945.

James, Robert Rhodes. *Gallipoli*. London: B. T. Batsford, 1965.

Katz, Shmuel. *Lone Wolf: A Biography of Vladimir (Ze'ev) Jabotinsky*. 2 vols. New York: Barricade Books, 1996.

Kedourie, Elie. *The Chatham House Version and Other Middle Eastern Studies*. London: Weidenfeld and Nicolson, 1970.

———. *England and the Middle East*. London: Bowes & Bowes, 1956.

———. "Young Turks, Freemasons and Jews." *Middle Eastern Studies* 7 (January 1971).

Manuel, Frank E. *The Realities of America-Palestine Relations*. Washington, DC: Public Affairs Press, 1949.

Meinertzhagen, Richard. *Middle East Diary 1917-1956*. New York: Thomas Yoseloff, 1960.

Nuttson, N. Y. "Agriculture Climatology, Physical Belts, and Crop Ecology of Palestine and Transjordan and their Analogues in the United States." Washington: American Institute of Crop Ecology, 1947.

Oke, Mim Kemal. "Jews and the Question of Zionism in the Ottoman Empire." *Zionism* (Fall 1986): 199-218.

Patterson, John Henry. *With the Judeans in the Palestine Campaign*. London: Hutchinson & Co., 1922.

———. *With the Zionists in Gallipoli*. London: Hutchinson & Co., 1916.

Picard, L. "Geological Studies of Aaron Aaronsohn." *Mad'a* (August 1959).

———. "History of Mineral Research in Israel." *Israel Economic Forum* 6, no. 3 (1954): 10-38.

Reinharz, Jehuda. *Weizmann: The Making of a Statesman*. New York: Oxford University Press, 1993.

Savage, Raymond. *Allenby of Armageddon: A Record of the Career and Campaigns of Field-Marshal Viscount Allenby*. Indianapolis: Bobbs-Merrill, 1926.

Scott, Charles Prestwich. *The Political Diaries of C. P. Scott, 1911-1928*. Edited by Trevor Wilson. London: Collins, 1970.

Sheffy, Yigal. "Institutionalized Deception and Perception Reinforcement: Allenby's Campaigns in Palestine, 1917-1918." In *Intelligence and Military Operations*. Edited by Michael I. Handel. London: Frank Cass & Co., 1990.

Stein, Leonard. *The Balfour Declaration*. London: Vallentine, Mitchell, 1961.

Storrs, Ronald. *Orientations*. London: Ivor Nicholson & Watson, 1937.

Thomson, Basil. *Queer People*. London: Hodder and Stoughton, 1922.

Tuchman, Barbara W. *The Guns of August*. New York: Macmillan Co., 1962.

———. *The Zimmermann Telegram*. New York: Ballantine, 1966.

Waldon, Louis B. *Hard Lying, Eastern Mediterranean 1914-1919*. London: Herbert Jenkins (undated).

Wavell, Archibald P. *The Palestine Campaign*. London: Constable, 1928.

Weizmann, Chaim. *The Letters and Papers of Chaim Weizmann*. Vol. 7. London: Oxford University Press, 1977.

Winstone, H. V. F. *The Illicit Adventure*. London: Jonathan Cape, 1982.

Hebrew

Aaronsohn, Alexander. *Sarah, shalhevet Nili* [Sarah, the flame of Nili]. Jerusalem, 1943.

Aaronsohn, Aaron. "Le blé, l'orge et le siègle à l'état sauvage," [French] *Bulletin of the Botanical Society of France* 61 (1909).

———. *Yoman Aaron Aaronsohn, 1916-1919* [Diary of Aaron Aaronsohn, 1916-1919]. Edited by Yoram Efrati. Tel Aviv: Karni, 1970.

Ben-Elkanah, Shlomo. "My Work in Finding the Grave of Avshalom Feinberg." In *Yosef Lishansky, ish Nili: Ketavim mikhtavim divre zikhronot* [Yosef Lishanky, a man of Nili: Writings, letters and memorials]. Edited by Yosef Nedava. Tel Aviv, 1977.

Ben-Zvi, Rahel Yanait. *Anu olim* [We go up (immigrate to Eretz Israel)]. Tel Aviv: Am Oved, 1959. English edition: *Coming Home*. New York: Herzl Press, 1964.

Dizengoff, Meir. *Im Tel Aviv bagola* [With Tel Aviv in exile]. Tel Aviv, 1931.

Hacohen, Mordechai Ben-Hillel. *Milhemet ha-amim* [War of the nations]. Tel Aviv: Tarpat, 1929.

Joffe, Dr. Hillel. *Dor ma'apilim* [Generation of brave pioneers]. Tel Aviv, 1939.

Katz, Shaul. "Aaron Aaronsohn: Reshit ha-mada ve-reshit ha-mehkar ha-hakla'i be-Eretz Yisra'el [Aaron Aaronsohn: The beginnings of science and the beginnings of agricultural research in Eretz Israel]," *Cathedra*, no. 3 (1977): 3-29.

Livneh, Eliezer. *Aaron Aaronsohn: Ha-ish u-zmano* [Aaron Aaronsohn: The man and his time]. Jerusalem: Bialik Institute, 1969.

———, Yosef Nedava, and Yoram Efrati. *Nili: Toldoteha shel he-aza medinit* [Nili: A story of political daring]. Tel Aviv: Shocken, 1961.

Nedava, Yosef, ed. *Yosef Lishansky, ish Nili: Ketavim mikhtavim divre zikhronot* [Yosef Lishanky, a man of Nili: Writings, letters and memorials]. Tel Aviv, 1977.

———. *Yosef, ish Nili: Aharit davar* [Yosef, a man of Nili: An epilogue] Jerusalem: Agudat Hashmonai, Merkaz le-hinukh ule-tarbut, 1986.

Neiman, Dr. Moshe. *Mi-Petah Tikva le'emek akhor* [From Petah Tikva to a gloomy valley]. Privately published in the 1940s.

Oppenheimer, Heinz Reinhard. *Tsemah 'ever ha-Yarden: Mifkad bikoret li-tsemahim asher ne'esfu u-miktsatam hugderu 'al yede Aharon Aharonson bemeshekh mas'otav (1904-1908) be-'ever ha-Yarden uva-Aravah* [The flora of Transjordan: Review of the plants harvested and identified by Aaron Aaronsohn in his expeditions (1904-1908) to Transjordan and Wadi el-Araba]. Translation of the French original *Florula transiordanica*. Palestine, 1934.

———. *Tsemah ma'arav hayarden* [Flora west of the Jordan]. Tel Aviv, 1940.

Reichert, Y. "L'zecher Aaron Aaronsohn [In memory of Aaron Aaronsohn]." *Hed Hahinuch* (1943-44): 11-12.

Samsonov, Aryeh. *The Book of Zichron Ya'akov*. Zichron Ya'akov, 1940.

Schneierson, Levi Yitzhak. *Miyomano shel ish Nili* [From the diary of a man of Nili]. Haifa: Renaissance Publishers, 1967.

K. Y. Silman (Mimeila). "Summer Lessons for Teachers at Zichron." *Hapoel Hatza'ir*, no. 24 (September 1912).

Slutzky, Yehuda, ed. *Sefer toldot ha-haganah* [A history of the Haganah]. Vol. 3, *Mi ma'avak le-milhama* [From struggle to war]. Tel Aviv: Am Oved, 1978.

Tolkowsky, Shmuel. *Yoman Tziyoni medini: London, 1915–1919; Li-kerat Hatzharat Balfur uve-'ikvoteha* [Zionist political diary: London, 1915–1919; On the making of the Balfour Declaration]. Translated into Hebrew from the French by Haim Ben-Amram. Edited by Devorah Barzilay-Yegar. Jerusalem: Hassifriya Hatziyonit, 1981.

Index

A

Aaronsohn, Alexander 29, 46, 66, 76, 78-79, 80, 88, 99, 107, 126-28, 155, 205, 214, 215, 217, 224, 228, 228n, 236, 245, 278n, 293, 294, 295, 303, 306, 312-13

Aaronsohn, Avner 274, 334

Aaronsohn, Efraim Fishel 27, 29, 43, 145, 152, 252, 269, 277, 293, 306

Aaronsohn, Haya-Rivka 275

Aaronsohn, Malka 27, 29-30, 76n, 177, 276

Aaronsohn, Miriam 258, 259, 260, 268, 306

Aaronsohn, Rivka 15, 19, 29 n. 5, 40-41, 46, 77, 78, 79, 80, 83, 86, 87, 88, 126, 127, 145, 203, 204, 205, 215, 217, 228, 228n, 236, 240, 240n, 251, 306, 307, 319, 329, 330

Aaronsohn, Sarah 15, 19, 29 n. 5, 40-41, 83, 84, 85-89, 97, 98, 100, 102, 119, 142, 143, 144, 145, 146, 149, 150-51, 162, 165, 167-68, 169-70, 171, 172, 172, 177, 180, 181, 187, 195, 203, 225, 227-240, 241-48, 251-61, 263-76, 281, 293, 295, 306, 309, 321, 329
  last letter 333-34

Aaronsohn, Sarah-Hinda 275

Aaronsohn, Shmuel (Sam) 29 n. 5, 127-28, 217, 258, 294, 306

Aaronsohn, Yedidiah 258, 259, 268, 306

Aaronsohn, Zvi 29 n. 5, 242, 242, 245-46, 252-53, 263, 272, 288, 292, 293

Aaronsohn House Museum 12n

Abdel Rahim Pasha 177

Abdul Hamid II 58

Abdullah (sailor) 138, 146

Aboulafia, Rafael 90, 133-34, 136, 137, 138, 142, 145 n. 6, 151, 174, 200, 205, 215, 231, 240, 240n, 259, 266, 294

Abu Arishi 271

Abu Rabaya, Hamad 298

Abu Rabaya, Hassan 298

Abu Safar, Salameh 298, 299

Abu Safra, Yussuf 297, 298

Acre 93, 140

Adana 293

Adel Bey 275, 276

Adler, Cyrus 17

Affula 149, 174, 229, 232, 241, 244

Agricultural Experiment Station, Jewish 18, 19, 23, 24, 25, 49, 73, 78
  Hadera branch 77, 97

agriculture 12, 13, 14, 16, 17, 19, 20,

22–23, 36, 37, 38, 40, 42, 43, 53, 63, 142, 142n, 157, 310, 316
agronomy 7, 15
Aharoni, Y. 58
Albania 64
Alberta 64
Aleppo 177, 278n, 291, 293
Alexander (Cairo lawyer) 207, 209, 312
Alexandretta 118, 161, 163
Alexandria 78, 79, 138, 145, 205, 208, 257
Algeria 61
Alhadeff, Yosef 171, 238
Allenby, Gen. 190, 191–98, 244, 310, 316, 328, 337
Alter, Albert 247–48, 271
Altshuler, Nakdimon 283
Amery, Leopold 188, 189, 303
Anatolia 36
Anglo-Palestine Bank 53, 71
Applebaum 333
Arab Bureau 79, 128, 129 139, 141, 210
"Arab revolt" 129, 131, 156
archeology 105
Argentine, the 28, 36, 37
Armenia, Armenians 73, 84, 107, 119, 273, 321–22
Ascherson, Paul 11, 12, 45, 57–58, 59
Athlit 18, 19, 23, 61, 78, 81, 82, 89, 90, 119, 120, 128 n. 3, 131, 132, 133, 136, 137, 140, 142, 143, 146, 147, 149, 152, 155, 156, 162, 167, 168, 169, 170, 180, 183, 184, 205, 214, 215, 217, 227, 232, 234, 237, 238, 239, 243, 248, 250, 252, 255, 257, 258, 265, 266, 270, 293, 294, 335
Atif (Effendi) 264–65

Auster, Daniel 292
Australians 145, 145 n. 6, 198
Austria 164
Avraham, Haim 85, 86, 87, 88, 89, 98, 143, 254
Avraham, Morris 98
Avraham, Mrs. Haim. *See* Aaronsohn, Sarah
Avraham, Ronya 98
Ayoubi, Shukri el 287, 290, 293
Azmi (Bey) 96

B

Baghdad 190
Baha-eddin 259, 266, 267
Balfour, Arthur James 141, 157, 219, 224, 329
Balfour Declaration 225, 304, 305, 308, 313, 318, 319, 322, 328
Beersheba 82, 169, 195–96, 200, 210, 212, 264, 265, 286
Begin, Menachem 301
Beirut 36, 78, 79, 88, 96, 118, 178, 179
Belinki 35
Belinkov 266
Belkind, Eitan 179, 263, 264–65, 289–90, 291, 292, 290, 291, 292
Belkind, Na'aman 82–83, 165, 169, 177, 178, 196, 199, 233, 243, 244, 246, 259, 261, 263, 264, 265, 267, 268–69, 270, 278, 284, 285, 288, 289, 290, 291, 313
Belkind, Olga 77
Belkind, Yisrael 77
Ben-Dano 36, 37
Ben-Elkanah, Shlomo 297–301
Ben-Hillel Hacohen, Mordechai 313
Ben-Shmuel 36

Bentwich, Norman 100, 140–41, 163
Benyamini (medical officer) 295
Berkeley (Calif) 15
Berkowitz, Esther-Leah 275
Berligne, Miss 139
Berligne, Eliahu 313
Berlin 7, 11, 12, 44, 45, 47, 48, 53, 59, 64, 83, 99, 100, 101–2, 103, 106, 122, 143, 166
Berman, Mrs. 139
Bernhardt, Olga 5, 6
Bernstein, Leibl 142, 146–47, 150, 174, 205, 266, 267, 294
Bernstorrf 288–89
Billings (Montana) 16
Bir el Bedawish 335
Blake 60
Blanckenhorn, Max 45, 51, 52, 54, 55–56, 57, 58, 59
Blumberg (family) 98
Blumenfeld, Efraim 279
Bornmuller 12
botany 7, 11–15, 19, 38–39, 40, 41, 44, 52, 60, 105
Boulogne 331, 340, 341
Boutagy, Charles 79, 80, 145 n. 6, 146
Brandeis, Louis Dembitz 17, 64–65, 108, 306, 308, 317, 327–28
Bremen 61
Brill, Abraham 285
Brinn, Ze'ev 68
Britain, British 6, 7, 8, 9, 26, 51, 54n, 64, 65, 69, 71, 71n, 72, 76, 77–85, 88, 89, 90, 91–93, 95, 101n, 102, 103, 104–5, 106, 107, 108, 110, 111–23, 125n, 126, 127, 128, 129, 129 n. 5, 130–34, 138–42, 143, 144, 145, 145 n. 5, 146, 147, 148, 150, 152, 155–56,

158, 159n, 161, 162–66, 169, 170, 171, 172, 173, 175, 178, 181, 183, 187–88, 190–91, 195, 196, 198, 203–9, 211, 212–15, 218, 219–20, 222, 223–25, 227, 229, 231, 232, 240, 241, 242, 243, 245, 247, 249, 255n, 257–58, 260, 269, 272n, 280, 283, 283n, 285, 286, 287, 292, 293, 294, 295, 298, 301, 303–19, 322, 323–28, 329–30, 336n, 337, 340–41
Bronstein, Menashe 82, 150, 230, 255, 256, 258, 266, 267, 268, 270, 293
Brusse, Captain 118
Bulgaria 164
Bullitt, William C. 323
Bureau of Plant Industry (USA) 13
Buxton, Capt. 325

C

Caesarea 258, 335
Cairo 79, 119, 128, 139, 142, 145, 152, 155, 156, 159, 161, 167, 170, 175, 179, 183, 184, 188, 191, 200, 205, 215, 231, 237, 238, 239, 243, 249, 250, 255, 258, 260, 267, 268, 269, 281, 294, 295, 306, 310, 312
California 14, 17, 20, 23, 48, 49
Canada 64
capitulations 171
carrier pigeons 214, 231, 257
Cecil, Lord Robert 189
Chetwode, General Philip 195
Chicago 64, 306, 307
Chtaura 35
Churchill, Winston 191, 337–38
Clayton, Gilbert 121, 128, 139, 162, 191, 214, 310, 316, 319
Clemenceau, Pres. 327

Cohen, Efraim 70
Cohen, Haim. *See* Schneierson, Levi
Cohen, Tsadok 28
Cohn, Oskar 166
Committee of Union and Progress (Turkey) 59, 114, 115
Community Relief Fund 230
Constantinople 58, 74, 83, 85, 86–87, 88, 91, 95, 96, 97, 98, 99, 100, 101, 103, 114, 118, 122, 126, 143, 144, 147, 148, 180, 236, 255, 293, 333 n. 3
Cook 65, 72
Copenhagen 7, 73, 102, 103, 104, 105–6, 122, 125, 135, 138, 215
Corfu 64
Council of Ten (at peace conference) 325, 329
counterespionage, British 7
Couzeniera (family) 36, 37
Cowen, Joseph 116, 309
Cowans, Sir John 163
Crosthwaite, Captain 158
Curzon, Lord 303, 322, 326
Cyprus 170, 204, 239

D

Damascus 83, 96, 99, 106, 149, 179, 180, 203, 229, 269, 281, 283, 284, 292, 333
    Khan el Basha prison 284, 292
Dardanelles, the 91–92, 161
Davidescu, Binyamin 82
Dawson 160
De Haas, Jacob 325, 327
Dead Sea 45, 56, 57, 58
Deedes, Sir Wyndham 93, 145–46, 157, 161, 183, 184, 185, 190 n. 4,

191, 209, 211, 213, 214, 258, 316, 319
Delhamiyeh 172
Denmark 7, 100, 143, 147, 220
Department of Agriculture (US) 7, 13, 16, 19, 63, 64, 65, 101, 103
Dera'a (Edrei) 55, 229, 241
Derby, Lord 163, 189
Dick, A. 38
Dixon 325
Dizengoff, Meir 204, 243, 248, 249, 250, 256, 257, 278, 282, 284, 285, 286, 311
Djemal Pasha 73–75, 81, 85, 95, 114, 119, 127, 164–65, 166–67, 165, 177, 187, 189, 190, 190 n. 4, 214, 223, 241, 285, 286, 287, 288, 289, 310, 318
dry farming 16, 20, 23
Dushkin, Alexander 5, 100, 102, 110

E

Eastern Mediterranean Intelligence Bureau (EMSIB) 132, 136, 182, 184, 233 n. 7, 257, 258
economic structure, Jewish people's 21
Eder, David 195, 197, 309
Edmonds, William 132–33, 134, 136, 138, 139, 140, 141, 142, 146, 156, 157, 163, 170, 182, 183, 184, 211, 214, 257, 258
Egypt 8, 63, 71, 71n, 78, 80, 82, 83, 90, 102, 107, 112, 119, 120–21, 127, 128, 131, 132, 133, 134, 137, 139, 140, 143, 144, 147, 149, 155, 156, 158, 166, 169, 170, 171, 173, 174, 187, 190, 193, 203, 205, 215, 219, 223, 231, 233, 237, 238, 245, 246, 248,

252, 255, 256, 257, 258, 259, 260, 263, 266, 286, 311

Egyptian Expeditionary Force (EEF) 8, 112, 155, 191

Ehrlich, Avner 293

Ehrlich, Shabtai (Shepsel) 280, 281, 283, 293

Eizenstein, Leib 30

Ekron 144

El Arish 42n

El Jama'a 172

England. *See* Britain

Enver Pasha 175, 177, 241

Eretz Israel. *See* Palestine

Ericssen, Dr. 100

Eshkol, Levi 301

F

Fairchild, David 13-14, 16, 17, 19, 57, 61, 63, 65, 72, 101, 103, 111

Feisal (s. of Hussein) 129, 322

Fakhri-eddin 259

Falkenhayn, General 175, 201, 241

Famagusta 152, 233 n. 7, 267

Feilding, Everard 141, 142, 158, 162, 185

Fein, Avshalom 199-200, 203, 233, 264, 265, 269

Feinberg, Avshalom 8, 9, 19, 63, 75, 76-78, 79-81, 82-83, 85, 86, 87-88, 89, 90, 95, 96, 97, 101, 102, 107, 112, 120, 122, 127, 133, 137, 139, 142, 143, 144-45, 145 n. 5, 149, 152, 155, 157, 167, 168-69, 172, 174, 217, 227, 228-29, 236, 237, 240, 245, 246, 247, 263, 297-301

Feinberg (family) 173, 243

Feinberg, Fanny 76

Feinberg, Meir 77

Feinberg, Tsilla 83, 88, 101-2, 120, 143, 147, 148, 299, 330

Feinberg, Yisrael 76, 76n

Feitelson 333

Fertile Crescent 12

Fichman, Ya'akov 279

First Aliyah 25, 66

Fisch, David 265

Fitzmaurice, Gerald 114, 115, 132, 141

Flahaut, Prof. 39, 40, 44, 60

Flexner, Bernard 325, 327

Foreign Office (Britain) 84, 114, 115, 119, 156, 162, 166, 187, 189, 208, 209, 213, 219, 303, 322, 326

France 31, 60, 113, 140, 193, 307, 329, 341

Frankfurter, Felix 17, 64, 108, 109, 216, 308, 313, 327

G

Galilee 11, 12, 32-33, 39, 52, 55, 140, 142, 165, 177, 279, 281, 317

Gallipoli 91-93, 113, 131, 189, 190, 191

Gaster, Moses 113, 123, 123 n. 10

Gaza 79, 93, 118, 140, 163, 170, 177, 189, 190, 191, 192, 193-96, 197-201, 212, 241, 244, 247, 257, 286, 337

Gedera 265

Gelberg, Tova 180, 230, 243, 274 n. 9, 293

General Headquarters (British) 121, 128, 139, 156, 157, 158, 159, 161, 166, 172, 173, 178, 181, 185, 191, 203, 205, 206, 207, 210, 214, 223, 232, 243, 259, 294, 295, 306, 319 geology 12, 39, 40, 41, 45, 52, 55–56, 105, 160

Gerard, Luther 101, 105

Germany 7, 84, 91, 100, 102, 125n, 164, 166, 187 Germans, 211, 288–89, 337

Ghanem, Elias 174, 270, 278

Ghanem, Nasser 174, 266

Gideonites 67

Giladi, Yisrael 232

Gintsburg, Shepka 264, 267

Glatzano, Paulette 177

Glazebrook, Consul 144

Gluskin, Ze'ev 205-6, 207–9, 210, 213, 223, 248, 311, 312

Golomb, Eliahu 315, 316

Goor, Mordechai 298

Graham, Sir Ronald 158-59, 162, 166, 188, 189, 209, 212, 303, 305

Graves, Philip 140, 157, 184, 185

Great Britain. See Britain

Greenberg, Uri Zvi 301

Grey, Sir Edward 92

Gribbon, Walter Harold 9, 78, 111–12, 117, 118-19, 120, 121–22, 128, 132, 134, 135, 136, 139, 141, 143, 155, 225, 323, 325, 328, 330, 330n

Grignon (France) 14 n. 3, 31, 32

H

Haas, Emmy 178

Hacohen, Mordechai Ben-Hillel 165n

Hadani, Ever 300

Hadera 57, 76, 83, 145, 149, 234, 242, 243, 258, 260, 333
  Agricultural Experiment Station branch 77, 97

Haifa 14, 28, 82, 93, 118, 162, 164, 165,

232, 243, 255, 257, 260, 266, 278n, 337

Haim, David 38, 57

Haimson, Albert 325

Hall, Reginald 7

Halperin, Yitzhak 150, 265, 267, 268, 270, 288, 293

Hamagen 82, 168, 229, 231

Hamara 280, 281

Hamburg 102

Hamilton, Sir Ian 92, 158

Hanin, Yehezkel 168

Hankin, Mendel 249, 256, 257

Hapoel Hatza'ir (journal) 233

Hapoel Hatza'ir (movement) 23

Hardinge, Lord 115

Haritia 81

Hashomer 168, 169, 229, 231, 232, 233, 237, 244, 249, 250, 253, 256, 279–80, 281, 286, 288, 293, 300, 301, 316

Hassan Bek (torturer) 277, 278n

Heck 105

Hedjaz 57, 58, 175

Hefter, Shmuel 232, 279

Hermon, Mount 11, 12, 13

Hershkowitz 272

Herzl, Theodor 42n, 45, 52, 221, 329

Hibat Zion 38, 42, 52–53

Hilgard, Prof. 15, 18, 61, 64

Hirsch, Baron 28, 36

Hirsch, Venitziani 28

Hodj 200, 263, 264

Hogarth, David George 129

Hoofien, Eliezer 249, 311, 312

Hornstein, Dvora 275

Horowitz, Menachem 280

House, Col. 323

Hovevei Zion. *See* Hibat Zion
Hoz, Dov 315, 316
Hoz, Yitzhak 88
Hurwitz, Moshe 30
Hussein, Sharif 128–29

I

Ibrahaim Pasha 162
Idelson, A. Z. 43
Italy 193, 307, 329
Izzet Pasha 58–59

J

Jabotinsky, Vladimir (Ze'ev) 71n,
  101n, 106, 116, 123, 155, 156, 159,
  187, 188, 189, 208, 211, 220, 221,
  222, 300, 303, 304, 305, 314–16, 319,
  328
Jaffa 71, 74, 93, 118, 144, 164, 165, 166,
  187, 206, 242, 243, 289, 292, 310,
  312, 315, 318, 335
Japan 329
Jefferson, E. B. 330, 340
Jericho 54
Jerusalem 51, 74, 140, 144, 159, 162,
  164, 166, 169, 181, 192, 193, 242,
  283, 284, 289, 311, 314, 318
Jerusalem-Jaffa agricultural zone 142
Jewish Colonization Association (ICA;
  PICA) 30, 37–38, 42, 52
"Jewish labor" 24
Jewish Legion 71n, 101n, 116, 155,
  187, 188, 189, 211, 219, 220, 221,
  303, 315
Jewish National Fund 18, 22
Jezreel Valley 162, 177, 191
Joffe, Bezalel 249, 313

Joffe, Hillel 37–38, 39, 68, 99, 222, 270,
  273n, 274–76
Joffe (Rogoff), Rahel 38–39, 47, 60, 61
Johannsen, Prof. 102
Jones, Seymour 139, 157
Jordan River 54
Jordan Valley 55
Josephus Flavius 160, 309
Judea 63
Judean desert 51

K

Kahanov 206
Kalverisky, Nahum 285
Kantrowitz, Yaacov 284
Karkur 279, 281
Karpelus, H. 299
Kashta, Abel-Hamid el 298
Katz, Shaul 20
Kidston, George 115, 219
Kirkwall (Scotland) 5, 7, 8, 103, 110
Kistamuna (Turkey) 112, 143
Kitchener, Lord 91, 92, 114
Kitchener-Condor survey 158
Klausner, Yosef 23
Klein, Major 148
Koernicke, Friedrich 11, 12n, 13, 45
Kotschy, Prof. 11
Kowalsky 176
Kozlovsky, Meir 280
Kressenstein, Kress von 178, 199, 212,
  264
Kut el Amara 190

L

Labor movement (Palestine) 233
Lansing, Robert 308, 329
Lante, General von 177

Larnaca 233, 237

Lawrence, Thomas Edward (T. E.; "Lawrence of Arabia") 130, 210, 339

Lebanon 63

Levi, Sylvan 309

Levi, Yosef 275

Levontin, Pnina 240, 240n

Levontin, Zalman David 53–55, 309

Lidano, Miriam 275

Liebman, Batya 27

Lifschitz, Moshe 300

Lipsky, Louis 65

Lipson, Eliezer 179

Lishansky, Ivriah 256, 269, 272, 273n, 300, 301

Lishansky (Yanait), Rahel 24, 24 n. 17, 89, 96–97, 315, 316

Lishansky, Rivka 269, 272, 273 nn. 6, 7, 300, 301, 329

Lishansky, Tuvia 256, 269, 272, 300, 301

Lishansky, Yosef 82, 142, 144–45, 145 n. 6, 146, 152, 167, 168–69, 170–71, 172, 172, 176, 180, 181, 199, 204, 227, 228, 229, 231, 232, 233, 235, 237–39, 242–51, 253, 256–61, 263–64, 265, 266, 267, 268–70, 272, 273, 273n, 278, 279–84, 283n, 285, 286, 287–88, 289, 290–91, 295, 297–301, 306, 316

Livneh, Eliezer 46, 50, 93, 318

Lloyd George, David 111, 116, 155, 156, 162, 189, 190, 191, 192, 194, 219, 220–21, 319, 325–26, 327, 337

Lloyd, George 172, 185

Loeb (family) 126

Loeb, Albert 109, 126

Loeb, Anna 109

Loeb, Prof. 18

London 6–9, 104, 105, 106, 115, 121, 122, 127, 128, 131, 132, 135, 136, 147, 155, 166, 197, 198, 203, 205, 212, 217, 222, 224, 248, 294, 317, 322, 327

First Avenue Hotel 6

Kew Gardens 64

Scotland Yard 6, 7, 8

War Office 9, 92, 104, 105, 111, 112, 113, 121, 131, 155, 156, 306, 307, 340

Lowther, Gerald 114

Lubrani, Eliezer 278

Ludvipol, Avraham 256, 257

Lulu, Farida 293

Luz, Kadish 299

Lyndon-Bell, General 196

M

Ma'an 55

MacDonogh, George 111, 117, 194–95, 225, 323

Mack, Julian 17, 64, 65, 69, 72, 73, 106, 108, 125–26, 215, 216, 308

Mack, William. *See* Aaronsohn, Aaron

Mackindoe, Capt. 325

Madorsky 333

Magnes, Judah Leib 5, 17, 99–100, 102, 102 n. 6, 106, 110, 125, 126, 216, 228n

Magnesia 36, 37

Malcolm, James 140, 182, 183, 185, 207, 321, 322

Maltzen, Dr. Baron von 177

Managem (ship) 151, 152, 165, 168, 169, 171, 182, 196, 200, 204, 204, 206, 207, 227, 230, 233 n. 7, 239,

242, 243, 255, 257, 259-60, 263,
   265-66, 267, 268, 269, 278, 294, 295
Margolius 206
Maritain, Jacques 63
Marr, Wilhelm 60
Marshall, Louis 109, 125, 126
Masdar, Frayah Farhan el- 298
Maude, Gen. 190
Maugham, Major 120
Maxwell, General 223
Maziya, Ronya 284
McRury, Captain 157, 167
Medina 175
Meier, Walter 309
Meinertzhagen, Richard 198, 304, 330,
   339
Meirowitz, Menashe 265
Menahemiya 168
Mendelsohn, Von 105
Mesopotamia 203, 327
Metulla 32, 33-35, 37, 41, 281
Middle East Committee (of the British
   War Cabinet) 318
Mikve Israel 21
Milner, Lord 329
Mizrahi, Eliahu 264, 265
Mograbi 30
Monckton, Lt. 312
Money, General 310, 316
Montagu, Edwin 159n, 213, 303, 304
Montgomery, Philip 101
Montpellier 14, 39, 40, 44
   University of 14, 60, 61
Morgenthau, Henry 101, 103
Mosseri, Jacques 139, 206, 209, 312
"mother of wheat" (triticum
   dicoccoides) 11, 12, 56
Mount Carmel 118

Mount Herzl 299, 301
Mount Nevo 55
Muhram (Effendi) 58
Murray, General 161, 162, 163, 163,
   170, 188, 190, 191, 195, 315, 337

N

Nadav, Zvi 279
Nahmani, Yosef 279, 280, 283
Naian 179
Napoleon Bonaparte 162
Narunsky, Hersh. See Feinberg,
   Avshalom
Nashashibi, Fuad 280, 281, 283
Nasser, Naguib 284
nature studies, teaching of 20-21
Nazareth 140, 159, 273, 277, 278n
Neale, A. C. B. 198
Nebi Rubin 283
Nedava, Yosef 273, 301
Negev 63
Neiderman 274
Neiman, Mendel 174, 178
Neiman, Moshe 174-75, 181, 232, 241,
   244, 281, 285, 286, 287, 288, 293,
   313
Neuhartdorf 336
Neville (French general) 163
Neville, Major 160
New York 19, 61, 103, 306, 307
Newcombe 79
Nielson, Prof. 102
Nili Organization 153, 162, 165, 169,
   171, 173-85, 196, 203-4, 211, 212,
   224, 225, 227-40, 242-50, 251, 254,
   256-57, 259, 263-74, 277, 278-79,
   282, 284, 285, 287, 288, 290, 291,
   292, 293, 294, 303, 307, 310, 311,

313, 315, 316, 299, 300, 311, 312–13,
315, 316
Nissanov, Zvi 280
Nordau, Max 329
Nugent, Col. 184

O

Oppenheimer, H. R. 19n, 56
Orel, Binyamin 281, 282, 283
Ormsby-Gore, Captain 139–40, 141,
142, 142n, 157, 190, 225, 303, 304,
307, 309, 316, 318, 319, 330
Osman Bey 272, 273, 275, 277
Osterhout, Prof. 15
Ovsievitz 34, 35

P

Paget, Sir Roger 7–8, 103–4, 138
Palestine 8, 12, 13, 14, 15, 16, 20, 22,
25, 27, 29, 32, 37, 38, 39, 43, 44, 45,
46, 51, 53, 55, 56–57, 58, 64, 65, 66,
69, 70, 71n, 72, 73, 77, 79, 83, 84, 85,
88, 90, 93, 101n, 103, 104, 106, 107,
111, 113, 115, 116, 125, 126, 131,
133, 135, 137, 139, 140, 141, 145,
146, 147, 148, 156, 157, 158, 159,
160, 161, 164, 165, 166, 169, 172,
178, 179, 181, 184, 187, 188, 189,
190, 191, 192–93, 194, 195, 197, 204,
205, 206, 207, 208, 209, 211, 213,
214, 219, 220, 221, 222, 223, 224,
225, 227, 239, 241, 243, 246, 256,
277, 278n, 287, 293, 300, 304, 305,
306, 307, 308, 309, 310, 311, 312,
313, 314, 316, 317, 318, 319, 321,
322, 323, 324, 325, 326, 327–28, 329,
330, 335–36, 337, 340. *See also*

Athlit; Hadera; Haifa, Jerusalem;
Rehovot; Petah Tikva
Palestinology 25
Paris 32, 35, 64, 317, 324, 330
Pascal, Batya 281, 282
Pascal, Lorette 281–82
Pascal, Miriam 281, 282–83
Pascal, Peretz 142, 145 n. 6, 167, 174,
205, 206, 207, 209, 211, 214, 281
Patterson, John Henry 71n, 315, 319
Péguy, Charles 63
Petah Tikva 21, 22, 164, 165, 176, 263,
264, 279, 281, 282
Petra 55
Philipsberg, Lucy 50
Pichon, Stephen 329
Pickard, L. 56
Poalei Zion 314
Port Said 123, 127, 136, 137, 138, 139,
142, 145 n. 6, 146, 147, 168, 169,
170, 196, 200, 214, 215, 233, 234,
237, 258, 260, 295
Post, George 11, 12
Primrose, Neil 340, 341
public health 67

R

Raab, Baruch 146, 150, 151
Rabin, Yitzhak 301
Rafa (Rafiah) 162, 297, 298
Raghem, Nasser 231
Ramet, Henry 340
Ramle 181, 229, 241, 242, 244, 283,
289
Rann, Binyamin 297, 299
Raschaya 11
Ras-el-Ein (Rosh Ha'ayin) 141
Rayak 179

Reclam, German 118
Red Cross 317
Rehovot 265, 283
Reichert, Israel 20
Reuters New Agency 166
Riklis, Pinhas 279
Rishon Lezion 76, 82, 177, 233, 264, 291, 300
Rivniker, Yitzhak 272
Robertson, Sir William 93–94, 113, 117, 161 n. 4, 163, 191, 192, 194, 197, 330n
Rodenheimer, Prof. 43
Romania 53, 83, 89
Roosevelt, Theodore 65
Rosen 264
Rosenberg, Yitzhak 232, 244, 245, 248–49, 253, 256, 257, 278–79, 288, 293
Rosenheck 309
Rosenwald, Julius 17, 22 n. 12, 64, 109, 126, 216, 308
Rosenwald, Mrs. 108, 109
Rosh Pinna 12, 56
Rothman, Nissan 243, 265, 293
Rothschild, Baron Edmond 21, 28–29, 30, 31, 32–34, 36, 37, 41, 166, 317
Rothschild, James 117, 309
Rothschild, Lord 116, 303
Rothschild, Yaacov 29
Rovina, Hannah 301
Ruhama 177, 200
Rumeilat tribe 298
Ruppin, Arthur 70, 148, 148n, 222, 289
Russia 38, 53, 84, 91, 187, 190, 305, 318

S

Sacher, Harry 325
Sahara desert 61, 105
Salaman, Radcliffe 315
Salonica 115, 191, 194
Samaria 39, 51, 142
Samsonov, Aryeh 28, 29
Samuel, Herbert 113, 116, 123
San Francisco 64
Sanana 298
Saporta, Daniel 52
Savage, Raymond 195
Scandinavia 100, 101
Scheid, Eliyahu 29, 32, 33, 34, 35
Schiff, Jacob 18, 70, 109
Schneierson, Levi ("Liova") Yitzhak 96, 97–98, 99, 143, 147–49, 150–53, 170–71, 172, 182, 196, 200–201, 203, 205, 215, 231, 233, 234–36, 237, 239, 243, 253, 257, 259, 260, 266, 267, 268, 269, 294, 295, 306, 313
Schneierson, Mendel 263
Schneierson, Pinhas 280
school teachers 20
Schubert 178, 179
Schwartz (family) 333
Schwartz, Ahuva 275
Schwartz, Freda 275
Schwartz, Reuven 150, 151, 152, 178, 182, 247, 271, 278
Schweinfurth, George 11, 12, 13, 45, 57, 59
Scott, Charles P. 221
Sea of Marmora 58
Second Aliyah 25, 66
Sheikh Zuwaid 144
Shochat, Manya 88

Shochat, Yisrael 88
Sidna Ali (Arsuf) 335
Sidon 118
Sieff, Israel 50, 309, 312
Simon, Leon 325
Simpson, Col. 132, 133, 136, 139, 140
Sinai 82, 93, 95, 113, 144, 162, 264
Skaletsky, Baruch 137, 138
Smith, Captain 134, 136-37, 141, 143, 144, 146, 157, 182, 183-85, 254, 255, 267
Smuts, General 190, 191, 337
Smyrna 58
Sokolovitz, David 177, 181, 244
Sokolow, Nahum 116, 123, 166, 205, 208, 209, 210-11, 220, 223, 224, 303, 305, 322, 329
Soskin, Selig (Evgeny) 18, 38, 40, 41-42, 43, 44, 46, 47, 49-50, 53, 59, 65, 102
Soskin, Sonia 46-50, 59, 102
Special Committee for Aid to the Deportees 206-7, 311-12
Sternberg, David 334
Storrs, Ronald 128, 311
Strauss, Nathan 17, 67, 70, 222
Strauss, Oscar 17
Suarez, Edgar 208, 214
Sursouk family 35-36
Suss, Edouard 199, 264, 265
Svalof (Sweden) 102
Sverdlov, David 315, 316
Sweden 7, 100
Swingle, Walter 17, 19, 64, 65, 72
Sykes, Mark 112-13, 114, 115-16, 121, 123, 128, 132, 141, 166, 187, 189, 190, 191, 223, 225, 303, 304, 306, 321, 323, 328

Sykes-Picot Agreement 113, 140
Syria 63, 69, 71, 93, 161, 164, 203, 287, 290, 317, 337
Syria-Palestine 12, 69, 93, 132
Szold, Henrietta 17, 18, 64, 65, 80, 95, 103, 109, 120, 136, 215-16, 217, 228n

T

Taarav, Netanel Hacohen 291
Talaat Pasha 289
Tantura 162, 336
Tardieu, Andre 329
Taylor, Lt. 157
Tchlenov, Yehiel 68, 220, 222, 305
Tel Adashim 279, 287
Tel Aviv 164, 165, 243, 282, 309, 310
Tel es Sammaq 336
Tel Shariya 177
Thomson, Sir Basil 7, 8-9, 111, 112, 143, 160, 323
Thon, Joshua 70
Thon, Yaakov 249, 250
Tiller 178
Titus 162
Tolkowsky, Shmuel 221, 330
Traill, Captain 120, 121, 122
Transjordan 51, 75, 142, 326
Treidel, Yosef 41, 42, 44, 58
Trumpeldor, Yosef 71n, 116, 189, 189n, 223
Tsifrin, Haim 30
Tulkarm 141, 172, 241, 242
Tunis 49
Tunisia 61
Turkey, Turkish 5, 6, 7, 8, 9, 17, 25, 37, 41, 46, 50, 53, 54, 58-59, 69-71, 72, 73, 74, 75, 76, 77, 78, 79, 80-83,

84-85, 87, 88, 90, 91-93, 96, 97,
98-99, 100, 101, 104, 105, 106-7,
108, 111-12, 114, 115, 117-19,
125-27, 130, 132, 133, 135, 138, 141,
142, 144, 147, 149, 151, 155, 159
161, 162, 164, 166, 167, 168, 171,
172, 173, 174, 175, 177, 178-79, 181,
188, 190-91, 192, 194, 195, 196, 197,
198-200, 201, 202, 205, 206, 207,
211, 212, 216, 217, 220, 222, 223,
227, 229, 230, 232, 238, 241-42, 243,
244, 248, 251, 255, 256, 257, 258,
259, 260, 261, 263-76, 277-81, 283,
287, 288-93, 297, 298, 299, 308, 316,
318, 321, 322, 335-36, 337
Department of Agriculture 85
Tuvion. *See* Lishansky, Yosef
Tyre 118

U

United States 13, 14-15, 16, 17, 18, 57,
59, 61, 64, 65, 67, 70, 72, 80, 101,
103, 125, 143, 166, 189, 192, 207,
217, 249, 305, 307, 308-9, 313, 317,
318, 323, 329
University of California at Berkeley 15,
64
Ussischkin, Menachem Mendel 324

V

Valetta 215
Vansittart, Robert 326
Vespasian 162
Vienna Science Museum 11
Vienna 41, 53, 60

W

Wadi-Sarar 241

Waldon, Louis B. 200-201, 260,
266-67, 268, 294
War Trade Intelligence Department
(WTID; Britain) 117, 122
Warburg, Prof. Otto 7, 11, 18, 44, 45,
47, 51-52, 53, 55, 59, 65, 68,
100-101
Warming, Prof. 105
Washington, D.C. 16, 306
water 54, 159-61
Webster, Charles 323-24
Weitz, Naftali 47, 68, 139, 145 n. 6,
157, 174, 206, 207, 209, 222, 239,
248, 312
Weizmann, Chaim 50, 106, 116, 123,
155, 166, 204, 205, 208, 209, 210-11,
213, 219, 221-22, 223, 224-25, 248,
256, 303, 304, 305, 307, 309, 310,
312, 313, 316-17, 319, 322, 323, 324,
326, 327, 328, 329
Weizmann, Vera 330
Wexler 209
Wilbushevitz, Nahum 172, 255n
Wilbushevitz, Shoshana 180, 255,
255n
Wilkansky (Volcani), Yitzhak 310, 311
Wilner, Frank 181
Wilner, Hugo 181
Wilson, Sir Henry 323, 324, 325
Wilson, Woodrow 64, 105, 125n,
308-9, 323
Wingate, Sir Reginald 128, 141, 162,
166, 204, 208, 209, 211, 212, 213,
214
Winstone, H. V. F. 341
Wise, Stephen 327
Wolffsohn, David 101
Woolley, Leonard 8, 9, 9n, 80, 81,

89–90, 95, 103, 112, 120, 134, 137, 143, 144
World Zionist Organization 220
Wormser 60
Wright, Maj. Gen. 160

Y

Yanait. *See* Lishansky (Yanait), Rahel
Yavetz, Ze'ev 30
Yavne'el 280, 281
Yissud Hama'alah 281
Yohanan of Gush Halav 309
Young Turks 58, 69, 114, 115
Yudelewitz, David 205–6, 207

Z

Za'arub, Shakhta 298
Zamarin 29
Zeldin family 333
Zeldin, Yehuda 146, 150, 231, 270, 273, 293
Zerubavel, Ya'akov 67
Zichron Ya'akov 8, 12n, 15, 19, 20, 27–28, 31, 36, 37, 41, 43, 46, 49, 56, 66, 67, 77, 78, 80, 81, 83, 88, 89, 90, 95, 98, 99, 101, 103, 116, 120, 141,

143, 145, 152, 174, 175, 180, 200, 214, 242, 245, 247, 248, 250, 254, 258, 259, 261, 264, 269, 270–76, 277l, 278, 278n, 280, 293, 295, 341
Zion Mule Corp 71n, 156, 189
Zionism 13, 18, 21, 22, 24, 27, 44, 45, 60, 64, 66, 70, 71, 80, 101, 105–6, 113, 115, 133, 156, 158, 159, 208, 213, 219, 293, 303–4, 305, 307, 308, 313, 317, 322, 329
  Committee for the Exploration of Eretz Israel 45
Zionist Commission 307, 308–9, 310, 312, 315, 316, 318
Zionist Committee (London) 308
Zionist Conference (Baltimore) 307
Zionist Organization 14, 52, 55, 63, 101, 208, 309, 324
  Greater Actions Committee 319n
Zionist Organization of America 64, 69
Zionists 18, 38, 51, 52, 65, 101, 106, 116, 123, 155, 166, 187, 212, 220, 232, 248, 285, 303, 324
Zlocisti, Theodor 100